THE
CHARTER
SCHOOL
LANDSCAPE

THE CHARTER SCHOOL LANDSCAPE

Sandra Vergari

UNIVERSITY OF PITTSBURGH PRESS

Published by the University of Pittsburgh Press, Pittsburgh, Pa., 15260

Copyright © 2002, University of Pittsburgh Press

Manufactured in the United States of America

Printed on acid-free paper

10 9 8 7 6 5 4 3 2 1

Library of Congress Cataloging-in-Publication Data
Vergari, Sandra.
    The charter school landscape / Sandra Vergari.
            p. cm.
Includes bibliographical references (p.   ) and index.
    ISBN 0-8229-4180-5 (cloth : alk. paper)
  1. Charter schools—Political aspects—United States. I. Title.
    LB2806.36 .V47 2002
    371.01—dc21

                                              2002000266

DEDICATED TO MY PARENTS,

DIANE AND DAN

Contents

Acknowledgments

I want to express my heartfelt appreciation to my parents, Dan and Diane, and my brothers, Paul and Doug, for their invaluable support and encouragement over the years.

Thanks to each of the contributors to this volume for their enthusiasm and commitment to quality. Special thanks are due to Rick Hess for his reliable friendship and counsel and to Michael Mintrom for setting an inspirational example of the gold standard in academe. I also thank the anonymous reviewers for helpful comments on the manuscript.

I want to thank the students in my classes over the years, especially students in my educational administration and policy studies (EAPS) courses at the University at Albany, who have thoughtfully passed along useful articles and information and who have engaged me in lively discussions about education reform. I continue to learn a great deal from my students and the experiences they relate from the field. I appreciate the diligence of several graduate assistants who have worked with me at U-Albany: Xiaoying Chen, Brian Goodale, Aidong Wu, Shuang Wu, and Huaying Zhang. Thanks also to Carm Colfer, EAPS secretary, for consistently cheerful, prompt, and competent responses to my various requests.

Finally, thanks to Niels Aaboe, Deborah Meade, and Dennis Lloyd at the University of Pittsburgh Press, to Carol Sickman-Garner for her skillful copy editing, and to Ilana Kingsley for constructing the index.

This project was supported in part by grants from the Research Foundation of the State University of New York and the State of New York/United University Professions Individual Development Awards Program.

THE CHARTER SCHOOL LANDSCAPE

1 • Introduction

Sandra Vergari

DURING A TIME of intense interest in how to improve public education, the charter school policy innovation is among the most dynamic and hotly debated education reform issues today. Minnesota adopted the nation's first charter school law in 1991, and a decade later, thirty-six additional states and the District of Columbia (D.C.) had charter school statutes. The first charter school opened in Minnesota in 1992. In the 2000–2001 academic year, over 2,000 charter schools were in operation across thirty-four states and D.C., with a total enrollment of about 500,000 students, and continued growth was anticipated (Center for Education Reform 2001d). Interest in charter schools has also emerged north of the border, where a charter school law was adopted in 1994 for Alberta, the sole Canadian province with such legislation. Across the United States, 70 percent of charter schools report having waiting lists (RPP International 2000).

While *The Charter School Landscape* focuses largely on charter school politics and policies at the state and local levels, the reform has also received tangible and significant support from the federal government. The federal Public Charter Schools Program (PCSP) was first authorized through a provision included in the 1994 reauthorization of the Elementary and Secondary Act of 1965 and later amended in the Charter School Expansion Act of 1998 (P.L. 105-378) (see Leal 1999). Over time, the federal appropriation for charter schools has risen swiftly: $6 million in fiscal year (FY) 1995, $18 million in FY 1996, $51 million in FY 1997, $80 million in FY 1998, $100 million in FY 1999, and $145 million in FY 2000 (SRI International 2000; Leal 1999). The PCSP provides funds for charter school planning and start-up and for research and information dissemination on the policy innovation. Former president Bill Clinton favored the innovation and called for 3,000 charter schools by 2002. In 2000, Congress approved $25 million for a new Charter Schools Facilities Financing Demonstration Program to help find ways to make facilities financing more available and affordable to charter schools. President George W. Bush also supports charter schools and proposed an increase in funding for the PCSP to $200 million for FY 2001. Charter schools are public schools and thus also eligible for other federal education funds.

The Charter School Concept in Theory and Practice

Charter schools are publicly funded entities that enjoy freedom from many of the regulations under which traditional public schools operate. Regardless of personal opinions on this controversial and multifaceted policy innovation, readers of this volume are likely to agree that various operational and political features of charter school policy are intriguing subjects for analysis. Operationally, charter schools have been characterized as "quasi–public schools" that straddle the boundary between the public and private realms (Witte 1996, 161; Loveless and Jasin 1998). Politically, the reform has attracted support from both the left and right ends of the ideological spectrum. Some supporters view charter schools as an interim step on the way to a full voucher system of education. Others view charter schools as the best means by which to preserve public education by provoking traditional public schools to reform and thereby head off the threat of a full voucher system.[1]

As originally conceived, and as expressed in many charter school statutes, the charter school concept is aimed at responding to demands for greater choice and accountability in public education and at providing opportunities for innovation in school governance, administration, and pedagogy (Nathan 1996). Charter schools are legally and fiscally autonomous educational entities operating within the public school system under contracts or charters. The charters are negotiated between organizers and authorizers. The organizers may be teachers, parents, or others from the public or private sectors. The organizers manage the schools, and the authorizers monitor compliance with the charter and applicable state and local rules. The charters contain provisions regarding matters such as curriculum, performance measures, governance, and operational and financial plans. The authorizers are public entities such as local school boards, state school boards, universities, cities, and statutorily created charter school authorizer boards in Arizona and D.C.

Charter school advocates emphasize that authorizers other than (or in addition to) local school districts should be permitted in order to break the "exclusive franchise" of school-district control over public education (Kolderie 1990a, 1994).

A majority of charter school states permit an entity other than the local school board to authorize charter schools. In addition, many charter school laws allow appeals of rejected charter school applications to the state board of education or another appeals entity (see Vergari 1999).

Charter schools may be established in several ways. An existing school might convert to a charter school, a charter school might be formed as part of an existing school (constituting a "school within a school"), or a charter school might emerge as an entirely new entity. Nearly three-fourths of charter schools in the United States are new start-up charter schools (RPP International 2000). In practice, the policy reform is quite diverse, as charter schools have adopted a variety of managerial and pedagogical approaches. Some schools are operated fully or in part by educational management companies (EMCs), and others emphasize the role of parents and teachers in school governance; some charter schools emphasize math and science, and others accentuate the arts or foreign languages; some focus on training students for an occupational trade, and others focus on preparation for university; some schools use a "back-to-basics" pedagogical approach, and others have chosen alternative curricula.

A Decentralized "Marketplace" of Public Education

Public choice theorists apply economic principles to politics and favor the marketplace over government as the central institution in society (A. Schneider and Ingram 1997). Reflecting public choice tenets, charter school advocates maintain that a market-based approach to the delivery of education can produce better-performing schools. When parents exercise their exit option and send their children to charter schools rather than traditional public schools, they issue powerful market signals (see Hirschman 1970). When a student exits a traditional public school, the public funds allocated for that student now belong to the charter school rather than to the school district. Thus, the opportunities created by attracting new students and the threats associated with losing students due to competition are expected to make all schools more responsive to the demands of their "customers"— local families.[2] In remarks prepared for an address before the 2001 annual meeting of the National Education Association, U.S. education secretary Rod Paige mentioned charter schools and avowed: "It's tempting to pretend public schools are exempt from the law of supply and demand. They are not. This pretension will destroy our system" (Paige 2001). However, if the hypothesized benefits of competition in public education are to occur, a supply of schools sufficient to meet consumer preferences is as important as demand. Statutory caps on the number of charter schools, for example, prevent the operation of a competitive marketplace (Cibulka 1999).

Market theory assumes well-informed consumers, yet in practice, consumer information "can be scarce, costly, and unevenly distributed" (Henig 1999, 74). This means that some families may lack ample access to accurate information about charter schools.[3] When producers have more or better information than consumers, the problem of asymmetric information impedes a healthy marketplace, and government regulation may be used to address the market failure (see Munger 2000; Weimer and Vining 1999). Thus, Kemerer (1999, 176) asserts that the state has an important role to play in disseminating information about school choice opportunities. Finn, Manno, and Vanourek (2000, 128) propose a system of "accountability-via-transparency," in which so much is known about a charter school that it can be "regulated" by observers (including authorizers) through market-style mechanisms, rather than by bureaucratic "command-and-control structures."

Some analysts argue that the political and bureaucratic factors that constrain effective governance in school districts can be avoided through the decentralized governance embodied in school choice reforms such as charter schools (Chubb and Moe 1990). The charter school idea is rooted not only in market principles but also in theories of direct democracy (Cibulka 1999). Critics of the traditional public school system assert that intrusive school boards, stringent teacher certification requirements, collective bargaining rules, and various regulations pertaining to curricula and other facets of school operations obstruct innovation and excellence in education. Charter schools enjoy the freedom to make their own decisions on issues such as personnel, curricula, and contracting with nonprofit or for-profit entities. This autonomy allows charter schools to implement new methods of education delivery that may prove more effective and efficient than those commonly used by school districts. In practice, however, some charter schools have struggled with decentralized management (Griffin and Wohlstetter 2001). In theory, operational and pedagogical practices that prove successful in charter schools can be replicated in traditional public schools. Moreover, the publicity enjoyed by successful charter schools is expected to place increased pressure on the traditional public school system to reform, thereby improving accountability throughout public education.

Charter schools must abide by federal and state regulations pertaining to health and safety, disabled students, and civil rights; they may not charge tuition, and admissions policies must be nondiscriminatory. Nonetheless, Ted Kolderie, a founder of the charter school concept, asserts: "Charter schools are schools of choice. Most regular schools aren't. Some things that would raise questions at a school to which students are assigned might be perfectly OK at a school where enrollment is voluntary" (Kolderie 1995, 6). The fact that families and teachers choose a charter school—as opposed to being assigned to it—means that the school has the potential to promote a productive sense of community among teachers, parents, and students. In addition, teachers might play a direct role in school decision making and enjoy flexibility to use their preferred instructional methods. However, as indicated in this collection, teacher empowerment may not be a common practice in charter schools operated by EMCs.

Charter School Laws

State governments have displayed an increasingly active interest in education policy over the past two decades (Mintrom and Vergari 1997b; Wirt and Kirst 1997; Lewis and Maruna 1996). The adoption of charter school laws in a majority of the states (see table 1.1) and the frequent adoption of amendments to these statutes are salient examples of this interest. Moreover, the adoption of robust charter school laws over the opposition of traditionally powerful education interests, such as teachers unions, demonstrates that the power of an idea sometimes prevails over the power of established political interests (see Kingdon 1995; Majone 1989; Reich 1988; Derthick and Quirk 1985).

Nearly all of the charter school laws examined in this book lean toward the "strong" or "permissive" end of the spectrum, and such laws generally promote the proliferation of charter schools. Indeed, the states with permissive charter school laws typically offer the most fruitful and dynamic settings for analysis of the charter school movement. The relatively restrictive Alberta law provides an instructive contrast: the province had just ten charter schools in 2000–2001. Examination of the Alberta case yields useful findings on the types of factors that can inhibit the growth of charter schools.

Charter school laws differ significantly across the states (RPP International 1999a; Vergari 1999).[4] Political exigencies of the legislative process have resulted in enabling laws that diverge in various ways from the charter school ideal (Hassel 1999a). In practice, therefore, charter schools exist along a continuum of autonomy (Wohlstetter, Wenning, and Briggs 1995). Certain features of the laws have had a major impact on the extent to which charter schools have proliferated

Table 1.1

Diffusion of a Policy Innovation: Charter School Laws in North America

1991	1992	1993	1994	1995
Minnesota	California	Colorado	*Alberta*	Alaska
		Georgia	Arizona	Arkansas
		Massachusetts	Hawaii	Delaware
		Michigan	Kansas	New Hampshire
		New Mexico		Louisiana
		Wisconsin		Rhode Island
				Wyoming

1996	1997	1998	1999	2001
Connecticut	Mississippi	Idaho	Oklahoma	Indiana
D.C.	Nevada	Missouri	Oregon	
Florida	Ohio	New York		
Illinois	Pennsylvania	Utah		
New Jersey		Virginia		
North Carolina				
South Carolina				
Texas				

in given jurisdictions and on the overall nature of the charter school movement within these jurisdictions. For example, some charter school laws permit only school districts to authorize charter schools. Other laws permit additional types of charter school authorizers, such as the state board for charter schools in Arizona and university boards in Michigan. Over 80 percent of charter schools are located in states with multiple authorizers or "strong" application appeals processes (Center for Education Reform 2001a). Alberta, Minnesota, North Carolina, and Texas are among a dozen jurisdictions that permit private schools to convert to charter status; most charter school laws permit only public school conversions (RPP International 2000). Massachusetts, Florida, and New York, among other states, have caps on the number of charter schools permitted, while Wisconsin is among several states without such caps.

Political battles over charter school legislation have not concluded with the adoption of charter school laws. In states with charter school laws, both supporters and opponents of the reform have pressed state legislators to keep charter schools on the policy agenda. Across the states, lawmakers have adopted significant amendments to charter school laws. To date, the amendments have typically been aimed at creating more fertile ground for the growth of charter schools. A notable exception is Michigan, where some of the amendments have served to create a more restrictive environment for charter schools.

Differences in charter school laws reflect different facets of the political context in each jurisdiction. Across the United States and Alberta, there are some instructive patterns in the political dynamics that have shaped the adoption and implementation of the charter school policy innovation. State politics scholars Bernick and Wiggins (1991, 73) assert that "the governor is the major policy actor in state government . . . no other individual has the potential to play as important a role." When it comes to education policy, governors are now much more likely to take political chances and commit themselves to reform agendas than they were a couple of decades ago (Lewis and Maruna 1996). Indeed, a common pattern across the United States is that governors have often championed the charter school policy innovation.

For any given jurisdiction, the adoption of a charter school law is not a sufficient condition for the viability of reform. The content of the law matters, of course, and so does the political context for policy implementation. Consider the extreme examples of Arizona and Alberta. The charter school movement in Arizona has enjoyed a constellation of political forces that has fostered a proliferation of charter schools in the state. On the other hand, the charter school movement in Alberta suffers from a dearth of politically powerful allies, and as a result, there are few charter schools in the province.

Organization of the Book

The dynamics of the charter school movement merit careful attention from scholars, policy makers, school administrators, teachers, students of policy reform, and others interested in education reform. The twelve jurisdictions examined in this volume are diverse in terms of geographical location, the year that enabling legislation was adopted, the key features of the charter school law and amendments, the number of charter schools, and the political and technical dynamics of policy adoption and implementation. In short, these eleven states and Alberta are rich sites for analyses of how the charter school idea has been interpreted and implemented across North America.

The chapter authors are well-qualified experts on their respective jurisdictions. The authors include academics in the fields of public policy, political science, and educational administration and researchers with direct experience in the charter school arena. The public discourse regarding charter schools is often passionate, normative, and politically motivated. There is a need for more reflective and scholarly discussion of the charter school innovation, its performance to date, and its implications for public policy. Readers of this volume may identify pro- or anticharter tones in some of the chapters. However, the authors have taken care to back up their claims with sound logic, data, and references, and the chapters complement each other in both tone and content. Thus, the relative enthusiasm for charter schools apparent in the chapter by Joe Nathan, a policy entrepreneur who helped launch the charter school movement in the United States, is counterbalanced by the comparatively reserved assessment of Michael Mintrom, a professor of political science who has tracked the reform over the past decade.[5] Overall, then, the chapters provide readers with a collection of credible data and assertions such that the volume cannot be neatly categorized as either pro- or anti–charter schools.

The chapters to follow include analyses of Minnesota (the state with the first charter school law) and of such other early charter school states as California, Michigan, Massachusetts, and Wisconsin; of states with charter school laws that were adopted in the mid-1990s, such as Florida and North Carolina; and of New York, which adopted its law only in late 1998. As indicated in table 1.2, during the 2000–2001 academic year, the number of charter schools across the twelve jurisdictions examined here ranged from twenty-three in New York to more than four hundred in Arizona, and growth was expected in virtually every case.

Each of the chapters focuses on one of the jurisdictions and systematically addresses several common items for analysis: the charter school law in the jurisdiction, the politics of policy implementation, charter school accountability, controversies and trends, and prospects for the future. Within these common parameters, each chapter emphasizes significant issues specific to the state or province under study that offer lessons for analysts and policy makers across all jurisdictions. Different issues are prominent across the jurisdictions due to their different stages in the implementation process and their respective legal, technical, and political contexts. In both theory and practice, the charter school innovation is multifaceted. Implementation of charter school policy has led to multiple outcomes and implications for how we think about public education. *The Charter School Landscape* illuminates the nature of this diversity and complexity by identifying and systematically analyzing key patterns that have emerged a decade after

Table 1.2

Charter Schools in Operation, 2000–2001

State	Number of Charter Schools	State	Number of Charter Schools
Alaska	16	Mississippi	1
Alberta	*10*	Missouri	21
Arizona	402	Nevada	7
Arkansas	4	New Hampshire	0
California	314	New Jersey	54
Colorado	76	New Mexico	11
Connecticut	16	New York	23
D.C.	33	North Carolina	92
Delaware	7	Ohio	68
Florida	149	Oklahoma	6
Georgia	38	Oregon	12
Hawaii	6	Pennsylvania	65
Idaho	11	Rhode Island	3
Illinois	22	South Carolina	9
Kansas	13	Texas	192
Louisiana	21	Utah	8
Massachusetts	40	Virginia	2
Michigan	183	Wisconsin	87
Minnesota	64	Wyoming	0
Total, North America	**2,086**	**Total, United States**	**2,076**

Sources: Authors of this volume; Center for Education Reform, Washington, D.C.

the first charter school law was adopted. Following is a discussion of several key issues that are addressed throughout the volume.

The Public Bargain: Accountability in Exchange for Autonomy

The charter school policy innovation is one of several recent education reforms aimed at altering the accountability mechanisms in the delivery of education (Mintrom and Vergari 1997b). The "new accountability" in public education refers to a performance-based system of evaluation, as distinguished from one that is compliance based (Fuhrman 1999; Tucker and Clark 1999; Cibulka and Derlin 1998; Cohen 1996; Elmore, Abelmann, and Fuhrman 1996; Ladd 1996). Accountability measures are focused on the outputs of the educational system, rather than on the inputs. With the exception of high-stakes testing, the charter school policy innovation is perhaps the most prominent performance-based education reform strategy in the United States today.

A key component of the charter school concept is the notion that accountability for rules is replaced by accountability for performance. Charter schools engage in a bargain with the public: in return for relief from the bureaucratic rules and regulations imposed on traditional public schools, charter schools are supposed to be held to a higher standard of accountability for results (Nathan 1996). If a charter school does not meet the provisions of its charter, fails to uphold applicable state and local statutes and rules, or lacks support from parents, teachers, and students, it is to be closed.

The trade-off between autonomy and accountability may sound straightforward in theory, but observations of practice across jurisdictions suggest a more complex picture. The ultimate power to revoke a charter is politically tenuous and likely to be "too crude a tool for true accountability" (Fiske and Ladd 2000, 299; Hess 2001). As of December 2000, eighty-six charter schools (about 4 percent of the total charter schools ever opened in the United States) had closed due to failure. An additional twenty-six charter schools had been consolidated into their local school districts for a range of reasons (Center for Education Reform 2001c). Diversity in charter school accountability systems across jurisdictions, and even within jurisdictions, results from differences in the political contexts of individual charter schools, state standardized-testing requirements, the contents of individual charter documents, charter school authorizer philosophies and practices, and the workings of market-style mechanisms of accountability such as parental oversight (Vergari 2000, 2001). That said, a consistent finding across jurisdictions is that the same dilemmas that confront those who seek to engineer greater accountability in the traditional public school system similarly confront the charter school movement. Charter school accountability systems are complicated by technical challenges, capacity limitations on the part of both charter schools and authorizers, and political factors (Vergari 2000; Hassel and Vergari 1999).

Some analysts place a great deal of faith in the ability of market mechanisms to address accountability concerns (see Finn, Manno, and Vanourek 2000). However, Arsen, Plank, and Sykes (1999, 85) avow that the market in and of itself does not hold schools accountable: "The choices of educators and parents may not always correspond to the purposes of public education." The findings presented in this volume are consistent with the recurring thread in previous research that finds that charter school accountability in practice has yet to meet the robust performance standards of the charter school concept as expressed in theory.[6] Yet there is evidence that charter school authorizers are learning from direct experience and each other and are working to develop feasible frameworks for holding charter schools accountable (Vergari 2000, 2001). Massachusetts is widely recognized for having developed a "model" charter school accountability process. Instructively, this model is not without expense. The chapter by Paul Herdman suggests that the model may not be feasible in other states or even over the long term in Massachusetts.

In theory, charter schools are autonomous educational entities. However, charter schools are fundamentally public schools and therefore subject to public-sector oversight. Regarding practice, then, Priscilla Wohlstetter, Noelle C. Griffin, and Derek Chau demonstrate how charter school autonomy has evolved over time and has been limited in significant ways in California. Similarly, Michelle Godard McNiff and Bryan C. Hassel review several regulatory issues, including the contentious issue of special education, that have presented challenges for charter schools in North Carolina.

Charter schools are bound by federal statutes and regulations pertaining to students with disabilities, and analysts have raised questions about the extent to which charter schools are providing ample access and services to special education students. The federally funded National Study of Charter Schools and evidence at the state level indicate that charter schools overall are serving fewer special education students than public schools are in charter school states. According to RPP International (2000), charter schools in the United States have consistently served a lower percentage of students with disabilities than all public schools in charter school states. In 1998–1999, 8.4 percent of charter school students were disabled, while the percentage of students with disabilities in all public schools in charter school states was 11.3 (RPP International 2000, 36).[7]

Charter school advocates Finn, Manno, and Vanourek (2000, 159) acknowledge that some charter schools do not adequately serve special education students and that "this situation needs fixing." They suggest that, prior to the issuance of a charter, the authorizer should ensure that the proposed school will have the necessary staff to do what it says it will do and that no student will be denied admission due to disability. They assert that just as parents of nondisabled students must evaluate a charter school carefully, parents of disabled students should also "be careful school shoppers. If they want the full panoply of government-imposed procedures and services, they may be happier elsewhere" (2000, 158). They further maintain that just as a traditional school district might send a disabled student to a school across town that is better able to meet the student's needs, every charter school need not accommodate the need of every disabled student. Finally, the authors note that many school districts do not provide adequate services to special education students and contend: "The real special education issue is not whether charters are adequately serving disabled youngsters but whether they are able to serve them *differently* than conventional schools. . . . Charter schools are *meant* to be different, even in special education. To insist that they model themselves on conventional schools in their treatment of disabled youngsters is akin to saying that every hospital must perform every operation in exactly the same way" (2000, 160). These positions are not without controversy. Ted Kolderie has noted: "It's unfair to expect the charter system to be perfect; it is fair to ask that it improve on the present system or show the potential to improve over time" (1995, 7). Indeed, when public dollars are at stake, it is important to analyze whether a policy outcome that is *different* than the norm is actually *better* than current policy or other policy options. Importantly, the conclusion of such an evaluation will depend largely on the core value(s) (e.g., choice, equity, efficiency, excellence) favored most strongly by the analyst.

Technical and Political Issues Faced by Charter Schools and School Districts

Finn, Manno, and Vanourek (2000, 110) observe that "most charter schools get off to a late, rushed, and hectic start." In addition, since precious public funds follow students who leave traditional public schools to attend charter schools, school districts in which charter schools are located are often less than enthusiastic about their development. In my analysis of New York, I review challenges and controversies pertaining to one of three charter schools that opened just months after the passage of the charter school law. In their examination of Florida, Tracey Bailey, Carolyn Lavely, and Cathy Wooley-Brown discuss political tensions and technical difficulties that have arisen between charter schools and their authorizing school districts.

Courts and Public Policy

Interest groups regularly turn to the courts after attempts at legislative and administrative remedies are exhausted (Heineman et al. 1997). Courts are major agents in policy making and implementation, and in recent decades, the judiciary has had a significant impact on public education (Wirt and Kirst 1997). In many states, charter school opponents have engaged in court-based strategies for containing or reversing reform. As indicated in several chapters here, a number of state-level court decisions have affected the charter school arena. The category into which a policy issue is classified determines the design of the policy intended to address the issue (Kingdon 1995). In at least one state, the question arose as to whether charter schools must be classified as public schools. In her discussion of several legal questions surrounding charter schools in Wisconsin, Julie F. Mead reviews an attempt by the city of Milwaukee to have charter schools classified officially as private rather than public schools.

Equity and Democratic Values

Charter school opponents lament the diversion of public funds from traditional public schools to charter schools and express skepticism about adequate public oversight of charter schools. Critics also point out that charter schools operate under certain favorable conditions not enjoyed by traditional public schools, such as relief from state and local regulations, low student-teacher ratios, high levels of parental involvement, and the ability to cap enrollments. Observers of charter schools and other school choice initiatives have also suggested that charter schools may foster greater social and racial stratification, fail to uphold democratic values, and undermine the socialization functions of public education in a diverse democracy (see Bosetti 1999; Henig 1994, 1999; Guttman 1987). Critics also suggest that students whose parents or guardians are relatively uninvolved in their educational development will be left behind in a market-based system of public education. School choice proponents respond that "there will always be some parents who are more informed, more alert, and more aggressive at finding the best schools for their children" and that the imperative is to design a choice system that alleviates rather than exacerbates existing inequities (Viteritti 1999, 13).

Charter school proponents point to the inequities evident in the traditional public school system and suggest that charter schools enhance equity by offering new options for underserved populations. Indeed, charter schools are aimed at providing low-income families with the types of educational options that were previously available only to wealthy families able to afford the tuition of private schools or the expense of residing in neighborhoods with good public schools. Equity advocates emphasize that the charter school policy innovation does not address the broader socioeconomic, structural causes of disparities in student achievement between children from wealthy and poor families (Fuller 2000). Nonetheless, Nathan (1996, xiii) notes that "acknowledging enormous problems *outside* schools does not mean that educators cannot do a much better job at helping youngsters *inside* schools."

One of the early concerns of charter school opponents was that charter schools would engage in cream-skimming—in other words, that their student populations would have disproportionate numbers of White, wealthy, academically talented students. This phenomenon has not generally materialized, since many charter schools are serving large numbers of minorities and students "at risk."[8] According to RPP International (2000), in 1998–1999, charter schools enrolled a larger percentage of students of color than all public schools in states with charter schools. The percentage of White students served by charter schools declined slightly over the preceding three years. In addition, charter schools served a slightly higher percentage of students eligible for a free or reduced-price lunch than all public schools in charter school states (RPP International 2000). However, in their review of Alberta, Lynn Bosetti and Robert O'Reilly note that charter schools there are largely products of a middle-class movement. Similarly, Eric Hirsch reports that the charter school movement in Colorado is largely a suburban phenomenon. Lance D. Fusarelli also raises questions about equity and diversity in the Texas charter school system.

Diverse Uses of the Reform

The charter school concept means different things to different interests (see, e.g., Wells et al. 1999). Its multifaceted quality explains the broad political appeal of the idea and makes it an intriguing subject for analysis from a variety of perspectives. For instance, in some districts, charter schools have eased overcrowding. Joe Nathan notes that the Minnesota charter school law has provided a new option for small rural public schools that were facing the prospect of being closed by their districts.

Public Education for Profit

One of the most controversial features of the charter school landscape is the presence of for-profit EMCs. The literature on public-private partnerships suggests that conflicts of interest between the two sectors are a key obstacle to successful partnerships. Most notably, the profit motive may conflict with public-policy obligations to society (Rosenau 2000). Indeed, the public and private sectors have different orientations. For example, the private sector is focused on reaping returns on investments and achieving corporate goals, while the public sector is oriented toward democratic decision-making processes and the achievement of social goals (Reijniers 1994). In his chapter on Michigan, Michael Mintrom discusses the increasing presence of EMCs in the operation of charter schools in that state.

Systemic Change

While opponents of the charter school concept might prefer to view the measure as a distraction or as confined to a marginalized series of niche schools, advocates hold fast to the tenet that charter schools have the potential to provoke systemic change. As noted earlier, a competitive public school marketplace is hypothesized to encourage accountability from traditional public schools as well as charter schools. Thus, Kolderie (1995, 7) avows that "the real purpose" of charter school reform is "to cause the main-line system to change and improve." Similarly, Hassel (1999a, 129) asserts that "the *full* promise" of the charter school reform includes systemic change. However, highly successful, highly experimental ideas do not diffuse rapidly in public education (Hassel 1999a; Elmore 1996). In addition, district responses to the introduction of competition may not lead to systemic reform. School districts may turn to the courts or the legislature for relief from the competitive threat; use the alleged costs of a charter school as a basis for threats about cuts in popular programs; or choose to ignore charter schools, viewing them as "pressure valves" for the welcome exit of disgruntled parents (Hassel 1999a, 136–41). Rofes (1998) found that school districts in which charter schools were located had not typically responded with swift, dramatic improvements. However, federally funded research on the impact of charter schools on school districts found that about half of the forty-nine districts examined in the five-state study reported that they became more customer-service oriented, increased their marketing and public-relations activities, or increased their communications with parents. All forty-nine districts made changes in education and/or operations that district leaders attributed to the presence of charter schools (RPP International 2001). In their chapter on Arizona, Frederick M. Hess and Robert Maranto provide various examples of how charter schools there appear to be spurring responses from the traditional public school system.

In total then, the chapters offer the opportunity to draw useful comparisons across twelve diverse jurisdictions, to become more aware of the political and policy issues that have shaped the contours of the charter school landscape, and to contemplate the key policy questions raised by the charter school concept as implemented. In the concluding chapter, I synthesize the findings and perspectives presented in this volume, highlighting key similarities and differences across jurisdictions and raising questions for further inquiry and reflection. Are charter schools just "another flawed educational reform" (Sarason 1999), a "dismal failure," and a "wasteful experience" (Good and Braden 2000, 176–77)? Do these schools signal the "reinvention of public education" (Finn, Manno, and Vanourek 2000, 16–17)? Or are they something in between these extremes? We shall return to these questions in the concluding chapter.

2 • Minnesota and the Charter Public School Idea

Joe Nathan

IT STARTED WITH people, a napkin, and a pen. "It," in this case, is the charter idea. This chapter describes how that idea was shaped in Minnesota and how Minnesota has used the charter idea to help accomplish important educational goals. Recently, Harvard University and the Ford Foundation recognized the charter idea as one of the nation's best public policy initiatives. This chapter also discusses some of the successes, dilemmas, and challenges that Minnesota faced and from which other states might learn.

What Led to the First Charter Public School Law in North America?

The charter idea developed from previous Minnesota experience with public school choice. Since the early 1970s, the state's two largest school districts, Minneapolis and St. Paul, have offered choice options within the districts. For example, with help from a major federal grant, Minneapolis decided to offer four distinctive options in one section of the city, beginning in the fall of 1971: a K–12 "free school"; a K–6 open school; an elementary "continuous progress school"; and a traditional elementary school with graded, self-contained classrooms, dubbed a "contemporary school." Providing options within the school district proved very popular, and within five years, the last three options were available in every section of the city. Additional options were also created, including a Montessori public school.

Similar activity took place in St. Paul, where the district opened a K–12, 500-student "open school" in September 1971. The open school was the result of an effort started by four mothers that quickly grew to a multiracial group called

"Alternatives Inc.," with a mailing list of more than 1,000 people. As of summer 2001, the St. Paul Open School had just completed its thirtieth year of operation.

By 1980, public school choice options in both Minneapolis and St. Paul were available to all kinds of students. These districts generally did not follow the path of many districts in establishing magnet schools that required passing admissions tests to enroll. Indeed, a large federal study found that more than half of the nation's secondary magnet schools and more than a quarter of the nation's elementary magnet schools use admissions tests (Steel and Levine 1994).

At a 1988 conference convened by the Minneapolis Foundation, several school reform activists met one evening after hearing two speakers—Al Shanker, president of the American Federation of Teachers, and Sy Fiegel, one of the architects of the East Harlem public school choice plan in New York City. At the conference, Fiegel had described East Harlem's efforts to increase student achievement and reduce discipline problems. Fiegel, then–East Harlem superintendent Anthony Alvarado, and a few others had decided to ask teachers for ideas about new, small "schools within schools," which would provide options available to students and educators. The results of this initiative were very encouraging (see Fiegel 1993).

Shanker had described the frustrations many teachers felt in school systems. He noted, for example, that educators in many districts had tried to create the kind of schools within schools that Fiegel described. Shanker stated: "Many schools within schools were or are treated like traitors or outlaws for daring to move outside the lock-step and do something different. Their initiators had to move heaven and earth to get school officials to authorize them, and if they managed that, they could look forward to insecurity, obscurity, or outright hostility" (Shanker 1988).

After hearing Shanker and Fiegel, five people sat down to chat. The five included Barbara Zohn, president of the Minnesota Parent Teacher Student Association; Elaine Salinas, education program officer of the Urban Coalition in Minneapolis–St. Paul; Ted Kolderie, a former journalist and director of the Citizens League (a well-respected Minneapolis-based public-policy group); Ember Reichgott, a Democratic state senator from a Minneapolis suburb; and myself.

This group had worked closely over the previous several years on legislative initiatives that expanded public school choice in Minnesota. These included:

- the Post-Secondary Option Law (1985), which allowed high school juniors and seniors to attend colleges and universities, with state funds following the students, paying all tuition and lab and book fees;
- Area Learning Centers and High School Graduation Incentives (1987), which allowed twelve- to twenty-one-year-old students who were not suc-

ceeding to attend a public school outside their district or a private nonsectarian school, with a contract from a local school board; and

- Open Enrollment (1988), which allowed students ages five to eighteen to move across district lines as long as the receiving district had room and the transfer did not harm efforts to racially integrate schools.

The group agreed that while Minnesota families now had a good deal of power to make a choice among public schools, there were very few choices. That is, very few school districts had yet decided to provide different kinds of schools from which families could select. The group thought, as Ted Kolderie put it, that it was "time to open up more options on the supply side of education."

For the previous several years, alternative school advocates and groups around the nation had been urging that groups of parents and teachers be allowed to create new options within public education (Nathan 1989). In response, California assemblyman John Vasconcelos had introduced legislation requiring that if at least twenty parents agreed to send their students to a newly developed educational option, a school district should open the program. However, this legislative proposal was not approved.

The Minnesota coalition thought that the state could not just rely on local school districts to offer options. After all, school boards already had the power to offer different kinds of schools, yet less than a handful of Minnesota's more than 400 districts were doing so. The group was frustrated by the fact that most Minnesota districts had not followed the lead of Minneapolis and St. Paul in offering educational options. Moreover, they were concerned that because of seniority provisions, innovative inner-city schools sometimes had to accept faculty who did not support the schools' approaches. Group members also knew that several distinctive public schools in Minneapolis and St. Paul had significant waiting lists and that the districts nonetheless did not seem eager to replicate these schools.

Thus, the group was eager to see more high-quality educational options for Minnesota families. The group had also seen the value of Minnesota's Post-Secondary Option Law. The law expanded opportunities for thousands of students and helped stimulate improvements in the K–12 system. Fundamentally, the group thought that giving groups of parents and teachers a way to get approval of new schools outside of the existing school district system was a critical public-policy issue.

Why was the word "charter" used? In his talk, Shanker had mentioned the term "charter," which he had picked up from a New England educator named Ray Budde. For the previous fifteen years, Budde had been urging school districts to do what European kings had done for explorers—give them a "charter" to explore (Budde 1988). Budde wanted local districts to give educators a "charter" to create new approaches to teaching math, reading, or other academic subjects. Shanker went further, suggesting that local districts give teachers a chance to create new schools, as the East Harlem school board had done (Shanker 1988).

The Minnesota group liked the idea of more options but concluded that the state's experience showed that school choice initiatives could not rely solely on local school boards. So, on that evening in 1988, members of the Minnesota group wrote their ideas down on a napkin: public school options, use of a charter or contract, and some group other than a local board to authorize or sponsor the pioneering educators. Ted Kolderie added a critical element to this list—the idea of a trade: more responsibility for performance in exchange for more autonomy. This formula had been suggested a few years earlier by Tennessee governor Lamar Alexander, then chair of the National Governors' Association. Alexander wrote, "The Governors are ready for some old-fashioned horse trading. We'll regulate less, if schools and school districts will produce better results" (Alexander 1986, 3).

Influenced by Minnesota's experience with public school choice and building on the ideas of Budde, Shanker, and Fiegel, the group came up with the charter idea—a fundamental rethinking of how public education is offered. The idea goes to the heart of how states provide public education. Kolderie describes this new kind of policy in a paper that is widely regarded as the founding document of the charter school movement: "The States Will Have to Withdraw the Exclusive" (Kolderie 1990b). The states, Kolderie proposed, should permit other groups, besides local school boards, to offer and authorize public education.

What Is the Charter Idea?

The Minnesota group developed the following key ideas, which have formed the basis for charter school laws.

1. The state will give more than one publicly accountable organization the power to authorize or sponsor new kinds of public schools. Such entities could include the state board of education, local school boards, cities, public universities, county boards, et cetera.

2. The sponsors will develop a "charter," or contract, with a group of people who want to create a new kind of public school or want to convert an existing public school to a charter school.

3. The contract will specify improvements in student achievement that the school will have to produce in order to have its contract renewed.

4. The charter school is public. It is nonsectarian. It may not charge tuition. It may not have admissions tests of any kind. It must follow health and safety regulations.

5. Existing public schools may convert to charter status, and this should happen if a majority of the teachers in the school vote to convert.

6. There is an up-front waiver of state and district regulations and rules about curriculum, management, collective bargaining, and teaching. States may specify student outcomes. However, determining how the school operates should be up to the people who establish and operate it. The charter school concept trades bureaucracy for accountability, regulation for results.

7. The charter school is a school of choice. It is actively chosen by faculty, students, and families. No one is assigned to attend or work in a charter school.

8. The charter school is a discrete entity. The law may let the founders choose any organizational type available under general state law or may specify an organizational type, such as nonprofit. As a legal entity, the school has its own board. There is real site-based management. Teachers, if employees, have full rights to organize and bargain collectively. However, their bargaining unit is separate from any district bargaining unit.

9. The full per-pupil funding allocation moves with the student to the charter school. This amount should be roughly the average state allocation per pupil or the average in the district from which the student comes. If the state provides extra funds for students from low-income families or with disabilities, these funds should also follow the students.

10. Charter school teachers should be protected and given new opportunities. Teachers may take a leave from public school systems and while on leave will retain their seniority. They may continue to participate in the local or state retirement programs. New teachers may join state retirement programs. They may be employees or organize a professional group through which they collectively own and operate the school.

The Seed Sprouts

The number of charters in Minnesota has increased steadily since the original law was passed in 1991. As of May 2001, sixty-four charter schools were in operation, with several additional schools scheduled to open in September 2001. Charter schools have been created in urban, rural, and suburban areas of the state.

Table 2.1

Evolution of the Minnesota Charter School Law

	Number of Charter Schools Permitted	Sponsors	Lease Aid	Number of Charter Schools in Operation
1992	8	Local school board	$0	1
2001	Unlimited	Local school board; public or private university; nonprofit with yearly budget of more than $1 million; state education department on appeal	Lesser of $1,500 per pupil unit or 90 percent of lease	64

The Minnesota charter school law has changed steadily to reflect the interest that educators, families, and legislators have shown in this idea. As indicated in table 2.1, the most dramatic changes include the following.

- The elimination of caps on the number of charter schools permitted. Originally, eight charter schools were allowed statewide. The current legislation permits an unlimited number of charter schools.

- An expansion of eligible sponsors to reflect the original idea. Originally, Minnesota legislation permitted only local school boards to sponsor charter schools. Today, public or private postsecondary institutions, the state commissioner of education (called the commissioner of the Department of Children, Families and Learning in Minnesota), and nonprofit organizations with at least a $1 million annual budget, in addition to local school boards, can sponsor charter schools. Each of these groups must have the approval of the commissioner of the Department of Children, Families and Learning.

- Provision of lease aid. Originally, the state provided no funds to help charter schools with building costs. Today, the legislature provides up to 90 percent of the cost of a lease or $1,500 per pupil, whichever is less. The 2001 legislature allocated more than $17 million for lease aid for the 2002 and 2003 fiscal years.

- Provision of start-up funds. Originally, the state offered no money to help charter schools start. In addition to serving as a "pass-through" for federal start-up funds, the 2001 legislature allocated more than $3 million in state money for the next two fiscal years to help with start-up expenses.

Table 2.2

Student Demographics in Charter Schools and All Public Schools in Minnesota

	White	Black	Hispanic	Asian/Pacific
Charter Schools	51.9%	26.7%	3.4%	10.3%
All Public Schools	82.2%	7.2%	3.0%	4.5%

	American Indian	Free/Reduced Lunch	Disabled	Limited English Proficient
Charter Schools	7.0%	60.1%	13.6%	10.0%
All Public Schools	3.1%	26.8%	10.9%	3.4%

Source: RPP International 2000

Note: Data for Minnesota charter schools come from 1998–1999 data supplied by charter schools. Racial and disability data for all public schools come from 1997–1998 U.S. Department of Education Statistics Common Core of Data. Income statistics for all public schools come from 1994–1995 U.S. Department of Agriculture Statistics. Limited English Proficient statistics for all public schools come from 1996–1997 U.S. Department of Education statistics.

Who Attends Minnesota Charter Schools?

Minnesota charter schools consistently have enrolled a higher percentage of students representing communities of color, low-income students, students whose knowledge of English is limited, and disabled students than the average public school in the state. Minnesota public schools, on average, enroll about 82 percent White students and 18 percent students of color. However, Minnesota charter schools enroll, on average, 52 percent White students and 48 percent students of color. See table 2.2.

Oversight and Accountability

As the founding state for the charter school idea, Minnesota has examined a series of questions over the past decade. Would anyone want to open a charter school? Which families would be interested in attending charter schools? How would a sponsor hold a charter school accountable? Would a sponsor actually close a charter school? Ten years of experience with the charter school concept now permit at least partial responses to several of these questions.

As of May 2001, nine charter schools had been closed by their sponsors. The

Minneapolis School District closed a charter school because after three years, the school had little record of improving student achievement. The state board of education closed a charter school it sponsored for essentially the same reason. St. Paul closed several charters it sponsored because of financial and academic problems. And a charter in an American Indian–controlled area was closed for several reasons, including intense disagreements about the purpose and direction of the school. In each case, charter school proponents supported the sponsor's decision to close the school. They insisted that closing ineffective schools was one of the central features of the charter idea.

One of the first key questions that Minnesota charter school founders and sponsors had to consider was how charter schools should be held accountable. In particular, how much progress should a school have to make over a three-year period in order to justify its existence? In many ways, this is a new question in education. The original Minnesota charter school law envisioned that Minnesota charters would participate in the state's outcome graduation standards, just like all other public schools. However, for several years charters had to develop their own graduation requirements, as the state phased in its standards over the last seven years. Nevertheless, like other public schools, Minnesota charters are now using the state standards.

Minnesota charter schools are also expected to participate in the statewide testing program. Minnesota currently administers statewide tests in the third, fifth, and eighth grades. Students are required to pass the state's eighth-grade reading, writing, and mathematics tests in order to graduate from high school. The 1998–1999 school year was the first in which the third- and fifth-grade tests were given and the third in which the eighth-grade tests were given.

Can charter schools improve student achievement? The answer from several Minnesota charter schools has been yes. Evaluations of several charter schools—including Minnesota New Country School, New Visions School, City Academy, Twin City Academy, and Community of Peace—show they are improving student achievement. Whether measured by traditional nationally normed standardized reference tests, writing tests scored by outside experts, or other means, a number of Minnesota charter schools have demonstrated the ability to make a clear, quantifiable, positive impact on student achievement.

Overall, the demographics and test scores of Minnesota charter school students are similar to those of other students in Minneapolis and St. Paul. The average student in these districts and the average charter school student score below the statewide average. Interpretations of the data vary. Some have used these statistics to suggest that charter school students are not doing as well as proponents pre-dicted. Others point out that in most cases, charter school students do about as well as or better than urban students. Moreover, in terms of funding, charter schools continue to receive less per pupil than the average public school in the state and more than $1,500 less per pupil than in the Minneapolis or St. Paul public schools (Mandala 1998). Some have argued that it is a sign of strength that charter schools score as well as the urban districts, despite the fact that they are funded at well below the level of the state's two largest urban districts. It is important to inter-pret the test results cautiously, since 45 to 55 percent of the students in the char-ter schools had attended those schools for less than a full year. Thus, the tests were actually measuring what the students had learned in their previous schools.

In addition to having students take the state-mandated tests, many charter schools have suggested other forms of accountability. These include proposals that students should demonstrate at least one year's growth on national norm–referenced tests for each year they attend the charter school; that the percentage of students who score in the bottom quartile on nationally normed standardized tests should decrease; that student writing skills should increase, as measured by various tests of writing; and that there should be reductions in the number of stu-dents involved in the juvenile justice system.

Charter School Issues Now under Discussion

One of the ongoing issues in the Minnesota charter school movement has been how to help sponsors carry out their duties in a responsible manner. The over-whelming majority of Minnesota's charter schools—about 90 percent—are not sponsored by the state. The relationship between these nonstate sponsors and the state education department is a subject of continuing discussion. In the last few years, the state education department has started to hold workshops not only for people who want to create new charter schools but also for groups that are con-sidering sponsorship of a charter school or are actually doing so. These "sponsor meetings" have covered a vast array of subjects, including governance, account-ability, and "who is responsible for what" in the state's charter school system, and these discussions are ongoing.

Sponsor responsibilities were highlighted in the 2000–2001 school year when several charter schools made headlines. The schools were closed because they lacked funds to continue, because academic achievement was low, or because of a combination of factors. Some legislators and journalists charged that several charters had not submitted audits, had not used standard accounting procedures, and had tolerated conflicts of interest involving for-profit organizations that helped to operate and were trying to help govern charter schools (see Drew and Lonetree 2001; Locke 2001). The 2001 state legislature required that the state education department provide training sessions for charter school boards in the areas of finance and accountability.

Another ongoing discussion involves the role of for-profit organizations and charter schools. Some Minnesotans question the role in charter schools of large out-of-state management companies, which help operate 10 to 15 percent of Minnesota's charter schools. Concerned about possible conflicts of interest, the 2001 Minnesota legislature insisted that representatives of such organizations should not be on the boards of charter schools. The vast majority of Minnesota charters are not run by for-profit companies, but many schools purchase some services (such as accounting and legal assistance) from outside providers.

Over the last few years, the state education department has provided more guidance to schools and sponsors. For example, the state has strongly encouraged the use of pre- and posttesting for charter school students. Such a practice permits the charter school to obtain a benchmark measure of student achievement against which to track progress over time. The state has also convened teams of state education department staff to visit each charter school and to offer feedback about its strengths and weaknesses. Several charter school sponsors have asked the state to share copies of the reports that these visits generate.

Minnesotans continue to discuss ways to improve the supervision that sponsoring organizations provide to the schools. Some sponsors have a staff member who visits the sponsored school(s) regularly. Other sponsors have been known to ignore the sponsored school(s) for years. The legislature has authorized sponsors to charge schools they sponsor a certain amount of money to pay for evaluation services. But many charter advocates think more effort is needed to improve the work of sponsors.

During the 2000 legislative session, the state's charter school association encouraged the legislature to remove its requirement that the state education department also review a charter application before it can be approved by the sponsor. State officials successfully opposed this provision, arguing that the state offers "quality control" for contracts developed between other charters and sponsors.

Another major issue being intensely reviewed involves charter school buildings. Minnesota's legislation prohibits charter schools from owning buildings.

The rationale behind this was originally that charters would not have enough money to purchase buildings. However, as the charter movement has matured and as a number of charter schools have had their charters renewed, this issue is being revisited. Some charter school advocates assert that these schools should, at some point, be able to purchase buildings and apply state assistance not only toward lease costs but also toward purchase price. For instance, some advocates suggest that a charter school should lease during its first three-year charter contract. But if that charter is renewed, the argument goes, a charter ought to be able to purchase its building. Building ownership increases the stability of a charter school. At this point, the prohibition on owning a building remains. However, many charter advocates will keep working on this issue.

Charter Schools and Education Reform in Minnesota

What about the impact of the charter school movement on the larger education system in Minnesota? This is not an easy question to answer. However, several changes in Minnesota schools over the last decade appear to have been influenced, at least in part, by the charter school movement.

Growth in the Number of Alternative Schools

In 1989, approximately 4,000 students attended alternative public schools in Minnesota. By 2000, the number had grown to more than 101,000 (Minnesota Department of Children, Families and Learning 2000). Alternative schools generally are secondary programs for students who have not succeeded in traditional schools. Some of the people who started alternative schools earlier in the 1990s started charter schools later in the decade. Over time, it became increasingly obvious to school districts—rural, suburban, and urban—that there were teachers who would start charter schools if the districts did not create alternative schools for students. As a result, there has been dramatic growth in the number of school districts that have started alternative schools.

Growth in the number of alternative schools and the number of students served by such schools is probably not solely a result of the charter movement. It became clear to many school districts that there were growing numbers of students for whom traditional junior and senior high schools were not working. However, the fact that people could (and would) create charter schools if districts did not respond probably had an influence on many districts that started and/or expanded their alternative schools programs.

Innovative Practices among Charter Schools

Several Minnesota charters have been recognized for their innovative practices. The Minnesota legislature has awarded hundreds of thousands of dollars to the New Visions Charter to help train educators and families who wish to be more effective with students with some form of disability. The Bill and Melinda Gates Foundation awarded the Minnesota New Country School in Henderson, Minnesota, more than $4 million to help promote replication of the school. The school is run by a cooperative owned by the teachers who work in the school. Minnesota New Country also provides one computer and workspace for each of its students and uses a project-based individualized approach in which students make public presentations of what they have learned at least three times a year. City Academy, the nation's first charter, has hosted both former president Bill Clinton and former U.S. education secretary Richard Riley, who have praised the school and encouraged others to learn from it. One of City Academy's innovations involves the way it shares space with a St. Paul city recreation building, thus making better use of existing space and more efficient use of tax funds.

More Options in Rural Communities

Some of the strongest, most popular Minnesota charter schools are in rural areas. The charter idea has helped demonstrate that providing more choice among public schools is possible in rural as well as metropolitan areas. In several cases over the past few years, rural school districts decided to listen to families pleading with them not to close a relatively remote elementary school that was a part of a larger district. Instead, community members in Hanska, Echo, Lafayette, and Nerstrand were granted charters by local school boards allowing them to keep these schools open as charter schools. School boards noted that granting these charters was generally a much more positive and politically popular action than closing the schools. There are numerous instances of people in small towns opposing bond proposals for years after the larger school district had closed their local elementary school. However, in cases in which the larger district approved the creation of a charter school rather than closing a school, parents and community members tended to support local school bonds.

Growth in the Number of Public School Options
Serving a Cross Section of Students

In several Minnesota communities, such as Rochester and Forest Lake, proponents of expanded options within the district explicitly noted that they would
prefer to create an option within the district but would create a charter school if
the district declined to work with them. In Rochester, the school board agreed to
create a school based on E. D. Hirsch's Core Knowledge curriculum. The Forest
Lake board created a Montessori public school option. In both cases, proponents had suggested that they might create a charter if the district would not accept their proposals.

A decade ago, most public school choice options serving a cross section of
students were located in Minneapolis and St. Paul. As of mid-2001, dozens of
such options, including schools within schools and magnet schools, were now
located in rural and suburban districts throughout the state. The charter movement is not totally responsible for this growth. However, as school boards have
considered the development of new options in suburban and rural areas, the fact
that educators and parents now have new opportunities—via charters—to create
programs if districts are not responsive has not gone unnoticed.

Changes in the Union Response

One final point might be made about a shift within the state's largest teachers
union, the Minnesota Education Association (MEA). As the original charter
school legislation was being reviewed, an MEA lobbyist sent a letter to all Minnesota state senators strongly opposing the idea (Furrer 1991). Accompanying
the letter was a four-page statement insisting that the charter idea was "a costly
hoax" and that it risked "creating elite academies for the few."

Two years later, the state MEA newspaper ran a major article on charter schools
that featured Milo Cutter, who is the cofounder of City Academy in St. Paul, the
nation's first charter school, and an MEA member (Berglund 1993). Significantly,
the article praised City Academy. While the MEA and Education Minnesota, the
organization that resulted from the merger of the MEA and the Minnesota Federation of Teachers, have not taken a leadership role in helping members to start
charter schools, most observers say that within the last few years, the union has
not tried hard to repeal the charter law or to vigorously oppose efforts to expand
the number of charters permitted.

Concluding Comments

The strong support charter schools received from the Republican-controlled Minnesota House and the Democrat-controlled Minnesota Senate in the 2000 and 2001 legislative sessions suggests that support for charters crosses the political spectrum in Minnesota. Legislators from both parties have served as strong public advocates for charter schools.

Nearly a decade of experience with charter schools is enough to answer several critical questions that were raised when the charter school idea was first proposed in Minnesota. Will educators be willing to risk their jobs to carry out their dreams? The answer is clearly yes. Will the charter schools they found in Minnesota serve primarily affluent, wealthy students doing well in traditional schools? The answer is clearly no. Will sponsors actually close charter schools that do not appear to be improving student achievement? Here, the answer appears to be yes. Will charter schools actually improve student achievement? While definitive assessments of all charter schools have yet to be completed, evidence from a number of Minnesota charter schools clearly demonstrates that they have improved student achievement. Will the charter school movement stimulate change and improvements in the larger educational system? While the results are not conclusive, there have been significant responses from school boards, generally in the form of creating new educational options within the district.

Moreover, a number of districts, including both Minneapolis and St. Paul, are delegating more decision-making power to the school site. While the charter school movement cannot be given total credit for the trend of decentralized decision making (a trend apparent in many parts of the country), various mass-media reports have pointed out that charter schools do have control over their own budgets and personnel. This information dissemination has led some educators in district-run public schools to push for similar opportunities in their own schools.

In my view, the charter school movement is often misrepresented by critics who say that the ultimate rationale for charter schools relies on markets. Some opposed to the charter idea have called it a step toward privatization in public education. In some states, many of the schools are run by private corporations. But in Minnesota, birthplace of the idea, the charter school movement has been seized by veteran and young teachers who recognize that this idea gives them a chance to carry out their dreams. Thus, it is the ultimate form of teacher empowerment, as well as a move to expand opportunities for youngsters. Therefore, the charter idea is more accurately seen as an expression of faith in educators and in the power of education to make a positive difference in the lives of youngsters.

Perhaps most importantly, the charter school movement is about hope. Conversations I have had with legislators in more than twenty-two states suggest that this concept of hope is one of the fundamental reasons that the charter movement has spread so widely. At a time when many questions are being raised about the influence of public schools, the charter movement stands out as a place where educators, parents, and community groups can and have joined together, believing that they can make a major, measurable difference in the lives of youngsters.

This frightens some people, who prefer to argue that schools cannot have much influence on children from troubled backgrounds. Charter school advocates argue that problems outside schools, such as violence, racism, and crime, must be addressed. But they also insist that problems outside schools should not be used as an excuse for little progress within those schools. The dramatic growth of the charter school movement suggests that this hopeful, optimistic view about the potential of these charter schools to make a positive difference in children's lives is winning many supporters.

Minnesota charter schools are offering new ideas for curriculum, facilities, and organization to educators, families, and policy makers throughout the nation. In Minnesota, as in many other states, the charter school movement appears to be one of the concepts Victor Hugo was referring to when he wrote that "stronger than all the armies of the world is an idea whose time has come."

3 • Charter Schools in California

A Bruising Campaign for Public School Choice

Priscilla Wohlstetter, Noelle C. Griffin,
and Derrick Chau

IN 1992 CALIFORNIA became the second state to enact charter school legislation. By the 2000–2001 school year, California was first in the nation in the number of students enrolled in charter schools, with nearly 115,582 of the national total of about 500,000 charter school students (California Department of Education 2001; Center for Education Reform 2001e). California was second only to Arizona in the number of operating charter schools.

California charter schools were distributed across many different parts of the state by the beginning of the 2000–2001 school year. Of the state's fifty-eight counties, thirty-eight had charter schools. Both large and small districts had granted charters—ranging from the massive 700,000-student Los Angeles Unified School District (with thirty-seven charter schools in 1999–2000, including the Crenshaw/Dorsey charter complex of sixteen schools) to the tiny 700-student Eastern Sierra Unified School District (with one K–12 charter school). Most California charter schools were located in urban areas; however, about a quarter of the state's charter schools were in rural counties.

In this chapter, we trace the evolution and impact of the charter school law in California. Features of the educational and political contexts, such as a diverse student population, poor student achievement, an inconsistent statewide testing program, and provoucher political forces, have influenced the development and refinement of the charter school law over time.

The California Charter School Law

In analyses of charter school laws, California's is ranked among the laws that include all the provisions central to the charter school idea, making California a

Figure 3.1

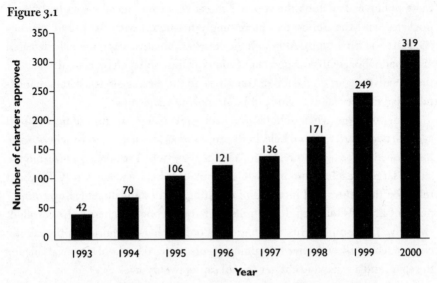

Source: California Department of Education 2001; Charter Schools Development Center 2001

"strong" charter school state (Bierlein 1997; Hassel 1999). The original California charter school law started off relatively strong, and over time, the law was amended to further strengthen in practice the basic principles that led to the initial legislation. Thus, it is not surprising that the number of charter schools in California has increased consistently since 1993, as shown in figure 3.1.

The Beginning

When Republican governor Pete Wilson signed into law the initial Charter Schools Act of 1992, sponsored by state senator Gary Hart (D-Santa Barbara), he also vetoed a competing charter school bill, sponsored by another Democrat, Assemblywoman Delaine Eastin. Thus, the tale of charter school reform in California began in the state legislature with a duel between two Democrats, who respectively were chairs of the Senate and Assembly education committees.

Charter school legislation in California was proposed during the same time period as a school voucher initiative—Proposition 174 (2 November 1993). The voucher initiative would have entitled parents to an annual scholarship amount of about $2,600 per child for use at a public or private "scholarship-redeeming" school (Legislative Analyst's Office 1993). The voucher initiative was led by one of the state's top business leaders—the chair of the California Business Roundtable—and voucher proponents included chief executives from around the state.

State policy makers took the voucher threat seriously—its sponsors had "deep pockets," and the public was increasingly frustrated with the public schools (G. Hart and Burr 1996). Although the voucher initiative was ultimately defeated at the ballot box, with 70.2 percent of voters against and 29.8 percent of voters for the initiative, it garnered enough votes to send the message to legislators that educational choice claimed wide public support in California.

Thus, in 1992, when school vouchers were rising on the public's reform agenda, two charter school bills, both proposed as alternatives to vouchers, were introduced in the legislature. Eastin's bill, AB 2585, had strong support from the state's largest teachers union, the California Teachers Association (CTA), and reflected the values and interests of the education establishment. Key components of Eastin's bill included requiring charter school teachers to be certified, collective bargaining rights for charter school teachers, requiring approval of a charter school by collective bargaining agents, a charter school approval role for the state, and a statewide charter school cap of twenty-five.

In the end, Governor Wilson rejected Eastin's bill on the grounds that it failed to embrace the basic principles of the charter school concept—local control, responsiveness to clients, and school choice. Wilson's reaction was also political: he detested the union lobbies and did not much care for Eastin, who had strong ties with labor.

SB 1448, which ultimately became the Charter Schools Act, was crafted by Senator Hart to foster local control of schools: "We . . . wanted the process of developing charter schools to remain local . . . the schools to be administered under the terms of a broad charter petition, and . . . to invest the locally elected school board with the power to approve the opening of a charter school" (G. Hart and Burr 1996, 38).

Hart's bill allowed for the creation of new-start charter schools, as well as charter schools converted from existing traditional public schools. The bill required that charter school developers define the school's educational program and specify measurable student outcomes in the charter. The bill also set the renewable term of the charter at five years. An application for a charter school had to be approved by at least 50 percent of the teachers at an existing school or 10 percent of a district's total teachers. Local school boards were vested with primary authority for approving charters. Hart's bill also exempted charter schools from most state and local educational codes and from collective bargaining agreements. Further, teachers in charter schools were not required to have a teaching credential. Finally, under SB 1448, the number of charter schools statewide was capped at 100, with a maximum of 10 per district.

From the outset, SB 1448 won support from the California School Boards Association (CSBA). In agreement with Hart, the CSBA viewed the charter school concept as a way to return control to local communities and to lessen the influence of the state's powerful collective bargaining laws (G. Hart and Burr 1996).

On the other hand, many education interests opposed the bill. According to Hart, the usual bargaining and compromise that traditionally characterize the legislative process were absent here: "We wanted to keep the bill as simple and flexible as possible to allow many charter school alternatives. We were fearful that once we started to accept amendments to reinsert statutory 'protections,' we would be deluged with such requests. . ." (G. Hart and Burr 1996, 39). Consequently, few interest groups had their views represented in the bill. The state parent-teacher association wanted to include prescriptive language about the nature of parent involvement. The California Teacher Credentialing Commission wanted all charter school teachers to be credentialed. The CTA wanted all existing collective bargaining rights explicitly protected. In Hart's view, all of these issues were best determined locally by charter school developers, rather than by the state. The only provision Hart added to his bill, in an attempt to obtain support from the teachers unions, was the requirement that a specific percentage of teachers approve a charter application. Unfortunately, the provision did not lessen the opposition of the CTA and instead had the deleterious effect of angering other school personnel unions, who viewed the provision as explicitly excluding their members from any role in the development of charter schools (G. Hart and Burr 1996).

Eventually, both charter school bills—SB 1448 and AB 2585—were sent to a legislative conference committee. However, as Hart observed, "it was quite apparent that reaching a compromise between our bill and Eastin's would be very difficult" (G. Hart and Burr 1996, 39). Ultimately, the two bills were sent to Governor Wilson, who signed SB 1448 into law and vetoed Eastin's bill. The California Charter Schools Act of 1992 took effect on 1 January 1993.

California's Evolving Charter School Policy

Charter school advocates argue that student performance is enhanced when schools are autonomous, self-governing organizations. Like those in most other states, California's charter school law initially featured a mix of provisions—some that encouraged the development of autonomous charter schools and others that limited their development. In subsequent years, legislative amendments have generally strengthened charter school autonomy along three dimensions: autonomy from the district and state, autonomy inside the school, and autonomy of parents and students (Wohlstetter, Wenning, and Briggs 1995).

Autonomy from the District and State

A key assumption underlying the charter school movement is that district and state regulations stymie innovation in public education; thus, in order for charter schools to become high-performance organizations, they need to be deregulated. The original 1992 law granted California charter schools a mega-waiver, exempting them from most local and state education codes. Charter school autonomy was further strengthened by 1998 amendments pertaining to charter approval. One such amendment allowed parents (rather than only teachers) to sign petitions for new start-up charter schools.[1]

Under California's original charter school law, local and county school boards were the initial charter-granting agencies. But these boards were allowed to deny charters for virtually any reason with no reporting requirements. Charter applicants had to follow a cumbersome appeals process, involving an appointed ad hoc appeal panel of teachers and district governing board members, as well as a final appeal to the county board of education. The 1998 amendments provide that in cases where a local or county school board denies a charter school application, the applicants may appeal directly to the county board of education and/or the state board of education (SBE) for charter (Premack 1999). The 1998 amendments also require local school boards to report specific reasons for denying charter school applications.

Other amendments to the California law have firmly established the legal status of charter schools. Under the 1998 amendments, charter schools may now organize as nonprofit corporations, and the charter-granting agency is protected from liability for charter school operations. Also clarified was the fiscal relationship between the district and the school. The 1992 California law tied charter school funding to average daily attendance and the per-pupil amount of the "base revenue limit."[2] During the early years of implementation, districts extracted financial concessions from or levied high overhead charges on charter schools (Premack 1999). In 1998, revisions to the law allowed charter schools to receive funding directly from the state and limited district charges to actual oversight costs, which helped curtail high district overhead charges. Building on this new funding system, amendments in July 1999 simplified state funding to charter schools by organizing a new block grant that allocated the funding by formula (Premack 1999).

Hart was interested in promoting local school autonomy, and the original California charter school law prescribed a fairly small state role. The SBE was given formal responsibility for recording charter school approvals and for reviewing appeals from local or county school districts. Later, as financial support for charter schools increased, the California Department of Education (CDE) assumed responsibility for distributing federal and state funds, including planning grants, to charter schools. The state legislature, however, retained its oversight role, mandating evaluations of the charter school program. The Legislative Analyst's Office commissioned a statewide evaluation of California charter schools in 1997 and is commissioning a second, which is due to be completed in 2003.[3]

Overall then, the balance of power was vested primarily at the local level. Charter authorizers, typically school districts, were obligated to oversee their approved charter schools. The law requires schools to specify in their charters the details of their educational programs, including assessment strategies. Authorizers then use these assessments (which by law must include the state-mandated standardized test) when considering charter renewal. Occasionally, authorizers in larger districts, like Los Angeles and San Diego, have contracted with external evaluators to assist with oversight. In 1997, the Los Angeles Unified School District contracted with a team of researchers to assess the district's charter schools just before five of the schools were up for renewal (Izu et al. 1998). The evaluation was subsequently used by the district in its decision to renew the schools' charters.

District discretion was bruised a bit by the 1998 amendments (AB 544), which shifted the burden of proof for charter rejection to charter authorizers. While authorizers previously had discretion to simply reject a charter application with no explanation, the presumption has now shifted in favor of the applicants: authorizers are required to grant charters unless factual findings can be given to support rejection. This change made it much more difficult for district or county authorizers to reject charters.

Autonomy inside the School

A second type of autonomy concerns the extent of control charter schools have in the areas of governance, personnel, student admissions, curriculum, and budgeting (Wohlstetter, Wenning, and Briggs 1995). In California, limitations on this type of autonomy have focused largely on the mission of the charter school and decisions about which students to serve. As in Colorado, California legislators expressed a preference for having charter schools serve at-risk students; however, in contrast to Rhode Island and Texas, the California charter school law did not establish a precise number of at-risk charter schools or a percentage of at-risk students to be enrolled in charter schools statewide (ECS and NCSL 1998). However, another provision in California's original charter school law required charter schools to maintain an enrollment that reflects the racial and ethnic balance of the general population residing in the school district.

In recent years, legislators have turned to refining their definitions of what constitutes a charter school and who is eligible to attend. With the 1998 amendments, charter school students were required to meet the public school minimum-age requirements. According to Eric Premack, director of the Charter Schools Development Center at the Institute for Education Reform in Sacramento, the amendment was an attempt to establish some funding equity between charter schools and other public schools. Noncharter public schools cannot enroll under-age students and receive the usual K–12 funding for them. The amendment required the same of charter schools and so forced all public schools—charter and noncharter—to operate preschool and child-development programs that are funded separately (and at a lower rate) from the K–12 system (Premack 1999).

In 1999, the legislature required charter schools to offer a specified, minimum number of minutes of instruction and maintain written records documenting all pupil attendance.[4] These modifications effectively curtailed the discretion enjoyed by non–classroom based charter schools (e.g., home study and distance learning). But they also represented a compromise among policy makers who wanted to dissolve charter schools that were networks of homeschoolers and those who favored educational diversity within the population of charter schools.

With influential teachers unions in California, the issue of teacher credentialing has been hotly debated since the charter school concept was first introduced in the legislature. The original charter school law contained no requirements that teachers have a state teaching credential. Nevertheless, charter schools in practice tended to hire credentialed teachers. A 1998 study found that 79.5 percent of teachers in California charter schools were credentialed, not too much lower than the percentage (87.3) for all California public schools (RPP International 1999b).

With strong backing from the CTA, legislators revised the initial charter school law in 1998 to require that all teachers in charter schools have a state credential, thereby limiting charter school control over who is hired. A year later, the legislature allowed all public schools, including charter schools, to hire teachers through an alternative route: individuals who possess a post-baccalaureate degree and five years of related work experience qualified for a preliminary, two-year teaching credential.[5] Public school teachers hired through this alternative route must complete preservice training and an additional professional development program to receive a permanent credential from the state's credentialing commission after four years. Thus, this amendment provides charter schools with the opportunity to recruit and hire noneducators as classroom teachers. At the same time, teacher standards were preserved, since alternative-route candidates were required to work through the California Commission on Teacher Credentialing.

In addition to activity on the credentialing issue, teachers unions have fought to preserve collective bargaining rights for charter school teachers. In the first generation of charter schools in California, some charter operators negotiated a leave of absence from the union for their staffs during the school's first five years (SRI International 1997). At the end of that initial period, teachers who had previously worked in traditional public schools were faced with the decision of whether to remain at the charter school or transfer to a district-run school and maintain the benefits they had accrued with the district.

In April 1999, Democratic assemblywoman Carol Migden introduced a highly controversial amendment that attracted attention from charter school stakeholders and analysts nationwide. Migden's AB 842 proposed that all charter school staff become employees of the authorizing district and be subject to the district's collective bargaining agreement—in effect, mandating collective bargaining in all California charter schools. Charter school advocates were particularly concerned that Migden's amendment was a serious departure from the commonly understood definition of a strong, or even genuine, charter school law. According to Premack, the bill would have taken away the most important freedom that charter schools have: "It would not only force them to bargain collectively, but to bargain as part of the existing bargaining units" (Billingsley and Riley 1999, 1). Even Oakland's Democratic mayor, Jerry Brown, who has a history of strong support from unions, blasted the bill: "The proposal takes the side of the state teachers union against parents who are struggling to take control of their children's education because a failed education system has sold them out. . . . These courageous parents will not be defeated now by distant political machinations over which they have no voice or control" (DelVecchio 1999). Ultimately, AB 842 lost its support among lawmakers, and in its stead, Governor Gray Davis signed AB 631 into law in October 1999. AB 631 gave each charter school the option of being part of the district's collective bargaining unit or of becoming an independent entity for collective bargaining purposes (Premack 1999). AB 631 set a 31 March

2000 deadline for charter schools to declare their collective bargaining status as to whether teachers wanted to be unionized or not.

Autonomy of Parents and Students

Wohlstetter, Wenning, and Briggs (1995) argue that consumer sovereignty is enhanced when parents and students have an expanded set of options within the public school system. In the original legislation, California policy makers restricted the number of charter schools to a cap of 100 with a maximum of 10 charter schools per district. After considerable deliberation, however, the California SBE used its broad-ranging waiver authority in 1997 to waive the cap. The SBE approved charter schools beyond the limit such that, at the time the cap was removed in 1998, a total of 136 charter schools had already been approved in the state. The 1998 amendments allowed 250 charter schools in the 1998–1999 school year and an additional 100 schools each year following. As of March 2001, the SBE had recorded 370 approved charter schools, including those in all-charter districts (Charter Schools Development Center 2001).

Despite the initial cap of 100 charter schools, California's charter school law was designed to enhance parent and student choice. Charter schools could be brand-new schools, as well as conversions from traditional public schools. Any individual or group—including parents—that secured approval from at least 50 percent of teachers at an existing school or 10 percent of a district's total teachers could apply to open a charter school. (With the 1998 amendments, parents were allowed to sign charter petitions.) Parents and students had the freedom to choose any charter school in the state. Further, California, like many other states, recognized the link between consumer information and consumer power: the original law required that charter schools issue periodic progress reports to the community, including parents.

The original California charter school law and subsequent amendments have stimulated the creation of charter schools by increasing options for their development. The amended law allows multiple entities to serve as charter authorizers, including public school districts, county offices of education, and the SBE. In addition, California charter schools are allowed in their applications to define their own degree of autonomy, from schools that continue to be fiscally "dependent" on the local district to schools that are extremely autonomous and that operate "independently" as their own school districts. This provision, in effect, encourages a larger number of schools to go charter, including some that are not able or willing to take on the responsibility of full fiscal autonomy.

Finally, the state legislature has tried to stimulate the development of new-start charters. Amendments in 1999 increased the maximum loan amount available through the Charter School Revolving Loan Fund from $50,000 to $250,000. The amendments, which were intended to ease the burden of development costs, also extended the repayment period from two years to up to five years.

California's Charter Schools

In March 2001, 314 charter schools, including those in all-charter districts, were operating in California, representing 3.6 percent of all the state's 8,761 public schools (California Department of Education 2001). While this number is high relative to other states, the percentage of public school students in California attending charter schools remains quite small—2 percent (California Department of Education 2001; Charter Schools Development Center 2001).

Schools

In the beginning, most California charter schools were preexisting public schools that converted to charter status. (Unlike some other states—for example, Michigan —California's charter law does not allow private schools to convert to charter status.) More recently, there has been a significant rise in the number of new-start charter schools in California, and the overall distribution has switched in favor of new-starts (67 percent) over conversions (33 percent) (California Department of Education 1999). This distribution now mirrors national statistics: across all states with charter schools about 70 percent of the charter schools are newly created (RPP International 2000).

Some evidence points to operational differences between new-start and conversion schools. New-start schools tend to be more autonomous and often organize as independent legal and fiscal entities (Premack 1996). New-start schools also are on the whole more innovative than conversions (Patterson 2000b). By contrast, conversion schools tend to remain closely aligned with their authorizing districts and rely on the districts for most centralized services. A few conversion schools, however, have moved away from their authorizing districts to become self-sufficient.

Although the evidence is sparse, motivations for charter applicants in California appear to be similar to those in other states. In its 1997 study of California charter schools, SRI International found that five of the twelve charter schools studied in-depth were started because their founders wanted to pursue new ideas or extend previous reform efforts. Other motivations included desires to increase parent involvement and to gain autonomy within an existing school system. In RPP International's (2000) national study of charter schools, the reasons given for starting charter schools were much the same. The majority of charter schools (58 percent) indicated that their most important motivation for charter school creation was to "realize a vision." The study also found that parental involvement (3 percent) and increased autonomy (9 percent) were reasons for starting charter schools.

Interestingly, while about a quarter (23 percent) of charter schools nationally were founded to serve special populations, this motivation did not surface in the top five reasons for charter school creation in California (RPP International 2000; SRI International 1997). While a number of state charter school laws have specific set-asides for special populations (e.g., at-risk students), the California law does not, and few schools maintain statistics on the number of at-risk students they serve.

Most California charter schools are small. Nationally, the median student enrollment in charter schools is 137, compared to 475 for all public schools (RPP International 2000). Similarly in California, the overwhelming majority of charter schools enroll fewer than 500 students. In the 1999–2000 school year, the smallest reported charter school in California enrolled 3 students and the largest enrolled 4,500.[6]

SRI International's (1997) study of California charter schools found that new-start charter schools tended to be smaller, averaging 244 students, while conversion charter schools averaged 620 students. In sum, enrollment in California's charter schools tends to be larger than the national charter school average (132) but smaller than the average state enrollment of 767 students per school.

Some of the enrollment-size differences in California charter schools may be related to grade-level configuration. Nationally, the grade-level configuration of charter schools differs considerably from district-run public schools. Charter schools, both nationally and in California, feature K–8, 6–12, and K–12 configurations far more frequently than district-run public schools (RPP International 2000). Charter schools with these grade configurations accounted for over 45 percent of California's charter schools according to 1999–2000 school year data (Charter Schools Development Center 1999). Further, it is noteworthy that while elementary schools account for almost half the number of California charter schools, a significant percentage (16) of charter schools span kindergarten through the twelfth grade. By contrast, California public schools with K–12 configurations account for less than 1 percent of all California public schools.

Observers have noted that California charter schools are especially innovative in their governance arrangements. Charter school constituencies—including teachers and other staff, community organizations, and parents—have pushed for shared governance. For example, some California charter schools are "principal-less" schools, while the principal's responsibilities in some others are shared between two people. Several community organizations, including the Conservation Corps and the Urban League, operate as nonprofits and manage charter schools in California. Since 1997, Edison Schools, Inc., has received contracts from districts and from nonprofit charter holders to manage charter schools. In March 2001, Edison Schools, which is the only educational management company active in the state, operated seven charter academies in California (approximately 2.2 percent of the state's operating charter schools).

In terms of educational services, many California charter schools have worked to change the traditional structure of schooling by lengthening the school day, extending the school year, establishing lower student-teacher ratios, offering Saturday classes, using individualized educational plans, and creating on-line "virtual classrooms" with a computer on every desk of every student. There has been little research on the educational focus within California charter schools. In SRI International's (1997) study, researchers conducted a statewide survey and found that most California charter schools (71 percent) reported that their educational programs emphasized all disciplines equally. A few charter schools reported an emphasis on particular disciplines or subjects, including technology (9 percent), English/language arts (9 percent), science (7 percent), and math (6 percent). Some California charter schools have also associated with other major education reform efforts, including Accelerated Schools and the Coalition of Essential Schools.

While the majority of California charter schools (184, or 77 percent) feature classroom instruction, a notable number of charter schools (55, or 23 percent) have experimented with delivering educational services in nontraditional ways (California Department of Education 1999). As shown in table 3.1, home study is the most popular type of alternative instruction. A few charter schools rely on distance learning and independent study. The prevalence of nontraditional instruction pushed the state legislature to regulate instruction time and student attendance in California charter schools, as noted earlier.

Table 3.1

Types of Alternative Instruction in California Charter Schools

Type of Classroom Instruction	Number of Charter Schools	Percentage of California Charter Schools
Home Study	33	13.8
Distance Learning	12	5.0
Independent Study	10	4.2

Source: California Department of Education 1999

Closures

California has experienced few charter school closings due to charter nonrenewal or revocation. By March 2001, thirteen schools (or 3.5 percent) have been forced to close: nine had their charters revoked, largely for mismanagement or inappropriate use of funds; four did not have their charters renewed, most because the schools opted not to renew and decided to convert back to noncharter status. Thus far, no California charter schools have been closed on the basis of poor student performance. This outcome may be due partly to the large number of conversion charter schools in the state. Many conversion schools had previous experience with site-based management, and this may have eased the transition to self-governing charter status (Wohlstetter and Griffin 1998). The persistence of charter schools in California also may relate to a well-developed technical assistance network that offers support services such as site visits to individual charter schools, training workshops for groups of charter school developers and operators, and ongoing information dissemination about the California charter school law and current implementation issues.

Students

Students in California charter schools reflect some of the diversity of California's population as a whole. Like other public institutions, charter schools cannot discriminate against any student on the basis of ethnicity, national origin, gender, or disability. Further, the charter school law requires that each school maintain an ethnic balance reflective of the general population of the district in which the charter school is located.

In terms of ethnicity, the percentage of non-White students in California charter schools (59.4) is larger than that of White students enrolled in charter schools

Table 3.2

Demographics of Charter Schools Compared to All Public Schools
in California, 2000–2001

	Percentage White	Percentage Black	Percentage Latino	Percentage Asian/Pacific Islander	Percentage Other
Charter Schools	40.6	17.3	32.8	5.0	4.3
All Public Schools	35.9	8.4	43.2	11.0	1.5

Source: California Department of Education 2001

(40.6) (California Department of Education 2001). When students in California charter schools are compared to students in all California public schools (see table 3.2), some other differences emerge. While charter schools tend to enroll higher percentages of Black and White students than California public schools in general, California charter schools also tend to enroll lower percentages of Latinos and Asians/Pacific Islanders.

Students who attend California charter schools include in significant numbers English language learners (ELLs), students with disabilities, and children from economically disadvantaged families. However, when compared to the entire California public school population, the percentages of such students enrolled in charter schools are relatively low. For example, while ELL students composed 24.9 percent of California public school students in 1999–2000, the percentage of ELL students in charter schools was roughly 17 (California Department of Education 2001; RPP International 2000). Similarly, the percentage of economically disadvantaged students in California charter schools in 1999 was 31.1, but statewide such students accounted for 47.3 percent of all public school students. Students with disabilities were enrolled in charter schools at close to the same rate—just 6.4 percent of the total charter school enrollment in 1999—as in California public schools (9.6 percent in 1998). This compared to approximately 11 percent in all states where charter schools are located (RPP International 2000).

Trends and Controversies

California charter schools have faced a number of political and technical challenges in the years since the adoption of the charter school law. At the same time, unique supports for the charter school community have developed.

Support Services for Charter Schools

Particularly noteworthy is the Institute for Education Reform at California State University, Sacramento. The institute's Charter Schools Development Center, modeled after England's Grant-Maintained Schools Foundation (Wohlstetter and Anderson 1994), provides technical assistance, training, and resources to California charter school developers, operators, charter-granting agencies, and policy makers. Funding for the center comes mostly from private donations and minimal fees for services and publications.

Charter schools in California have also benefited from the California Network of Educational Charters (CANEC), a nonprofit organization founded in 1993 that operates an E-mail list serve and publishes a monthly newsletter to promote information-sharing among charter school participants and policy makers. A combination of business, government, and private support allows CANEC to fund a lobbyist in Sacramento. CANEC also sponsors an annual conference (the largest state-level charter schools conference in the country) to help build bridges among charter schools and to strengthen links between charter school research and practice (Patterson 2000a).

Although a charter school "industry" has emerged and grown quickly in California, this growth has not been without controversies. The key implementation issues in California center on three areas: the authorizing process, student selection and admissions, and school accountability.

The Authorizing Process

As described earlier, the California charter school law allows multiple entities to serve as authorizers for charter schools, including public school districts, county offices of education, and the SBE. While charter school applicants may enjoy having multiple authorizers from which to choose, the authorizing system has also resulted in conflicts over the chartering process and charter oversight.

As of May 2001, California charter schools are able to "shop around" across school districts for an authorizer. As a consequence, some school districts grant charters to schools beyond district boundaries. The district doing this most frequently is the Twin Ridges Elementary District (Nevada County), which has chartered schools within its boundaries, as well as in Napa and Mendicino Counties. Twin Ridges has established a cooperative support-service arrangement whereby each charter school contributes a fixed percentage of its budget into a pool (Feller 2001). The pool is used to provide business and legal services, insurance, staff development, special education, and other services to the schools within the cooperative. While charter schools authorized outside their school districts' boundaries accounted for only 4 percent of the total number of charter schools in California by May 2001 (Charter Schools Development Center 2001), "authorizer shopping" is controversial. The arrangement, of course, angers the CSBA, which views it as a loss of control for local school boards, while charter school advocates, who support the idea of multiple authorizers, consider Twin Ridges among the "state's most sophisticated and thoughtful charter-granting agencies" (Patterson 2000b; Premack 2000).

There have also been tensions between districts and the state regarding planning grants to charter school developers. The CDE determines which charter school developers merit planning grants, and these decisions are made independently of charter authorizers. This process, thus, sets the stage for a situation in which a charter school may receive a planning grant from the state but subsequently have its charter application denied by the local school district. Moreover, some districts feel pressure to approve charter applicants that the state already has funded. In such cases, local authority to select which charter school developers to approve is, in effect, usurped.

To partially remedy this problem, the CDE developed a plan that requires a district's (or county office's) signature on a planning-grant application. This would eliminate the problem of the CDE awarding a grant to developers who were then unable to find a district or county to act as coapplicant. A more direct solution— outlawing the authorizing of charter schools outside district boundaries—was introduced into the California state legislature in 1999 (AB 696). However, AB 696 was eventually revised, with completely new language not pertaining to out-of-district chartering, and was passed in May 2000 with minor effects on California charter schools (Charter Schools Development Center 2001). Charter school proponents referred to it as "a bill in search of a purpose," since the overwhelming majority (96 percent) of charter schools are located in the district that granted their charter (Patterson 2000b).

Finally, the option of establishing either a fiscally dependent or fiscally independent charter school in California continues to force the question of precisely what constitutes a "real" charter school. By opening the door for schools that are not able or willing to take on the responsibility of full fiscal autonomy, the option of fiscal dependence arguably attracts a larger number of schools to seek charter status. However, questions remain as to whether the fiscally dependent schools are truly charter schools. Some observers have called these "faux" charter schools (Vanourek, Manno, and Finn 1997), and researchers have noted little distinction between fiscally dependent charter schools and schools operating under district-run site-based management (Izu et al. 1998; Wohlstetter and Griffin 1998). Thus, California's experience suggests that fiscal dependence extends beyond fiscal issues; fiscally dependent charter schools also tend to be dependent in many other facets of school operations, including personnel, curriculum, and instruction decisions.

Student Selection and Admissions

Opponents argue that charter schools are tools for cream-skimming—that they will disproportionately serve White, upper-middle class students, rather than providing educational opportunities for all ethnic groups (University of California, Los Angeles 1998). Partially in response to this charge, the California charter school law requires that each school describe in its petition how the school will achieve an ethnic balance reflective of the general population within the territorial jurisdiction of the school district in which the charter school resides.

In practice, meeting this ethnic diversity requirement has been a challenge for many charter schools. During the 2000–2001 school year, California charter schools averaged 40.6 percent White students, while California schools as a whole averaged 35.9 percent White students (California Department of Education 2001). For some charter schools in the state, this situation was more acute: in about one-fifth of California's charter schools, the percentage of White students was more than 25 percent higher than the state average (SRI International 1997).

For many charter schools, the diversity situation is aggravated by conflicting requirements in law, as well as conflicting goals in charter petitions. While all California charter schools must set forth a plan for achieving ethnic representation, all conversion charter schools must give enrollment preference to students who were already enrolled at the school (Izu et al. 1998). As a consequence, if the geographic area surrounding the school is not ethnically representative of the district as a whole, the two goals—giving priority to local students and replicating the district's ethnic balance—become incompatible. While diversity of charter school students has been an issue high on researchers' agendas (RPP International 2000;

Izu et al. 1998; University of California, Los Angeles 1998; SRI International 1997), few California policy makers have voiced concern regarding the issue. As of May 2001, no charters had been revoked in cases where the charter school student population did not meet the ethnic balance of the district.

Transportation is another problem limiting the ability of some charter schools to attract an ethnically diverse student population (University of California, Los Angeles 1998; Izu et al. 1998). Due to effective lobbying from unions representing school bus drivers and mechanics, authorizing districts are not required to provide transportation for charter school students (Premack 2000). Although some school districts continue to provide student transportation for conversion charters, district transportation is not generally available to students in new-start schools or to new students in conversion schools. For charter schools located in ethnically homogeneous areas, the lack of district transportation often interferes with schools' intentions to attract an ethnically diverse group of students.

Beyond ethnic diversity, some critics express concern that California charter schools are free to set admissions requirements "if applicable." The University of California, Los Angeles, Charter School Study (1998) cited several criteria that charter schools have developed as mechanisms for enrolling students whose characteristics are deemed the most desirable. Such criteria include admissions preferences based on residence (as described earlier), academics, and discipline. Some charter schools, for example, have explicit student codes of conduct for attendance, academic progress, and behavior. Violation of these codes can lead to student suspension or expulsion. Critics have suggested that these codes favor more advantaged students, particularly in terms of the academic-standards criteria. Economically advantaged students may have had access to higher-quality education in the past and thus may be better prepared to meet schools' academic standards. In practice, however, there is little evidence to support this claim: there is no data to suggest, for instance, that charter schools with student codes of conduct attract more advantaged students. Indeed, many charter schools with such policies have as their mission to serve students in the most disadvantaged communities.

Another controversial aspect of student selection concerns parental involvement requirements. The majority of California charter schools (75 percent) require that a parent or adult sign a contract with the school when enrolling a child (SRI International 1997). These contracts typically cover parents' acceptance of school rules and parental involvement requirements. Parental involvement contracts thus are used as a condition of admitting a child to a charter school, and students, likewise, can be expelled if parents do not meet their involvement requirements.

In surveys of parents and teachers in Los Angeles charter schools, many reported great satisfaction with parental contracts, arguing that such contracts helped promote better communication between parents and schools (Izu et al. 1998). The evaluation of charter schools in Los Angeles also found high degrees of parental involvement across a variety of socioeconomic backgrounds. Indeed, a charter school in South Central Los Angeles serving primarily economically disadvantaged families had a demanding parental contract and evidenced the strongest parental involvement among all charter schools in the area (Izu et al. 1998).

However, there is some concern that economically disadvantaged families may be less able to meet parental involvement requirements. Such families typically have fewer resources (time, money) than more advantaged families, and so, critics argue, they opt not to send their children to charter schools because they are not able to meet the demands for parental involvement (University of California, Los Angeles 1998). At this point, there is no evidence to suggest that parental involvement contracts present a problem for less affluent parents. To the contrary, a few evaluations have highlighted how charter schools have structured their programs to enable parents from all socioeconomic levels to contribute (see, e.g., Izu et al. 1998; SRI International 1997).

School Accountability

One of the most consistently cited benefits of charter schools is increased accountability for student outcomes. If charter schools do not meet educational goals, their charters can be revoked and the schools will go out of business, unlike other public schools, which are allowed to remain open. Proponents of charter schools argue that increased accountability will produce both higher-quality education and improved student achievement (Nathan 1996).

Studies of California charter schools have consistently found that strong accountability is lacking, partly due to deficiencies in the chartering process and partly due to the statewide testing system, which has been in flux since California first enacted its charter school law (University of California, Los Angeles, 1998; Izu et al. 1998; SRI International 1997). Although California charter schools are required to include educational goals in their charters, a majority of schools reported few consequences for not meeting these goals. For example, SRI International (1997) found that while 85 percent of California charter schools provided some sort of student achievement data to their authorizers, only 4 percent reported that their authorizers had taken any action in response to the data. As suggested by the charter school closings in California, authorizers have been more diligent on matters of fiscal and administrative accountability (University of California, Los Angeles 1998; SRI International 1997).

Some deficiencies in the accountability system have been attributed to the nature of charter school applications, particularly among the first generation of California charter schools. Several studies concluded that charter school applications were characterized by vague goals and outcomes, which were difficult to define and measure (University of California, Los Angeles 1998; Izu et al. 1998; Wohlstetter and Griffin 1998). As charter authorizers in California have gained more experience, the specificity they require from charter school developers likewise has increased. This area, however, continues to be a challenge and is the focus of much technical assistance for authorizers in the state.

As noted earlier, California charter schools are required to administer statewide assessments to track student achievement. When the charter school law went into effect in 1993, the state used the California Learning Assessment System (CLAS). However, controversy over CLAS, which featured performance-based testing, led the state to discontinue its use or the use of a state assessment system of any sort until 1998, when California adopted the Standardized Testing and Reporting (STAR) system, which mandates the Stanford Nine achievement test (SRI International 1997). In 1999, the Stanford Nine achievement test also became the basis for the new Academic Performance Index (API), which is the cornerstone for Governor Gray Davis's school accountability system. The API includes a numerical score for each school and a decile ranking for comparison with other schools statewide. The future API system will incorporate high school exit-exam results and attendance and graduation rates, as well as results on the Stanford Nine achievement test, into API scores for schools.

Beyond changes in the state testing and accountability system, many authorizing districts also experienced changes in their own district-level assessment programs. Many districts used the California Test of Basic Skills (CTBS) at the time the first charter schools were opened and then used CLAS; in 1997 some districts switched back to CTBS, but by 1998 all districts administered the Stanford Nine achievement test. All of these changes in the standardized testing process made it very difficult for charter schools and charter authorizers to track changes in student achievement over time and to compare charter school students to students in other public schools as part of a systematic accountability process.

Conclusions

Several unique characteristics of the charter school process in California have shaped the experiences of legislators, authorizers, and educators. First, the California charter school law is dynamic: it has been amended numerous times and will likely be subjected to further refinements. The law has evolved in response to lessons learned from the initial implementation process and also from the feedback of multiple stakeholders. Many of these changes increased charter school autonomy. However, this was not always the case; a few decisions, such as the change that put age limits on charter school students, curtailed local discretion. Overall, there has been a trend toward supporting the development of charter schools, as evidenced by the steady increase in the number of charter schools since initial passage of the California charter school law. This support, moreover, has come from Democrats and Republicans alike. During most of the period between 1992 and 1999, there was a split in partisanship between the executive and legislative branches, with a Republican governor and a Democratically controlled Assembly and Senate.

Second, the lack of ethnic diversity among charter school students, particularly in comparison to other public school students, remains an area of controversy for charter school critics. Given the overall heterogeneity of the California student population, California charter schools continue to face issues of diversity, equity, and access. The U.S. Justice Department recently blocked three predominantly Black charter schools on the grounds that they promoted racial separation in school districts, despite parents challenging old desegregation orders to protect their charter schools (McQueen 2000). In California, there are no signs of lawmakers or the courts taking steps to address racial diversity, suggesting that the issue is likely to be left to charter school authorizers. Providing transportation or additional technical assistance to charter schools in ethnically diverse or minority areas might increase the overall diversity of charter school students, but there currently are no plans in place for such assistance.

Finally, the struggle over the definition and implementation of external accountability for California charter schools continues. There is still confusion about what charter schools should be held accountable for and through what mechanisms their performance should be monitored. Although authorizers are moving toward requiring greater specificity in charter applications, relying on school districts as the primary charter-granting agency (with authorizing, oversight, and renewal responsibilities) is considered by some observers to be a huge policy mistake. Critics argue that many district officials dislike the charter concept and so are often disinclined to exercise competent oversight or incapable of doing so.

The implementation of a statewide assessment system, now underway in California, could help remove some barriers to a stronger accountability system for charter schools. As the state's new accountability system—the API—matures, holding charter schools accountable may shift to become a shared responsibility of the state and local levels. Regardless of the division of responsibility, perhaps the central and most difficult policy challenge in the California charter school system is how to establish a balance in the charter school approval, oversight, and renewal processes that supports the charter school concept yet is tempered by high-quality oversight.

4 • Letting a Thousand Flowers (and Weeds) Bloom
The Charter Story in Arizona

Frederick M. Hess and Robert Maranto

ARIZONA IS THE only state with something approaching an institutionalized free market in public education. Marrying the entrepreneurial and antibureaucratic philosophy of the wide open West, a dominant Republican party, relatively weak teachers unions, and an executive branch that at least in the 1994–1998 period aggressively promoted charter schools, Arizona provides a milieu in which charter schooling has rapidly grown into a prominent and discourse-shaping feature of the state's public school system. Arizona is thus a useful laboratory, demonstrating how a large-scale charter school system can evolve and how it affects schooling.[1]

In 1994, Arizona adopted the law that quickly fostered the nation's most expansive charter school system. The law allows public, private nonprofit, and for-profit schools to open as charter schools. In addition, private schools can convert to charter status. For the first six years of the program, up to twenty-five charters annually could be granted by the Arizona state board of education (SBE), with another twenty-five granted by an activist and consciously political state board for charter schools (SBCS). In addition, local school boards were allowed to charter. Several school boards generated revenue by issuing charters for operators in other parts of the state, charging substantial "administrative fees." In 2000 the legislature amended the law to remove the twenty-five-charter cap on the two state boards but also to stop local school boards from chartering distant schools. Finally, a single charter holder can open multiple sites. In short, the Arizona charter school law has few of the restrictions typical of charter laws elsewhere (Hassel 1999a). Accordingly, as of January 2001 Arizona had 270 charter operators with an estimated 402 charter school campuses, approximately 20 percent of the total number of charter schools in the United States.[2]

The Adoption of the Arizona Charter School Law

As in many states, Arizona parents and legislators expressed increasing concern about the mediocre performance of the state's students during the late 1980s and the early 1990s. The *Arizona Republic,* the state's dominant daily newspaper, editorialized on several occasions about the need to improve state schooling.

In Arizona, student scores on the National Assessment of Educational Progress (NAEP) tests put the state in the bottom third of the forty-one states participating in the state-level assessments in 1992. Moreover, only about 27 percent of Arizona students took the ACT assessment, the dominant college-entrance exam in the state. In 1994, only 50 percent of Arizona seniors went on to higher education, the eighth-lowest rate in the nation (Miller 1998). Finally, as of 1990, Arizona's dropout rate of 14.4 percent significantly exceeded the national average of 11.2 percent (U.S. Bureau of the Census 1997). Constituents pressured legislators to do something significant to improve public education. School vouchers and charter schools, both of which were gaining increasing national attention during the early 1990s, were proposed by conservative state legislators as potential solutions.

School choice advocates found fertile ground in Arizona. Arizona is one of the most politically conservative states in the nation. Save for 1996, Arizona has voted Republican in every presidential election since 1952, usually by wide margins (D. Berman 1998, 60). Arizona's governor, both of its senators, and five of its six U.S. representatives are Republican (Barone and Ujifusa 1999, 5). The Goldwater Institute, a prominent promarket think tank, provides moral support and resources to school choice advocates, and the state's culture is receptive to arguments for market competition and for downsizing the public sector. Indeed, the success of market-based competition for public services has made Phoenix a vanguard in the movement to reinvent local government (Osborne and Gaebler 1992; Osborne and Plastrik 1997).

Most significantly, Republicans had unified control of the legislature and the governor's office when Arizona's charter school law was adopted. Republicans held solid majorities in both houses throughout the early 1990s. After the 1992 elections, Republicans held thirty-five of the sixty House seats and eighteen of the thirty Senate seats. In the 1994 elections, they gained three additional House seats and another Senate seat. These gains gave the Republicans over 60 percent of the seats in both chambers after 1994. Republican Fife Symington served as governor from 1990 until 1997, when he was forced to resign under indictment

(Timmons-Brown and Hess 1999). The dominant political position enjoyed by Republicans allowed them to use the threat of voucher legislation to squeeze union and Democratic opponents of school choice into accepting compromise charter school legislation.

Legislative sponsors placed both voucher and charter school bills on the policy agenda. The influential Arizona Education Association (AEA) and the less powerful Arizona Federation of Teachers (AFT) opposed both reform initiatives, worrying that the proposed legislation could threaten the professional status, job security, and working conditions of professional educators. According to the AEA, as of 1998, approximately 79 percent of Arizona's teachers were AEA members; AFT leaders claim fewer than 10 percent. The AEA and the AFT argued that because charter schools would not be required to hire certified teachers, they would undermine the professional teaching force, subverting standards and opening the door for unqualified teachers to serve in charter schools. Even more distasteful to the AEA and the AFT than the proposed charter legislation, however, were the proposals for school vouchers.

Interestingly, and with crucial implications for the resolution of the charter school battle, the AEA was politically crippled in 1994 when it was forced to settle with the state attorney general regarding charges that the union had violated campaign finance laws. Attorney General Grant Woods allowed the union to pay a $4,000 civil penalty for making $67,500 in illegal political contributions to its political action committee in the 1990 and 1992 elections ("Teachers Union" 1994). The result was a union weakened and lacking moral authority even as it sought to blunt vigorous pro–school choice efforts.

In March 1993, two opposing bills were introduced in the Arizona legislature, one in the Senate and one in the House. Senator Bev Hermon (R), chairwoman of the Senate Education Committee, and Senate Majority Leader Tom Patterson (R) cosponsored the Senate legislation (SB 1200). SB 1200 proposed to funnel state aid directly to individual schools through a charter school system. It was thought that this would redirect much decision-making power from school boards to teachers and parents, give parents a choice of where to send their children, eliminate some education mandates, and ultimately increase student achievement. Aid would be based on student enrollment and would be sent directly to the school to cover operating costs. Any school that received a charter could have the charter renewed after an initial three-year period if it demonstrated that it had met its stated charter goals.

Charter school supporters liked the bill's assurance that a charter applicant who was turned down by the local school district could seek approval from another school district governing board, the SBE, or the SBCS (Keegan 1999, 190). This provision meant that local school boards would not be able to squeeze out competitors or retain control over entry into the local educational market. Patterson envisioned charter schools "as a little escape valve to the bureaucracy and domination of the public school districts" (Schultze 1993). Although SB 1200 passed in the Senate by a vote of sixteen to nine, the House did not act on the bill (Timmons-Brown and Hess 1999).

HB 2125, introduced in 1993, focused on funding initiatives—a decentralized decision-making fund, a New Arizona School Fund, and a School Improvement Fund. Bill sponsors intended the decentralization provisions to shift decision-making power down from the district level to individual schools; the New Arizona School Fund was essentially a charter school program under another label.

The incorporation of a number of educational programs into HB 2125 was supposed to soften the threat posed by the charter school proposal. As part of the strategy to incrementally enhance school choice while avoiding conflict with those concerned about equitable participation, HB 2125 sponsors also proposed to fund transportation costs for all students participating in open-enrollment plans and to fund a variety of at-risk, kindergarten, and preschool "model" programs.[3] HB 2125 was held in committee and was not reported out.

Charter school advocates enjoyed their first real success in the spring of 1994. They gained political traction in February 1994 when Representative Lisa Graham Keegan (who would go on to be elected as Arizona's superintendent of public instruction in November 1994) introduced HB 2505. Keegan was a second-term representative known as a champion of educational issues. In HB 2505, she proposed a $23 million education initiative that was most notable for its school voucher program. By offering an alternative that would permit public education dollars to flow to private schools, Keegan energized public school critics even as she made charter schooling appear much more palatable to those who had previously opposed charter school legislation (Timmons-Brown and Hess 1999). Keegan's proposal sparked national attention from leading conservatives. The directors of Empower America, Ronald Reagan's education secretary William Bennett, and George H. W. Bush's housing and urban development secretary Jack Kemp, touted Arizona as the state where the school voucher campaign would succeed (Germond and Witcover 1994).

As initially proposed in February 1994, HB 2505 included provisions for charter schooling, expansion of advanced placement programs, decentralization, school report cards, "Twenty-First Century Schools," open enrollment, preschools for at-risk children, and training dollars for teachers. This broad-based approach to reform was intended to soften the hostility to vouchers and to help present them as part of a larger effort to enhance education.

Almost simultaneously, Senator Bev Hermon introduced SB 1375, which offered many of the same programs as Keegan's bill—with the notable exception of vouchers—and at a lower cost. The slimmed-down SB 1375 cost only $10 million, a substantial difference from the $23 million of HB 2505. Nonetheless, both bills were criticized as measures that would undermine public schooling. Opponents argued that vouchers or charters would lead the most accomplished students to abandon the public schools and would deprive these schools of desperately needed funding. The education reform debate shifted as a result of Keegan's move and centered on the question of whether reform legislation ought to include a voucher program (Timmons-Brown and Hess 1999).

Conservative forces, including Governor Fife Symington, Keegan, and leading business interests, were adamant about including vouchers in any educational reform package. Several leading Republican legislators trumpeted their support for the inclusion of vouchers in any legislation. Meanwhile, the education establishment—particularly the AEA, the AFT, the Arizona School Boards Association (ASBA), and the Arizona School Administrators (ASA)—refused to consider any reform measure containing a voucher proposal. The threat that voucher legislation would indeed pass escalated as SB 1375 was held in committee while HB 2505 made its way to a floor vote. However, moderate Republicans feared that controversy over the voucher initiative would hold up other desired education reforms, such as charter schools. Thus, a third consecutive year of legislative stalemate seemed likely.

By April 1994, a consensus in support of charter schools began to emerge, though conservative lawmakers still insisted that any school choice legislation include private schools. Heated arguments flared. Democratic state senator Stan Furman rejected any voucher provision that would permit public funds to flow to private schools: "We are dealing with public money. We are dealing with public schools." Keegan countered, "It is the public's money. It is for the purpose of educating children, not the maintenance of a [public school] system" ("Private School Choice" 1994, 5). After HB 2505 passed by a vote of thirty to twenty-eight in the House on the last day of its regular session in 1994, the Senate narrowly rejected the bill by a three-vote margin. This left the reform-minded Republican majority without a major education initiative.

Over the summer, Governor Symington won legislative approval for a special session to consider the charter school issue. In special session, Keegan introduced HB 2002, a simplified and slimmed-down substitute for her controversial and more expensive HB 2505. The new bill dropped the voucher school proposal but retained charter schools, decentralization, school report cards, at-risk pre-school dollars, and open-enrollment provisions.

The key charter school opponents reconsidered their strategy during the summer session. Fearing resurgence of a voucher school initiative and unsure of their ability to beat it back after their narrow spring victory, they decided to endorse charter school legislation. Prominent in this repositioning were the ASBA, the ASA, and the AEA. Keegan welcomed this change of heart and argued that she had always intended to use the voucher initiative to serve as a red herring that would distract unions from focusing on their opposition to charter schools. Keegan explained that her strategy was to introduce her charter school proposal, HB 2002, only after HB 2505 had drawn the unions' fire and left them willing to contemplate compromise legislation. A Republican state legislator recalls that the debate over vouchers and support for charter schools from the Democratic National Committee (DNC) pushed school choice opponents into public stands in favor of charters:

> The DNC had sent a letter out to legislators saying that "charters . . . look like they're the coming thing, and they might not be that bad," and so the whole deal [for opponents of the bill] was there are so many good things about this bill, it's just not right that you have put this poison pill [of] vouchers in there. . . . So [we] said to them "OK, if we took vouchers out, would you vote for the bill?" And they all said "Oh yeah. . . ." And so we took vouchers out . . . and . . . they said . . . "we have to talk about this charter school legislation," and we said "no" because they were all on very public record 'cause they had been squirming about having to vote against the education reform bill. . . . The deal was, we take vouchers out and you vote for the bill . . . and the [public] vow was enforceable.

By June 1994, conservative proponents had sacrificed the voucher initiative in order to advance a "strong" charter school bill.[4] With reluctant support from the teachers unions, the ASA, and the ASBS, charter school advocates smelled victory. Near the end of the three-day special session in June, charter school legislation was enacted.

A "Strong" Charter School Law

The Arizona charter school law stands as one of the "strongest" such laws in the nation, offering freedom from most public education regulations. Particularly note-worthy are provisions regarding sponsors and funding. Three governing bodies were permitted to grant charters: school districts, the SBE, and the newly created SBCS. In permitting entities other than the local school district to authorize charter schools, the law broke what charter school theorist Ted Kolderie (1990) has called the "exclusive franchise" held by school districts. Although the SBE and the SBCS were each allowed to approve twenty-five charters per year, school districts were allowed to issue unlimited numbers of charters. The existence of several authorizers meant that the possibility of receiving a charter was much greater than if only one governing body was authorized to approve charter schools.

The legislation also provided relatively generous funding for charter schools. New charter schools were eligible to receive start-up grants of up to $100,000 for each of their first two years of operation, though state officials report that the mean grant was $21,800. Start-up funding for charter schools is provided after application approval, subject to the condition that projected per-pupil spending will be comparable to the average statewide per-pupil expenditure. This provision was included to ensure that charter school operators would not pocket start-up funds by launching shoestring operations. In 1997, the *Arizona Daily Star* estimated that the state allocated approximately $33 million to charter schools, roughly $4,040 per charter school pupil (Tapia 1997). Arizona Department of Education (ADE) officials estimate this figure as 5 to 10 percent below mean per-pupil expenditures of Arizona district schools, though it is more than for some low-income districts with limited local tax bases.

The charter school law also includes provisions to protect teacher employment benefits. A charter school teacher maintains his or her rights of certification, retirement, and salary status if the teacher was previously a teacher in the school district. The ability of charter school teachers to return to district schools was also protected by legislative language mandating that teachers would not have to forfeit their salary status or benefits if they left for a charter school and then returned to the district. This provision helped reduce teacher opposition to charter schooling and increased the number of teachers willing to teach in charter schools.

Policy Implementation

Charter schools and the regulatory authorities, such as the SBE and the ADE, encountered many problems due to the hurried manner in which the charter school law was implemented. The charter legislation was approved on 17 June 1994, and it took effect just three months later—on 16 September 1994. No appropriation had been tied to the legislation, and there was little time for the ADE to develop a regulatory framework. Thus, the beginning of the 1994 school year was marked by confusion and frustration. The state was ill equipped to deal with inquiries and applications by those wishing to open charter schools for fall 1995.

Despite these complications, charter schools proliferated rapidly. Fifty-five charter campuses operated during the 1995–1996 school year. As table 4.1 shows, that number increased to 119 in 1996–1997, 222 in 1997–1998, 272 in 1998–1999, and 351 in 1999–2000. By fall 2000, 402 charter school campuses were serving approximately 55,000 students, about 6.3 percent of Arizona's public school enrollment. Not everyone who received a charter actually opened a campus, and some charters were the consequence of applicants simply switching from one charter authorizer to another. For example, when two small, low-income districts on the Navajo Reservation that had chartered about two dozen schools (charging operators for their charters) announced that they would rescind their charters en masse, the schools chartered through different districts or through one of the state-level authorizers.

The rapid growth of the charter system demonstrates significant demand for different education options and a ready supply of entrepreneurial teachers, administrators, and social workers wishing to supply those options. Analyses suggest that as of fall 1999, about 13 percent of Arizona charter school operators represented private school conversions to charter status. In contrast, 25 percent of operators were former district school administrators, 25 percent were businesspeople, 23 percent were former social workers, and 23 percent were former district school teachers, with 11 percent started by parents, college professors and administrators, and charter and private school teachers. (The percentages add up to over 100 percent since some schools are operated by teams and since many operators have varied backgrounds.)

The supply of alternative education could not have been produced without the political activism of the newly formed SBCS and the revenue-maximizing strategy of a few local school districts. In contrast, the SBE was less active. By fall

Table 4.1

Charters Granted in Arizona by Year and by Board

Board	1995	1996	1997	1998	1999	2000	2001
State Board for Charter Schools	25	20	25	25	26	32	55
State Board of Education	20	24	10	6	7	14	5
Local School Districts	5	20	10	29	23	16	2
Total Charters Granted Each Year	50	64	45	60	56	62	62
Total Campuses Open[a]	55	119	222	272	351	402	460 (est.)
Total Number of Charter School Students	7,500	16,000	26,000	34,000	39,000	54,000 (est.)	N.A.
As Percentage of Arizona Public School Students	1.0	2.0	3.3	4.4	5.0	6.3	N.A.

Source: Policy and Planning Staff, the Arizona Department of Education

Note: Not all charter holders open campuses, and the number of charters includes those issued for schools switching from one chartering authority to another.

[a] These are estimates. There is some confusion at to the exact number of campuses, since charter operators do not always count adjacent or nearby sites as separate campuses.

1998, the SBCS had granted 110 charters, while the SBE had granted 62 (Maranto and Gresham 1999, 100). The aggressive attitude of the SBCS levied political pressure on the SBE to authorize more schools. A member of the SBCS bragged to us that they had "done a lot of analysis looking for loopholes [in the regulations]" as part of a concerted effort to increase the rate of charter expansion.

School districts had granted just thirty-five charters between 1995 and 1997, although they were the only authorizers unencumbered by a charter school cap. Virtually all were chartered by two low-income Navajo districts, Window Rock and Ganado. These districts chartered schools that operated in other districts, charged the operators substantial fees ranging from a flat $3,000 to 9 percent of revenues, and used this money to help fund their district schools. Under pressure from the state, Window Rock and Ganado ceased this practice and rescinded their charters in 1998, prompting other districts in need of revenue—rapidly growing Higley and rural Peach Springs and Snowflake—to take over the role.

There are obvious financial incentives for school districts to approve charters operating in other districts, but not in their own districts. In Arizona, state subsidies accounting for a mean of 57 percent of K–12 education expenditures follow enrollment; thus a charter school opening in or near a particular district could reduce that district's budget, while one opening in a distant district would have no impact. Second, as noted, the charter law empowers local districts to issue an unlimited number of charters. Third, the extent to which districts are required to carefully supervise their charters is unclear, making districts very attractive authorizers for charter operators who want to avoid much supervisory interference. Due to the ambiguity in the law regarding charter school accountability, school districts can approve charters without assuming the headaches of oversight. Interviews suggest that Window Rock, Ganado, and Snowflake did little to oversee "their" charter schools. Opinion is divided as to whether Peach Springs adequately monitors its charter schools. In spring 2000, a bill signed by the governor ended the practice of school districts chartering schools operating in other districts, with a grandfather clause for existing schools.

In contrast to other actively chartering districts, Higley staff visit each charter school site at least quarterly; provide advice on complying with state and local regulations; and, through contractors, manage charter financial records. Higley officials report that they gain about $1.2 million in revenue from charter schools but that they spend about two-thirds of that on support for charters. Indeed, Higley may provide better oversight than either state board. Both the SBE and the SBCS are understaffed and lack the resources to visit their charter sites on even an annual basis. Notably, some Higley and Peach Springs charter schools are switching to SBE or SBCS status, since those bodies do not charge administrative fees.

Both nationally and in Arizona, charters serve a variety of age groupings, though few Arizona charters are middle schools. In 1998, of the 255 charter campuses open or approved to open, nearly half crossed conventional age groupings, while 72 were essentially high schools and 55 were essentially kindergarten or elementary schools (K–5). Only a handful of the charters were for middle schools. Elementary charter schools were the most common because they were the easiest for charter operators to open and to run. Whereas high schools are expected to provide relatively expensive services, such as sports teams, musical opportunities, and well-equipped science laboratories, the demands on elementary schools are simpler and more straightforward. The more homogenous services provided by elementary schools also make them more affordable, because high school operators have to attract a larger group of students in order spread the costs of differentiated services.

Consistent with the national trend, Arizona charter schools are generally small.

In part, this is due to the fact that many charter entrepreneurs create their schools because they want to create close-knit and familial learning communities. When Arizona charter schools were surveyed in 1998, the median number of students in the elementary schools was 110. In stark contrast, the similar figure for district elementary schools was 590. Similarly, charter secondary schools had a median enrollment of 65 students, while the district secondary schools had a median enrollment of 871 (Maranto and Gresham 1999, 107–8).

Charter operators are relatively unconstrained in determining their curricula, and there is much variation among schools. Stout and Garn (1999) report that as of fall 1998, roughly 47 percent of charter elementary school students attended content-centered schools, typically advertising a "back-to-basics" approach. Thirty-five percent of students attended child-centered schools, usually Montessori or "Montessori-like" programs. The remaining 18 percent attended schools with a wide range of other curricula, including bilingual, arts-based, and Waldorf programs. Our analysis of charter school demographics and mission statements finds that as of fall 2000, 87 (64 percent) of the 136 charter secondary schools in operation with identifiable missions were for at-risk students, most of whom had failed in district schools.

One career official in the ADE has explained that because most students attending charter high schools are at-risk students who are likely to inflate dropout statistics, the public schools are not particularly concerned about competing for the students. ADE officials noted that some district school officials call the ADE to ask about charter school options for their at-risk students and use the charter schools as a resource for those students. Some charter school operators also view their role as cooperative—rather than competitive—and seek to locate in districts where they are welcome. One such school is Portable Practical Educational Preparation Training for Employment Center (PPEPTEC). The second-largest charter franchise in Arizona, PPEPTEC is a nonprofit that provides basic literacy and vocational training at fourteen campuses around the state and opens schools only where welcomed by the local school district.

Oversight and Charter School Accountability

In Arizona, the Republican state legislature and governor nurtured and protected the state's charter schools. State authorizers and financial and special education regulators have not closed schools for inadequate compliance with special education regulations and untimely paperwork. Instead, they have worked with operators who seemed to act in good faith. Indeed, in one case the ADE charter school office helped a troubled charter school for at-risk youth to apply for and win a federal grant for curriculum development. The resulting in-service training helped turn the school around, and it survived.

Part of the effort to nurture charter schools was the conscious decision of policy makers to limit the funding for regulation and administration of the charter school system. This was done to prevent a new bureaucracy from developing around the reform. One of the consequences was that ADE financial and special education regulators were forced to share responsibility for implementation, approval, and oversight with chartering authorities and the state attorney general. In addition, even as ADE responsibilities were expanding, Superintendent of Education Lisa Graham Keegan cut staff by 27 percent. As a result, the ADE was constantly scrambling to catch up to changing circumstances and found itself with little opportunity to plan strategically or anticipate change in the charter school arena.

Charter school authorizers have three fundamental responsibilities: processing and acting upon applications for new charter schools, monitoring charter schools' compliance with their charters, and determining whether charters should be renewed or terminated (Hassel and Vergari 1999). Staffed largely by charter supporters and encouraged by the legislature to focus on getting new schools launched, the SBCS focused on the application process rather than oversight. Surprisingly, the less aggressive and less procharter SBE was also found to focus more on application issues than on oversight (Garn and Stout 1999). Early on, both boards were overwhelmed by interested charter entrepreneurs. During the first round in fall 1994, 105 applications arrived. Most of the applications came from teachers rather than profit-making enterprises. During the 1997–1998 application cycle, the boards developed a three-step approval procedure, which consisted of completing the application, getting it approved, and signing the accountability contract once the school had opened. Once schools actually opened, authorizers had little or no contact with the schools unless parental complaints or ADE financial or special education regulators called failings to their attention.

In theory, charter school accountability criteria should be set out in the charter. In practice, early charters in particular did little to specify student achievement levels, and charter supporters and opponents we interviewed agreed that accountability requirements were generally superficial, a finding in accord with Garn and Stout (1999). Both the SBE and the SBCS required charter schools to complete an annual written report detailing outcomes and progress toward the goals in their charters. However, the authorizers did not initially mandate any particular format for these reports, and decisions about what information to include were made by charter operators. (By 2000, the SBE had developed a format for reporting.) Charter operators and ADE officials frequently termed the annual reports a mere formality. SBCS operators were expected to make an annual oral report to the board, in conjunction with the written reports, but these tended to be informal and unsystematic. The SBE and the SBCS had an informal goal of visiting each of their charter schools annually but lacked the staff to do this.

After receiving complaints from a number of charter school faculty and parents about unresolved problems in charter schools, the ADE introduced a charter school monitoring program during 1996–1997 to supplement more special education and financial monitoring by the ADE and to fill the void, since authorizing bodies (with the notable exception of Higley) did not monitor charter schools. One administrator recalled that the ADE would hear "horror stories" from the field but that neither the ADE nor charter authorizers had any way of independently monitoring the schools or knowing how valid the complaints were (Garn and Stout 1999, 151). Two ADE members worked full time on the project, with assistance from several dozen ADE staffers, as well as charter operators, district school officials, and university professors. The program began informally, with efforts to respond to and investigate specific complaints from parents, teachers, and charter opponents, but by the fall of 1996, a more systematic monitoring approach was in place.

ADE monitoring teams examined seven general dimensions in accord with the ADE's interpretation of the charter legislation: (1) purpose of the charter; (2) special area emphasis, curriculum design, and innovation; (3) student assessment program; (4) operational structure; (5) parent and student satisfaction; (6) school finance, reporting, enrollment, and verification; and (7) statutory and statement of assurances review (Garn and Stout 1999, 152).

In theory, the ADE oversight process was intended to yield comprehensive reports on charter school activities and performance. However, when the reports were publicly released, they were generally in the form of handwritten notes. Summary sheets for the monitor to complete were part of each reporting packet. These sheets were intended to permit the evaluator to summarize the performance of the school—whether it was complying with the law and with its charter. In fact, two scholars found the summary sheets blank or missing in roughly two-thirds of the monitoring reports they analyzed in 1998. Most of the monitoring notes were not formally typed up, the information from the reports was not formally collated or passed on to a coordinator, and neither the charter school authorizers nor the charter school boards heard much about the monitoring visits (Garn and Stout 1999, 153).

Charter School Closures

Despite this relaxed approach to regulation, nineteen charter sites closed during the charter program's first four years, with five more by January 2001, most in part for financial reasons. ADE officials believe that the schools that closed typically suffered from a combination of mediocre educational programs, which led to low enrollments, which led to financial irregularities. ADE officials reported that three for-profit charters—Success Schools, Alternative Learning Center, and Arizona Vocational Training, which accounted for fourteen of the closed campuses— were each threatened with losing their charters. Each had expanded too quickly and was unable to survive state sanction. Notably, all of the charter closings and warnings were for financial abuses, rather than because of solely pedagogical or curricular concerns.

In order to help parents make informed choices in the education market and thus hold charter (and other public) schools accountable, the ADE uses school report cards. These report cards are available on the Internet and include standardized test scores, disciplinary and criminal statistics, personnel data, and the school's mission statement. Where comparable, district and state mean test scores are also provided.

Challenges

One oversight challenge emerged due to the system of funding charter schools based on per-pupil enrollment. Since parents often apply to several schools in Arizona's plentiful charter school pool and since they do not always opt to attend when admitted, operators find it difficult to predict fall enrollments. This is particularly problematic given the small sizes of the charter schools. In some cases, charter school operators overestimated fall enrollments and received overpayments, which they had to refund. In the first four years of the charter law, the ADE agreed to generous repayment plans to avoid forcing schools into bankruptcy, but officials report that this is no longer the case.

Charter schools have made efforts to interpret regulations to their best advantage, and not necessarily in ways consistent with the spirit of the law. For instance, like other Arizona public schools, charters are paid for student transportation costs on the basis of vehicle miles traveled. The subsidy is set at $1.95 per vehicle mile traveled, on the assumption that busing costs are high. Certain charter schools collected the subsidy, paid parents $.30 a mile to transport their own children, and then pocketed the difference, for a statewide profit of about $3.6 million in 1996. As a result, the legislature modified the legislation so that schools are now reimbursed at a flat rate of $174 per student for transportation expenses. This subsidy is paid regardless of whether the schools provide transportation (Hartley 1999, 200).

In order for a market-based system to work as intended, it is crucial that customers have sufficient information to make good decisions (Garn and Stout 1999). If parent-customers are not making such decisions, then good school performance will go unrewarded, and ineffective schools will have little incentive to improve. Just what constitutes "sufficient" information is open to debate, as a long line of political science research has suggested that most people make most decisions based on very little information (Popkin 1991). Nonetheless, market discipline can be imposed, because the vague directives of a small number of rational individuals may be enough to provide direction (M. Schneider et al. 1998). Whether Arizona's chaotic and imperfect administrative accountability system, combined with market accountability through parental decisions and based on school report cards, is sufficient to ensure charter school accountability is a question subject to debate (Maranto et al. 1999, 241–43).

Responses to Charter School Competition

One of the key contentions for market-based school reform is that competition will compel all schools—including traditional district schools—to improve (Kolderie 1990a; Chubb and Moe 1990). Because schools that lose students will lose per-pupil funding, charter advocates suggest that public schools will seek to improve their performance and offer new services in order to retain current students and attract new ones. However, there is also reason to believe that the structure of schooling and the nature and training of school personnel may inhibit their ability or desire to respond to market pressures. With its hundreds of charter schools, Arizona provides a valuable opportunity to examine this hypothesis.

Anecdotal evidence suggests that Arizona district schools, in a manner consistent with the findings of previous research, have reacted to competition from charters in a variety of ways. First, it is important to note that most districts do not evince any visible reactions. This is due in part to the fact that Arizona public schooling has grown rapidly throughout the 1990s, dwarfing losses due to charter enrollment and leaving many school districts hurting for space. It is also due to the structure of public school systems, in which administrators are poorly equipped to monitor their systems, to evaluate the competition, or to compel their employees to respond to the threat posed by charter schools (Hess 1999).

Five regions in the state—generally more urban regions such as Tucson, Phoenix, and Flagstaff—have shown clear evidence of a competitive response to charter schools. Some districts have sought to provide improved service when confronted with visible charter competition. The Roosevelt School District, an inner-city Phoenix district hit hard by competition from charters, sent letters to all charter parents in the district to ask why they had left the district schools and explain how the district would serve them better in the future. The nearby Isaac School District had teachers and administrators home-visit all their parents to address concerns. Since 1996, the largest district in the state, Mesa Unified, has conducted customer-service training for teachers and staff and developed a program to welcome charter parents who may wish to return to district schools. In addition, Mesa regularly sends staff to the SBCS office to study charter school applications in order to check up on the competition.

Districts have also sought to provide curricular programs that are in particular demand. In some locales, observers have suggested that the spread of charter schools has forced district schools to place more emphasis on phonics instruction. Along with several smaller districts nearby, Mesa also started to offer all-day kindergarten after nearby charter schools offered this option. Traditional school districts have also stepped up their public relations efforts, including an increased effort to advertise in newspapers. The Flagstaff School District distributes leaflets comparing district test scores with those of neighboring districts, and the Mesa School District has taken to advertising in newspapers and local movie theaters.

Research conducted in 1998 suggests that district schools with collegial work environments give their teachers more power over curricula and internal school operations (Hess, Maranto, and Milliman 1999). These schools appear to find it easier to foster productive work relationships and to involve teachers more fully when they have a history of cooperation to build upon. Thus, because charter schools are often launched by energetic and respected teachers, school districts may be more likely to cooperate with innovative teachers in order to keep them in the fold.

Finally, competition can also provoke negative responses. Charter operators insist that some district officials seek to squash competition by spreading rumors asserting racism or that charter schools are in fragile fiscal condition. Some district teachers who decided to found or teach at charter schools report being ostracized by their former colleagues. Moreover, charter operators complain that district schools are sometimes unwilling to accept transfer credits from charter schools, while district officials counter that some charter schools offer nonstandard courses.

Controversies

Three key conflicts that have emerged in Arizona relate to the church-state relationship, the education of disabled children, and concerns about nepotism. Charter critics have worried that religion has crept into some charter schools. For instance, Heritage Academy had a curriculum that included the teaching of creationism (Kull 1996), while the NFL-YET Academy in South Phoenix was found by a charter school board official to have a prayer and a picture of the Virgin Mary hanging on an office wall (Pearce 1998). Critics have also argued that charter schools practice both subtle and overt discrimination against disabled children in order to escape the expenses associated with providing for them. For instance, one account reported that an attorney for the Arizona Center for Disability Law had received more than 200 calls from charter school parents during the 1997–1998 school year (Hartley 1999, 202). The absence of bars to nepotism in charter schools has led to cases in which family members have served as board members or employees at schools where questionable behavior was found to have taken place (Hartley 1999). State senator Mary Hartley introduced a bill to outlaw nepotism in charter schools in the 2000–2001 legislative session, but it failed to win passage.

Conclusions on the Charter School Movement in Arizona

The Arizona experience demonstrates just how significant charter schooling may prove to be. In less than five years, charter schools have become an institutionalized element of the state's educational system. The political success of the charter school advocates has reshaped the way policy makers and educators discuss accountability and schooling, encouraging those wishing to put more emphasis on output (test scores) and less on input (funding and compliance). Further,

ADE parent surveys show that while only 38 percent of district school parents gave their schools an A+ or A, 61 percent of charter school parents did (Center for Market Based Education 2000). However, it is important that analysts neither romanticize nor demonize charter schooling. Charter schools in Arizona have not proved to be a panacea, but neither have they wrought widespread harm. Rather, they have unleashed untapped entrepreneurial energy, have allowed some families to find schools they prefer, and have led to some malfeasance and isolated disasters. Whether these consequences are positive or negative on balance is difficult to state. The answer depends largely on what one thinks of the existing Arizona public schools; how one conceives of the mission of schooling more generally; and, in particular, how one feels about whether schooling should be controlled by parents and education providers or by elected and appointed officials in school districts.

On a more general level, there are several larger implications that emerge from an examination of the charter school movement in Arizona. Perhaps most interesting is the central paradox of market-based educational reforms: the extent to which the impact of charter schooling depends upon political support. Without the threat of a voucher law, Arizona would not have passed a strong charter law. Further, supportive legislators and regulators have helped charter schools to develop and grow. Under a less promarket regulatory regime, Arizona charter schools would not have flourished. Similarly, the Arizona experience suggests that educational markets benefit from a strong central authority that provides information to parents and polices the system, missions in which the ADE has not always proven effective.

Arizona has demonstrated that charter schooling can unlock enormous entrepreneurial energy from parents and teachers. While charter schools are not inventing new modes of education out of whole cloth, they are making alternatives, such as Montessori schools, available to thousands of families.

Finally, despite the rapid growth of charter schooling in Arizona, it does not appear that charter schools will replace district schools at any point in the near future. The number of charter campuses doubled or nearly doubled in the second and third years of the charter law but has increased by only 22 percent, 29 percent, and 15 percent in the years since, with another 15 percent increase expected for fall 2001. The charter sector has added roughly an additional 1 percent of the total public school market share each year, for a gradually slowing relative rate of growth. In part, this may be because some districts and traditional schools are seeking to make changes to retain students and teachers.

Table 4.2

Comparisons of Academic Performance: Percentage of Schools Posting
One Year Academic Growth (from 1998 to 1999) by Grade and Subject

	Percentage of Schools Posting Gain from Grades 3 to 4	Percentage of Schools Posting Gain from Grades 4 to 5	Percentage of Schools Posting Gain from Grades 5 to 6	Percentage of Schools Posting Gain from Grades 6 to 7	Percentage of Schools Posting Gain from Grades 7 to 8
Reading					
All Public Schools[a]	87	27	84	53	82
Charter Schools	80	31	75	63	82
Number of Charter Schools[b]	(25)	(26)	(15)	(16)	(16)
Math					
All Public Schools	77	67	90	46	48
Charter Schools	85	54	82	65	60
Number of Charter Schools	(27)	(28)	(17)	(17)	(20)

Source: Policy and Planning Staff, the Arizona Department of Education

[a] This category includes charter schools. The number of charter schools has been a small enough portion of the state total that the ADE has not calculated the district public school total separately from that of all public schools (including charter schools).

[b] Most existing charter schools could not be included in this data set due to insufficient numbers of students in a single grade. For inclusion in the state calculations, schools must have at least eight students continuing from one grade to the next.

Three lingering questions remain unanswered. Perhaps most important, it is not yet clear whether charter schools do a significantly better job of educating students than do district schools. In part because the state moved from Iowa Tests to Stanford Nine tests in the second year of the charter reform, there is no time-series data by which to judge student performance. In a comparison of the two sectors, Stout and Garn (1999, 168–69) report that charter school "student achievement as measured by the Stanford Nine test looks just about the way one would expect, given the audiences of the schools, and very much like scores reported in district public schools."

More recent analyses by the authors suggest that charter schools boast annual mean gains in student achievement virtually identical to those in district schools. As table 4.2 shows, the scant evidence available suggests that charter and district schools seem to be equally likely to produce a "standard" academic year of gain in reading and math. This analysis was conducted by the ADE for students taking state achievement tests in 1998 and 1999 who remained in the same schools from one year to the next. For reading scores, charter schools do better for two grades, district schools do better for two grades, and the sectors are tied for a third. For math scores, charters do better for three of the five grades, but for each subject, the difference is marginal. Given that most Arizona charter schools are less than four years old, such achievement results can be viewed as successful, though perhaps less successful than school choice proponents had promised.

Of course, these are relatively blunt, methodologically unsophisticated, school-level comparisons. In contrast, Lewis Solmon of the University of California, Los Angeles, Kern Paark of Arizona State University, and David Garcia of the ADE used an analysis of covariance (ANCOVA) method to analyze the individual performances of 35,000 district students and 5,500 charter students, examining sector (charter or district), previous year test scores, race, primary language, absences, special education status, and grade level to predict student performance on the Stanford Nine. The authors find that charter students do consistently better in reading and no worse in math. The reading effects are statistically significant, equaling one-tenth of a standard deviation, for a .10 effect size. While modest, this compares favorably with such interventions as reducing class size or the length of the school day (Solmon, Paark, and Garcia 2001). In short, charter schools do seem to improve student achievement, though not so much as market proponents expected.

Second, while the evidence thus far suggests that charter schools tend to serve disadvantaged populations—particularly at the high school level—and that they do not seem to be promoting segregation (Milliman, Maranto, and Gresham 1999), there is uncertainty about the long-term implications for equity.

Finally, none of the evidence to date can address the fundamental questions posed by the debate about whether the democratic ethos necessitates that we make educational decisions as a community, rather than as individual consumers and producers. Where charter schools are concerned, there is much still to learn about and from Arizona. The continued growth of the charter school system and new evidence from other states will offer invaluable opportunities to better understand the politics and the educational effects of charter schooling in the years ahead.

5 • Michigan's Charter School Movement

The Politics of Policy Design

Michael Mintrom

IN MICHIGAN, CHARTER SCHOOLS—referred to formally as "Public School Academies"—represent part of a broader policy initiative to establish a quasi-market in public education, with extensive parental choice and far-reaching use of nongovernmental entities for the delivery of educational services.[1] In this chapter I review the politics that have accompanied Michigan's charter school movement. I then discuss the evolution of the charter school community, focusing on the schools and their students, the authorizing agencies and the Michigan Department of Education, and the role played by private management companies.

For the most part, my assessment of the contribution of Michigan's charter schools to the broader terrain of public education is positive. Nonetheless, the charter school movement in Michigan has too often betrayed an ideologically driven, antigovernment penchant. This has resulted in occasional negligence in the choices that have been made about how to hold the charter schools accountable for their actions and how to placate public concerns about these schools.

Michigan's charter school movement has helped set the conditions for even more radical policy change, such as the introduction of educational vouchers. Advancing the public use of private interests in the delivery of public education inevitably raises questions about how to balance the rights of private individuals and organizations against public interests. These questions have been raised during the evolution of the charter school community. How seriously they are addressed in the coming years will play a critical role in determining the success or failure of efforts to further harness market forces for the delivery of public schooling.

The Politics of Policy Design

Since the late 1980s, various interests in Michigan have voiced support for the introduction of education vouchers, in line with the approach first proposed by Milton Friedman (1955, 1962). However, education vouchers have been expressly forbidden by the Michigan Constitution since 1970, when a ballot initiative effectively ended a fervent debate over the merits of state funding for private schools.[2] To promote school choice and eventually attain sufficient electoral support to secure constitutional change, a coalition called TEACH Michigan became increasingly active during the 1990s.[3] Following the lead of several other states, in 1991, Michigan adopted an open-enrollment law that allowed for intradistrict school choice. But this law did not fulfill the wishes of voucher advocates.

When brinkmanship politics led the state legislature to temporarily abolish local property taxes as a source of school funding in the middle of 1993, supporters of increased school choice, Republican governor John Engler among them, saw their chance to couple this kind of reform with school finance reform (Vergari 1995). Voucher supporters, including Paul DeWeese, the founder of TEACH Michigan, saw the adoption of charter schools as a useful interim policy change.[4] As DeWeese has observed, charter schools offered a means to introduce school choice "in an incremental . . . non-threatening kind of way, so that [citizens] could look in their own community or . . . region . . . and . . . identify choice schools that were getting government money, they could see them working . . . and . . . see . . . the parents happier because their kids were in schools that they thought were better."[5]

With strong support from Governor Engler, the legislature adopted a charter school law in December 1993. At the same time, a law was adopted making provision for interdistrict open enrollment across public schools. In addition, the legislature proposed a new school finance mechanism to be introduced subject to voter approval. In a March 1994 referendum, Michigan citizens voted to cover more than 70 percent of public school funding through an increase in the state sales tax.

Within the space of just a few months, the key components of a system of public school choice that would eventually exhibit many features equivalent to those of an education voucher system had been put in place. On the educational demand side, Michigan parents had been granted greater public school choice, both through open enrollment and through the possibility of sending their children to newly created charter schools. On the supply side, allowing the creation of charter schools held the promise of greater program diversity in public education. Moreover, the much greater reliance placed upon state (as opposed to local-level) funding of schools ensured that school funding would more closely follow enrollment levels. This would give public schools—including charter schools— strong incentives to respond to parental and student concerns about school policies and practices.

In contrast to the charter school laws previously adopted in Minnesota, California, and Massachusetts, the 1993 Michigan law was quite permissive.[6] In particular, the law authorized a range of public entities, including local school districts, intermediate school districts, community colleges, and state universities, to serve as charter school authorizers. The law also gave considerable autonomy to charter school organizers with relief from many provisions of the state school code. Further, it did not include a cap on the number of charter schools in the state. This distinguished the Michigan law from previously adopted charter school laws. However, one apparent deficiency of the law was that it did not include charter school start-up money.[7]

In what turned out to be a false start, 8 Michigan charter schools began operating in the 1994–1995 school year. However, none remained in operation under their original charters because the constitutionality of the charter school law was challenged and state funding to the schools was blocked by a court injunction.[8] By 2000–2001, over 180 charter schools were in operation, enrolling more than 58,000 students. While impressive, this rapid growth of charter schools has occurred against a backdrop of much partisan political battling, court rulings, and the passage of a new charter school law in 1994—subsequently amended in 1995 —to address potential constitutional anomalies in the 1993 law.

In July 1997, the Michigan Supreme Court ruled that the state's 1993 charter school law was indeed constitutional and that charter schools established under it were public schools qualifying for state aid. By then, seventy-eight charter schools were established and operating with state funding. They were doing so in accord with the revised charter school laws adopted in 1994 and 1995 respectively. Thus, in terms of day-to-day operations, the court ruling had few obvious implications for the state's charter schools. However, two points should be noted. First, had the 1993 law been declared unconstitutional, charter school opponents might have gone on to challenge the constitutionality of the charter school laws that superseded it. Second, in affirming the constitutionality of the most permissive version of Michigan's charter school law, the court removed a threat to the long-term viability of the charter school movement.

The court ruling was especially important for allaying the fears of investors who had previously shown reluctance to lend money to charter school operators for start-up and other costs. Shortly after the court ruling, Gary Cass, then director of charter schools for the Michigan Department of Education (MDE), said, "We're getting calls [from financial institutions] because they know the schools are constitutional." James Goenner, then executive director of the Michigan Association of Public School Academies observed, "This is a green light for the financial markets. . . . It's full speed ahead."[9]

The legislative and judicial turmoil surrounding the creation of charter schools in Michigan kept the permanency of the broader institutional context in doubt until the start of the 1997–1998 school year. The stability that now obtains has come at a cost. In particular, the authorizing legislation for charter schools has grown successively more restrictive. Currently, all teachers in Michigan charter schools are required to be certified, the schools must operate in accord with the Michigan School Code, student performance must be assessed using the Michigan Education Assessment Program (MEAP) test for primary school students and the High School Proficiency Test (HSPT) for high school students, and caps have been placed upon the number of charters that can be issued by state universities. These changes have restricted the extent to which charter schools can experiment with innovations, although opportunities clearly remain for imaginative school leaders to try out new approaches to management, pedagogy, and curriculum development.

In considering how best to introduce policy innovations, decision makers face a dilemma. On the one hand, potential problems can be avoided by the gradual introduction of a new program like charter schools, as has been the case in many states, such as Minnesota and Colorado. Initially, only a few charter schools were allowed in these states, but the numbers have been steadily increasing. This might be construed as a sound approach to policy implementation, because problems may be found and dealt with prior to widespread adoption. On the other hand, small-scale policy innovation reduces the potential for political support to build and leaves the new program vulnerable to strangulation. In Michigan, the loathing of charter schools by powerful enemies, such as the Michigan Education Association (MEA), was palpable from the outset. Thus, building a vibrant, politically strong charter school movement was a top priority for supporters of the innovation. Governor Engler went to considerable effort to ensure that many charter schools were authorized and established, even while legislative efforts were made to remove constitutional anomalies from the authorizing legislation and as constitutionality issues were debated by state circuit court and supreme court justices.

While many might dispute the added value of some charter schools and others might wince at some of the stories of charter schools that opened their doors before they were ready, few will deny that these schools now represent a permanent addition to Michigan's educational community. In addition, political opposition to the schools has begun to subside, and support appears to be on the rise. Even an MEA official observed in 1998: "I know that in some [charter] schools good things are happening. We need to know that ... so we can learn from the competition. Charter schools are here, and probably here to stay, so we should learn what we can and change where we need to change."[10]

Surprisingly little effort has been made in Michigan to track public opinion on charter schools. In the middle of the 1997–1998 school year, a representative sample of Michigan residents were asked their opinions on public education in the state, charter schools, and the voucher concept.[11] When asked their opinion on charter schools, 63 percent of respondents said that they supported them. However, 56 percent said that there should be limits placed on the number of charter schools that are allowed to operate in the state. When asked their opinion on state-funded vouchers that would allow parents to send their children to the public, private, or parochial school of their choice, 59 percent of respondents voiced support.

Table 5.1 summarizes several aspects of Michigan public opinion on charter schools. The partisan nature of support and opposition is clearly evident. Respondents who identified themselves as supporting the Republican party or as Independents were much more likely to support charter schools than Democratic party supporters. The survey results also reveal greater support for charter schools among those expressing dissatisfaction with the performance of their community's public schools. Those living in urban areas were much more supportive than those living in suburbs, African Americans were more supportive than Whites, and those from low-income households were much more supportive than those from high-income households. In sum, these survey results indicate that, four years after the Michigan legislature adopted its first charter school law, this policy innovation enjoyed broad support across socioeconomic and racial groups in the state. In addition, they suggest that charter schools are viewed positively by those who cannot leave the public schools of which they disapprove by either moving to the suburbs or enrolling their children in private schools.

Table 5.1

Michigan Public Opinion on Charter Schools, 1997–1998

Opinion	Support	Indifferent	Oppose	Don't Know
All Respondents	62.6%	7.1%	23.4%	6.8%
By Grade Given to Public Schools				
A	52.7%	8.2%	30.9%	8.2%
D or F	81.4%	6.2%	10.3%	2.1%
By Community				
Urban	70.1%	4.8%	21.1%	4.1%
Suburban	57.1%	10.2%	22.8%	9.8%
By Race				
White	62.3%	7.6%	23.8%	6.3%
African American	68.5%	2.4%	20.5%	8.7%
By Household Income				
Up to $19,000	73.3%	8.6%	12.1%	6.0%
From $20,000 to $79,999	61.0%	7.3%	25.0%	6.6%
By Party Identification				
Republican	67.9%	9.1%	17.9%	5.1%
Democrat	52.3%	7.4%	31.6%	8.6%
Independent or Other	65.9%	5.4%	22.8%	5.9%

Source: Vergari and Mintrom 1998

The Evolution of the Charter School Community

Public policy initiatives typically represent incremental additions to present policy settings, and for good reason (Lindblom 1968; Tyack and Cuban 1995). However, as a result of deliberate design decisions and political antagonisms, this has not been the case for Michigan's charter schools. Here we find the universe of charter schools superimposed upon the universe of Michigan's traditional public school system. While proximate, these universes operate in near-complete separation. The charter school universe can be divided into several parts: the schools, the students attending the schools, the authorizers, the Public School Academy Program of the MDE, and the private management companies that provide services for many of the schools.

In 1995–1996, the first full year in which charter schools operated with state funding, 41 schools in Michigan were designated as Public School Academies.

Table 5.2

The Growth of Michigan's Charter School Community

School Year	1995-1996	1996-1997	1997-1998	1998-1999	1999-2000	2000-2001
Students in Charter Schools	4,815	12,698	20,710	34,319	50,000	58,326
Charter Schools in Operation	41	78	108	138	173	183
Active Authorizing Agencies	11	16	19	20	21	21
Schools Using Educational Management Companies (EMCs)	7	19	54	82	110	119
EMCs Providing Services to Charter Schools	4	10	18	23	31	34

Sources: Michigan Department of Education 1997, 1998; Michigan Association of Public School Academies 1999, 2000. Compiled by author.

The total enrollment in these schools stood at 4,815. Of these schools, a considerable number were conversion schools—that is, formally private schools that transformed themselves to operate using public money. While many charter school laws allow traditional public schools to convert to charter school status, the Michigan law is uncommon in that it allows for both traditional public school and private school conversions. The 41 schools obtained their charters from eleven authorizers: three state universities, six intermediate school districts, and two public school districts. The Charter Schools Office at Central Michigan University (CMU) was by far the most commonly used authorizer in the state. Of the 41 charter schools operating in 1995–1996, 26 (63 percent) had CMU as their authorizer. In 2000–2001, the number of charter schools operating in Michigan had climbed to 183, and enrollments stood at 58,326. (This represents about 3.5 percent of Michigan's 1.6 million school students.)

As the number of charter schools in the state has steadily increased, there has been an accompanying growth in the number of active authorizers (see table 5.2). Nonetheless, CMU has remained a key authorizer, responsible in 2000–2001 for 59 (32 percent) of the state's charter schools.[12] In 2000–2001, twenty-one authorizers were active: eight state universities, seven intermediate school districts, five public school districts, and one community college. The increasing diversity of authorizers has no doubt been driven by the legislative cap that has for several years limited to 150 the number of charter schools that can be sponsored by state universities. Further, the limited number of public school districts serving as authorizers suggests that administrators in the traditional school system remain wary of the competition for students that accompanies the introduction of charter schools. That said, the increasing diversity of authorizers can also be viewed as yet another indicator of the growing acceptance of charter schools in the Michigan educational community.

In addition to the rapid growth in the number of charter schools in Michigan and in the number of active authorizers, there has been notable growth in the number of private, for-profit companies offering a range of management services to the charter schools. In 2000–2001, thirty-four management companies were providing services to charter schools in the state. More than anything else, this presence of for-profit companies signals the potential for publicly funded education to be successfully delivered privately should government choose to retreat— in part or even completely—from this traditional area of activity.

The Charter Schools and Their Students

Michigan charter schools are typically small. In 2000–2001, the average enrollment was 320 students, while traditional schools tended to have enrollments averaging above 500. (Of the 183 charter schools in operation, only 34 had student populations above 500.) Many of Michigan's charter schools have started by offering classes at just the kindergarten and early-grade levels. They have then grown by one grade per year, thus meeting the needs of the cohort of oldest students in the school.

Charter schools operate on funds provided by the state and disbursed through their authorizers. The amount of funding per student is equal to either the level of per-student state aid provided to traditional schools in the relevant public school district or $6,500, whichever is less.[13] Since this is a relatively low amount of money for charter schools to operate on, many have attempted to keep personnel costs low by offering benefit packages to staff that contain more limited contributions to retirement plans than those in the state employee plan and by employing younger, inexperienced teachers. There has also been a tendency for schools to find creative ways to reduce their reliance upon certified teachers. One common approach involves using classroom aides and parent volunteers to maintain low student-to-adult ratios, when the student-to-teacher ratios are otherwise quite high.

The Michigan funding formula provides a disincentive for organizers to locate charter schools in those (typically more affluent) school districts where local funding makes up a relatively high proportion of combined state and local funds.[14] The funding formula produces another quirk. School personnel often observe that students in primary grades are less expensive to teach than those in high school grades. This helps to explain why, out of the 183 charter schools operating in 2000–2001, 141 (77 percent) offered classes starting at the kindergarten level, while only 3 (2 percent) offered exclusively middle school grades (i.e., grades 6–8) and only 39 (21 percent) offered classes exclusively in some or all of the high school grades (i.e., grades 9–12).

Charter schools can be found scattered across Michigan in urban, suburban, and rural locations. However, they tend to be concentrated in the high population centers. In 2000–2001, close to half the schools were located in the state's two largest metropolitan areas: sixty-three (34 percent) in and around Detroit and twenty-seven (15 percent) in and around Grand Rapids. Using demographic figures for the charter schools in operation in Michigan in 1998–1999, I found a tendency for these schools to be located in school districts with student population demographics that differ substantially from those of the public school student population in the state as a whole. In particular, charter schools are more likely to be found in districts with greater percentages of African American and Hispanic students and lower percentages of White students (see table 5.3). It should be noted, however, that the demographics of Michigan's charter schools appear on average to closely follow those of the districts in which they are located.

Standardized Tests

Proponents and opponents of education reform initiatives, especially of those falling under the rubric of school choice, often support their arguments and assertions by referring to student test scores.[15] In Michigan, debate over the merits of charter schools is rekindled annually with the release of the MEAP and HSPT results. These tests are administered by the MDE to all students in selected grades in all public schools across the state, including charter schools. For example, in the fall of one year, all fourth and seventh graders might be tested in mathematics and reading. The following spring, all fifth and eighth graders might be tested in

Table 5.3

Charter School Demographics in Perspective, 1998–1999

Unit	White	African American	Hispanic	Native American	Asian and Pacific Island
All School Districts in Michigan	75.7%	18.5%	3.0%	1.0%	1.7%
School Districts Where Charter Schools Have Located	51.4%	40.9%	5.0%	1.0%	1.7%
Charter Schools	49.4%	43.4%	4.0%	1.9%	1.3%

Source: Michigan Department of Education 2001

Note: The figures for charter schools are based on information from 133 schools.

science and writing. Meanwhile, the HSPT is administered to all eleventh graders in four subjects every spring.

While these tests tell something about the progress being made by individual students, they tell us essentially nothing of value about the comparative strengths or weaknesses of charter schools and traditional public schools. There are two obvious reasons why this is so. First, the tests do not allow analysts to track individual student progress over time. Second, there is no way to control for the selection mechanisms that have led some students to enroll in charter schools. That said, looking at the reported results of recent tests aggregated to the school level, it appears that students in charter schools have generally performed at a much lower level than those in traditional schools.

In analyzing average test scores over the three-year period from 1996–1997 to 1998–1999, I found that students in only 17 percent of charter schools performed better overall than students in the traditional public schools located in the same school district.[16] Among other things, since the oldest charter schools had been operating for less than four years when the tests were administered, it might be that the low scores reflect the quality of the education that students experienced before entering charter schools. In addition, efforts of charter school leaders to develop innovative curricula might have placed their students at a disadvantage when compared with those students in schools following the Michigan curriculum guidelines from which the contents of tests are derived. But given the nature of currently available information, we can only speculate here. This suggests that

Michigan policy makers should put considerably more effort into establishing appropriate assessment measures for tracking student performance across all Michigan public schools. This must be done if meaningful comparisons across schools are to be made.

In order to operate effectively, all markets require the transmission of appropriate levels of information between buyers and sellers. Often, it falls to government to ensure that such information is supplied. In the absence of high-quality, easily understood information about the comparative performance of schools, parents and students can do little more than rely upon gossip and superficial judgments as they attempt to "shop" for a school. Thus, in Michigan, there exists a high risk of market failure due to information asymmetries.

Special Populations of Students

Some states keep records on the number of charter school students defined as at risk, special education, bilingual, and so on.[17] In Michigan, such records are not being maintained at the state level. Some charter school authorizers attempt to keep records for the schools they oversee, but the effort is often haphazard. Better record-keeping procedures are needed regarding the presence and treatment of children with special needs in charter schools. Even so, under present conditions the accuracy of such efforts would remain in doubt because of the incentives faced by both parents and schools. I know of instances in several schools where the special educational needs of students were not identified until after several months of attendance. Sometimes, parents knew that their children had been categorized as having special needs in their former schools. But such categorization had led to stigmatizing. The parents wanted to transfer their children to charter schools to avoid labels and to make a fresh start. (In many cases, the smaller size of the charter schools and the individualized instruction occurring in some of them also held appeal for parents of children with special needs.)

At the same time, charter school administrators face an incentive to ignore signs of special needs among students. Where financial resources are tight, it is inevitable that, especially for borderline cases of special need, efforts might be made to avoid the cost of bringing in special education teachers or contracting with intermediate school districts and private corporations for special education services. Incentive problems of this sort could be addressed, but it would take sensitivity in policy development to make improvements without replicating the stigmatizing effects that special education programs in traditional public schools appear to have generated. Meanwhile, anecdotally, it seems that charter schools are seen as bastions of hope for some families whose children have been treated as the proverbial "square peg in a round hole" in traditional public schools.

Missions and Expectations

Many charter schools have been established with particular missions or educational goals (e.g., some focus on a liberal arts education, some emphasize Afrocentrism, and others emphasize computer technology). When such specially focused charter schools open, some almost inevitable clashes tend to arise between the expectations of school organizers and those of some students and parents. These clashes occur because, while others have been "pulled" to the school because of the nature of the program on offer, some parents and students—who have also made deliberate choices—have been "pushed" from unhappy situations, so that any alternative school would be valued.

In the idealized product market of the economic textbook, why people choose to "buy" a given product is always treated as immaterial. And, indeed, the satisfaction any individual gets from driving a particular model of car is not affected by whether other drivers of the same model choose it because of its intrinsic characteristics or simply because they have been dissatisfied with all their previous cars. Schooling is different. The opposing reasons why particular families choose a given charter school can have material consequences for the school climate, and some charter schools in Michigan have experienced turmoil as a result. With time, expanding choices, and increased information about what particular charter schools have to offer, instances of such problems may decline. However, at present, it is common to hear charter school principals talk about such clashes of expectations. Sometimes, schools have had to completely alter their mission to better meet the needs of their students. At other times, strong leaders with excellent communication skills have been able to find ways to ease internal tensions.

The Authorizing Agencies and the Michigan Department of Education

Under a voucher system like that proposed by Friedman, schools are held to account by students and their parents. If one school is deemed to provide an unsatisfactory product, customers can go elsewhere. Government involvement is relegated to the "approval" of the schools that may be attended: "The role of government would be limited to insuring that the schools met certain minimum standards, such as the inclusion of a minimum common content in their programs, much as it now inspects restaurants to insure that they maintain minimum sanitary standards" (Friedman 1962, 89).

In the charter school model, authorizers are intended to perform the limited governmental role of issuing contracts (charters) to schools and then ensuring that the schools operate in compliance with agreed terms. In Michigan, aside from disbursing state school-aid payments to charter schools, the major function of authorizers involves overseeing charter compliance. While a few intermediate school districts and public school districts have served in this capacity, the most active authorizer offices have been housed at state universities.[18] In 1995–1996, three such agencies, typically called "charter school offices," oversaw 31 (76 percent) of the state's 41 charter schools. In 2000–2001, eight such offices oversaw 146 (79 percent) of Michigan's 183 charter schools.

These charter school offices have come under considerable public pressure because they represent the primary conduit through which anything like "the public will" can be imposed upon charter schools. Thus, the offices have often been caught in the midst of broader battles over the degree to which charter schools should be held directly accountable to parents versus the broader public.[19]

Oversight regulation of charter schools is not a particularly complex task (compared with, say, the regulation of nuclear power plants), but university authorizers in Michigan have been subject to political scrutiny. The literature on regulatory enforcement suggests that these two conditions, lack of technical complexity and political salience, will have divergent implications for the behavior of agency staff. Limited technical complexity—and, hence, the lack of professionalized norms and guidelines—permits staff to come to their own "common sense" understandings of how to achieve regulatory compliance. Under such circumstances, agency staff might promote compliance through cooperation, developing trust relationships with those they must regulate and providing technical assistance where they can (Gormley 1998). In contrast, political salience and the continual threat of criticism for regulatory permissiveness can lead agency staff to "go by the book," thus exhibiting behaviors that the regulated organizations interpret as "regulatory unreasonableness" (Bardach and Kagan 1982).

The charter schools office at Grand Valley State University (GVSU) appears to work with charter schools in accord with a cooperative model. At an informal monthly meeting, office staff bring together the principals of the schools they oversee.[20] If office staff have received several inquiries on the same compliance issue from school principals, they will use this meeting as an opportunity to have an expert provide advice about remedial actions. In addition, principals report that these meetings provide excellent networking opportunities and reduce the isolation that they have sometimes felt as principals in all types of schools, charter or otherwise.

In contrast to the GVSU office, the charter schools office at CMU appears to operate in a policing capacity, typically going by the book over compliance issues.[21] School officials have expressed annoyance over receiving violation citations following a routine visit from agency staff, when cited problems could have readily been noted and addressed during the visit. For all this formality, the CMU office has frequently missed serious instances of noncompliance (see Michigan Office of the Auditor General 1997). By neglecting to establish closer informal arrangements with and among charter schools, CMU might also have missed opportunities to develop a stronger, more cohesive charter school community.[22]

In contrast to the authorizers, the MDE has played a low-key role in the charter school movement. The activities of the department's Public School Academy Program have been restricted to two areas: distributing federal funds to charter schools through competitive grants; and monitoring the growth of the charter school movement and providing periodic reports to the state board of education (SBE) and the legislature. The MDE is the only government agency in Michigan that, at least in principle, has both the responsibility and the capacity to take a leadership role in generating high-quality information on the nature and effect of the charter school movement. But by deliberate design, the MDE has received insufficient resources to perform a leadership role. Staffing of the Public School Academy Program has been restricted to one supervisor and one secretary.

Despite good intentions, MDE staff are rarely able to meet legislative reporting deadlines. An overstretched staff and turnover at the supervisor level have also mitigated against the development of an institutional memory concerning the charter school movement. To date, the most thorough evaluation work on charter schools has been produced by third parties under contract to the MDE (Horn and Miron 1999; Public Sector Consultants and Maximus 1999). These studies have contributed to our broader understanding of what is going on with charter schools in Michigan. However, no institutional support exists to convert such one-shot observations into standard operating procedures to support continuous, careful monitoring of these schools and their broader effects.

Those who decry "big government" might applaud the limited MDE role in the oversight and coordination of charter schools. But such exuberance is misplaced. Poor, untimely record-keeping provides the perfect camouflage for those who seek to use the machinery of government for their own selfish ends—public servants and private entities alike. Although superficially reducing the potential for waste and abuse of government resources, eviscerating the monitoring means that more serious forms of waste and abuse at different levels can go unchecked. The report of the Michigan Office of the Auditor General (1997) on the Charter Schools Office at CMU indicates a need for more careful scrutiny of various aspects of the charter school movement. It would make sense for the MDE to play a greater monitoring role.

The Private Management of Public Schools

The most prominent educational management company (EMC) on the national scene is Edison Schools, Inc., which managed 113 public schools (many of them charter schools) in seventeen states in 2000–2001.[23] Charter schools often turn to EMCs for assistance when day-to-day operations become overwhelming for school organizers or when schools need help securing loans (see Schnaiberg 1997). This has especially been the case in Michigan because the university-based authorizers (the most common type in Michigan) and the MDE have deliberately not provided such assistance to charter schools.

Boards of the (nonprofit) charter schools contract with the (for-profit) companies to provide management services. Typically, the EMC takes a cut of about 12.5 percent of the school's revenue for these services. During 2000–2001, 119 (65 percent) of the 183 charter schools in Michigan made some use of EMCs. These numbers give a strong hint that privatization of school management services was an intended consequence of the design of Michigan's charter school framework. But a closer look reveals an even more interesting pattern. Of the 146 charter schools authorized by universities in 2000–2001, 112 (77 percent) made use of EMCs. In contrast, of the 37 charter schools authorized by other entities (mostly intermediate school districts and school districts), only 7 (19 percent) contracted with EMCs.

These numbers surely reflect differences in availability of administrative support from the authorizers. But they probably also reflect a degree of hostility toward EMCs on the part of people closely associated with the administrative structures that accompany traditional public schooling. In interviews, some charter school principals have told me that they are not interested in working with EMCs because they do not believe that people should treat public education as yet another site for capitalist accumulation. But these same principals would like to have some external support for their schools, just as traditional public schools can turn to district offices for support.

In education circles and the popular press, EMCs are usually characterized as large organizations that operate schools along the same franchise lines as McDonald's operates hamburger joints and Starbucks operates coffee houses. But an analysis of EMCs operating in Michigan reveals a more nuanced situation. Of the thirty-four EMCs operating in the state in 2000–2001, nineteen (56 percent) were providing services to just one school each. Another nine (26 percent) were providing services to from two to four schools each. Just six companies (18 percent) were providing services to five or more schools. And even among this "big six" considerable variation could be found. Despite all the publicity associated with the company, Edison Schools was running just five schools in the state. Three other companies were running from seven to eleven schools each. The two largest EMCs were National Heritage Academies (NHA), which was managing twenty-two schools, and the Leona Group, which was managing nineteen.

While there is clearly a great degree of variance in the scope of the EMCs operating in Michigan, the actual operating procedures or management philosophies of the companies also vary in ways that are interesting and important. NHA is developing a chain of schools using Christian schools as "an economic model." J. C. Huizenga, who has provided several million dollars of financial backing for the company, has observed: "It's not strictly on an altruistic basis. . . . It's done with the expectation of significant returns."[24] The schools emphasize back-to-basics teaching and the development of "moral character" in the students. NHA controls all the revenues coming into its schools and engages in micromanagement of all aspects of school operations, including curriculum, staffing, and the contracting of maintenance and janitorial services. The Leona Group is somewhat more respectful of local control. For example, it gives schools latitude on questions to do with curriculum and pedagogy. Nonetheless, this EMC has often been rumored to emphasize cost-cutting, and it has been known to micromanage schools toward this end.

Among principals of charter schools that do not use EMCs, resistance has been based partly on a fear of losing local control and being required to cut costs by increasing school size. Some schools do not need help from an EMC because they rely on their (nonuniversity) authorizers for administrative support. Others have their own competent business managers or board members with legal, accounting, and management expertise to offer. Clearly, EMCs are a major feature of the charter school landscape in Michigan. They are providing financial brokerage services, management support, and advice integral to the smooth operation of the schools.

While some EMCs might be limiting the chance for parents, students, and teachers to have a say in the development of school policy, this phenomenon is by no means widespread. By dealing with the business aspects of the schools, EMCs allow others to focus squarely upon educational matters. Nonetheless, the encroachment of EMCs into traditional areas of government service delivery should be subjected to close scrutiny. At present, it is difficult to know whether the charter schools case heralds the start of a larger trend in the delivery of public education. Even if carefully managed, expansion of the role of private companies in this area is likely to meet with much political debate and resistance.

The Development and Diffusion of Innovative Practices

Charter schools have introduced a competitive dynamism to the delivery of public education in Michigan. They have also provided opportunities for developing creative approaches to schooling. But what is the likelihood that charter schools will serve to transform the broader system of public education? Ted Kolderie, a longtime advocate of the charter school model, recently reiterated its primary purpose: "The purpose of 'charter schools'—of letting somebody else offer public education—is not just to create schools. For those who enact the laws it is to create dynamics that will cause the mainline district system to change and to improve. The charter schools, helpful as they may be to the students who enroll in them, are instrumental" (1997, 2–3).

In a comparative study of innovation in Michigan's charter schools and a matched set of traditional public schools, I found that some charter schools are developing interesting innovations but that many appear to be simply replicating much of what is found in traditional public schools (Mintrom 2001). Based on this study, I contend that policy makers who expect market forces to be enough to propel the spread of innovations from charter schools to traditional public schools might be waiting a long time. Two matters need to be considered. First, what features of the organizational design of a school serve to prompt or inhibit the *development* of innovative practices? Second, what features of the broader institutional structure serve to prompt or inhibit the *diffusion* of innovative practices across schools (both charter and traditional)?

Identifying the antecedents of innovation in schools can be complicated. Pincus (1974) argues that the incentives and constraints faced by individuals have an important bearing on how much they are prepared to innovate. Thus, the competition and school-based management that are part of the charter school model would appear to enhance the opportunities for innovation. More work needs to be done to assess how stakeholder involvement and the structuring of deliberations influence the likelihood of experimentation in school programs. Here, the role and influence of EMCs also merit further examination.

For innovative practices to diffuse across schools, a major precondition is that high-quality information can freely circulate among school leaders. Several formal and informal arrangements appear to be facilitating information transfer across the charter school community. The efforts of charter school authorizers and 'of some EMCs to bring school leaders together on a regular basis are serving to build and maintain networks through which ideas and suggestions for innovation rapidly diffuse. In addition, the Michigan Association of Public School Academies and the Michigan Resource Center for Charter Schools keep the charter school community informed about school-level developments. However, far fewer opportunities exist for information transfer between charter schools and traditional public schools. Competition among schools for students and resources can engender suspicion and animosity, and this has certainly been the case in Michigan. Thus, those who would like to see "the mainline district system" change and improve in response to the presence of charter schools might need to think of ways to give the "hidden hand" of the market some visible nudging. In my view, innovation awards for charter schools, developed along the lines of the Ford Foundation's annual Innovation in American Government awards, could spur the transfer of innovative ideas from charter schools to traditional schools.

Conclusion

In adopting a permissive charter school law, Michigan policy makers sought to make public use of private interests to improve the overall performance of the state's system of public education. Judged in terms of creating opportunities for ambitious individuals and groups to establish new, diverse approaches to delivering publicly funded schooling, the policy has been very successful. There is much that is exciting and potentially system-changing about Michigan's charter school movement. Of course, problems have emerged, but many have been addressed through incremental legislative and administrative changes. These problems, in and of themselves, do not suggest that the overall initiative was mistaken.

Some of the thinking that guided aspects of Michigan's charter schools policy, while not mistaken, might have been misguided. Some design choices betray a naive faith in markets and an ideologically driven belief in the virtue of competition. Policy makers would do well to remember that even straightforward exemplars of market-based delivery of goods and services (e.g., supermarkets and the airline industry) are affected on a day-to-day basis by a combination of private and governmentally devised policies and practices. Education is a more socially contingent product than most others. Thus, the claim that the delivery of public education would necessarily be improved by placing it in the hands of private organizations should not go unchallenged.[25] Yet the increasingly secure presence of privately managed charter schools in the new education "marketplace" is likely to prompt further interest in using school choice and the private delivery of education services to transform public schooling.

Given this political momentum for increasing use of school choice arrangements, policy scholars and policy makers must think carefully about what set of institutional arrangements would strike the appropriate balance between, on the one hand, harnessing private interests for public purposes and, on the other, preserving a lively public space for democratic deliberation of how (public and private) policies can be shaped to improve our lives. The debate over charter schools and school choice more generally provides an opportunity for—indeed *necessitates* —serious thought about these broader issues of public-sector management.

6 • Colorado Charter Schools

Becoming an Enduring Feature of the Reform Landscape

Eric Hirsch

Since 1993, when Colorado became one of the first states to enact charter school legislation, the number of charter schools in the state has grown. In 1999–2000, over 2 percent of Colorado's pupils attended sixty-nine charter schools across the state. During the 2000–2001 school year, seventy-six charter schools were in operation, and an additional seven charter schools were scheduled to open during the following year.[1] These schools appear to be doing well, in most cases outperforming district and state averages on the state standardized test, while managing long waiting lists. Recent legislation and the political climate in the state point toward continued charter school expansion.

Yet the charter school movement in Colorado also raises questions about equity, especially regarding the number of charter schools serving at-risk students and issues of geographical and ethnic diversity. While charter schools are outperforming state averages, they are doing so with largely suburban populations in charter schools that overwhelmingly utilize core curriculum models. School districts serving predominantly minority communities, such as Denver, Aurora, and Alamosa, have been leery of the charter concept, choosing not to sponsor significant numbers of charter applicants, whereas rapidly growing suburban districts like Jefferson, Boulder, and Douglas Counties have numerous charter schools. Further, only one-quarter of charter schools serve a higher percentage of racial/ethnic minority students and students eligible for free or reduced-price lunch than their chartering district (Colorado Department of Education 2001).

While the current political and educational landscape almost assures the continued growth of charter schools in Colorado, issues of diversity and dissemination of best practices will need to be addressed in order to ensure the vitality of the charter school movement in the state over time.

The Colorado Charter Schools Act

Unlike most major education reforms in the state, Colorado's charter school legislation, SB 93-183, passed during the first year it was proposed (1993). When the legislation was drafted and debated in Colorado, only Minnesota and California had enacted charter school laws, and only two charter schools, both in Minnesota, were in operation. Numerous factors came together to move charter schools onto the legislative agenda and through the legislative process.

First, the policy agenda had already been set with previous reform initiatives that focused on expanding choice opportunities and providing school districts with greater flexibility. In 1990, the legislature adopted the Public Schools Choice Act, creating a statewide interdistrict choice program, and a bill defeated in 1992 aimed to make school districts largely free of rules and regulations. Although it failed by a 62 percent to 37 percent margin in 1992, the Choice School Reform ballot initiative—a plan to give parents a voucher worth 50 percent of existing per-pupil expenditures to use at any public, private, or parochial school—created an urgency to discuss market-based educational approaches. Charter schools were seen by some as the first step toward a full choice system including vouchers, and other supporters saw the policy as a compromise that would defuse the voucher movement.

Second, support for charter schools was bipartisan. Then Republican senator and now governor Bill Owens and Democratic representative Peggy Kerns cosponsored SB 93-183. Some moderate Republicans and liberal Democrats lined up against the bill, but a largely bipartisan coalition pushed the legislation through both chambers and ushered it through a deeply divided conference committee. According to Kerns (1999), the bill likely would not have made it out of appropriations—little information on the fiscal impact of the policy was available—had Republicans been the sole sponsors of the legislation.

Third, Roy Romer, then governor and a Democrat, strongly supported the legislation and was supportive of choice within public education. Governor Romer addressed the Democratic caucus before the House vote to urge the bill's passage. His support not only provided leadership but also fostered the bipartisan coalitions that developed in support of the legislation.

Finally, various policy entrepreneurs were supportive of charter school legislation.[2] The Colorado Children's Campaign played a vital role in working with individual legislators and the community in support of the idea of charter schools, and other groups were also active supporters of the charter school policy reform. The Colorado Education Association (CEA) and the Colorado Association of

School Boards (CASB) eventually supported, or at least did not oppose, modified versions of the legislation.

While gubernatorial and partisan variables have been found to be important factors for predicting the passage and strength of charter school legislation in other states (Mintrom and Vergari 1997c), many facets of the Colorado law are unique due to the timing and the actors involved in the state. With little research to draw upon, legislators and other stakeholders were unsure of what role charter schools should or could play in education reform. Further, stakeholders shaped charter school authorization and finance decisions to ensure a primary role for local school districts. Following are several key provisions of the Colorado charter school law, as it was originally passed.

- *Sponsorship and appeals.* In a context in which local school districts have constitutional control over instruction (Article IX, sec. 15) and in which there is a strong local-control ethos, it is perhaps not surprising that school districts were made the sole chartering authority in Colorado. However, in cases where a school district rejects a charter school application, there is an appeals process to the state board of education (SBE) that allows a decision to be remanded back to the local school board if the SBE believes that the decision was contrary "to the best interests of the pupils, school district, or community."[3] If the local board still denies the charter, a second appeal to the SBE can be made, and the SBE can require a district to approve a charter school.

- *Charter school finance.* The charter school and the school district in which it is to be located negotiate the level of funding, using at least 80 percent of the district's per-pupil operating revenues (which do not include capital reserve funds). The 80 percent figure was the result of negotiations among legislators, the CASB, and the CEA. The lower funding figure for charter schools was intended not only to cover overhead costs to districts for overseeing charters but also to cushion the political and financial blow of district responsibility for charter sponsorship.

- *Waiver of rules and regulations.* Waivers from local policies are negotiated with the district. The charter school and school district must apply jointly to the SBE for waivers from any state rules and regulations.

- *Sunset provision and limits on schools.* In an effort to symbolize that charter school reform was an experiment (Kerns 1999), the legislation was enacted for only a five-year period. Further, the number of charter schools permitted was capped at sixty. The cap, like the finance provisions, worked to ease the opposition of groups such as the CASB and the CEA that worried about the impact of charters on traditional public schools.

- *At-risk students.* Sixteen of the first sixty charter schools approved (prior to 1

July 1997) were required to be "designed to increase the educational opportunities of at-risk pupils."[4] With no experience to draw upon, legislators feared that charter schools would mainly serve "white, well-to-do kids who want to leave the public schools" (Kerns 1999). However, a broad definition of "at-risk" and the reluctance of high-poverty and minority districts to sponsor charters have led to few charter schools designed specifically to serve populations that are truly at risk.[5]

Changes to the Charter School Law

Since the passage of the Charter Schools Act, the legislature has made numerous changes to the law. In what is perhaps the most important change, charter schools were made a permanent part of education reform in Colorado when the law was reauthorized in 1998 without a future sunset provision. In another victory for charter school supporters, caps on the numbers of at-risk and other charter schools were also removed. These changes lend support to the argument that the charter school reform in Colorado has progressed from being a policy experiment to being an institutionalized feature of public education in the state.

Other legislative changes fit within a general pattern of providing additional resources and opportunities for charter schools. In 1999, the legislature adopted new finance regulations under HB 99-1113, approved by Republican governor Bill Owens. In this instance, it is instructive to consider the role of the governor in state policy making, since enhancements of charter school finance had previously been passed by the legislature but vetoed by former governor Roy Romer. The new funding formula, effective beginning in the 2000–2001 fiscal year, requires that school districts provide a minimum of 95 percent of the district per-pupil revenues for each pupil enrolled in a charter school. Districts with fewer than 500 students have a different minimum level of funding, which essentially will be 85 percent of district per-pupil revenues.

Recent legislative changes have also provided additional resources for financing charter school facilities. The new funding rules provide charter schools with a percentage of per-pupil revenues versus per-pupil operating revenues—meaning that charter schools receive a minimum dollar amount to devote to a fund created for capital reserve purposes or for the management of risk-related activities. Legislation from 1998 (SB 98-82) expanded the list of eligible beneficiaries of the Colorado Educational and Cultural Facilities Authority (CECFA) to include charter schools, enabling CECFA to issue tax-exempt bonds on behalf of charters. Another bill, SB 99-52, extended this access by clarifying the status of charter schools as governmental entities for the purpose of tax-exempt financing, allowing any charter school to seek bonds from private issuers at a public rate. Providing tax-exempt bonding access to charters helps alleviate problems for operators who struggle with attaining traditional loans in the face of a lack of knowledge about the charter concept, little collateral, and a charter term of five years compared to a thirty-year mortgage (see Hassel 1999b). However, these funds must be paid back, unlike direct-facilities funding in states such as Arizona and Florida and lease aid in Minnesota.

The 2001 legislative session ushered in significant reforms to improve capital funding for charter schools. SB 01-129 requires that charter schools receive an additional 130 percent of state capital reserve funds in addition to the 95 percent that had already been included in the 1999 finance reforms. This money—no administrative fees can be kept by the sponsoring district (as is the case with per-pupil operating revenues)—will be given to the charter school in one lump sum. Further, the bill requires that school districts include charter schools in all bond elections, allocating a portion of local bond revenue to the charter on a per-pupil basis. A separate bill (SB 01-237) delayed the implementation of this provision until 1 July 2002.

Despite these policy victories for charter school supporters, legislation to permit entities other than school districts to authorize charter schools continues to struggle. One of the fundamental tenets of charter school advocates is that school districts should not have exclusive authority to authorize charter schools (Kolderie 1992, 1994; Nathan 1996). A bill to create a statewide charter school district with the SBE as the chartering authority failed to win approval in 1999 and 2000. Other efforts to extend sponsorship to universities and the state have struggled since the original law was enacted. Much of the opposition to extending sponsorship appears to be connected to strong views of local district control expressed by state policy makers.

A new provision enacted in 1999 allows entire school districts to apply for charter school status. Thus far, one district in the rural, western area of the state has undertaken the necessary procedures. If the number of charter districts in other states that allow them, such as Texas and California, are any indication, few Colorado districts are likely to employ this new opportunity.

The change that may have the greatest impact over time is a new provision passed in 2000 as part of the governor's education reform plan (SB 00-186). Under the new act, every school in the state will receive a report card grading its performance and improvement in academic achievement. Each year, schools will be assigned a letter grade—A, B, C, D, or F—based on overall academic performance on the state assessment. Schools with the lowest 2 percent of scores on the exam will receive an F. A school that receives this grade must convert to an "independent charter school" or submit a school improvement plan to the state. If upon completion of the first school year under the improvement plan the school again receives an F, then the school district must convert the low-performing school to an independent charter school.

A review committee will solicit proposals from any individual, group, company (nonprofit or for-profit), university, or other school district to operate an independent charter school within the same building.[6] Rent will not be more than one dollar per month, and the school will assume all operations and maintenance costs of the facility. Students already enrolled will be eligible for attendance at the independent charter school. After hearing the recommendations of the review committee, the SBE will select an applicant charter school operator to recommend to the district. The commissioner or a designee will then assist the selected applicant in negotiating an independent charter with the local board of education.

The independent charter school will be given a charter for four years and adhere to many of the same provisions as other charter schools (e.g., regulatory waivers must be requested, and the charter application must contain information similar to that required for other charter schools). If the independent charter school receives an F during its third year of operation, the SBE will issue a new request for proposals. After the fourth year, if a majority of the parents vote in favor of renewing the independent charter application, the renewal process will be similar to that of other charter schools. The parents may also vote to become a traditional school under the local district, returning the operation of the school to the local board of education.

How independent charter schools will interact with other charter schools will not be seen for at least another year. However, the schools have the potential to create an expansive, parallel charter school population in the state.

The Charter School Landscape in Colorado

Although created to extend new learning opportunities to at-risk and low-achieving students, the charter school movement in Colorado has not served such populations as well as they have been served in other states. Charter schools nationally enroll students that have similar demographic characteristics to students in all public schools or serve a higher percentage of students of color than their surrounding districts (RPP International 2000). In Colorado, however, the charter community is less diverse. In 1999–2000, 14.4 percent of charter school students were eligible for free or reduced-price lunch, versus 28.2 percent statewide.[7] Of charter students, 26.6 percent are ethnic minorities, compared to 29.4 percent in all Colorado public schools. For both categories, 58 percent of charter schools served a significantly lower population of students of color and those eligible for free or reduced-price lunch (Colorado Department of Education 2001).

Suburban Emphasis

The relatively low percentage of at-risk students being served by charter schools in Colorado is due in large part to the local district sponsorship model. While there has been tremendous growth in the number of charter schools, this growth has been in isolated pockets rather than across the state. Three-quarters of the state's charter schools are on Colorado's "Front Range" between Colorado Springs and Greeley. About 40 percent are in the greater Denver region. Charter schools have been established disproportionately in suburban settings. The Jefferson County R-1 School District has authorized eleven charter schools, Adams County and Boulder have seven, and Douglas County RE 1 School District has authorized five. These largely suburban districts are experiencing rapid expansion and increases in student enrollments. These factors have cushioned the financial impact of charter schools, as the new schools have helped the districts to address facility and class-size needs.

The results of this suburban emphasis are seen not only in the composition of the charter school student populations but also in the types of charter schools established. Parents in these suburban communities are demanding back-to-basics charter schools that employ E. D. Hirsch's Core Knowledge sequence. Indeed, at least twenty-three charter schools in the state—40 percent of charter schools studied in the recent Colorado charter schools evaluation—use the Core Knowledge sequence (Colorado Department of Education 2001). A substantial number of these schools are in suburban Denver. Efforts to support Core Knowledge schools by the Challenge Foundation and the early success of the first Colorado charter school—Academy Charter—have also boosted the popularity of Core Knowledge with charter applicants.[8] Core Knowledge has been criticized by some analysts as being Eurocentric and as focusing on rote memorization over critical thinking approaches.

There are several examples of charter schools using other reform models—

Expeditionary learning, Montessori, and Paideia—and catering to special populations of different types of students. For example, the Passage Charter School was developed by the Delta/Montrose Pregnancy Prevention Initiative and focuses on students who are pregnant or parenting. Prairie Creeks Charter School is a joint effort of four school districts to serve eight at-risk students using the PLATO Integrated Learning System. Colorado charter schools rarely have traditional grade-level configurations, and almost all are newly established schools. Finally, Colorado charter schools, as is the case nationally, tend to be small: 42 percent enroll 200 students or less, compared to 24 percent of all public schools in Colorado (Colorado Department of Education 2001).

In 1999, 17,822 students attended Colorado charter schools, representing over 2 percent of the state's student population. Student enrollment in charter schools grew 23 percent between fall 1998 and fall 1999, compared to 1.7 percent in all public schools, 0.6 percent in nonpublic schools, and 10.1 percent in home schools.[9] The Core Knowledge focus and suburban setting have helped to recruit students back from nonpublic and home schools. Although there is tremendous variation in the data, some charter schools have drawn as many as 44 percent of their students from home schools and up to 15 percent from private schools (Clayton Foundation 1999). Most charter schools report waiting lists (Clayton Foundation 1999). Denver-area charter schools report waiting lists from 25 students to over 1,000 in Core Knowledge charters in Cherry Creek and Jefferson County (Cummins 1997).

Urban districts are beginning to become more interested in the charter school concept, with the urban Aurora public schools opening two charter schools and Denver continuing to sponsor additional schools, raising the Denver district total to seven. Charter school advocates point to such factors as particular personalities on school boards and fear of competition from charter schools as reasons for school districts' reluctance to become involved with charter schools.

Regulatory Freedom

Although there is no formal state-level mechanism to catalyze information-sharing between charter and traditional public schools, much can be learned about perceived barriers to educational innovation by examining from which laws, rules, and regulations charters seek waivers. While these waivers allow charter schools greater flexibility, they may also have detrimental effects on the qualifications and compensation of personnel. Waivers of state policies must be requested jointly with the board of education of the district in which the charter school is located. (The district sponsoring the school may waive local regulations.) If the SBE does not provide written denial of a waiver request within forty-five days of the proposed waiver, it is considered granted.

For the sixty-three charter schools with state waiver information on file as of September 1999, fifty-nine received at least one waiver, with others seeking as many as thirty-three.[10] Only four charter schools had not requested any waivers, and a total of 944 waivers had been granted to fifty-nine charter schools (Colorado Department of Education 1999). The most popular waiver requests were from the Teacher Employment Act. Fifty-three schools asked to be waived from C.R.S. 22-63-401, which requires that teachers be subject to district-adopted salary schedules. The fiscal restraints faced by charter schools, especially those receiving less than 100 percent per-pupil operating revenues, appear to be strong incentives for seeking this waiver. The waiver has allowed charter schools to pay teachers less than the salary schedule mandates and channel the savings to other priorities. However, such waivers have apparently not deterred teachers from working in charter schools. Interestingly, a recent evaluation found that charter school teachers cited the charter school educational philosophy and the opportunity to work with like-minded colleagues as far more important that compensation packages (Clayton Foundation 1999). The salary waiver helps explain the large disparity between the average salaries of charter school teachers ($26,446) and those of traditional public school teachers in Colorado ($38,163). While an extreme example, the average teacher salary at Boulder Preparatory High School was $12,275, compared to its sponsoring district's average of $42,663 (Colorado Department of Education 2001).

Other components of the Teacher Employment Act have been waived for numerous charter schools. As of 1999, forty-nine charters had asked to be waived from having to hire certified teachers. As a result, 63 percent of charter school teachers have a certificate, 11 percent report a certificate from another state, and 16 percent are actively working toward certification. Waivers from statutory procedures to dismiss teachers were requested by forty-eight schools, and forty-six asked to be waived from requirements regarding the renewal and nonrenewal of probationary teacher contracts (Clayton Foundation 1999).

These waivers indicate that provisions pertaining to teacher certification, compensation, transfer, and dismissal are all perceived as impediments to charter school creativity and innovation. This could be the case. But given a growing body of research demonstrating the impact of teacher quality (as traditionally measured by years of experience, certification, and education level) on student achievement (Darling-Hammond 1997; Sanders and Rivers 1996; Greenwald, Hedges, and Laine 1996; Ferguson 1991), the waivers could have a detrimental effect on student performance over time.

The second most frequently granted waiver pertains to the employment and authority of principals. The waiver, requested by fifty-two charter schools, allows charter schools to hire administrators without certificates. Again, the flexibility comes with some consequences, as almost one-third of charter schools in the state have employed three or more principals/chief administrators since opening (Clayton Foundation 1999). More than one-third of charter schools have lead administrators with less than two years of experience in the field of education, with an average administrator tenure of two years. The impact of this leadership instability has not been well examined and merits careful analysis. In one noteworthy case, Alpine Charter School in Dillon requested a waiver from statutes governing principals and then went through six principals between its establishment in 1996 and its closure in 1999.[11]

The third area in which charter schools frequently request waivers pertains to state statutes regarding local school boards. Many of these waivers transfer powers from the local school board to the charter school. Fifty-one charter schools have received waivers from local board control over hiring, evaluations, and other personnel decisions. Freedom from school board policies regarding textbooks and curriculum, conduct and discipline, school calendar, selection of staff, termination of employment of personnel, and in-service training have all been frequently requested. Waivers of compulsory attendance requirements, the establishment of kindergartens, fingerprinting of licensed personnel, and the creation and maintenance of food-service facilities have all been granted to multiple charter schools. To date, the SBE has been willing to grant virtually all waivers requested.[12]

Oversight and Accountability

As the sponsoring entity, the local school district is largely responsible for charter school accountability through the charter-renewal process, occurring every three to five years. Renewal applications must include a report on charter school progress toward achieving the objectives and pupil performance standards specified in the initial charter agreement and a financial statement disclosing expenditure information (C.R.S. 22-30.5-110). But as is the case in most states, the statutes include more information on reasons for charter revocation than a clear delineation of state and local responsibilities for overseeing charter schools (Banks and Hirsch 1998; RPP International 1999a). For this reason, there is wide variation across the state in the level of district interaction with charter schools, as well as in the performance expectations for charter schools (Clayton Foundation 1999).

As a means to assist school districts and charter schools with accountability matters, the Colorado League of Charter Schools has undertaken a project aimed at ensuring that charter schools are accountable and meeting their goals during their first five years. The program, piloted in fifteen charter schools during 1998–1999, has two stages. Stage one occurs during the application process, when the league works with the charter applicant and the district to foster agreement on an accountability process. Stage two involves various steps to facilitate accountability through data gathering, external site visits, and self-study. It appears that the league's efforts have not gone unnoticed, as several districts across the state have adopted components of this accountability plan in their oversight of charter schools. The program, however, is voluntary, and the results of the data gathering and external site visits that are part of the process are not compiled and systematically analyzed and distributed.

At the state level, the SBE is charged with overseeing the charter school program by compiling charter school evaluations from local boards, reviewing information regarding requests for waivers from state regulations and policies, and comparing charter school pupil performance with the performance of comparable groups of pupils in other public schools. A federally funded evaluation study of the program has been performed annually over the past four years in order to gather information about the effectiveness of the Charter Schools Act and provide data on charter school performance. There are additional accountability measures at the state level, as charter schools do not receive blanket waivers from participation in state-required programs. Charter schools must participate in the state assessment program and adhere to district and state accreditation standards.

Colorado Student Assessment Program

Charter schools, like all public schools in the state, participate in the Colorado Student Assessment Program (CSAP). The assessment, a criterion-based exam consisting of open-ended and multiple-choice questions, measures whether students have achieved proficiency levels by meeting state standards. The test was given in reading and writing in the fourth and seventh grade in 1999–2000.[13] Tests were also administered for the first time in fifth-grade math and eighth-grade math and science. Data are available from the 1999 CSAP for thirty-one charter schools on the fourth-grade assessment and twenty-six charter schools on the seventh-grade test.[14]

By virtually all measures, charter schools are performing well as a group, although there is tremendous variation within the charter school population. As indicated in table 6.1, the percentage of students performing at or above proficiency levels in charter schools is above the state average on all four tests, especially in writing in both grades. Charter schools adopting the Core Knowledge sequence have done particularly well, vastly outpacing statewide averages, while charter schools with experiential curricula are performing at more modest levels. However, many of the Core Knowledge charters are in suburban settings and serve less diverse populations. A handful of charter schools, mostly serving at-risk students, had fewer than 10 percent of students achieving at proficiency levels in 1999. Some of the highest-performing schools in the state are charter schools— Jefferson Academy Elementary Charter School was named one of five John Irwin Colorado Schools of Excellence—and some of the poorest-performing schools are charters, as well.

The generally high performance levels of charter schools can also be seen in a comparison to their sponsoring school districts. On all four tests in 1999, a majority of charter schools had a greater proportion of students performing at proficient or advanced levels than the school districts in which they are located. Fifty-eight percent of charter schools (eighteen out of thirty-one) had higher averages than their school districts on both fourth-grade tests, 62 percent had higher averages on the seventh-grade reading test, and 85 percent outperformed their districts on the seventh-grade writing test.[15] These figures are similar to the patterns found in the 1998 CSAP scores. In 1998, over three-quarters of the charter schools examined in an evaluation study outperformed the average scores in their sponsoring districts (Clayton Foundation 1999).

Somewhat different results were found in a recent CDE analysis comparing the fourth-grade test scores among some charter schools and traditional public schools that were matched according to having 0–20 percent of their populations composed of minority students and 0–20 percent of their students eligible for free or reduced-price lunch. Both groups had a greater proportion of students performing at proficient or advanced levels for both reading and writing than statewide averages. However, while charter schools did slightly better than the traditional

Table 6.1

Percentage of Public School Pupils at or above CSAP Proficiency Levels, 1999

	Fourth-Grade Reading	Fourth-Grade Writing	Seventh-Grade Reading	Seventh-Grade Writing
Statewide	62%	33%	56%	40%
Charter Schools	69%	45%	67%	58%
Core Curriculum	76%	54%	71%	64%
Experiential Learning	53%	28%	52%	42%
Other	55%	31%		

Source: Colorado Department of Education, Unified Grants Office, 2000

public school grouping, the differences between the two groups were not statistically significant.[16] Results were similar for 2000. Across the matched samples, the statewide traditional public school average was 77 percent of students scoring at proficient levels or above, compared to 78 percent for charter schools. Analyses cannot be done for schools in other demographic categories, as an insufficient number of charter schools in Colorado report serving higher percentages of minority students and students eligible for free or reduced-price lunch.[17]

Thus, while charter schools are undoubtedly performing well as a group, that success appears to be due in part to the small percentage of at-risk students attending charter schools. Traditional public schools serving students with similar socioeconomic backgrounds are attaining similar results.

Accreditation Standards

Under 1998 legislation and recent SBE rules and regulations, each school district will need to address a number of academic indicators involving CSAP benchmarks; third-grade literacy results; advanced placement passing grades; and other measures such as dropout, student attendance, and graduation rates. All districts are expected to reach an intermediate benchmark of 80 percent of students at proficient and advanced levels. Districts have three years to increase the proportion of students at this level by 25 percent. If these goals are not met, districts are placed on academic watch for one year and then probation for a year, after which the district will lose state accreditation. In 1999, only four charter schools had students scoring over 80 percent proficiency on both the reading and writing exams (all at the seventh-grade level).

School districts will now sign a six-year accreditation contract with the SBE, which sets accreditation targets for each public school, including charter schools. Given that charter schools already have unique agreements with their districts, their targets may look somewhat different than those for traditional public schools. But with each district establishing agreements with every school in the district, state content standards and CSAP scores promise to play a more prominent role for all schools in Colorado. The impact of these changes on charter schools remains to be seen. The accreditation standards should enhance accountability by clarifying expectations placed on charter schools. However, the heavy emphasis on state curriculum standards and CSAP scores may also impede charters from engaging in innovation and emphasizing curricula and approaches that are not tailored specifically toward improved CSAP scores.

Controversies

Controversies surrounding the charter school movement in Colorado have focused on three main issues: charter school sponsorship, charter school finance, and the impact of charter schools on traditional public schools.

Charter School Sponsorship and Appeals

Allowing for multiple sponsors is a key aspect of "strong" charter school laws (see, e.g., Dale and DeSchryver 1998). Nationally, sponsorship does appear to play a key role in the number of charter schools approved. More than 80 percent of charter schools are located in the twenty-six states that have multiple sponsoring entities or an appeals process accompanying local district sponsorship (Center for Education Reform 2001a).

The appeals process has been well employed in Colorado and is at least partly responsible for the relatively high percentage of students attending charter schools. In total, at least twelve schools exist, in part, because of the role played by the SBE in resolving disputes between school districts and charter applicants (Clayton Foundation 1999). As of 31 December 2000, the SBE had heard eighty-five appeals under the Charter Schools Act. Of those, thirty-three district decisions were upheld; twenty-two appeals were dismissed; twenty-one were remanded to the district for reconsideration; and, in three cases, the SBE ordered the establishment of a charter school (Colorado Department of Education 2001).

The SBE's directive that the Denver school board sponsor the Thurgood Marshall Charter Middle School application has been the subject of numerous lawsuits challenging the appeals process.[18] In September 1999, the Colorado Supreme Court resolved the six-year-old case, ruling that SBE power to require school districts to sponsor charter applicants in appeal cases is constitutional. The crux of the decision lies in the court's belief that the SBE, in exercising its constitutional responsibility for the general supervision of education, has the power to impose its opinion regarding the best interests of pupils, school districts, and communities across the state without infringing on a district's control of instruction.

While this court decision ensures that the appeals process will remain a part of Colorado's charter approval process, many advocates believe that the decision has further implications, opening up an avenue for establishing new authorizers. In a state with a long cultural and legal adherence to the principle of local control, the decision might remove any constitutional barriers to moving toward an alternative charter school sponsorship model involving the SBE. Legislation permitting state authorization of charter schools will assuredly be proposed, and a rancorous debate over the appropriate role of the local and state boards regarding charter schools, and perhaps other education reform issues, is likely to follow.

Charter School Expenditures and Revenues

Until the 2000–2001 school year, charter schools negotiated a revenue rate during the application phase that was at least 80 percent of the district's per-pupil operating revenues (not including capital reserve funds). The charter school pupil count is included in the school district's pupil enrollments. Funding is then distributed to the charter school by the sponsoring district. Of the charter schools that participated in the 2001 evaluation study, about one-quarter received a funding rate at 90 percent or less of their sponsoring district's per-pupil operating revenues, and about 30 percent received 100 percent or more (Colorado Department of Education 2001).

While some school districts provide all of their charter schools with at least 100 percent of per-pupil operating revenues, others have used the 80 percent funding floor as an absolute level for allocating charters; only applicants requesting the minimal level of funding are approved. It appears that both charter school operators and school district personnel are unhappy with this system. Charter school operators argue that they should receive the same allocation as other public schools. Instructional expenditures suffer due to the lower funding levels, as rent and other fixed costs are not fully covered. Already dissatisfied with the financial impact of charter schools, school district officials often argue that the 20 percent funding gap does not sufficiently cushion the blow of losing revenue to charters and does not adequately compensate districts for new administrative and oversight responsibilities presented by charter schools.

A recent study compares the per-pupil revenues and expenditures in five Colorado charter schools to their sponsoring districts. In a comparison of major expenditures—on instruction, administration, and operations and maintenance —charter schools in four of the districts spent at least 80 percent as much as their sponsoring district (Hirsch and Anderson 1999).[19] See table 6.2. However, the charter school located in the rural Moffat 2 School District spent only 41 percent as much as the district spent overall per pupil. As the 80 percent revenue floor applies to per-pupil operating revenues, having capital revenue streams such as bonding that bring in additional funds can greatly affect overall expenditure levels. These allocations have a direct impact on the amount charter schools can spend relative to traditional public schools on instructional expenses, as well as other services.

Further exacerbating the effects of these revenue discrepancies are issues faced by charter schools as a consequence of their small size. As charter schools are smaller educational units, they cannot enjoy the same economies of scale as large school districts. For example, in the same study, two out of five of the charter schools spent more per pupil than their sponsoring district on administrative costs (Hirsch and Anderson 1999). In one case, the charter spent four times the amount of the district. On the other hand, by utilizing a part-time administrator who also teaches, the Moffat charter school was able to spend only 8 percent of what the sponsoring school district spends on administration. In three of the charter schools, operations and maintenance costs were also greater than in the sponsoring school district. This is not surprising, as about half of charter schools in the state rent or lease facilities, with almost two-thirds of those paying rent out of their operations budget (Colorado Department of Education 2001; Clayton Foundation 1999).

With lower per-pupil revenues than districts, charter schools have cut costs mostly in the area of instruction, through hiring less experienced teachers (Colorado Department of Education 2001; Hirsch and Anderson 1999; Bomotti, Ginsburg, and Cobb 1999). Statewide, the average teacher salary in charter schools was $26,446, compared to $38,163 in traditional public schools. Charter school teachers have less experience—3.9 years versus 13 years in traditional public schools—

Table 6.2

Major Per-Pupil Expenditures, 1997–1998

	District	Charter School	Relative Spending
Moffat 2	$10,171	$4,171	41%
Eagle County RE50	$5,719	$5,497	96%
Littleton 6	$4,182	$3,560	85%
Colorado Springs 11	$4,226	$3,774	89%
Jefferson County R-1	$3,565	$3,041	85%

Source: Hirsch and Anderson 1999

and fewer have master's degrees than in traditional public schools (Colorado Department of Education 2001; Clayton Foundation 1999). Further, charters are spending less on employee benefits (as a percentage of teachers' salaries) than are traditional school districts (Hirsch and Anderson 1999).

Beginning in 2000–2001 charter schools receiving less than 95 percent of per-pupil operating revenue will receive additional funds under the newly approved funding formula, and all charter schools will receive the state allocation for capital reserves. Starting in 2001–2002, charter schools will received an additional 130 percent of capital reserve funds, and in 2002, districts will have to allocate a per-pupil proportion of any funding raised through local bond initiatives. But charter operators still do not foresee an equal playing field. Many are worried that districts already handing over more than 95 percent may use the opportunity to renegotiate charter agreements at lower revenue levels. Also, any services provided by the district will be purchased back by the charter school at the actual per-pupil cost. With little itemized information on the scope or cost of services provided by districts under the old revenue system (Hirsch and Anderson 1999), it is difficult to predict whether charter schools will end up paying more for services such as insurance, payroll, security, and central office support. Under SB 01-129, an annual audit will be conducted (starting in July 2002) to determine if the 5 percent administrative costs charged by districts were actually provided to charter schools.

Impact on Traditional Public Schools

Advocates often argue that charter schools will act as "laboratories of reform." Successful innovations demonstrated in charters can be emulated and thus engender systemic change (Bierlein 1997; Nathan 1996). However, similar to the patchwork distribution of charter schools across the state, the effects of charter schools on the traditional public school system are sporadic. While there are examples of reforms that may not have occurred without the pressure placed on school districts by charter schools, "few pressure points have spilled over into districts" (Kerns 1999). This is not surprising given that the "strong majority" of school districts do not have a formal mechanism in place for sharing the experiences of charter schools with other schools in the district (Clayton Foundation 1999, 156). Charter school personnel typically interact with only their sponsoring school district or with other charter and alternative schools and do not have opportunities to regularly interact with their peers in traditional public schools (Clayton Foundation 1999).

Charter school operators, however, believe that there have been subtle impacts. Sponsoring school districts have been more responsive to parent concerns regarding curriculum and have provoked other school districts to reevaluate accountability (Clayton Foundation 1999). There are also various anecdotal examples of changes that may not have occurred in the absence of charter schools.

- The Poudre School District did not have a traditional public school that used Core Knowledge prior to 1993, despite requests from parents. Immediately after the passage of the Charter Schools Act, the district designated a Core Knowledge school.

- When the Douglas County RE 1 School District received an application for a charter school aimed at "talented and gifted" students, the district instead created a traditional public school to cater to the same student population.

- Dolores County RE 2 and Moffat 2 School Districts, in part as a result of the success of charter schools using Core Knowledge, have been investigating the possibility of converting their entire districts to the Core Knowledge program.

The state recently received $350,000 (FY 2000) from the U.S. Department of Education for dissemination grants aimed at facilitating the sharing of successful innovations between new charter school operators and traditional public schools. However, there are strained relationships between charters and some districts due in part to district perceptions of the negative financial impact of charters and feelings that charters have unfairly heightened criticism of traditional public schools. This state of affairs suggests that significant systematic change that nurtures productive communications between charter and traditional public schools is not likely.

Conclusions

The future of charter schools is not in doubt in Colorado, and given the current political context, all indications point to continued growth. In reauthorizing the Charter Schools Act in 1998, without a cap on the number of schools that can be established or another sunset provision, the legislature sent a clear message that charter schools are a permanent part of education reform in Colorado.

This attitude is not exclusive to the legislature. The commissioner of education and the SBE have also been supportive of charter schools as an education reform. Governor Owens, a cosponsor of the original Charter Schools Act, has written numerous letters of support on behalf of charter school applicants throughout the state. Moreover, the CDE has reorganized to ensure that charter schools are "an integral part rather than an appendage" of departmental programs (Windler 1999). For example, there is now a unified grants office to ensure that charter schools receive the same access to grant opportunities as traditional public schools.

The key question for state policy makers and other stakeholders is how to ensure that charter school growth is spread more systematically throughout the state, rather than isolated in suburban communities in the Denver–Colorado Springs–Fort Collins areas. The Denver city school district has become more accepting of charter schools, to the point of not only sponsoring seven schools but also creating its own charter school (Pioneer Charter School). Certainly implications of the application appeals process and the Colorado Supreme Court case played a role in Denver's new thinking. However, other districts have been successful at acting in a preemptive fashion to discourage applicants from even bringing proposals to the local board.

Legislation establishing the SBE as an alternative sponsor would allow charter applicants to bypass reluctant local school districts and could serve as a significant catalyst for the creation of a more diverse charter school movement in the state. Policies providing additional financial or facilities support to charter schools that are designed to work with at-risk students could also help to spur the creation of additional charters in urban communities. The Colorado League of Charter Schools is also working to create and support charter schools that serve urban communities and at-risk students.

In addition, independent charter schools authorized under SB 00-186 may also play a significant role in a few years. As most "F" schools have been projected to be in Denver and other urban areas, the rules mandating independent charter schools may necessitate the creation of charter alternatives in these districts. While independent charter schools are technically different from the existing charter schools, they will likely shape the views of local school board members, either creating new supporters or solidifying opposition to the charter school concept.

Clearer statutory requirements regarding charter school oversight might also address some of the funding inequities and strained school district–charter school relationships that have developed in some districts. A formal advisory board or other group at the state level that could mediate when problems between sponsoring districts and charter schools arise could also be beneficial. That same group might also facilitate a better documenting and sharing of best practices in both charter and traditional public schools. In Colorado and nationally, school districts have not often responded to charter schools in the ways that advocates had envisioned (Rofes 1998). Better, more formalized mechanisms of mediation and information exchange will be necessary if charter schools are to remain an integral part of education reform in the state.

7 • The Massachusetts Charter School Initiative

A Model for Public School Accountability?

Paul Herdman

MASSACHUSETTS HAS CREATED what many consider to be a model accountability system for charter schools (Finn, Manno, and Vanourek 2000; Hill et al. 1999). States across the nation are creating central assessments and moving toward focusing on schools rather than districts as the unit of analysis; in other words, schools are being given increased autonomy in exchange for more accountability (Fuhrman 1999). Given this trend, the question of balance between local and central control becomes important. Since charter schools are seen as "the country's most aggressive version of school decentralization" (Odden and Busch 1998, 48), examining the governance relationships between charter schools and their authorizers may have implications for how districts could be governed. This chapter provides an overview of the Massachusetts charter school initiative with a focus on how its accountability policies might inform the governance of public schools in general.

Political Origins

In order to understand the evolution and trajectory of the Massachusetts charter school initiative, it is important to examine its political origins. As Marshall, Mitchell, and Wirt (1989, 6) point out: "In state capitals, when policies are formulated to change education systems, the values of *people* . . . are transformed into a set of statements (policy) about the way things *must be done.*"

The Massachusetts charter school law (Chapter 71, sect. 89, of the Massachusetts General Laws) was a small provision of the Massachusetts Education Reform Act of 1993 (MERA). MERA was an omnibus act that called for adequate district funding across the state (C.70, MGL) and the establishment of state standards and assessments at all levels of the school system (C.69, MGL).

Since Massachusetts is a Democratic stronghold, it is reasonable to question how charter schools—an initiative often thought of as the first step toward vouchers—ever became law in the state. In fact, when Scott Hamilton, a former Massachusetts associate commissioner of education, first began his assignment, he likened the Commonwealth's charter schools to "palm trees in Bangor [Maine]."[1] Examining the perspectives of those who influenced the creation of the charter school law may help unravel this enigma.

The Players

Five major players from the public and private sectors shaped the Education Reform Act and, by extension, the charter school law: Governor William F. Weld (R); the cochairs of the Joint Education Committee—Senator Thomas Birmingham (D) and Representative Mark Roosevelt (D); Paul Reville, president of the Massachusetts Business Alliance; and William Edgerly, president of CEOs for Fundamental Change.[2]

There was no groundswell calling for charter schools. Representative Roosevelt, the legislator credited with championing the charter legislation, said he got the idea from Ted Kolderie, the charter school pioneer in Minnesota. Reville went so far as to describe charter schools as an "eleventh-hour add-on" (Herdman 2000, 39). So why did the charter idea take hold despite heavy opposition from the state's teachers unions? In short, the charter legislation in Massachusetts was passed because, like many charter laws across the United States, it was a reasonable political compromise that both liberals and conservatives could support (see Hassel 1999a; Pipho 1993).

The Intents

Each of the players involved in crafting the law supported one or more of the following three purposes: (1) innovation, (2) choice and competition, and (3) accountability. Reville saw the intent of charter schools as "a R[esearch] and D[evelopment] branch of the system as a whole" (Herdman 2000, 39). Weld and Edgerly saw charter schools as a means of infusing competition into the system. Edgerly, a former banker, argued that "the system couldn't be changed from the inside" (Herdman 2000, 39).[3] Birmingham saw charters as a means of providing more choices for parents. He said that "children shouldn't be penalized for an accident of birth" (Herdman 2000, 39). As Roosevelt accurately summarized,

Table 7.1

Purposes of the Massachusetts Charter School Law

Major Intents	Purposes of Charter School Law (C.71, s.89, MGL)
Innovation	To stimulate the development of innovative programs within public education
	To provide opportunities for innovative learning and assessments
	To provide teachers with a vehicle for establishing schools with alternative, innovative methods of educational instruction and school structure and management
	To provide models for replication in other public schools (added in 1997)
Accountability	To hold teachers and school administrators accountable for students' educational outcomes
	To encourage performance-based educational programs
Choice and Competition	To provide parents and students with greater options in choosing schools within and outside their school districts

"There is no clear intent [in the charter school law] because there were *many* intents" (Herdman 2000, 38). As indicated in table 7.1, innovation is the most prominent intent of the law, followed by accountability, and then by choice.

The Law and Its Amendments

The original Massachusetts charter school law set in motion a controlled experiment. If the charter law in Arizona is seen as letting a thousand flowers bloom, the Commonwealth's law might be seen as tending the garden carefully. Governor Weld's Executive Office of Education (EOE) was given the power to create just twenty-five charter schools, and these schools were to be scrutinized vigilantly.

Original Provisions of the Law

The major provisions of the original Massachusetts charter school law were as follows.

- *Number of schools.* The law called for a statewide cap of twenty-five schools and municipal caps of no more than five schools in large urban districts and no more than two in all other districts. Further, the total charter school enrollment could not exceed three-quarters of 1 percent of the state's public school enrollment.

- *Access.* While students (and their siblings) located in the charter school's district of residence would have admissions preference, students from other districts were also eligible to apply. The charter school had the option of using district transportation or providing its own via an average transportation allotment per student.

- *Governance.* A governing board composed of local community members would oversee each charter school. These boards were legal entities empowered by the Massachusetts education secretary to oversee all school functions. In turn, the secretary had the power to grant and revoke all charters.

- *Length of charters.* Charter terms would be for five years.

- *Personnel.* Charter schools were not bound by local bargaining agreements nor required to hire certified teachers. If a charter school did hire a public school teacher, the teacher could take a leave of absence from the district for up to two years, and the charter school would pay into the teacher's retirement fund.

- *Finances.* Charter schools would receive an Average Cost per Student (ACS) for each student enrolled. This ACS equals "all" educational expenses for a given district, divided by its total population. (The ACS does not include capital expenses.)

- *Accountability.* The law simply stipulated that the EOE was required to develop measures of academic success.

Since Ted Kolderie inspired the Massachusetts charter law, it seems appropriate to compare its initial design to Kolderie's ideal charter law (1994). Consistent with Kolderie's definition, the law provides school-level governing boards with maximum control of personnel and other budgetary decisions. However, contrary to Kolderie's ideal, the law limits the supply of charter schools by establishing caps on the growth of the initiative and providing that only *one* body (the EOE) can authorize charters.

Amendments

Over time, several important amendments were made to the charter school law. In 1996, the EOE was eliminated as a part of Governor Weld's efforts to reduce big government. As a result, charter school authorizing powers shifted from the secretary of education to the state board of education (SBE). This was an important shift, because rather than being overseen by a nimble fifteen-person policy office, the charter school initiative would now be under the auspices of the Massachusetts Department of Education (MDE), a much larger and more deliberate body. This shift would also bring the charter school initiative closer to mainstream education interests, thus perhaps blunting its ability to serve as a catalyst for significant systemic change.

RAISING THE CAPS

In 1996, several major amendments to the law served to both enhance and hobble the growth of the initiative. Proponents of charter schools, frustrated by the lack of available charters and the substantial waiting lists at existing charter schools, successfully lobbied the legislature to increase the cap on charters. The cap was doubled from 25 to 50 charter schools. However, 37 of these slots would be for "Commonwealth" charter schools and 13 for "Horace Mann" charters. The former would continue to be independent of local districts, reporting directly to the state, while the latter would *not* be independent of the district structure. Horace Mann applicants would need to garner approval from the local bargaining unit and the superintendent in order to apply for a charter from the state. Further, once approved, Horace Mann employees would be members of the local bargaining agreement, and the school would need to negotiate its per-pupil allocation with the district. In 2000, an act relative to charter schools (C.227, MGL) increased the number of available Horace Mann charters to 48 and Commonwealth charters to 72, for a total of 120. However, since the state cannot grant more than 7 Horace Mann or 7 Commonwealth charters in a given year, the Commonwealth will not reach it charter school limit until at least 2006.

The enrollment caps were also changed. At the state level, the cap on charter school enrollment began at three-fourths of 1 percent of the state's total enrollment, and the cap was removed completely in 2000. However, the total growth of the charter school initiative is still controlled by the establishment of a fixed number of charters (discussed above) and municipal caps. At the municipal level, the cap was changed in 1996 from no more than five charters in any district to no more than 6 percent of a district's net spending. In 2000, this cap was changed to no more than 9 percent of a district's net spending (see table 7.2).

REREGULATING AND SOFTENING THE BLOW

Meanwhile, charter opponents voiced concerns about the charter movement. They argued that special needs students were being ill served, that the funding formula was unfair to districts, and that charters were not living up to their promise of being "laboratories of innovation."

Table 7.2

Summary of Massachusetts Charter School Law and Amendments

Provisions	Original Law (1993)	Amendments
Authorizer	Executive Office of Education	Massachusetts Board of Education (1995)
Number of Schools Allowed	25	120: 48 Horace Mann and 72 Commonwealth (2000)
Municipal Caps	No more than 2 charters in small districts and no more than 5 in larger districts.	Revenue going to charter schools cannot exceed 9 percent of the district's net school spending (2000).
State Enrollment Cap	Charter enrollment cannot exceed three-quarters of 1 percent of the total state enrollment in public schools.	No state enrollment cap (2000).
School Governance	School governing board	
Charter Length	Five years	
Professional Rights	Teachers can organize but are not obligated to be part of a collective bargaining unit. They can take a leave of absence from their district for two years and participate in the state retirement system.	The provisions remain unchanged for Commonwealth charter teachers. However, Horace Mann teachers are part of a collective bargaining unit (1996).
Finances	Average Cost per Student follows child.	
Transportation	A charter school may use the district's transportation services or receive an average transportation allotment from the district.	Charter schools are reimbursed from the state for the cost of their transportation expenses (1996).
District Reimbursement	Not specified in law[a]	Districts are reimbursed 100 percent for loss in revenue due to charter school enrollment in year one of the school's operation. District reimbursement is reduced over time to 60 percent, 40 percent, and 0 percent in the subsequent three years of the charter school's operation (1996).

[a] While this was not specified in law, districts were reimbursed through the state's foundation formula.

The legislative response was twofold. First, the legislature mandated a raft of studies and additional reporting requirements. These new amendments called for studies ranging from reports on charter school services to special education students to reports on the extent to which charter schools are serving as sources of innovation.[4] Additional reporting requirements ranged from mandates to collect more detailed enrollment information to a rule that potential charter school board members disclose all of their financial interests to the state ethics commission.[5]

Concerns about lost revenue as a result of charter school students leaving districts led the legislature to request an evaluation of the payment process and to reimburse districts for losses. KPMG Peat Marwick (1998) reported that the ACS—the cost calculation of all students in a K–12 district—was not only fair but may actually be unfair to charter schools because they are not eligible for state capital revenue. Nonetheless, the legislature voted to reimburse districts at 100 percent for loss in revenue due to charter school enrollment in year one of a school's operation, followed by 60 percent, 40 percent, and 0 percent reimbursements in the subsequent three years. It was clear that the majority in the state legislature did not support the notion that competition might improve public education.

Second, the Horace Mann legislation further softened the blow to districts. The theory behind this provision was that this new brand of charter schools would have less acrimonious relationships with districts and, therefore, increase the potential for sharing new ideas and practices. However, these new charters would also not challenge districts, in that they would not be taking any resources away from districts. The concern regarding Horace Mann charter schools, then, is that if the district and local bargaining unit need to sign off on the applications, these applications may not be very innovative.

The Controlled Growth of the Charter School Movement

The first fifteen charter schools in Massachusetts opened in fall 1995. Since that time, charter school enrollment grew, roughly, from 30 to 40 percent per annum from 1995 to 2000 and slowed to about 3 percent from 2000 to 2001. However, as indicated in table 7.3, most of the enrollment growth can be attributed to expansion in existing charter schools, rather than the creation of new schools. While the cap on Commonwealth charter schools was reached in 1999, seven Horace

Table 7.3

Growth of the Massachusetts Charter School Initiative, 1995 to 2001

Academic Year	Charter Schools in Operation			Total Enrollment	Average School Size	Percentage of State Enrollment[a]
	Common	*Horace*	*Total*			
1995–1996	15	0	15	2,623	175	0.25
1996–1997	20	0	20	5,329	252	0.52
1997–1998	24	0	24	6,623	276	0.65
1998–1999	30	4	34	9,896	291	0.97
1999–2000	34	5	39	12,771	328	1.25
2000–2001	35	5	40	14,072	361	1.4

Source: Massachusetts Department of Education 2001

[a] These figures are based on charter school enrollment divided by the 1997–1998 state public school enrollment of 1,018,900.

Mann charters were still available. By March 2001, forty-eight charters had been granted: forty-one Commonwealth and seven Horace Mann.

All regions of Massachusetts now have charter schools. The law gives priority to charter applications in "low-performing districts," so it is not surprising that 65 percent (twenty-six of forty) of the operational charter schools in 2000 were located in urban areas, followed by 27.5 percent (eleven) in suburban areas, and 7.5 percent (three) in rural areas.

Consistent with national data (P. Berman et al. 1998), Massachusetts charter schools do not appear to be siphoning off White and affluent students. Compared to statewide public school averages, charter schools serve a higher percentage of Black students (24 percent, vs. 9 percent statewide), a higher percentage of Latino students (14 percent, vs. 10 percent statewide,) and a higher percentage of low-income students (34 percent, vs. 25 percent statewide). However, the percentage of charter school students on Individual Education Plans is lower than the state average. Special education students compose 9 percent of the overal charter school enrollment, compared to 17 percent for public schools statewide. J. Wood (1999) reports that charter schools serve proportionally fewer special needs students overall and that this disparity is more marked when the numbers of students with more severe disabilities are compared.

On average, Massachusetts charter schools are small, but this may be changing. MDE data for 2001–2002 indicate that the average charter enrollment was 359 students. Projected enrollments for 2001–2002 range from 25 to 1,350 students per charter school, but an analysis by J. Wood (1999) indicates that charter schools are generally smaller than district counterparts at the elementary, middle, and high school levels. Despite this trend, about ten of the charter schools in operation in 2001–2002 will have 500 students or more, and many of these are expected to grow to more than 1,000 students.

Progress Relative to the Law's Intents

This section summarizes the progress made relative to the three intents noted earlier: innovation, choice, and accountability.

Innovation

Advocates hoped that charter schools would be laboratories of innovation—that fewer bureaucratic constraints would generate and inspire new and more effective means to educate children. To some extent this has worked—over forty-five charters have been awarded, representing a broad array of options. For example, two teachers in Boston created City on a Hill, a high school that promotes civic engagement through an academically rigorous curriculum. A founding group in Central Massachusetts—a group that included Coalition of Essential Schools (CES) founder Ted Sizer—created the Francis W. Parker School, which not only embodies the CES principles of critical thinking but serves as a resource center for other like-minded educators throughout the state.

Further, the charter school law opened the door to educational management companies (EMCs) like Edison Schools, Advantage, and Sabis International. These for-profit entrepreneurs, hired by charter school governing boards, provide a direct challenge to the traditional government-managed approach to public education. Thus, the charter school law provided an opportunity for the development of new ways to deliver and manage education.

Despite this freedom, Rosenblum Brigham Associates (1998) and J. Wood (1999) found that Massachusetts charter schools offered little in terms of pedagogy that could not be found in other public schools. J. Wood (1999) noted differences in charter versus district schools that she argued could be attributed to most small schools—for example, more personalized services and longer instructional days and years. Most charter schools fall into either a "progressive" (33 percent) or "traditional" (33 percent) approach (with the remaining third labeled as using hybrid approaches or as "alternative" schools serving out-of-school youth) (Massachusetts Department of Education 2001, 68). While the first two categories are broad enough to include everything from a "Core Knowledge" school, like the Benjamin Franklin Charter School, to the Hilltown Cooperative Charter School, based on the Regio Emilia approach, the issue is that these schools offer few totally new designs.[6] Rather, they offer "local innovations"—in other words, approaches not available in the district (Finn, Manno, and Vanourek 2000; Rosenblum Brigham Associates 1998). Moreover, the larger innovation seems to be the notion of truly giving schools the power to spend their resources in a way consistent with a particular mission.

A corollary to innovation is dissemination. Some charter approaches have led to ripple effects in districts. For example, the Lawrence School District instituted a school uniform policy soon after the two Lawrence charter schools did the same, and Boston created in-district charters known as pilot schools out of fear of losing some of its more innovative schools to charter status. However, there have been several limitations to using charters as vehicles for creating and disseminating new ideas.

With a couple of exceptions, charter schools are not having a great effect on the district schools that surround them.[7] Rosenblum Brigham Associates (1998) explains that the lack of sharing is due largely to animus between districts and charter schools over lost revenues. While there are some federal dissemination funds and the state has begun to convene conferences for the purpose of sharing best practices, prior to 1998, there were limited funds for such activities. Moreover, the "multi-layered administrative structure of districts" mitigates district efforts to respond to new ideas (J. Wood 1999, iv).

In addition, heavy administrative responsibilities and state accountability pressures may blunt the innovative potential of charter schools. The premise that charters would be freed from bureaucratic constraints has simply not materialized. Charters do have control of their budgets, particularly those funds dedicated to hiring personnel, but the charter school reporting requirements are generally heavier—rather than lighter—than those of district schools.

Charter school accountability relationships are "multi-dimensional" in nature (Hill et al. 1999; Wohlstetter, Wenning, and Briggs 1995). Rather than being responsible *solely* to the district's central office, as are most traditional public schools, charter schools are designated as "local education agencies" (LEAs) and need to fulfill the same reporting requirements as school districts. These reporting requirements are particularly complex, as they relate to meeting federal special education law.[8] In addition, charter school leaders have direct accountability relationships with a range of actors—their governing boards, parents, the mass media, and politicians.[9]

Some argue that the state's high-stakes testing program also works to thwart innovation. Ted Sizer, one of the founders of the Parker School, says that the Massachusetts Comprehensive Assessment System (MCAS) calls for a curricular approach that runs counter to the school's pedagogical beliefs. That is, the MCAS calls for a wide range of knowledge in several subject areas, while the Parker charter emphasizes depth versus breadth. Sizer notes: "There's a terrible contradiction.... If you want new kinds of schools, you've got to give them room. You can't say, 'Do what you want, but you must follow our frameworks and give our tests'" (Archer 2000, 19).

The relatively short time frame for charter renewal may also discourage innovation. The charter-renewal process occurs in the school's fourth year. This means that the performance of a charter school will be based, at least in part, on just 3.5 years of test data. Therefore, charter schools can ill afford to flounder for a year or two trying unproven approaches.

Choice

According to school choice theory, if charter schools can present more options for parents, district schools will work to provide better services to families in order to compete. However, despite a sizable demand in Massachusetts—MDE projections for 2001–2002 indicate that 11,162 students are on charter school waiting lists and that, on average, five students are applying for every charter school seat —most districts appear to have been able to absorb the losses and continue on unaffected (Rosenblum Brigham Associates 1998).

There are several reasons why the charter school initiative is relatively small in Massachusetts. These constraints deal with legal, human-capital, and financial limitations. First, the charter initiative cannot legally expand beyond the current statutory caps on municipal and state growth. Therefore, even with the passage of the 2000 amendments, the Massachusetts charter school initiative will not reach a tipping point at a state or local level. The caps of 120 schools and of a student enrollment total not to exceed 4 percent of the state's enrollment will not be reached until 2006 (at 14 schools per year). Further, districts will not lose more than 9 percent of their total budgets to charter schools. Therefore, growing at this rate, charters will likely provide little market pressure to change districts.

Second, even if the caps were lifted completely, as former governor William Weld proposed (Zernike 1996), there is a question as to whether there are enough competent founders to create an unlimited number of new schools. When proposing language for the amendments of 2000, the chairman of the SBE, James Peyser, said that the SBE was proposing an increase of ten charters a year for five years because the state received only about that many strong applications per year.

The third constraint on creating an unlimited supply of charter schools pertains to finances. Facilities and special education are the most problematic costs for charter schools. Because charter schools do not have access to capital funds, the cost of finding, renovating, and financing a facility often dominates all other expenditures (see Herdman and Millot 2000; Loveless and Jasin 1998; Manno et al. 1997). For example, paying off the $12 million debt that the Renaissance Charter School in Boston had to invest to get started in 1995 influences to this day the rate at which the school expands its enrollment and how it spends its operational dollars.

Adequately meeting the needs of special education students has also been a challenge for Massachusetts charter schools. Without the economies of scale of a large district, charter schools face the possibility of providing a range of special needs services that exceeds available revenue. Charter schools have generally responded with creative solutions to this challenge—such as providing all students with individual education plans, sharing a single provider across several schools, or applying jointly to access federal funds—but meeting the needs of all students is still a formidable task.[10]

Accountability

In theory, charter schools will produce good results or face the possibility of having their charters revoked. In the 1996 policy report "Massachusetts Charter School Initiative" (Massachusetts Department of Education 1996, 3–4), the state's accountability policy is prefaced as follows: "For the first time in the history of public education, public schools are being allowed to set their own standards, demonstrate performance against those standards, and—most importantly—face the consequences of being shut down if they fail to demonstrate success in helping children learn the core academic subjects." Further, some believe that this high-stakes incentive will push charter schools to outperform their district counterparts.

There are two types of accountability: compliance based and performance based. While my focus is on the latter, the former cannot be ignored. MDE Program Quality Assurance staff review charter schools for compliance with special education laws in the same way that districts are evaluated. A comprehensive study of charter school special education practices is currently being conducted, but to date, the MDE reports that several new charter schools have been slow to establish the procedures necessary to be in full compliance.

Fiscal compliance is also very important. Of the 4 percent of charter schools that have failed nationally, the vast majority of failures have been due to poor financial management (DeSchryver 1999). In addition to requiring them to complete an independent audit annually (a threshold not required of other public schools), the MDE has required all charter schools to conduct their finances using a common chart of accounts. Further, all charter school business managers are now required to participate in financial training provided by the MDE and the inspector general.

In contrast to compliance with regulations, accountability for performance is more difficult to measure and enforce. Consistent with national trends, virtually no Massachusetts charter schools have been shut down solely for performance.[11] All but one of the fifteen original charters granted in 1995 were renewed by the SBE in 2000. The one exception, Youth Build Boston, returned its charter in 1997 after it demonstrated clear academic, financial, and organizational deficiencies. Two other schools had their charters revoked for a combination of insufficient funds, poor academic performance, and/or noncompliance with their charters.[12]

It is not yet clear whether the accountability incentive to perform will in fact push student test scores up. Charter school scores on the MCAS for the first two years have been mixed. Some schools have excelled, while others have done about the same or worse than the district average (Malone 1999).

However, despite these concerns, Massachusetts is monitoring performance in a way that is breaking new ground. The details of the charter school accountability policy can be found in the "Accountability Handbook" on the MDE website (<http://www.doe.mass.edu/cs.www>). The policy builds on two assumptions: first, that the state needs to generate reliable data to ensure public dollars are being well spent; and second, that mission-driven schools will yield better results, so the system needs to respect the unique visions of each founding group. The resulting policy attempts to find a balance between comparable and customized performance data.

Three questions guide all aspects of the state's charter school accountability policy: (1) Is the academic program a success? (2) Is the school a viable organization? and (3) Is the school faithful to the terms of its charter? The state begins with a stringent application review process. Only 43 of 202 applicants (less than one in four) were awarded charters up until 2000. The charter school engages in a self-review process during its first year of operation to develop its own *account-ability plan.* This plan lays out the school's performance goals for the next four years. These goals relate to projected MCAS performance, as well as school-specific goals. Schools have received up to $10,000 from the state's portion of federal charter school start-up funds to complete their plans. Once approved by the state, the accountability plan becomes an amendment to the school's charter.

The state utilizes a mix of paper and on-site reviews to monitor the school's performance. At the end of each academic year, each school submits an *independent fiscal audit* and an *annual report* on its financial status and progress toward its goals. In years two and three, the state conducts one-day *site visits* to verify and augment the annual report data. The teams generally consist of three to five citizens (e.g., representatives from business, teaching, school administration, and the MDE). Using prescribed protocols, the teams review student work and interview teachers, parents, administrators, and students. In the school's fourth year, it presents its case for renewal in a twenty-five-page *renewal application.* The state follows with a three- to four-day *renewal inspection.* The renewal inspection costs $19,000 per visit on average. It is commissioned by the MDE and conducted by SchoolWorks, an outside evaluation team. This mix of data is used to evaluate whether a charter will be renewed.

The Massachusetts charter school accountability policy is fairly straightforward, but when it was codified in 1997, it was the most comprehensive approach to accountability in the country. Today, charter authorizers in jurisdictions such as Chicago, Washington, D.C., Connecticut, and Colorado have built on the Massachusetts model. The policy is promising because it uses a mix of comparable and customized data. Comparable data, in the form of MCAS scores and financial audits, are essential in order to ensure some measure of reliability and validity. Perhaps more importantly, the state has also given credence to a school's unique goals. By collecting customized data, the state demonstrates a respect for each school's goals, helps schools maintain a focus on their missions, and engenders school-level buy-in to the accountability process.

While this government-oversight model may be the most promising element of the charter movement in Massachusetts, it has limitations. State accountability systems are characterized by challenges in three areas: technical complexity, insufficient capacity, and political instability (Elmore, Abelmann, and Furhman 1996). These challenges seem to apply to the Massachusetts charter school initiative.

TECHNICAL COMPLEXITY

The current accountability policy is strong in that it creates relatively clear expectations up front and gathers data relative to those expectations using multiple formats. However, the policy does not definitively answer some critical questions. For example, how good is good enough? That is, what does "significantly improved" actually mean? If a school states in its accountability plan that 60 percent of its students will perform at the proficient level in math and only 54 percent do, should that school's charter be revoked? A second unanswered question is: To what should a charter school be compared? Some would argue that comparing the performance of a charter school to a district school is statistically invalid, given the different size and composition of the samples. However, others would argue that unless the charter school can outperform the average district school, why bother? A third question is: What is a reasonable time frame in which to judge a school's success? Some may argue that measuring a school's success in three-and-a-half years simply does not allow enough time to make a high-stakes decision.

INSUFFICIENT CAPACITY

At the charter school level, it is unclear whether these schools have the training to use the data they receive to improve performance. At the state level, it is unclear how much data can or should be collected. Schools are complex institutions, so it makes sense to gather as much information as possible. The site visits and inspections are helpful instruments for providing a full profile of the school, catching problems early, and leveraging needed changes at each school. However, the state's resources are limited. So the issue becomes how to allocate those resources most effectively. Outsourcing the inspection process to consultants addresses the limitations posed by having a small staff in the charter schools office and also provides staff with some professional distance from the process. However, the overall cost of the renewal inspection process will likely become prohibitively expensive as the initiative grows. Further, monitoring schools in this way is a new venture for the MDE, so it will take some time before staff can recognize problems and even more time before it can discern ways to help.

POLITICAL INSTABILITY

Despite the empirical merit of the data, politics will inevitably play some role in decisions to renew or revoke charters. To mitigate political influence, the accountability process should be as clear, or "transparent," as possible (Finn, Manno,

and Vanourek 2000). Unlike Chicago's preestablished rubric of expected performance, the Massachusetts accountability policy is intentionally somewhat subjective. Scott Hamilton, the former associate commissioner of education, addressed
this concern by arguing that the decision to renew or revoke a charter should be
seen in the same light as the legal standard of "beyond a reasonable doubt."[13]
Thus, the question of how good is good enough will be answered by a series of
precedents. This approach works well when decision makers have a common
understanding of the intent of the accountability policy, but it may leave schools
vulnerable to new interpretations of policy when the decision makers change.

The Massachusetts charter school accountability policy is worth emulating,
but it is still a work in progress. It strikes a balance between comparable and customized performance data, collects a rich body of data, and continues to improve. Despite these strengths, the technical flaws of the accountability policy are
significant and, if not addressed, could erode the credibility of the process. The
renewal process is the lynchpin. When a charter school comes before the SBE at
the end of its five-year charter, there must be a real chance that it might lose its
charter; otherwise, all the steps leading to renewal—the accountability plan, annual reports, and site visits—will simply become empty rituals.

Privatization versus Reregulation

The Massachusetts charter school initiative is at a crossroads. While amendments to raise the cap on charter schools passed in 2000 (C.227, MGL), pressure
is mounting to marginalize the charter movement. The growing resistance may
be fueled by fears of privatizing public education. Like much of the nation, Massachusetts is debating the merits of vouchers and for-profit EMCs. Unfortunately
for Massachusetts charter supporters, this link between charters and vouchers
may be serving to sway public opinion against charters. As Hassel (2000, 4) notes:
"If policymakers or the public are unclear about the distinction between charter
school and voucher programs, charter schools must carry the baggage of anti-
voucher sentiment as they vie for support from politicians." Massachusetts is a
strong labor state; thus, in this political context, rather than charter schools being
the "camel's nose under the tent" of vouchers (Hassel 2000, 5), discussions of
vouchers may be hurting support for charters.

Concerns about privatization first surfaced in earnest during the 1997–1998
charter application cycle. A furor erupted about the number of applicants that

had decided to contract with EMCs (Stein 1998). To that point, five (20 percent) of the twenty-four operational charter schools were managed by EMCs. However, in 1998 four of the thirteen new Commonwealth and Horace Mann charters were awarded to schools working with EMCs. This represented about 30 percent of the total number of new charters and half of the new Commonwealth charters. As of 2001, almost 20 percent of operational charter schools (eight of forty-two) were managed by EMCs.

The Reregulators

Opposition to privatization is well entrenched. Scott Harshbarger, the former attorney general and the Democratic gubernatorial nominee in 1998, has said simply, "I do not accept the notion that injecting the for-profit element will improve the system" (Stein 1998). Organized labor is the most ardent opponent of charter schools because they are not required to hire certified teachers. In describing the motivations of unions, Steven Wilson, former CEO of Advantage Schools, has simply said, "This is not about ideology. It is about a loss of power and money" (Stein 1998).[14]

The tactics of charter opponents have been to lobby against increasing the cap or to hobble the initiative via added regulation or taking time to complete more studies. The amendments cited earlier are representative of some of the efforts to reregulate the charter initiative; however, there are many other such efforts. Harshbarger called for background checks and greater scrutiny of EMCs. His stated concern was that there was insufficient oversight of the $32 million in public dollars going to these companies (J. Hart 1998). Senator Marc R. Pacheco and other lawmakers attempted to block EMCs outright by filing legislation to prohibit EMCs from running the state-funded schools. Pacheco explained: "The law clearly says no for-profits can apply for a charter. . . . It does not address the fact that not-for-profits created by a for-profit can in effect be a front for a for-profit. That is what we believe is what's happening with for-profits running schools" (Hayes 1998).

A more subtle reregulation tactic is to ostensibly agree with the charter concept but request more information. For example, Kathy Kelly, president of the Massachusetts Federation of Teachers, has said that her group will ask that the cap on charter schools be kept in place until there is an "an impartial and complete evaluation of what current charters are doing and what they contribute to public education" (Daley, Vigue, and Zernicke 1999).

What About Improved Performance?

Those closest to the situation, MDE staff and charter school founders, have attempted to bring the debate back to student outcomes. When asked about EMCs, Scott Hamilton replied: "I don't care whether they are profitable. The management company has to please the board of trustees, and the board of trustees has to please us. . . . We are not asking these same questions about millions of dollars in state funds, for example, that go to textbook companies each year" (J. Hart 1998).

Julie Macuch, a parent founder of the Rising Tide Charter School, echoed a similar concern. She said that her school is using the Beacon EMC only for the school's back office responsibilities. As a result, Beacon will only receive 7 percent of the school's operating budget. Not only is this less expensive than most district administrative services, it is an essential service that this founding group of parents simply could not provide. "We went to them because they were able to take our vision and put it on paper. We are all parents," Macuch said. "We don't know how to run a school. Beacon will make sure . . . we do it correctly" (Hayes 1998).

Concerns About Privatization

There were three major concerns about EMCs in Massachusetts: that EMCs had an unfair advantage in the review process, that they were unwilling to share their innovations, and that they might compromise quality for profit.

First, some were concerned that the charter approval process was biased toward the more-polished EMC applications. At issue was whether this bias conflicted with the law's intent to create "innovative" schools; in other words, how could a "chain" be innovative? Massachusetts appears to be following the national trend of authorizers choosing a higher percentage of applicants with EMC partners because they represent a lower-risk investment (see Hill et al. 1999).

A second concern about EMCs focused on a dispute over intellectual property rights. SABIS International, Inc., an EMC contracting with two Massachusetts charter schools, was unwilling to share its curriculum with other public schools at no cost. Some were concerned that SABIS was not only restricting access to products created with public dollars but also inhibiting or blocking the dissemination of new ideas, rather than encouraging it. A 1997 amendment to the charter school law directly addresses this issue: "Charter schools shall not charge any public school for the use or replication of any part of their curriculum subject to the prescriptions of any contract between the charter schools and any third party providers" (C.71, s.89, ss.k., MGL).

Third, and perhaps most important, there is concern that EMCs will compromise service for profits. Opponents of EMCs argue that resources, excellence, and equity are linked and that the latter two will suffer in an effort to increase the former. A study did find that charters serve fewer special education students than district schools, particularly those with more severe special needs (J. Wood 1999). However, EMC supporters argue that the market will serve as a buffer against abuses. Niel Yanofsky, vice president of Fidelity Investments and an investor in Boston-based Advantage Schools, argues that, by law, students are selected by lottery and that therefore, charter schools need to accept any child that comes to their doors, including special needs students. He says, "If the school doesn't do a good job, the students won't come back. . . . One of the nice things about being for-profit is that you have to work to satisfy your customers" (Stein 1998).

Unfortunately for supporters of increased privatization in Massachusetts, the odds are stacked in favor of the reregulators. Even with the increase in the charter school cap, the initiative is not likely to reach the critical mass necessary to force the existing system to change dramatically. In the seven years since the enactment of the charter school law, interest groups (particularly those close to the Democratic base—teachers unions and civil liberties groups) have pushed the Democratic majority in the legislature to slowly constrict the original freedoms provided in the charter school law. The significance of this trend, what McDonnell and Elmore (1987) might call "regulatory recapture," is that it reduces the ability of charter schools to serve as true engines of change. Rapid growth and increased market pressure may not be the most lasting charter school effects. Rather, the basic bargain of autonomy for accountability may be the most important lesson charter schools bring to mainstream education.

Conclusions on the Massachusetts Case

Charter schools in Massachusetts began as "palm trees in Bangor." This was indeed a strange place for these seeds of change to have landed. Today, the growth of the movement is slow and steady, in large part because it directly challenged the educational establishment. Over the last seven years, the charter initiative has been incrementally hobbled with increased regulation, studies, and caps.

However, even if the charter school movement does not grow to its potential, it will still leave an important legacy. First, the schools created will continue to provide much-needed services across the state. Second, the enthusiastic and entrepreneurial educators drawn to this movement are reminders that the culture of public education can be changed.

Beyond the charter schools themselves, there are lessons to be learned about the governance of public education. Unlike the site-based management policy that came before it, the charter school initiative gave real power to local citizens to decide how to spend their educational dollars. Not only has this experiment provided insights into the challenges and benefits of creating autonomous, mission-driven schools, it has created a crack in the sheltered monopoly of public education. For good or ill, by giving charter school boards the power to choose their vendors, the door is now open to large-scale privatization of public education.

This Massachusetts charter experiment has also raised important questions about the appropriate balance between local and central control. While the charter school accountability system is still a work in progress, it has had a significant impact on the discourse in education circles and among policy makers. For instance, it has raised issues pertaining to the complexity of evaluating school performance and the need for subjectivity and multiple measures.[15] Second, it has brought performance, rather than compliance, to the fore in evaluating school success, and it has raised the importance of associating real consequences with failure to perform. The accountability system has also raised questions about the capacity needed at both the school and state levels in order for a decentralized system to work well. And finally, it has given voice to the tremendous demand for more options among the consumers of public education.

If the trend in public education continues toward giving individual schools more autonomy in exchange for more accountability and if one believes that mission-driven schools will outperform those responding to central office mandates, then the Massachusetts charter school initiative may be an important experiment in the quest to find the appropriate balance between central and local control.

8 • Wisconsin

Chartering Authority as Educational Reform

Julie F. Mead

WISCONSIN, WITH ITS HISTORY of progressivism, has become known as a pioneer state for various kinds of school choice.[1] Although not the first state to introduce charter school legislation, Wisconsin has joined the charter school movement in unique ways. Most notably, Wisconsin was the first state to grant chartering authority to a municipality and the first to use chartering authority to target a specific urban region of educational concern. The following discussion explores various facets of Wisconsin's chartering environment and the political, legal, and policy questions raised by the Wisconsin case.

Wisconsin's Charter School Statute

Wisconsin became a charter school state in 1993 with the passage of Act 16.[2] Initially this statute granted chartering authority only to school districts. The statute also limited the total number of charter schools to twenty statewide and restricted each school district to chartering no more than two schools. The state superintendent of schools had to approve each charter prior to implementation and could also withdraw approval for any charter school that failed to show significant student progress.

These restrictions were removed when the statute was revised in 1995 by the biennial budget bill (1995 Act 27). Changes also allowed school districts to collaborate to create a "shared" charter school. Another new provision permitted charter school teachers to form a separate collective bargaining unit if a majority of those teachers so voted. The revised statute also contained some significant provisions directed solely at the Milwaukee Public School District (MPS). These provisions included the creation of an appeals process that allows petitioners denied charters by MPS to appeal to the Wisconsin Department of Public Instruction (DPI). New provisions also required that MPS charter schools could not be considered "instrumentalities" of the district but must instead be independent from the district. Therefore, charter school personnel could not be considered MPS employees. Finally, several sections attempted to limit the ability of the Milwaukee Teachers Education Association (MTEA) to include issues regarding charter school employees as subjects for collective bargaining. Not surprisingly, these last provisions immediately generated litigation, as is discussed later in the chapter.

Additional amendments were adopted in 1997 (1997 Act 27 and 1997 Act 238). It is these additions that set Wisconsin's charter statute apart from other states' versions. Frustrated with the fact that MPS had chartered only one school and was prohibited from chartering more schools by an injunction and given the continuing problems plaguing the state's largest school district, Republican governor Tommy Thompson introduced legislation to grant chartering authority to the city of Milwaukee, the University of Wisconsin-Milwaukee (UWM), and the Milwaukee Area Technical College (MATC).[3] With the adoption of these provisions, Wisconsin became the first state to grant chartering authority to a municipality.[4] It also marked the first time that chartering authority had been used to target a specific locale. In contrast to states such as Michigan and North Carolina that grant chartering authority to universities more broadly, only UWM may charter schools in Wisconsin. Likewise, no municipality other than Milwaukee or technical college other than MATC was given chartering authority.

Significantly, the chartering authority granted to the three entities is restricted to the boundaries of the city of Milwaukee. Any charter school authorized by the city of Milwaukee, UWM, or MATC must be physically located within the city and may serve only Milwaukee pupils who met one of the following criteria in their previous school year: (1) the pupil was enrolled in the school district operating under Chapter 119 (MPS); (2) the pupil was attending a private school under s.119.23 (the Milwaukee Parental Choice Program [MPCP]); (3) the pupil was enrolled in grades K–3 in a private school located in the city of Milwaukee other than under s.119.23 (the MPCP); (4) the pupil was not enrolled in school; or (5) the pupil was enrolled in a charter school under this subsection (WI Stat. §118.40(2r)(c)).[5]

Other 1997 changes included a requirement that chartering authorities consider the fiscal impact on the district of a proposed charter school prior to granting the charter. Districts also gained authority to contract with a cooperative educational service agency (CESA) for the management and operation of a charter school.[6] Wisconsin also became one of only eleven states that permit private nonsectarian schools to convert to charter schools. Finally, school districts, including MPS, were given latitude to determine whether a charter school would be an instrumentality or a noninstrumentality of the district.

The most recent revisions to the statute occurred in 1999 (1999 Act 9) and 2001 (2001 Act 16). The 1999 revision changed the funding portion of the statute as applied to the charter schools authorized by the three special chartering authorities in Milwaukee by distributing a portion of the costs for these schools to all districts in Wisconsin. The previous funding provision deducted the costs of the program from the state aid targeted for MPS. In 2001 the legislature added the University of Wisconsin-Parkside (UWP) as a sponsoring authority on a pilot basis. UWP may charter only one school, which may not be a high school, may not enroll more than 400 pupils, and must be located in the Racine Unified School District.

As a result of the statutory evolution described above, the Wisconsin charter school law creates two sets of rules for chartering authorities. One set applies to all of the state's school districts, including MPS, and the other applies to the three special Milwaukee chartering authorities (the city, UWM, and MATC).

School Districts as Chartering Authorities

For school districts, a charter school may be created in one of two ways. Either the school district may begin the process of creating a charter school, or it may review a "petition" (application) for a charter. In the first instance, the district may create a charter school as long as it examines the fiscal impact on the district, ensures that it meets statutory requirements, and considers the alternatives available to families who do not want to send their children to the charter school. Districts may create charter schools independently or in cooperation with other districts. A district may even convert one or all of its existing public schools into charter schools. Similar to the charter school statutes in some other states, the Wisconsin statute requires that preference be given to charter schools focused on the educational needs of children at risk for school failure.

In the second instance, individuals or groups, either internal or external to the district, may petition a school district for charter approval. Districts may also approve the conversion of nonsectarian private schools into charter schools. Districts have authority to entertain petitions only for charter schools proposed within their geographic boundaries. The charter school statute specifies fifteen provisions that must be present in all charter school applications (e.g., descriptions of the educational program, governance structure, and facility).

Petitions must have the approval of 10 percent of the district's teaching force or 50 percent of the teachers employed by a single district school. This showing of support is required whether the petition seeks to convert an existing district or private school to a charter school or to create a start-up charter school. The district must hold a public hearing on the petition within thirty days of receipt. A petition to convert all of a district's schools to charter schools is also allowed. Districts may approve such petitions if they are signed by 50 percent of the district's teachers and if alternatives are available for students who do not wish to attend charter schools or who are not admitted to them. The statute does not indicate exactly how a district is to make public school options available to such students.

Petitions to MPS must be considered in a public hearing within thirty days of receipt. If the MPS board denies the petition, the petitioner may appeal to the DPI.[7] The DPI has thirty days to consider the appeal and issue a final decision. If a rejection is overturned, presumably the DPI would order MPS to issue the charter, as the DPI has no independent authority to issue charters under the statute. However, the statute does not detail further particulars of the appeals process. No judicial appeal of the DPI's decision is allowed. In contrast, the chartering decisions of all other school districts are final and not subject to appeal to the DPI.

All districts must determine whether a given charter school will be an instrumentality of the school district or independent. Districts employ only the personnel of charter schools that are instrumentalities. As such, any collective bargaining agreements in force would apply to instrumentality charter schools as they do to other district schools. Noninstrumentality charter schools are independent from the district for personnel purposes, and employees would not be included in the collective bargaining unit that serves school district personnel. The statute does require that any *private* schools converted to charter schools by MPS be noninstrumentalities of the district.

Although charter schools are relieved from compliance with most Wisconsin public school statutes, they do face some restrictions.[8] For example, charter schools must meet the "educational goals and expectations" set by the legislature for all public schools.[9] Second, they must administer the same state tests required of all public schools. Third, charter schools must ensure that all instructional staff, including all teachers, librarians, psychologists, social workers, guidance counselors, and administrators, hold proper state certification. Fourth, charter schools may not charge tuition. They may, however, employ selective student admissions policies as long as they do not discriminate on the basis of sex; race; religion; national origin; ancestry; pregnancy; marital or parental status; sexual orientation; or physical, mental, emotional, or learning disability. Fifth, charter schools must be nonsectarian in all practices. Finally, no student may be required to attend a charter school.

Once a charter petition is approved, the charter school and school district must enter into a charter contract. Charters may be granted for up to five years and must address each of the fifteen provisions required in a charter school petition. The statute does not specify or guarantee any particular level of funding. Thus, school districts and charter schools negotiate funding as part of the charter contract. Charter school students are counted in the district's child-count figures, and both general and categorical state aid is provided to the district for those students. The district then provides funding to its charter school according to the terms of the charter school contract.

Charter revocation may occur for one of four reasons: the charter school violated its contract with the chartering authority, the pupils failed to make sufficient progress toward the goals specified by state statutes, the school failed to adhere to "generally accepted accounting standards of fiscal management," or the school violated a provision of the charter school statute (WI Stat. §118.40(5)).

Responsibility for charter school oversight falls predominantly on the charter issuer. Each school district must notify the DPI that it intends to establish a charter school by 1 February of the school year before the school is to begin operation. Other than the appellate powers granted with respect to MPS petitions, the DPI has no authority to approve, revoke, or deny any charter petition. The DPI does keep records as to the number and type of charters established in the state for reporting purposes.

The Other Four Chartering Authorities

Groups seeking charters from the city of Milwaukee, UWM, UWP, or MATC apply directly to these authorities. The city of Milwaukee, UWM, and MATC may authorize charter schools only in Milwaukee and only serving Milwaukee students. In addition, schools chartered by one of these entities must, by law, be noninstrumentalities of MPS. There is one exception to this rule: "If the city of Milwaukee contracts with an individual or group operating for profit to operate a school as a charter school, the charter school is an instrumentality of . . . [MPS] and the board of . . . [MPS] shall employ all personnel for the charter school" (WI Stat. §118.40(7)(am)(3)). The same restriction does not apply to UWM or MATC, however. Finally, while UWM's chartering authority is vested in the university chancellor, no charter may be finalized without approval from the University of Wisconsin board of regents. Similarly, UWP may only charter a school geographically linked to the university's borders. That school is also, by definition, a noninstrumentality of the Racine Unified School District, and charter school personnel may be employees of UWP.

In contrast to the negotiation process that determines funding for charter schools authorized by school districts, funding for charter schools established by the city, UWM, UWP, or MATC is "equal to the sum of the amount paid per pupil under this paragraph in the previous school year and the amount of revenue increase per pupil allowed [under state funding statutes] in the current school year, multiplied by the number of pupils attending the charter school."[10] Essentially, the funding statutes create a formula that computes a per-pupil cost for the special Milwaukee charters and then distributes the total cost of these students among all 426 school districts in the state. As the Wisconsin Legislative Fiscal Bureau (2000–2001) explained for the 2000–2001 school year, "Each district's general school aids, including MPS's, will be reduced proportionately by a total statewide amount of $10.0 million or 0.3% each." Payments are made by the DPI directly to the charter school on a quarterly basis. There is no provision in the law for "start-up" funds, although groups seeking these special charters may request development grants from the state to assist with planning and start-up costs, as can groups affiliated with school districts.[11] While there is no statutory provision for administrative fees for the chartering authority, the city, UWM, UWP, and MATC are free to negotiate such fees as part of the charter.[12]

Other than the preceding provisions, charter schools authorized by the city, UWM, UWP, and MATC must meet the same requirements, are subject to the same restrictions, and face revocation for the same reasons as all other charter schools.

Policy Implementation

Although Wisconsin has had charter school legislation since 1993 and no charter cap since 1995, only 63 charters were approved and only 39 charter schools were operational as of the third Friday in September 1999. However, by the same point

Table 8.1

Wisconsin Charter School Statistics, 2000–2001

Total Number of Charter Schools Approved	92
Total Number Reporting as Charter Schools by the Third Friday in September 2000[a]	87
Number of Chartering Authorities	61
Most Schools Chartered by One Authority	7
Number of Total Approved Schools Serving District Cooperatives	15
Number of Schools Approved Serving At-Risk Students	51
Total Number of Students Served	10,523
Smallest Number of Students Served	8
Largest Number of Students Served	1,100
Number of Schools with 50 or Fewer Students	45
Average Number of Pupils per School	121
Number of Schools within Schools	38
Number of Noninstrumentality Charter Schools[b]	18
Number of Schools Operated by For-Profit Educational Management Companies[c]	1
Total Number Approved by UWM	1
Total Number Approved by City of Milwaukee	4
Total Number Approved by MATC	0
Total Number Approved by MPS	7
Total Number Approved by All Other Districts	80
Total Number of Charter Schools Closed in Wisconsin	3

Source: Wisconsin Department of Public Instruction

[a] Based on a pupil count taken the third Friday in September. The DPI has data for 83 schools operating as charter schools on that date. Schools that began operations later or that have not yet opened are not reflected in these numbers.

[b] Employees of noninstrumentality charter schools are not employed by any school district. These schools also serve as their own LEAs for the purposes of special education. They are not considered "part" of any school district, even though they may have received their charters from school districts.

[c] The charter for this school was granted to a nonprofit organization that subsequently contracted with the Edison corporation to operate the school. No charters have been granted directly to any for-profit educational management company.

in September 2000, the state counted 92 charters, with 87 schools operational (see table 8.1). Thus, charter schools constitute approximately 4 percent of the 2,134 public schools reporting data for the same period. The 92 approved schools were established by sixty-one different chartering authorities. The statutory preference for creating schools that serve children at risk for school failure appears to have been honored, as 51 of the 92 approved charter schools (55.4 percent) are designed for that purpose. In total, the 87 operational charter schools reporting in 2000–2001 educate 10,523 pupils, or just over 1 percent of the total number of public school students in Wisconsin.[13] In general, the schools are very small, with an average student body of only 121 students and with 45 schools (51.7 percent of operational schools) serving 50 or fewer students. The schools range in size from 8 to 1,100 students.

As of 2000–2001, fourteen school districts had established multiple charter schools. Not surprisingly, these districts tend to be some of the largest in the state. After its slow start, MPS now leads the way with seven approved charter schools. The next most active districts are Appleton and LaCrosse, with five schools each. As of 2000–2001, no district has exercised its authority to convert all of its schools to charter schools. In addition, the DPI had received no appeals of charter school petitions denied by MPS.

Of the three special chartering authorities in Milwaukee, only the city had charter schools operating in 1999–2000. Of its four schools, two were preexisting private schools that converted to public charter school status. Two other private schools had petitioned to convert to charter school status and were offered charters contingent on the successful negotiation of a charter contract. However, both schools later elected to remain enrolled as private participating schools in the MPCP, the state's private school voucher program. One of these schools, Bruce Guadalupe School, later petitioned for and received an MPS charter. It began operation as an MPS charter school in 2000–2001.

UWM has granted three charters and has finalized contracts with all three schools, the Milwaukee Academy of Science, the Milwaukee Urban League Academy of Business and Economics, and the School for Early Development and Achievement. The Milwaukee Academy of Science opened in the 2000–2001 school year. The other two schools planned to open in fall 2001. The Milwaukee Academy of Science is sponsored by the Milwaukee Science Education Consortium, a nonstock corporation that has connections to the Medical College of Wisconsin, Marquette University, and Alverno College. Both the Science Education Consortium and the Urban League will contract with Edison Schools, Inc. MATC and UWP have not yet exercised their chartering authority.

Similar to the trend nationwide, the number of charter schools in Wisconsin has increased steadily each year. In 1997–1998, there were only eighteen charter schools in the state. That number increased to twenty-four in 1998–1999. The 1999–2000 total of sixty-three approved charter schools, while modest in comparison to some other states, is nearly a threefold increase over the previous year's numbers. The increase one year later, from sixty-three to ninety-two, is equally dramatic. It is likely that the number of charter schools in the state will continue to rise. MPS, for example, received nine proposals for charter schools at the close of 1999 and continues to entertain charter proposals.[14]

In terms of curricula, Wisconsin's charter schools "have, in general, not provided the innovation that the Legislature may have intended," according to an official program audit (Wisconsin Legislative Audit Bureau 1998, 19). The report on the eighteen charter schools operating in 1997–1998 found that most charter schools resembled their parent districts in both programming and administration. The audit also found that traditional public schools that had converted to charter status had not altered their programming in significant ways. Perusal of the names of the ninety-two approved charter schools in 2000–2001 suggests that some additional innovation may have occurred since 1998. Four schools have titles that indicate a technology focus, two employ a Montessori approach, two focus on science and medicine, two others have a business and careers theme, one school has adopted the International Baccalaureate approach, another has a fine arts focus, and one school focuses on leadership.[15] Finally, other than schools designed to serve at-risk populations, there is no report of charter schools using selective admissions criteria.

Charter School Accountability

By law, the DPI has some, but very limited, oversight responsibilities related to charter schools. Basically, the agency's role is one of counting. It has no independent authority to charter and no authority to review the chartering decisions made by other entities, except in the case of MPS, where it can hear appeals of charters denied by MPS. It also has the authority to investigate complaints about charter schools, just as it does for other public schools. Since much of its monitoring authority over traditional public schools (e.g., requiring various reports and compliance documentation) is contained in the statutes from which charter schools are relieved, the DPI's direct monitoring authority is limited.

The University of Wisconsin board of regents has some oversight authority, but again, it is extremely limited. The charter school statute specifically grants chartering authority to the chancellors of UWM and UWP, not to each university itself. The only check on that authority is that the statute requires the regents' approval for any UWM or UWP charter contract. It is this approval process that allows the board to accept or reject the provisions of such a contract. Nonetheless, the board's authority ends there. It has no statutory authority to direct either university to charter any school or to revoke any charter. Of course, it could exercise de facto revocation by refusing to approve any subsequent contracts after the term of an existing contract expires.

Therefore, the real oversight of a charter school comes from the chartering authority. The law does not direct school districts or other authorities as to how to accomplish this task. Thus, the charter contract becomes very important in structuring the oversight role of the authorizer and in establishing conditions under which a charter may be revoked.

A comparison of a contract establishing a city of Milwaukee charter school with one establishing a UWM charter school provides an instructive example of the different approaches chartering authorities can take. The city contract with the Downtown Montessori Academy, one of the first city charter schools, contains two provisions relating to school oversight. The first ensures the city full access to the school's "books and records" and requires that annual financial audits be submitted to the city and that the school submit to an independent financial audit every odd-numbered year. This provision also requires the school to "retain an independent certified public accountant which accountant shall attest to the accuracy, validity and reasonableness of academic achievement and programmatic results reported by the Charter School." Another provision gives the city of Milwaukee the right to inspect the charter school facility, review records, and request reports about school operations.

The contract between UWM and the Milwaukee Urban League Academy of Business and Economics contains similar provisions. Annual budgets and audit reports must be submitted to the university, and the school must be open to inspection. In addition, the contract states that "the University shall evaluate and the Charter School agrees to be evaluated in, the areas of Academic Achievement, Educational Practice, Organizational Structure, and Parent Satisfaction." In another section of the contract, the school agrees to be open to university research, including, but not limited to, surveys, interviews, pupil testing beyond that which is statutorily required, and on-site research observers. Another section describes a code of ethics that members of the charter school board of directors must adhere to, including such items as not accepting or soliciting "anything of value" related to charter school business and not disclosing confidential information regarding the school.

It is also noteworthy that the university charter school contract incorporates as binding two state statutes that are among those that charter schools are exempt from following. Both relate to student rights and discipline or school safety. The first prohibits corporal punishment (WI Stat. §118.31), and the second forbids a strip search of a pupil (WI Stat. §118.32).[16]

Whatever one believes about the wisdom of such engagement, clearly the university has taken a direct and involved role in the oversight, if not the operation, of the schools it charters.

Findings from an Official Audit of the Charter School Program

Charter school oversight is also featured in the statutorily mandated financial and programmatic audit conducted by the Wisconsin Legislative Audit Bureau (LAB). The 1998 report pertains to the eighteen charter schools operating in 1997–1998.

Staff at sixteen of the schools reportedly did not know what criteria would be used to consider charter renewal or revocation. Moreover, several charters failed to address all fifteen statutorily required provisions. The report states: "Although the lack of formal oversight has not been a problem while charter schools have been closely affiliated with their districts, this may not be the case in the future" (Wisconsin Legislative Audit Bureau 1998, 6).

LAB also identifies several advantages of charter schools, such as the fact that charter school teachers can obtain flexible permits allowing them to teach more than one subject and the fact that charter schools offer the opportunity to experiment with different educational approaches (Wisconsin Legislative Audit Bureau 1998). Nonetheless, the report concludes that most of the charter schools mirrored their parent districts in programming and administration.

The audit discovered that most district-chartered schools generally received funding on par with traditional district schools. Charters aimed at the general student population spent slightly less per pupil than the average for other public schools ($4,458 for charter schools versus $4,918 per pupil for all schools in the districts in which the charter schools were located), while charters for at-risk students expended slightly more per pupil ($5,966 for at-risk charter schools compared to an overall average of $4,912 for all schools in those districts in which the charter schools were located). The difference for general education charter schools can be explained by the fact that "some administrative and overhead costs are not charged to the charter school but are spent by the districts on behalf of these schools" (Wisconsin Legislative Audit Bureau 1998, 31). The disparity in funding between at-risk charter schools and other district schools "is not surprising, given the additional costs of educating students at risk of failing or dropping out"

(Wisconsin Legislative Audit Bureau 1998, 31). Fourteen of the eighteen charter contracts failed to specify how the schools would be funded as required by statute. It is interesting to note that the one charter school to fail during this period, Kickapoo River Institute in the North Crawford School District, closed due to fiscal concerns.[17]

LAB also raised concerns about the funding of charter schools in Milwaukee: "Charter schools established by the city of Milwaukee, UW-Milwaukee, and Milwaukee Area Technical College may potentially have significant effects on MPS because the district loses general equalization aid for every student enrolled in these charter schools. . . . These schools may eventually compete with MPS for significant numbers of students" (Wisconsin Legislative Audit Bureau 1998, 7). Recall that students attending these Milwaukee charter schools may have never actually been enrolled in MPS. City students who were too young to attend school previously, who have attended private schools in Milwaukee under the MPCP program, or who are in grades K–3 at a non-MPCP private school are all eligible for charter school admission. These concerns motivated the changes enacted for the funding of the special Milwaukee charter schools in late 1999. No longer is MPS "penalized" for students' attendance at the city and UWM charter schools. Rather, all districts in the state, including MPS, share equally in the funding for these charter schools.

Auditors also found that seven of ten general education charter schools failed to use random selection processes for admissions and instead filled seats on a first-come, first-served basis. Such practices violate federal requirements that dictate that available seats be filled randomly from the applicant pool.[18] Moreover, LAB suggests that this problem contributed to the fact that charter schools did not adequately address the law's requirement that a charter school specify how it will achieve a racial and ethnic balance among its students that reflects the school district population (Wisconsin Legislative Audit Bureau 1998). Charter contracts in fourteen of the schools omitted this requirement. Charter schools created for at-risk pupils had minority student populations higher than the district at large, while general program charters had minority student populations smaller than other district schools (Wisconsin Legislative Audit Bureau 1998).

LAB found that general education charter student achievement results were slightly higher than the average achieved by their counterparts in their respective districts (Wisconsin Legislative Audit Bureau 1998).[19] However, the report noted that this conclusion was based on a limited sample of achievement scores. Many districts did not disaggregate charter school students' scores from other students' scores. In other cases, the number of students was too small to "permit their scores to be reported." Attendance rates at the eighteen charter schools compared similarly to district schools, with the exception of charter schools for at-risk students, which reported slightly poorer attendance.[20] Charter schools that maintained records on suspension rates likewise reported using suspensions in a manner similar to traditional public schools.

Finally, the report suggests additional ways to expand the charter school program should the legislature wish to do so. While cautioning lawmakers that they might not want to adopt further amendments until after they have information on the consequences of recent statutory changes, LAB suggests that chartering authority be granted to all thirteen University of Wisconsin campuses, all sixteen technical colleges, and the DPI (Wisconsin Legislative Audit Bureau 1998).

Charter School Controversies

Wisconsin's charter school law has spawned a number of controversies, including formal litigation. Each case provides an opportunity for policy makers to explore the intended and unintended consequences of the charter school movement.

Legal Challenges from the Teachers Union and Parents

The charter school program has been challenged in court three times, each time in Milwaukee. The MTEA filed the first two challenges in 1996 and 1998. Both involved essentially the same issue: that the charter school law had been enacted without proper process in violation of the Wisconsin Constitution because the provisions were included in budget bills instead of as single-subject bills. The MTEA's complaint stemmed from the fact that the law forbids charter school employees from being employees of the district in some instances.[21] In addition, at the time of the first suit, in 1996, the law included a provision, since removed, that prohibited collective bargaining on the subject of converting public schools to charter schools or on the impact of such action on the wages, hours, or conditions of employment of existing staff.

The trial court in this case, *Milwaukee Teachers Education Association v. Milwaukee Board of Directors,* determined that the union had sufficient likelihood of succeeding in its challenge and ordered an injunction prohibiting MPS from chartering more schools.[22] At the time, MPS had one charter school, Highland

Community School, which had been converted from a private school. Highland teachers were not employed by the district and were therefore not members of the MTEA nor bound by the contract between the MTEA and MPS. The Wisconsin Court of Appeals also heard the case, but declined to issue a ruling. Instead it certified the case for appeal to the Wisconsin Supreme Court after concluding that the issues involved exceeded the "error-correcting" charge of the appellate court.

The second such lawsuit was filed in July 1998 after the city of Milwaukee made its intention of chartering four schools known. Again the union challenged the constitutionality of the legislation's enactment as part of a multisubject bill, although the complaint did not challenge the substance of the act itself. The MTEA withdrew its complaint in the second case, after the largest school offered a charter by the city of Milwaukee, Bruce Guadalupe School, declined the charter.[23] The first suit was settled between MPS and the MTEA in 1999. The union dropped its appeal in exchange for a memorandum of understanding regarding the reconstitution of failing MPS schools and the reassignment of teachers in such instances. This settlement allowed the court's earlier injunction to be lifted, thereby permitting MPS to again entertain charter school proposals. Immediately following the settlement, MPS converted two of its existing schools to charter schools for 1999–2000 and considered additional charter applications.

The third lawsuit filed in connection with the charter school law was *Omegbu v. Norquist*.[24] It was filed in May 1998 against the city of Milwaukee and the state by a group of parents with children in MPS schools. It alleged that the program was improperly enacted by the legislature, that the city has no authority to approve charter schools, and that the statute creates a "dual system" of education that violates both the Wisconsin and the United States Constitutions. A federal district court judge dismissed the case on 30 March 2000 for failure to state a federal claim. The U.S. Court of Appeals affirmed that decision on 12 October 2001 (Docket No. 00-2111).

Are Wisconsin Charter Schools Public Schools?

Other controversies that have surfaced about the charter school program have not elicited formal legal complaints thus far. The first involved what some might consider a statutory omission. In the course of considering its new chartering authority, the city of Milwaukee raised the question of whether or not Wisconsin's charter schools are public schools. Unlike most state laws that create charter schools, Wisconsin's statute never explicitly defines charter schools as public schools.

The issue first came up at a planning meeting between representatives of the city, UWM, MATC, and the DPI to consider the new statute. Following that meeting, the DPI's chief legal counsel drafted a memo that concluded that charter schools were indeed public schools.[25] This conclusion was inferred from a discussion of the evolution of the chartering statute (beginning as it did with public school district chartering authority only) and a comparison to how private schools are referred to in other applicable statutes. For example, the memo notes that private schools enrolled in the MPCP are referred to as "private participating schools" throughout the statute. No such reference is made in the charter school statute. The Milwaukee city attorney's office also completed a legal analysis of the same question. That analysis concluded that Milwaukee city charter schools were "an entirely new classification of schools, similar to public schools for some purposes and similar to private schools for other purposes" (Letter from Office of City Attorney, 25 June 1998).[26]

Although this may appear to be a disagreement over an esoteric question, the stakes were actually quite high. The determination of public school status was important because it dictates the responsibilities charter schools have for students with disabilities. The city of Milwaukee maintained that the schools it chartered were not public and therefore not bound by the requirements of the federal Individuals with Disabilities Education Act (IDEA). In other words, charter schools authorized by the city would not be required to assure that each child with a disability had available a free, appropriate, public education. They would not be required to follow IDEA procedures nor to provide the specialized instruction and related services required for individual students. Rather, the city maintained that the schools were like private schools in relation to children with disabilities; that they needed only to accept those students who could be accommodated in existing programs. The city argued that since charter school attendance was voluntary, children with disabilities would be admitted only because of parental choice. If special education programming was an issue, parents could elect to avail themselves of the appropriate special education and related services available within MPS for their child. The DPI argued precisely the opposite. It maintained that charter schools were public schools and had the same obligations toward children with disabilities as did traditional public school districts. Legal scholars (Heubert 1997; McKinney 1996, 1998) have also articulated this view.

Seeking further guidance, the DPI wrote to the U.S. Education Department (ED) in August and September of 1998. Milwaukee alderman John Kalwitz, Mayor John Norquist, and Howard Fuller, a Marquette University professor, penned related letters.[27] Marshall Smith, acting deputy secretary, responded for the ED on 8 October 1998 (Letter from Marshall Smith, 8 October 1998).[28] The ED concluded that the public/private dispute was a matter of state law and deferred to the Wisconsin DPI on this matter. However, Smith offered various points in support of viewing charter schools as public schools. He noted that federal statutes supporting charter schools consider them public schools and "clearly contemplate that charter schools will provide special education and related services as public schools." Smith also noted that all other states consider charter schools to be public schools. Finally, the letter discussed penalties, such as the withholding of federal funding, that might occur should the state be found in violation of Section 504 of the Rehabilitation Act for failing to be certain that charter schools were providing a free, appropriate, public education.

Following this response, the city of Milwaukee capitulated and agreed that charter schools were public schools. However, the city requested that the DPI designate MPS as the local education agency responsible for serving charter school students with disabilities. The DPI refused this request, reminding the city that the charter statute specifically mandates that all city charter schools operated by not-for-profit agencies be noninstrumentalities of MPS. Therefore, MPS could not employ the charter schools' special education staff.

The DPI was unwilling to consider any compromise on the issue. As State Superintendent of Public Instruction John Benson wrote in a 14 October 1998 letter to legislators, "If the city is permitted to take this position relative to children with disabilities we wonder who will be next to be excluded." The dispute continued, and the DPI withheld a portion of the payments to the city's charter schools until it agreed that the schools had to comply with IDEA. Each of the charter schools had previously participated as a private school in the MPCP, so the DPI paid the schools at the MPCP per-pupil rate (then $4,895 per eligible low-income pupil), rather than at the higher charter school payment (then $6,052 per pupil). In fact, two schools that had petitioned to convert to charter school status and were offered city charters declined them, in part due to the special education issue.[29]

Eventually, the city of Milwaukee accepted the DPI's position. The application for a city charter now requires applicants to describe how they will serve students with disabilities, consistent with IDEA.[30] It is unknown whether this very public stance relative to children with disabilities has harmed the city politically or whether it will have ramifications either for the kind and number of applications the city receives or for students' willingness to apply to the schools it charters.

This dispute, of course, illustrates a principle that many do not fully understand. While a legislature may exempt charter schools from its *state* laws, it does not have the authority to exempt schools from *federal* laws and regulations. The contract between UWM and its charter schools makes this fact explicit by expressly incorporating a number of federal statutes into the contract itself and requiring charter schools to agree to compliance. Likewise, the constitutional principles that have been applied to public schools regarding freedom of speech and religion, freedom from unreasonable searches and seizures, and due process for students and teachers would arguably continue to apply in publicly funded charter schools. Charter schools are creations of the state, just like traditional school districts. Therefore, students do not "shed their rights" as a condition of participation in a charter school.[31]

Other Statutory Complexities

As is noted earlier, Wisconsin charter schools are exempt from the bulk of state statutes concerning education. The exemptions apparently created a loophole that allowed some charter school teachers and administrators to receive DPI permits without ever being subject to criminal background checks, as required for others seeking state certification (Wisconsin Legislative Audit Bureau 1998). In fact, LAB noted that two of three directors of the city's charter schools had never undergone such scrutiny. Therefore, LAB recommended that the legislature require the DPI to conduct criminal background checks on charter school teachers and administrators in a process similar to the requirements for licensed public school staff (Wisconsin Legislative Audit Bureau 1998).

UWM also seems to have identified two other potentially unintended exemptions. Recall that UWM charter school contracts require charter schools to comply with state statutes that prohibit corporal punishment and strip searches. Corporal punishment has long been prohibited in Wisconsin's public schools. However, unless reincorporated through the charter contract, as UWM requires, no such prohibition limits the authority of charter school officials. The statutory ban on strip searches appears in two places in Wisconsin statutes, once in the education provisions and a second time in the "crimes against children" provisions of the criminal code. While excused from compliance with the first through the charter school statute, charter schools, like all Wisconsin schools public and private, must comply with the second.

Another statutory issue concerns the requirement that charter schools be tuition free. Tuition became an issue when existing private schools sought conversion to charter school status through the city of Milwaukee. The private schools had currently enrolled students who fit none of the enumerated eligibility criteria. As noted earlier, those criteria affect only schools created by the city of Milwaukee, UWM, or MATC and limit attendance to students who meet one of the five eligibility criteria noted earlier.

Existing Milwaukee private schools may have students who do not fit any of these five categories. They may enroll tuition-paying students who are in grades 4–12 and have not participated in the MPCP. Some enrolled tuition-paying students may reside outside Milwaukee city limits and still attend the private school seeking conversion to charter school status. This creates a difficult choice for the private school, for the statute seems to suggest that if it converts to charter status, it must turn away enrolled students who fall outside the categories enumerated. UWM has avoided this problem by deciding to charter only new schools, rather than convert existing private schools to charter schools.

The city of Milwaukee solved its problem by including a contract provision that allows the schools to charge tuition to students "who are attending Charter School, but who are not doing so under sec. 118.40(2r), Stats. [the charter school statute]." Likewise, the city ordinance relating to charter schools states that "the school shall not charge tuition for pupils enrolled under the charter school program; however, the school may charge tuition for other pupils" (Milwaukee Ordinance 330-7). In other words, these provisions allowed the schools to convert to charter status without asking any enrolled students to leave. Rather, those students who did not fit any of the eligibility categories were allowed to continue to attend the school and pay tuition for the privilege, just as they had before the conversion.

In addition, a reading of this contract provision and city ordinance suggests that the school can accept newly enrolled tuition-paying students who do not meet one of the five statutory criteria. As LAB points out, this provision appears to directly conflict with the statute's clear prohibition on tuition (Wisconsin Legislative Audit Bureau 1998). However, recall that the statute does not grant the DPI or any other agency the independent authority to approve or reject charter contracts created by the city of Milwaukee or other chartering authorities. It is unclear what direct action they could take against a charter school charging tuition to some of its students under similar contract provisions. The DPI could investigate a formal complaint, if someone filed one (no one has to date). The agency might also have the authority to withhold any federal grant monies if it became aware of a problem.[32] Or the question might require a court of law to resolve any dispute on the propriety of the city's ordinance and related contractual agreements.

After discussing this problem, LAB recommended that "the Legislature amend statutes to allow charter schools established by the City of Milwaukee, UW–Milwaukee, and Milwaukee Area Technical College to charge tuition to non–charter school students or to enroll students at all grade levels in the charter school program, even if the students did not participate in the Milwaukee Parental Choice Program the prior year" (Wisconsin Legislative Audit Bureau 1998, 57). To date, there have been no changes to this portion of the statute.

Dilemmas Raised by Charter Schools Operated by For-Profit Companies

Another controversy came to light when UWM offered charters to the Milwaukee Academy of Science and the Milwaukee Urban League Academy of Business and Economics. A nonprofit group sponsors each school: the Milwaukee Science Education Consortium and the Milwaukee Urban League, respectively. However, both organizations have elected to contract with Edison Schools, Inc., for the operation and management of their schools. This development raised concerns within both the university community and Milwaukee about the propriety of an organization "profiting" from participation in the publicly funded charter program.

It is also fair to say that the university was under considerable political pressure to charter. It received nine proposals during its first year as a chartering entity, but of those that were invited to submit full applications, all eventually withdrew except the Science Education and Urban League groups. Both groups had strong community ties, and the local newspaper had already cited both proposals with approval. The university faced a difficult political and philosophical dilemma. Was contracting with an educational management company (EMC) sufficient justification for denying the proposals put forward by these two respected community groups? Ultimately, the university addressed its concerns with the following provision in the charter contract: "The Chancellor reserves the right to review and approve beforehand any Operation or Management Contract for the operation or management of the Charter School that the Grantee wishes itself to enter into with any third party. . . ."

UWM's experience also raises a question regarding the city of Milwaukee's authority to enter into a contract with an EMC. As mentioned earlier, the statute requires that "if the city of Milwaukee contracts with an individual or group operating for profit to operate a school as a charter school, the charter school is an instrumentality of [MPS, and MPS] shall employ all personnel for the charter school" (WI Stat. §118.40(7)(am)(3)). In other words, the city may—presumably like all Wisconsin chartering authorities—grant a charter directly to a group operating for profit.[33] But if it does so, any such school would by definition become an MPS school. However, if the city, like UWM, contracts with a nonprofit organization that then subcontracts with a for-profit management group, would the charter school be subject to this provision and therefore be an instrumentality of MPS? There is no clear answer to this question, but it has yet to be tested by the city. If the city did so, it would risk being accused of honoring the letter of this statutory provision, while ignoring its intent.

Not surprisingly, the decision of UWM to approve charter schools with ties to Edison Schools created some political problems with MPS staff. UWM has long-standing relationships with public schools in Milwaukee. A number of the schools have formal partnership agreements with UWM, and nearly all of the schools accept UWM student teachers. The UWM faculty committee charged with examining the statute and making recommendations to the dean of the School of Education and the chancellor was aware that the strongly unionized MPS teachers already felt pressured by the legislature's passage of the charter school law and the MPCP. Thus, the committee attempted to forestall problems by adopting a set of principles to guide UWM's charter activities. These ten principles included a commitment to sponsor charter schools that would "improve the overall education conditions for children who live in the City of Milwaukee"; "reflect 'best educational practices'"; "reflect linkages between and among the school families and community agencies"; be consistent with UWM's urban mission; reflect the diversity of the city of Milwaukee; embody principles of democratic management; and be subject to measures of success that "encompass both academic and social outcomes for children as well as consumer satisfaction." The principles also promised collaboration with other academic units of UWM as well as with the MPS board of directors, administrators, and teachers union.

Still, MPS staff were less than pleased with the prospect of UWM authorizing Edison-run charter schools and voiced concerns formally to the university's chancellor. For example, the principal and staff at Riverside High School sent a letter on 18 March 1999 warning that "as things stand, the positive relationship that has existed between UWM and Riverside is in serious jeopardy." The letter voiced concerns that charter schools would ignore the needs of at-risk learners and would be run by the Edison corporation, which the staff claimed had "not shown [it-self] to be a reliable, successful means for educating students," with "dismal" re-sults for its efforts in Baltimore. The letter then suggested that charters should include requirements that the charter school serve all children; meet all state as-sessment requirements; and make all records of student performance, attendance, and discipline available to the public.

The letter illustrates both misunderstandings of the charter legislation (the first two of the suggestions are statutory requirements) and the misgivings MPS had about the chartering process. There were rumors that schools and perhaps the district as a whole would refuse to accept UWM's student teachers as pun-ishment for authorizing charter schools that would employ Edison. The rumors appear to have been unfounded. Yet, to calm district fears, the university made early drafts of the charters available to MPS central administration and to the MTEA. A charter school contract template is also available on the university's Website (<http://www.uwm.edu/Dept/ccs/contract.html>). Only one of the char-ter schools that raised the concerns had opened as of the 2000–2001 school year. It remains to be seen whether the operation of these schools will have any further impact on the university's relationship with MPS and the MTEA.

Assessing the Wisconsin Charter School Movement

Despite the political controversies and technical complexities discussed earlier, the charter school movement can only be described as alive and well in Wiscon-sin. The increase in the number of charter schools shows no signs of abating. That said, to date, the legislature has not acted upon the LAB recommendations (Wisconsin Legislative Audit Bureau 1998). No bills are currently pending that would grant chartering authority to the state's universities and technical colleges nor to the DPI itself. In addition, there has been no legislative response to the issue of criminal background checks or the subject of tuition in limited circum-stances. Finally, there has also been no legislative action to consider state provi-sion of charter school start-up funds or other financial issues or to grant the DPI further oversight authority to ensure that charter schools fully comply with the current statute.

Although open to contention, it may be inferred from events that have tran-spired in Milwaukee that the legislature's goal of providing more educational op-portunities and spurring MPS to create and charter its own schools has been at least somewhat successful. Note that MPS and its teachers union settled the suit that was blocking further MPS charter schools after the legislature had authorized the city, UWM, and MATC to charter schools. Of course, without further research, there is no way to tell whether this settlement would have occurred absent that new authority or whether MPS would have pursued its current charter schools without the impetus provided by the other Milwaukee chartering authorities. Perhaps it would have. And, of course, the jury is still out about whether the charters created in Milwaukee can actually address the urban educational concerns there. Certainly the two Edison-managed schools will attract considerable scrutiny.

Likewise, the experiences of charter schools in Wisconsin in general and in the city of Milwaukee in particular suggest several avenues for further research. For example, what process is used and what issues surface when school districts and charter schools negotiate funding through the charter school contract? Have there been any ramifications, political or otherwise, stemming from the city's public stance with respect to charter schools' obligations toward students with disabilities? What processes are used and what issues surface as charter school authorities oversee the effectiveness of the schools they charter? What issues surface as charter schools begin the charter-renewal process? What are the specific provisions of charter school contracts, and how do they compare to the statutes from which charter schools are relieved? What are the ramifications, if any, of allowing a charter school to charge tuition to some of its students, as is apparently occurring in some charter schools in Milwaukee?

These questions deserve further study, and Wisconsin's charter schools provide a venue for such exploration. It also seems clear that Wisconsin's charter school law will continue to evolve as policy makers reflect on the effectiveness of charter schools as a tool for educational reform. Whatever the future holds, Wisconsin will continue to serve as a laboratory for the examination of various forms of school choice and their effect on educational opportunities and effectiveness.

9 • Parameters for Choice

Charter Schools in Alberta

Lynn Bosetti and Robert O'Reilly

THE PROVINCE OF Alberta adopted its charter law in 1994. To date, Alberta is the only Canadian jurisdiction to permit charter schools. Alberta's charter school legislation was introduced to the legislature by a Conservative government with a strong majority in the house. It was adopted in 1994 after minimal consultation with stakeholders and little legislative debate. The minister of education promoted these "term-specific" charter schools as a vehicle to revitalize public education by fostering innovation in the organization and delivery of education. The intent was that successful innovations would be shared with and eventually adopted by the public education system.

The Charter School Law in Alberta

Charter school advocates often characterize charter school laws as being "weak" or "strong" based on criteria such as the degree of charter school autonomy, the relative ease in attaining a charter, the potential for large numbers of charters to be granted, admissions criteria, and the opportunity to employ noncertified teachers (Wells et al. 1999; Premack 1996).

The Alberta charter school law is more restrictive than expansive in nature. The law reflects a cautious government that was willing to pass charter school legislation robust enough to leverage some change in public education but not so far-reaching or controversial as to signal an end to government-run public education and a move toward a deregulated voucher system. From the outset, the provincial government has consistently conveyed that the charter school law is intended to provide parents with more choice in addressing children's learning needs and to promote innovation in public education in order to enhance and improve student learning.

The Alberta charter school law can be characterized as "restrictive" in that it permits a limited number of charter schools (a cap of fifteen) to operate for a limited term of three to five years. A charter can be renewed for another limited term subsequent to two formal evaluations that attest to the success of the school in achieving its charter goals. Only the minister of education or a public school board may grant charters, and charter schools must operate under the provisions of the Alberta School Act. Charter schools must employ certified teachers, and admissions processes must provide open access to students and be nondiscriminatory in practice.

The law is strong in that it designates charter schools as legally autonomous entities and permits a variety of operators (i.e., individuals, groups, and nonprofit organizations). It also allows for existing private or public schools to convert to charter schools. Under the Canadian Constitution, education is under the jurisdiction of the provinces. However, some provinces are required to make accommodations within the public education system for the creation of Catholic school boards and of French public and French Catholic school boards. In other words, Canada has a dual public education system based on religion (Catholicism) and the French language.[1] Alberta is one of several Canadian provinces that are required to make such accommodations, and as a result, Catholic schools and French-language schools can become charter schools.

Alberta has a centralized school funding mechanism; consequently, school boards are not dependent on local tax levies but are allocated funding through the provincial government's grant-funding formula. Provincial policy dictates that the school funding follows the child. Consequently, charter schools are entitled to the same basic instructional grant and all supplemental grants (e.g., money for students with disabilities) that other public schools receive. In 1999–2000, the instructional and support grants per student were approximately $6,000.[2] The original charter school legislation did not provide any special start-up grants, and until 1999, Alberta Learning (the province's education agency) made no effort to assist charter schools with capital costs.[3] Charter schools were allocating between 10 and 15 percent of their total operating budget to leasing school facilities and had difficulty accessing leases for available school facilities in the traditional public education system. As a result of significant lobbying from the charter school sector, Alberta Learning has since introduced a variety of measures to assist charter schools with certain capital and leasing costs and has provided monetary incentives for local boards to lease existing facilities to charter schools.

The western province of Alberta has a population of approximately 2.9 mil-

lion (about 10 percent of the Canadian population). Although historically dependent on the cattle and agricultural industries, in the past forty years Alberta
has become increasingly dependent on the oil and natural gas industries. Most of
Canada's major oil corporations have their head offices in Calgary, Alberta. The
Progressive Conservative party (PC) of Alberta, under the leadership of Ralph
Klein, won the 1990 election on a platform of fiscal reform. The government promised to eliminate not only deficit budgets but also the provincial debt.

Through a coherent plan of fiscal restraint and with the good luck of increased
oil and gas prices, the government quickly brought in balanced budgets, achieved
significant surpluses, and, by 1998, eliminated the provincial "net debt." As part
of this reform, it reduced educational funding by 12 percent, reduced the salaries
of all those paid directly or indirectly by government (including teachers) by 5
percent, centralized the educational funding process through the control of local
school taxes, consolidated school boards from 141 to 68, and imposed spending
restrictions on school boards (Bruce and Schwartz 1997).

Under this government, Alberta Learning became a policy-driven agency and
focused its attention on the goals of educational accountability, efficiency, and
performance. Overall educational policy in Alberta was revised to include elements
of close government control of curriculum, fiscal accountability, and assessment
of student progress and teacher performance. The government favored models of
local school management, strong parental involvement, and public disclosure of
school progress and student achievement on standardized tests (Bosetti, O'Reilly,
and Gereluk 1998). These policies were based on trends that had been emerging
in Alberta for some years. For example, since the 1970s the Edmonton Public
School Board had experimented with school-based management, alternative
programs and schools, and open boundaries for student enrollment, and it was a
recognized world leader in the field of educational innovation (Caldwell and
Spinks 1998, 9).

During this time, there were consistent critiques of public education in Alberta, especially of the key mainstream players such as school boards and teachers unions. These complaints were part of general North American attacks on
public schools and included such Canadian critiques of public schools as those
written by Barlow and Robertson (1994), Lewington and Orpwood (1993), and
Nikiforuk (1993). Local critics challenged public schools for failing to provide
a rigorous curriculum, traditional teaching methods (including greater use of
phonics in reading), and teacher-centered pedagogy. The Alberta Chamber of
Resources, a provincial consortium of Alberta natural resource corporations,

published a document purporting to demonstrate that the Alberta curriculum was significantly inferior to that found in such countries as Hungary (Alberta Chamber of Resources 1993).

It was within this context that the minister of education, Halvar Johnson, a former school superintendent and one-time president of the Alberta Teachers Association, introduced the notion of charter schools to Alberta as a vehicle to leverage change in public education through innovation in the organization and delivery of education. While charter schools were born out of the desire of the minister, he had strong support from his deputy minister and staff and from a small but significant lobby group from within the PC caucus who were advocates of parent-controlled schools (Bosetti et al. 1998).

The Alberta School Board Association was not supportive of charter schools, and most school board members were unwilling to foster a charter school initiative that was the child of Alberta Learning. Under pressure from budgetary cuts and increased supervision by the government and suffering from a loss of support services, school board members looked askance at charter school legislation. There had been no consultation with school boards regarding the establishment of charter schools, and there had been minimal formal debate in the legislature when the minister of education introduced an amendment to the Alberta School Act that would empower him to establish charter schools.

The charter school legislation followed on the heels of legislation requiring all schools to have school councils composed primarily of parents, with some representation from teachers and the school principal. Although the draft legislation for school councils would have given parents extensive powers to control what transpired in schools, the final set of regulations made them advisory bodies to the school principal (O'Reilly 1995). Some school board members saw school councils and then charter schools as additional moves to reduce the influence of school boards, raising the concern that this might open the door to private-sector encroachment into the management of public education (Robertson 1999). However, to date, charter school legislation does not permit charter schools to be managed by the private sector.

Policy Implementation

In 1996, Alberta Learning released the *Charter School Handbook* and prepared draft regulations, and the first charter school was approved in July. As of 2000–2001, twelve charters had been granted: two had been closed, and ten remained operational. Of the original twelve schools, only one was located in a rural community, and it has since been closed. Two charter schools are in small urban centers, and the remainder are located in two of Alberta's largest cities. Of the twelve charter schools, three were conversions from private or independent schools, six were newly formed, and the other three were extensions of community-based educational programs or societies (e.g., the Society for the Education of Gifted Children, the Action for Bright Children Society, and a Community Services cooperative).

Most charter schools are housed in vacant public school facilities. One has been located in a renovated building in an army barracks (in September 2001, this school moved to school space made available by the local urban school board) and another in teaching facilities at a hospital. A few have obtained space not originally designed for school use, but the charter school founders have undertaken renovations to make the space suitable for teaching and learning and to meet necessary health, fire, and safety regulations.

Charter schools vary in size, drawing students mainly from educated, English-speaking, middle-income families. For example, 88 percent of charter school parents speak English as their first language, 77 percent have at least some post-secondary education, and 56 percent have a family income above $60,000. School populations range from less than 80 students to more than 600. In all but two cases, student enrollment has increased since inception, and retention rates remain high. Charter schools providing a structured, sequential teaching methodology have extensive waiting lists, and parents and teachers express overall high levels of satisfaction with their experiences in charter schools (Bosetti 1998). One such school has become the largest charter school in the province, with a population of 615 students housed in two campuses in different areas of the same city. The school has a lengthy waiting list.

Charter schools in Alberta cater to niche markets in the public education system. While they cannot discriminate in admission to the school, they in fact stream students by virtue of the kinds of programs and philosophical orientations they offer. For example, the missions of the charter schools reflect three different philosophical approaches to teaching and learning: traditional "back-to-basics" instruction; student-centered, "progressive," individualized-learning programs; and an interagency approach to addressing the educational needs of at-risk youth. Only two of the twelve charters that were granted by Alberta Learning were designed to serve children who were at risk or had special learning needs.

Three of Alberta's charter schools offer a traditional educational program for grades 1–9 that emphasizes teacher-directed learning, highly structured learning

environments, strict disciplinary policies, and a demand for high parental involvement in children's learning. In contrast, three other charter schools have offered a
more student-centered approach to teaching and learning, geared toward students
in grades 1–9. They have provided differentiated instruction to meet the diverse
learning styles of students and incorporate Gardner's (1993) theory of multiple
intelligences. These schools are aimed at self-directed or motivated learners and
those with a preferred learning style. Only one of these charter schools remains
operational.

A fifth charter school serves the needs of street-involved youth (ages twelve to
nineteen) who have dropped out of school or have been "shut out" of the public
education system. The educational program is designed to provide a safe environment for these students to acquire a basic education focused on life skills and
job readiness. One charter school, situated in Calgary's inner city, caters to students in grades 1–9 who are part of the Islamic community. Many of these students
are recent immigrants who require assistance in learning English as a second language. Three charter schools serve children who are academically gifted and/or
talented. One school caters to students who are in grades K–6, the other to students who are in grades K–9. The third school serves K–6 students who are mu-
sically talented, using the Suzuki teaching method. Finally, the remaining charter
school provides students in grades 4–6 with programs that emphasize science
and technology (Bosetti 1998).

The marketing of most charter schools is limited to public information meetings advertised in local newspapers and to word of mouth. Consequently, most
parents who are attracted to charter schools are informed and aware of the choices
available within public education or have personal connections with charter school
teachers or parents (Bosetti, O'Reilly, and Gereluk 1998).

Blurred Visions

In the minister of education's vision, charter schools were positioned to work in
partnership with school boards. As a consequence, those seeking a charter had to
apply first to a school board, and only after being denied at this level could they
appeal to the minister for charter approval. Charter schools were not provided
with start-up funds or capital grants because the minister anticipated that school
boards would provide surplus school space to charter schools. He also envisioned
that the superintendent of the local school board would also serve as the superintendent of the charter school.

This conception of charter schools as complements of local public school systems was generally not accepted by school boards. In the period leading up to the charter school legislation, local school boards, particularly urban ones, viewed themselves as under attack by Alberta Learning because of the government's aggressive restructuring of public education (e.g., consolidation of school boards, introduction of parent councils, increased funding to private schools, expanded standardized testing programs, and grade-twelve diploma examinations). Local school boards thus saw little incentive to support charter schools and viewed them as the children of the minister. Local boards were expected not only to grant charters but also to provide superintendent services, monitor and evaluate charter schools, and assist them in finding suitable physical space. In this climate local boards routinely dismissed applications for charters and offered little cooperation in providing charter school operators with access to vacant school facilities.

Lack of Leadership

Innovations such as charter schools can be expected to have growing pains as they struggle to define their character and place within the public education system. The charter movement began with strong governmental support and direction; however, in the three years following enactment of the legislation, support and enthusiasm appeared to diminish as the result of a number of unforeseen events (Bosetti 1998). In particular, there was significant turnover in key governmental positions. First, the minister who had introduced the legislation was shortly afterward given another post in government, and a new minister was appointed. Second, the deputy minister retired, his replacement lasted only several months, and an acting deputy minister was appointed. Third, the advocate for charter schools within Alberta Learning died unexpectedly shortly after the deputy minister retired. He had been given a special assignment to oversee charter schools; however, the position was redefined as 40 percent of the responsibility of another position. The person in this new position saw her role as being a manager rather than an advocate of the charter school program. Her position was abolished in a reorganization of Alberta Learning in 1998, and responsibility for charter schools was given to a general-purpose "Educational Response Team." By 1999, members of this team were viewed by charter schools as supporters of the charter school movement. The team has devoted the equivalent of a full-time position to oversee ten charter schools.

The next minister of education, Gary Mar, did not seem to have the same conception of charter schools as his predecessor. In particular, he did not see the role of local school boards as critical. It was also during his tenure that the relationship between Alberta Learning and the largest urban school board in the province deteriorated substantially. Charter school applicants were routinely rejected by local school boards, and on appeal they were almost certainly approved by the minister. In fact, while charter school applicants were required to first apply to a public board for charter approval, they did so with hopes that their charter application would be rejected so that they could appeal to the minister for approval, avoiding further conflict with local boards. By 1998 only one of the ten charter schools had had its charter approved by a local school board; the remainder had received their charters directly from the minister.[4] The minister demonstrated support for the concept of charter schools by granting charters; however, Alberta Learning was now directly responsible for monitoring and evaluating charter schools for compliance with their charters and provincial charter school regulations. Charter schools were left to create their own support network through a provincial organization, the Association of Alberta Public Charter Schools (ASAPCS), and an independent organization established the Canadian Charter Schools Centre to offer related research and professional development resources.

A noteworthy example of the effects of the lack of leadership from Alberta Learning occurred in 1997. The auditor-general of the province of Alberta noted in his annual report to the legislature that there were few accountability guidelines for charter schools and that those that existed were not being followed. In response to this report, Alberta Learning conducted a series of workshops for charter school board members concerning their responsibilities under the Alberta School Act. Chief among the topics discussed in these workshops were the facts that all charter schools had a limited-term charter and that renewal would be granted only if the results of the educational programs met the targets set in the schools' charters. This was met by consternation among the charter school operators, because they had presumed that if their schools functioned normally, demonstrated enhanced student learning, and were fiscally responsible, then their charters would be automatically renewed.

Cumbersome Regulations

The School Act specifies that each charter school must have a school board that is elected by parents of children enrolled in the school, must hire a secretary-treasurer as its chief financial officer, and must hire a school superintendent as its chief educational officer. The School Act also specifies that the superintendent should function as the chief executive officer of the board and the chief education officer of the school, overseeing the operation of the school and reporting to the minister annually. In practice, most charter schools rely on their principal as their key manager, and the superintendent plays a less significant role. Generally, the superintendent has provided some general advice to the board, supervised teachers in complying with the provisions of the School Act, and generally ensured that the school followed the official Alberta curriculum. The charter school boards hire teachers, set salary schedules and work conditions, and determine teaching methods and any curricular enhancements deemed fitting. The local board superintendents have rarely been consulted on these decisions.

There is little consistency in the quality or amount of time superintendents devote to charter schools. Their contracts vary from one half day to two days per month. Those charter boards experiencing internal tension and those schools with inconsistent leadership due to ever-changing principals require more guidance and support from the superintendent. In cases in which a charter school matures, the board gains experience in school governance, and when a strong principal is providing educational leadership, the superintendent role is diminished (Bosetti et al. 2000). There is a need for clearer guidelines for the role and responsibility of a superintendent of a charter school, particularly when the sponsoring authority is a local school board.

In addition to a school board, each charter school must also have a school council elected by parents of students. Under the School Act, the school council is advisory to the principal but also has the duty to ensure that the school programs are assessed and that the assessment results are reported to all parents annually. There is some confusion regarding the various roles and responsibilities of elected bodies (the charter school board and the charter school council, both elected by parents of students) and those of the principal and superintendent. In its workshops with charter school boards, Alberta Learning has devoted considerable time to clarifying these roles and responsibilities in light of the School Act. The charter school regulations were not explicit regarding these roles and responsibilities. Unlike members of other public school boards, members of a charter school board do not have access to the services, programs, or advice of the Alberta School Board Association, an organization that provides in-service training for school trustees in Alberta.

Poor Funding Regulations

The unique character and requirements of charter schools have not been recognized in the funding regulations. Schools and school districts receive grants from Alberta Learning that are sufficient to operate the schools. The grants are typically of three types: operating grants, which cover the total cost of instruction and administration, including maintenance of facilities; capital grants, which are based on an annual competition for new facilities and major renovations; and transportation grants, which charter schools can access if they can negotiate the use of existing transportation offered by local public school boards. Charter schools are eligible for the same per-pupil grants as all other public schools, including supplemental funding for special education and second language teaching. In 2000–2001 Alberta Learning allocated about $6,000 per student (which included the basic instructional grant and supplemental grants). Most charter schools also charge fees to cover additional expenses for students. The following fee structure is typical of most charter schools: a $100 student activity fee, $6 for a student agenda, a $25 family membership fee for the charter school society, and a $25 student supply fee.[5] In schools that provide their own transportation, parents pay between $20 and $40 per month. In other cases, parents are expected to transport their children to the school at their own cost.

Since the original intention of the legislation was that charter schools would be cooperative ventures with local school boards, charter schools were expected to hit the ground running. Initially no start-up funds were available, except that charter schools could receive an advance of up to two and a half months of the year's funding allotment prior to start-up. Charter schools were not eligible for any capital grants (grants for buildings). These funding issues were alleviated somewhat with revised funding regulations adopted in 1999. The new funding regulations provided funds for the costs of leasing school space and the possibility of capital grants for major renovation projects.

All charters are for a limited term, yet an organization with a three- to five-year life cannot enter into long-term lease arrangements or secure loans. This makes it difficult for charter schools to operate efficiently. Since they cannot obtain loans commercially, charter school operators have spent an inordinate amount of their first years' budgets on bringing their buildings up to the health, fire, and safety standards required in the School Act. These expenses were often met through lower teacher salaries and reduced spending on instruction and teaching supplies.

Charter School Accountability

The 1996–1997 *Annual Report of the Auditor General of Alberta,* given to the Alberta legislature, noted the paucity of regulations pertaining to charter school accountability (Province of Alberta 1997). The lack of accountability guidelines became a major issue a year later when the charters of two schools expired in June 1998. Although the regulations specified that renewal depended upon positive recommendations in two evaluations, it was not clear who would conduct these evaluations. By the fall of 1997, no such evaluations had been conducted, and Alberta Learning had not published the expectations and formats for such evaluations. Charter schools were uncertain of the criteria by which they would be assessed.

At the same time, Alberta Learning realized that although it had requested and received annual business plans from the charter schools, it had not asked for nor received definitions of each school's performance measures. Each school was required to demonstrate "improved student learning" from having implemented an "innovative, different or enhanced program," and the definition of these terms became critical (Alberta Education, Planning Branch 1997). The two charter schools up for renewal had not created mechanisms for demonstrating "improved learning." All they could report was the current level of achievement of students on government tests in a few basic subjects for grades three, six, and nine or on senior secondary course examinations. The remaining charter schools had records of other achievement data but generally not in a form that enabled the schools to indicate the extent to which the schools were meeting their objectives. Thus far, all charter schools applying for renewal have been successful, although the school with the poorest record of academic achievement has been warned to improve its results.

The charter school regulations also provide that charter schools are expected to demonstrate that they deliver unique and innovative programs and have an impact on student learning (Alberta Education, Planning Branch 1997). Charter schools are also expected to share their successful innovations with other public schools. These requirements put charter schools in an interesting position. If other public schools adopt a charter school's innovations, does this jeopardize charter renewal because the charter school is no longer unique? What does "unique and innovative" mean in this context? Charter schools must also offer "parental and student choice" and "increased learning opportunities" (Alberta Education 1996).

These concepts require further definition if charter schools are to be evaluated fairly.

In practice, it appears that if a charter school's students are achieving as well as could be expected, if the programs listed in the charter are actually being delivered, and if the school is being managed prudently, then the charter will be renewed. In each case, the final arbiter is the education minister. Although each charter school is responsible under the regulations for developing measures to indicate academic success, most rely on assessments conducted by Alberta Learning. There is some evidence that government-appointed evaluators are examining the extent to which charter programs have been implemented. For example, one school whose charter requires it to provide substantial programs in English as a Second Language (ESL) has been strongly encouraged in writing by the education minister to spend more resources on its ESL program and to hire more ESL-qualified teachers. The implication was that failure to implement the core programs listed in the charter would be grounds for rescinding the charter. Until these evaluation exercises began, approximately three years after the first charter was issued, the only reasons for terminating a charter had been financial malfeasance or inability to financially sustain a school.

In cases in which charter schools have had sponsoring school boards, the authority of the sponsoring board has been unclear. For example, in one case, the sponsoring board of the Centre for Personal and Academic Excellence Charter School determined that the school did not meet two conditions of its charter (relating to salaries of teachers and support staff and payment to the board for superintendency services) and requested that the charter be rescinded by the education minister. However, in response to a request from the school, the minister granted a new charter to the school directly, bypassing the local school board and effectively overruling the authority of sponsoring boards. By 2001, only one school had its charter granted by a local board (there originally were three). This state of affairs is counter to the original intent of the legislation to foster cooperative partnerships between local boards and charter schools.

Current regulations require that each school requesting charter renewal must have two independent evaluations. For the first round of renewals, the government hired private-sector evaluators to visit schools and prepare evaluation reports. The evaluations were based on the purposes of the schools as stated in their charters and evidence of success in meeting those objectives. More recently Alberta Learning has assigned its own officials (some of whom are retired superintendents) to assess charter schools. The bases for these assessments are checklists that focus attention on the charter; its objectives; the role and conduct of the charter school board; the role of the superintendent in fulfilling duties; and adherence to a substantial body of government regulations for schools in terms of safety, management, and curriculum.

To date, student performance on provincial assessment examinations, which are required of all schools, has not played a significant role in charter school accountability. Without any benchmarks or other standards for assessing the achievement of charter school students, if the results seem "reasonable" for the particular school, no further analysis is conducted. Only one charter school has been cited for poor performance.[6]

To date, two of the twelve charter schools approved have been closed. In 1997, the largest charter school (with over 700 students) was closed at the request of the charter school board due to alleged fiscal malfeasance on the part of the principal. There was also a significant division among the members of the board that made successful negotiation of its difficulties unlikely. The second school was the smallest charter school (less than 70 students), which surrendered its charter because the school was not financially viable. The charter school was turned over to the local school board, which continued to offer a version of the charter as an alternative program in one of the local schools.

In 2000, a third school that encountered problems in maintaining itself was in negotiations with its sponsoring school board to surrender its charter and become an alternative school under the local school board. However these talks fell through, and the school's charter was renewed by the minister. The school no longer has any affiliation with the local school board. The minister has warned a fourth charter school that it must be more successful in achieving its charter objectives and in aiding its students to improve their performance on provincial examinations. It is noteworthy that of the four schools encountering difficulties, only one has been cited for failure to provide a program that enhances student learning. The other three schools all had problems with governance and administration, particularly financial administration.

Evolution of Government Policy

Many of the preceding observations of Alberta's charter schools have been noted in earlier reports on charter schools (O'Reilly 1999; Bosetti 1998; Bosetti, O'Reilly, and Gereluk 1998) and have been recognized by participants in the charter school movement in Alberta and by members of the educational bureaucracy. Alberta Learning made some attempts at clarifying its expectations for charter schools and, in the spring of 1999, announced its three-year plan for the period 1999–2002 (Alberta Education 1999a).[7]

Role of the Superintendent

The role of the superintendent was clearly reinforced in a public statement by the education minister at the time that the charter of the Centre for Academic and Personal Excellence (CAPE) Charter School was conditionally renewed in July 1998. In a news release, the minister confirmed that the school would receive a new charter, even though the sponsoring school board had recommended against such a renewal because the school had allegedly failed to fulfill certain conditions of its charter. The minister would grant the new three-year charter with no role for the local board but with a clear role for the superintendent of the charter school. The minister stated: "[The charter school] must employ a superintendent, consistent with the requirements of the School Act. Under the Act, a superintendent must have a meaningful role as chief executive officer of the board and as chief education officer of the charter school. Also the superintendent must be able to effectively supervise the operation of the school and report to the Minister on a yearly basis" (Alberta Education 1998).

This public reaffirmation of the superintendent's role clarified the relationship between the charter school board and its superintendent. Nonetheless, the superintendent remains a part-time contract official for most charter schools, and the charter school boards rely upon their principals as their key managers. The superintendent is a key administrative figure in less than half of the ten charter schools in Alberta. The statement regarding the superintendent role indicates that the minister wishes to administer charter schools as if they are mini–school districts and will address them, for administrative purposes, as if they are school districts. However, the issuance of the statement did little to alter the relationships among superintendents, charter school boards, and charter school principals. Whereas the law requires superintendents to be chief administrative and educational officers responsible for the management of charter schools, in fact charter school boards expect their superintendents to serve an almost symbolic role of signing official documents; the charter school boards rely on their principals to fulfill all executive and educational functions. Most of the superintendents, who receive only modest stipends for their work, comply in these practices.

Initiatives Concerning Leasing of Space

In February 1999, the education minister announced further measures to encourage cooperation between local school boards and charter schools with respect to sharing school facilities (Alberta Education 1999b). Local school boards that lease space to charter schools would receive credit for the effective use of current space when they applied to the government for grants to build new schools or modernize current space. This measure was aimed at urban school boards that had surplus space in the city center and were unwilling to lease space to charter schools yet were applying to the government for capital grants to build new schools in rapidly growing communities at the edges of the boards' boundaries. Since the measure, only one urban board has freed up space in one of its schools for a charter school. The board has been rewarded with grants to build a school in a newly developed community. The irony is that in order to make the space available for a charter school, the board had to terminate its lease with a private school. The board has since announced that it will provide space for another charter school in one of its school buildings in the fall of 2001.

If a charter school leases space from a local school board, the school is eligible for provincial grants to cover the costs of the lease, as well as limited support for furniture and equipment to begin school operations. In specific circumstances where facility upgrading is required, the local school board is eligible for a one-time facility-improvement grant. However, such grants are not available to charter schools that do not rent space from a school board. Regulatory changes have also provided for grants to cover the cost of leasing private facilities; however, no public funds are available for modernization or capital improvements to a charter school that leases a private facility. In addition, charter schools are now eligible to apply for provincial grants for start-up support for furniture and equipment.

Overall, these regulations have had two impacts. The first reaffirms the original vision of the legislation, that charter schools would complement existing school boards. Whether this was a conscious intent of the regulations is debatable. For example, no mention of this objective was made in the various press releases announcing the changes. Both the minister and the deputy minister referred only to the more economical use of school space and the requirement that school boards either divest their districts of surplus school space or make it available to charter schools in order to receive funds for new buildings or renovations (Alberta Education 1999b).

The second impact of the new regulations was to provide more equitable funding to charter schools for facilities. The financial regulations finally recognize that most charter schools have to lease facilities either from school boards or from other private or public providers. The infusion of funds for facilities also greatly eased the difficult trade-off faced by charter schools. No longer would funds destined for charter school instructional services be diverted to pay for expenses associated with facilities. However, the new facilities grants do make charter schools more of an expense on the public purse.

Departmental Staff Support

Although support for charter schools was originally to be a small portion of the 1998 Educational Response Team mandate, charter schools have accessed the resources of the team quite heavily. Given various issues affecting individual charter schools, the leader of the team, Randy Clarke, has estimated that almost 40 percent of his time has been devoted to charter schools.[8] This appears to be an unanticipated allocation of public professional resources to charter schools. However, charter school operators now have direct access to an officer of the ministry who has reasonable access to senior managers and who will advocate for them within the bureaucracy.

The Role of Charter Schools in the Public Education System

The executive assistant to the education minister reiterated the theme of the charter school as a partner with school boards in public education in an address at a charter schools conference in Calgary in May 1999. Kelly Charlebois, speaking on behalf of Minister Gary Mar, emphasized that charter schools are a vital part of the public educational system: "The Minister's vision for charter schools is that you and public schools work together in one seamless public education system: that your goals and programs are linked together in compatible ways . . . so you can share the methods and structures you use so effectively. . . . To accomplish this vision, I urge you to explore a stronger partnership with the public school boards" (Charlebois 1999).

   Thus, the stated intent of the government of Alberta is to have charter schools and local school boards work together. However, there is little evidence that anyone has made much of an effort to make this a reality. Although charter schools might have something to gain from cooperation with school boards, school boards presently see little advantage to—and possible problems with—cooperating with charter schools. The problems include finding adequate space for charter school students, the uncertain accountability chain between the school board and the charter school, the concern of being seen as sponsoring educational practices with which significant proportions of the electorate may not agree, and the competition for students. The negative reaction of school boards to charter schools has done little to encourage charter schools to seek partnerships with school boards. The change in regulations concerning facilities may encourage some cooperation in areas where the school board does have desirable surplus schools, but school boards in general will require greater incentives to view charter schools as their partners. Such incentives may include financial inducements or a clarification of the rules by which charter schools would be accountable to local school boards.

Conclusion

The purpose of the Alberta charter school program is "to provide for an innovative, different or enhanced program to improve student learning" (Alberta Education, Planning Branch 1997). The political motivation for charter schools in Alberta stems from many forces. Some would argue that charter schools were introduced as vehicles to revitalize public education by providing parents and students with more options within the public sector and by fostering laboratories of innovation through stepping outside the bureaucratic constraints and resistance imposed by teachers unions and school boards. Charter school operators argue that they have demonstrated that they can operate effective schools with fewer resources, while maintaining the general objectives of enhanced student learning, fiscal accountability, and general school improvement.

Alberta charter schools have provided services in areas where the public system is somewhat deficient: services for children who are gifted and talented, for immigrant children who must learn English as a second language, and for street youth. Charter schools are also experimenting with pedagogical innovations, such as a Suzuki method–based curriculum and differentiated curriculum.[9] Finally, some charter schools provide alternatives for parents who want a school that is traditional in its teaching and standards and that manifestly proclaims a set of values consistent with the parents' beliefs. Such schools may have nonsectarian admission standards and curricula, but the school ethos is expected to mirror the parents' principles regarding discipline and social and political values.

Only a few charter schools appear to have the professional depth, commitment, and resources necessary to carefully document their programs and achievements and to make the results available for other schools. One charter school designed for gifted children has the backing of a strong, experienced community of professionals and parents who have long advocated for gifted children. The ABC Public Charter School and the Association for Bright Children (ABC), which supports it, have links with the Centre for Gifted Education at the University of Calgary; strong educational leadership at the school; and well-paid, highly qualified, experienced staff. To date, no other charter school in the province appears to enjoy such a combination of professional, administrative, community, and financial resources.

The government initially made a minimal investment in the charter school program. In Alberta, grants follow students, and charter schools receive the operating grants that school boards would otherwise receive; however, they originally received no capital grants. Due to changes in the regulations governing charter schools, the costs to the government for the charter schools have escalated. Charter schools now receive grants to cover the costs of leasing facilities and are eligible for capital grants. The Educational Response Team now devotes a substantial proportion of its time to charter school matters, and Alberta Learning has assumed responsibility for evaluating charter schools instead of relying on the schools themselves to provide suitable evaluations to the government.

It would appear that the government does not want a large number of charter schools in Alberta. A total of twelve has been approved over a five-year period, and ten remain. Although many groups have begun preparation of charter applications, there appear to be only two or three groups that are currently actively working on applications, and it is not clear if any of these groups have the resources to submit a successful application. Moreover, the only school designed for at-risk students is the result of leadership by social workers and teachers. The result is that support for charter schools in Alberta is essentially a middle-class movement.

The lack of leadership and support from the government has opened the way for the private sector to step in to support charter schools. Prominent among private groups has been the Society for the Advancement of Excellence in Education, an advocacy organization that is operating with considerable private-sector support. With little or no consultation with Alberta charter schools, the society raised private funds to create the Canadian Charter Schools Research and Development Center in Calgary. Traditional educational leaders in Alberta have not

been active in the charter school arena, although a few retired school superintendents and principals have lent their expertise to some charter school boards.

With very few exceptions, the children who attend Alberta's charter schools
have a variety of alternative choices within the public sector to meet their needs and
many more in the private sector. During the past decade, with the Alberta government policy of decentralized school management and the creation of school councils, school systems in Alberta have begun to provide a wide variety of programs of
choice within the public sector. For example, the Edmonton Public School Board
has over thirty programs of choice operating in over ninety-five public schools.
Although some programs of choice are currently oversubscribed, such as programs for gifted children, most are freely available.

Many of these alternatives either were in place before the charter school initiative or have been implemented as a result of a more general public demand for
choice. Therefore, the impact of the existence of charter schools on these alternatives within the public sector cannot be assessed easily. However, it is clear that
charter schools have provoked those who govern and administer public schools to
be more responsive to parent and student demands for more choice. For example,
one large urban board accommodated a number of charter school applications as
alternative programs within existing schools. Moreover, in another district, where
there are a number of charter schools, the school board has recently developed
additional programs for students who are gifted, increased services for ESL students, established a high school for the fine and performing arts, and established
a bilingual Mandarin-English school.

Since the adoption of the charter school law, there has also been an increase in
the number of private schools in the province. Traditionally, low-cost Christian
schools have characterized the independent school movement in Alberta. But
there has recently been an increase in the establishment of private schools that
cater to parents and students interested in academic excellence, preparation for
university, and more traditional approaches to teaching.

As all public schools become more responsive to community needs and as
school districts attempt to offer as much choice as the public requires, the demand for charter schools may taper off. While the Alberta government did decide
to devote more resources to the charter school program, it does not appear to be
willing to strongly advocate for a widespread system of charter schools. Both the
public and the government apparently still want to place major emphasis on the
traditional public education system. The lack of interest on the part of the government is further characterized by the fact that, in contrast to jurisdictions with

charter schools in the United States, the government has not commissioned a major assessment of the work of charter schools.

It appears that charter schools in Alberta are at a crossroads. If charter schools are to become a viable alternative within public education in Alberta, then the government has to take a more proactive role in providing the guidance and professional and administrative support necessary to ensure their success. Currently, charter schools are a wedge to leverage change in public education, rather than a dynamic alternative to the present public education system.

10 • Texas

Charter Schools and the Struggle for Equity

Lance D. Fusarelli

IN 1995, WITH THE enthusiastic support of Republican governor George W. Bush, the Texas legislature passed charter school legislation (SB 1) allowing for 20 state-approved open-enrollment charter schools and an unlimited number of district-approved campus charters. In 1997, the legislature increased the cap to 120 open-enrollment charters and unlimited additional charter schools if at least 75 percent of the students served by each additional school were at risk of dropping out. Texas had 192 charter schools in 2001, when lawmakers adopted a new cap of 215 charter schools statewide, with an exemption only for charter schools run by any of the state's thirty-five public four-year colleges and universities. The Texas charter school law is considered one of the strongest in the nation (Center for Education Reform 2001b). This chapter examines how the law is being implemented, with particular attention paid to equity issues.[1]

The Texas Charter School Law

The state board of education (SBE) approves all charters in Texas. SB 1 authorizes the SBE to grant open-enrollment charters to schools operated by a public, private, or independent institution of higher education; a nonprofit organization; a for-profit educational management company (EMC); or a governmental entity. Charters may not be granted directly to EMCs, but charter schools can contract with EMCs. Existing public and private schools can convert to charter schools in Texas. However, home-based schools may not convert to charter status. Charter schools are considered part of the public school system and must accept students regardless of where they live. A charter school may deny admission only to students who are adjudicated, who have been convicted of delinquent conduct, or who have been removed from their previous school because of disciplinary reasons. However, many charter schools are designed to work with just this type of "hard to educate" or "troubled" student.

Although open-enrollment charter schools are exempt from many state mandates, they are not exempt from regulations regarding class size, graduation, and accountability requirements or from laws related to bilingual and special education, textbooks, finance, and selected additional provisions. The SBE has the responsibility for adopting "criteria to use in selecting a program for which to grant a charter and procedures to be used for modifying, placing on probation, revoking, or denying renewal of the charter of an open-enrollment charter school" (Texas State Board of Education 1997a, 2).

Open-enrollment charter schools are the most common of the three types of charter schools permitted under state law. State law also allows school districts to apply for home-rule school *district* charters, designed to give parents and teachers more input into the delivery of education. These districts are subject to the same regulations as open-enrollment charter schools. No districts have applied for home-rule status, in large measure because the home-rule provision actually gives a district less freedom from regulation than if the district were to convert each of its schools to campus charter status, the third type of charter schools in Texas.[2]

Campus charter schools are public school conversions created by local school districts, and they receive less monitoring from the Texas Education Agency (TEA). However, campus charter schools have less independent authority from the local district than open-enrollment charter schools (which operate independently of a school district). Campus charters must give enrollment preference to district students, while open-enrollment charter schools do not have enrollment restrictions (U.S. Department of Education 1998). For a school district to convert a school to a campus charter, the parents of a majority of students and a majority of classroom teachers in the school must agree to the conversion. State law requires every district to adopt a board policy, application, and approval process for campus charters. There are no limits on the number of campus charters a district may award. In 2000–2001, 25 (13 percent) of the 192 charter schools in Texas were classified as campus charters; the remainder were classified as open-enrollment charter schools. Twenty (80 percent) of the 25 campus charter schools were in Houston.

Policy Implementation

As of January 2001, 192 charter schools were in operation throughout Texas, serving approximately 30,000 students (Kofler 2001). The number of charter schools grows every year, with some schools opening up midyear. In fall 1996, 17 charter schools opened in the state; in 1998, that number had grown to 90; a year later, 60 more schools had opened; and an additional 42 charter schools opened in fall 2000. Despite the growing popularity of charter schools in Texas, student enrollment in charter schools (30,000) represents less than 1 percent of the total student enrollment (4 million) in public schools in Texas. Similarly, the 192 charters that have been granted since 1995 represent only 3 percent of the total number of public schools (approximately 7,400) in Texas.

Demographic Characteristics

The majority of Texas charter schools are located in urban areas, and many are designed specifically to serve at-risk students. Table 10.1 contains a detailed demographic breakdown of charter school student enrollment, with a comparison to student enrollment in public schools throughout the state.

Compared with their overall enrollment in public schools, African American students are significantly overrepresented in charter schools, while their Anglo counterparts are underrepresented (see table 10.1). Approximately 38 percent of students enrolled in Texas charter schools are Hispanic, and 39 percent are African American, compared to 40 percent Hispanic and 14 percent African American in public schools (Texas Education Agency 2000a). The percentage of Anglo students enrolled in charter schools is about half the percentage of their enrollment in public schools statewide (22 percent and 43 percent, respectively). Nearly 66 percent of students enrolled in charter schools statewide are at risk of dropping out, compared to only 37 percent in traditional public schools (Charter School Resource Center of Texas 1999). On the other hand, children classified as gifted and talented are underrepresented in charter schools: only 2 percent of students enrolled in charter schools are identified as gifted and talented, compared to 8 percent statewide (Texas Education Agency 2000a).

Charter schools in Texas serve fewer numbers of special education and limited English proficient (LEP) students than public schools statewide. Only 7 percent of students enrolled in charter schools are classified as special education

Table 10.1

Student Demographics, 1999–2000

	Percentage in Charter Schools	Percentage in Traditional Public Schools
African American	39	14
Hispanic	38	40
Anglo	22	43
Other	2	3
At-Risk	66	37
Special Education	7	12
Limited English Proficient	3	13
Talented/Gifted	2	8

Sources: Charter School Resource Center of Texas 1999; Texas Education Agency 2000a

students, compared with a state average of 12 percent, and only 3 percent of students in charter schools are LEP, compared with a state average of 13 percent (Texas Education Agency 2000a). Since at least half of the charter schools in Texas are created to meet the needs of students most at risk of dropping out (a point made by advocates of charter schools), it would be expected that enrollment of special education and LEP students in charter schools in Texas would be *higher* than the statewide average. This raises serious questions of equity and social justice, particularly insofar as children labeled as "special education" or "LEP" are considered by many educators to be the children most difficult to educate. In 1999, the TEA's Department of Accountability and Accreditation conducted on-site formative evaluations of seventeen first-generation charter schools and found that only two schools had LEP programs in place—a particularly troubling statistic, since Hispanic students constitute nearly 40 percent of students enrolled in charter schools in the state (Smoot 2000).

These data raise several critical issues. Do charter schools, either explicitly or implicitly, discourage families with special education and LEP students from enrolling? Do charter school staff mislabel or fail to label students as special education and/or LEP to avoid providing the necessary services required for such students? Or are administrators and teachers in charter schools simply unaware of the identification of and requirements and accommodations for special education and LEP students? Much additional research is needed in this area to answer the serious equity questions raised by this preliminary data.

Another equity issue presented by charter schools in Texas pertains to teaching. With respect to staffing, one of the "strengths" of the Texas charter school law, depending on one's perspective, is that teachers in open-enrollment charter schools need not be certified by the state. Texas charter school students are much more likely to be taught by a noncertified teacher: 54 percent of teachers in charter schools are noncertified, compared to only 4 percent in traditional public schools. In 1999, charter school faculty had slightly lower percentages of master's and doctorate degrees (22 percent and 2 percent, respectively) than traditional public school faculty (26 percent and 4 percent, respectively) (Mabin 2000). Charter school teachers also had fewer years of teaching experience (about six), compared with an average of about twelve years for traditional public school teachers (Mabin 2000). Not surprisingly, Texas charter schools suffer from extremely high rates of staff turnover—annual staff turnover is 55 percent in charter schools, compared to 15 percent in traditional public schools (Smoot 2000). This makes it extraordinarily difficult to provide a sound, stable educational experience, particularly for at-risk students, who often lack stability outside the school environment.

On the other hand, Texas charter schools have higher percentages of minorities serving as faculty members, administrators, and board members than traditional public schools. According to 1999 data provided by the TEA, 33 percent of faculty in charter schools are African American, and 21 percent are Hispanic, compared to only 8 percent African American and 16 percent Hispanic teaching in traditional public schools statewide. Similar results are found among charter school administrators and board members. According to the TEA, in 1999, 31 percent of charter school administrators were African American, and 23 percent were Hispanic; similarly, 28 percent of charter school board members were African American, while 26 percent were Hispanic.

According to Brooks Flemister, former senior director of the TEA's division of charter schools, Texas charter schools are "mostly an urban phenomenon" (Waters 1999, 19). About forty charter schools operate in the Houston area, offering some students an alternative to the schools in the huge (235,000 students) Houston Independent School District (Waters 1999).

Operational and Educational Features

In Texas, charter schools come in all shapes and sizes—and change nearly every year as the schools add grade levels and as student enrollment grows. A review of existing schools reveals astonishing diversity in terms of size and grade levels served. Charter schools range in size from 23 students to 2,070 students, with an average enrollment of approximately 200 students (Texas Education Agency 2000b).[3] The average enrollment is misleading, however. Only six Texas charter schools have enrollments greater than 400 students, and 75 percent of the schools have enrollments of less than 250 students. This is considerably smaller than the average enrollment (638) in a traditional public school in Texas (Charter School Resource Center of Texas 1999). More than forty different grade-level configurations can be found among charter schools in Texas, with slightly more than a quarter consisting of grades 9–12.

In their first year of operation (1996–1997), Texas charter schools were characterized by low student-teacher ratios (12:1). In the second year (1997–1998), the average student-teacher ratio had increased to 16:1, about the same as the average for Texas traditional public schools, although the range among charter schools was quite broad—from a low of 4.9:1 to a high of 31:1 (Taebel et al. 1997; Texas Education Agency 1998). In the third year (1998–1999), the student-teacher ratio had climbed to 21:1 (compared to 15:1 in traditional public schools), although more than one-third of the schools had a ratio of less than 15:1 (Texas Education Agency 2000b).

The amazing diversity found among Texas charter schools in terms of size, structure, and location, coupled with a corresponding shift in the demographic composition of students, faculty, administrators, and board members, reflects an attempt to "restructure, re-engineer, and reinvent" urban education in America (Fusarelli 1999, 214). A growing number of people view the charter school movement as an opportunity to provide a more effective education to students who are ill served by the public school system as it is currently structured. When Houston Independent School District trustees approved thirteen campus charter schools to operate within the district, board president Don McAdams stated, "I think Houston is just seeing the beginning of a renaissance in education in its public schools. And I think these 13 charters are sort of the vanguard of a whole wave of creativity and innovation that is going to be coming up through the system" (Markley 1997b).

Many charter schools are taking advantage of their newfound flexibility, extending the school day and offering biweekly Saturday classes and mandatory summer school. Two charter schools were specifically designed to offer bilingual education programs, several charters have been granted to dropout-recovery high schools, some offer individualized instruction, and two provide distance-learning opportunities (Charter School Resource Center of Texas 1999). In several schools, teachers are reported to have developed their own curriculum. The most common educational practices reported are multiage grouping, mainstreaming, use of technology to enhance student learning, performance-based assessment, and project-based learning (Texas Education Agency 1998).

Oversight and Accountability

Charter schools, like other public schools, are part of the state accountability system, a system considered by many to be one of the best in the nation (Palmaffy 1998). Texas charter school founders and evaluators have a major advantage over those in other states in that a well-developed state assessment system is already in place. Charter schools are rated by the accountability system after operating for two years. They must meet the same standards as traditional public schools on the statewide test, the Texas Assessment of Academic Skills (TAAS), including the requirement that students pass the test in order to graduate (Fikac 1999; Texas Education Agency 1998).

Open-enrollment charter schools are subject to annual review by a state-appointed evaluation team. The team consists of members of two nonprofit corporations and three universities; two-thirds of the team is appointed by the SBE, one-third by the commissioner. The team interviews parents and students at the schools, monitors each school's progress, and reports annually to the SBE. Charter schools must also design their accountability programs to include more performance measures than traditional public schools, including achievement gains, nontraditional grading procedures, student products, and indices of parental and student satisfaction. Charter schools are required to submit annual reports to the TEA and the SBE (Charter School Resource Center of Texas 1998).

Seven Texas charter schools have had their charters revoked, and another ten schools have closed within the past two years (Kofler 2001; Mabin 2001; "Legislative Panel" 2000). Revocations have not been the result of low student performance or failure to meet student performance accountability requirements; rather, charters have been revoked for reasons such as inadequate fiscal accountability, including the accumulation of a large budget deficit, financial mismanagement and embezzlement, declining attendance, violation of laws relating to open meetings and records, and inaccurate student attendance record-keeping (Fikac 1999; Mabin 2001). Before the SBE decides to revoke a charter, several options are available, including placing the school on probation for the duration of its charter, unilaterally modifying the charter, lowering the school's accountability rating (a shaming type of punitive action), or the commissioner's appointment of a financial or program monitor or a special "master" to oversee the operation of the school.

Conflict has arisen over the necessity of overseeing a charter school system that serves less than 1 percent of the total public school population. According to Tom Canby, senior director of the TEA's financial audit division, "We are spending a disproportionate amount of resources on oversight of charter schools" (Eskenazi 1999, 37). There has been some dispute as to which TEA division has responsibility for oversight—whether it is the responsibility of the division of charter schools, the TEA's financial audit division, the outside review team, or a combination of these groups. During the 1999 state legislative session, the TEA requested authorization of twenty-four additional staff positions to help oversee the rapidly expanding charter school program; lawmakers approved only six additional positions (Fikac 1999). The TEA division of charter schools is woefully understaffed. As more charter schools are created, enrolling increasing numbers of students, the need for careful evaluation and assessment becomes greater than ever. In fall 2000, the House Committee on Public Education issued a report pointing out that the SBE and the TEA lack the capacity to effectively monitor charter schools. The committee further criticized the SBE for its failure to adequately screen charter applications ("Panel" 2000).

In addition to state-mandated accountability procedures, charter schools are subject to the ultimate accountability standard—parents whose children are enrolled in the charter schools. According to Allan Parker, president of the Texas Justice Foundation, "In the public school system, bad schools continue to put out students year after year. These [charter] schools have the quickest accountability in the state. . . . If parents don't like the school, they can take their kid out the next day" (Goins n.d.).

Refining the Application Process

To ensure that charters are "not just granted to anybody," the legislature and the SBE have made several changes in the application process for charter schools. The SBE uses a forty-five-member application review committee, appointed by board members and the education commissioner, to grade the written applications for charters. The application for charter status has been expanded to better assess the financial aptitude of a proposed charter holder. The new application includes a full-disclosure clause requiring applicants to list the names and contacts of board members who will receive compensation from the school. It also requires school officers to reveal any bankruptcies and the charter holders to disclose any liens against them (Eskenazi 1999).

Criminal background checks are now required of all charter school employees. Applicants are also required to disclose their intention to apply for a charter to the local community via the local newspaper. These changes reflect "lessons learned" from the earlier charter application procedures, an evolutionary process that is also occurring among charter-granting agencies in other states (Hassel and Vergari 1999).

Preliminary Performance Data

Under the TAAS system, schools are rated and classified into one of four categories —(1) exemplary, (2) recognized, (3) acceptable, and (4) low performing—based on clearly defined dropout, attendance, and TAAS percent-passing rates. In 1998, the first year for which performance data on charter schools in Texas are available, of seventeen charter schools rated, only one received the second-highest state accountability ranking of recognized; nine were judged acceptable; and seven received low-performance ratings based on test scores, dropout rates, and attendance (Fikac 1999). No charter schools were rated as exemplary in 1998. Texas accountability ratings for 1998 show that 59 percent (of seventeen) charter schools received an acceptable or higher rating, compared with 91 percent of Texas public schools overall (Texas Education Agency 1998). Nine of these seventeen charter schools enrolled a majority of at-risk students.

Charter school performance in the state's accountability system improved significantly in 1999. Of twenty schools rated, two received the state's highest rating of exemplary, and three were rated as recognized. In 2000, five schools were rated exemplary, seven were recognized, thirty-nine were judged acceptable, and twenty were rated low performing.[4] While only 59 percent (of seventeen) of charter schools in 1998 received a rating of acceptable or higher, this figure rose to 85 percent in 1999 (90 percent of traditional public schools had achieved such a rating). In 2000, 72 percent (of seventy-one) of charter schools were rated acceptable or higher, compared to 90 percent of traditional public schools. In other words, in 2000, about one in ten traditional public schools were rated as low performing, while one in four charter schools were low performing (Texas Education Agency 2000b; "Charter School Accountability Ratings" 2000).

Charter schools rated as low performing are required to develop a detailed improvement plan and receive increased attention (including site visits) from the TEA. The poor performance of charter schools under the state's accountability system has fueled critics' claims that the state has rushed too quickly in expanding charter schools beyond the twenty schools originally authorized under SB 1 ("Charter Schools Worse on TAAS" 1999).

Performance comparisons on the state TAAS test reveal significant differences between the performance of charter school and traditional public school students. Table 10.2 compares student performance according to ethnicity and economically disadvantaged status.

African American, Hispanic, and Anglo charter school students score lower on the TAAS (as measured by percentage passing all sections) than traditional public school students statewide; the performance gap ranges from 18 to 27 percent, depending on ethnicity (Texas Education Agency 2000a). Economically disadvantaged students scored 20 percent lower than similar students in traditional public schools. Overall, only 53 percent of charter school students passed all sections of the spring 2000 TAAS test, compared to 80 percent of traditional public school students.

While the data in table 10.2 suggest that charter schools are failing to match the performance of traditional public schools, it is premature to conclude that the Texas charter school experiment is a failure. Indeed, the data are somewhat misleading. What gets lost in student performance comparisons, such as table 10.2, is the vast difference in the size of the test-taking populations. Each charter school student taking the TAAS test exerts a greater impact on the percentage passing in each grade level because there are so few students taking the test, making valid comparisons with traditional public schools difficult. Also, the test-taking group is different in charter schools than in traditional public schools. Texas charter schools enroll nearly three times as many African American children (measured as a percentage of the student population) and nearly twice as many at-risk children as traditional public schools.

There are over 7,000 schools in Texas, only 192 of which are charter schools —and most charter schools have been in existence less than two years. Analyses of student performance over the last three years involve comparing a handful of

Table 10.2

Average Percentage of Students Passing TAAS (all sections), 2000

	Percentage in Charter Schools	Percentage in Traditional Public Schools
African American	41	68
Hispanic	54	72
Anglo	67	89
Economically Disadvantaged	50	70
All Students	53	80

Source: Texas Education Agency 2000a

charter schools with thousands of traditional public schools.[5] Is it realistic to expect significant gains in student performance in charter schools after only a few short years, when the vast majority of students' education has been in traditional public schools? As a result, the mixed performance of charter school students may not be indicative of low quality in the schools themselves. Senate Education Committee chair Teel Bivins, a longtime supporter of charter schools, noted: "This is a program that doesn't lend itself to instant evaluation" ("Charter Schools Worse on TAAS" 1999, 1). Because charter schools are so new, it may take years before solid, reliable school effects are reflected in student performance. As Vergari (1999, 400) observes, early student outcomes "may be more of a reflection of students' previous educational experiences than the performance of the charter school" itself.

Since nearly two-thirds of students enrolled in charter schools are at-risk, predominately low-income, minority children, a more accurate measure would be to compare student achievement in charter schools with that in traditional public schools with similar demographics. The majority of charter schools cater to students who have not done well in traditional education. TEA spokesperson Debbie Graves Ratcliffe has stated: "It's a victory that some of these kids are in school at all" (Walt 1998, A37). Some charter schools operate as dropout-recovery programs in which students need only a few credits to graduate or obtain their GED. John Turman, assistant superintendent for the New Braunfels School District near San Antonio, has stated: "The charter school[s] will provide a real education for expelled and troubled students. In the past they had nowhere to go . . . because we didn't have an alternative education program" (Sibley 1998, H9).

Not all indices of charter school student performance show poor results; some charter schools reported significant gains on the TAAS. Chase Untermeyer, SBE chair, concludes that "the world of charter schools in Texas . . . shows the full range from those doing brilliantly to those that are embarrassments and probably will be closed" (Fikac 1999). State representative Paul Sadler, House Public Education Committee chair, notes: "There's a general feeling in the Legislature that some time needs to go by so we can evaluate these programs" (Fikac 1999).

Although preliminary student performance data are not encouraging, parents and students report satisfaction with charter schools throughout the state. More than two-thirds of at-risk students attending charter schools report that the charter schools they attend offer smaller classes, more personal attention, better-quality teachers, and teachers who care more about students than the schools the students had previously attended (Texas Education Agency 1998). However, TEA data indicate that student satisfaction levels declined from 1996 to 1999. In 1996–1997, approximately 88 percent of parents and students attending charter schools for at-risk students expressed satisfaction with their schools, giving them a grade of A or B. By 1999, student satisfaction had declined to 74 percent; levels of student dissatisfaction with charter schools increased from 4.3 percent in 1996–1997 to 12.4 percent in 1998–1999. Nonetheless, over half of charter school directors reported having waiting lists in 1998 and 1999 (Texas Education Agency 2000b).

Expansion and Segregation Concerns

A major, ongoing controversy is the expansion of charter schools in Texas. The program was initially conceived as a pilot program of 20 charter schools. The original plan had wide bipartisan support (Governors Ann Richards and George Bush supported the bill). As noted, the cap was later increased to 120, with unlimited additional charters for schools serving mostly at-risk children. In 1998, in response to mixed reviews of the academic and financial performance of charter schools, the SBE recommended that the legislature grant no additional charters until the existing charter schools had proven successful (Hood 1998). However, in 1999, under political pressure, the SBE announced the creation of three new charter award cycles. A December 2000 House Committee on Public Education report criticized the SBE for granting some charters under political pressure from the Republican leadership (Kofler 2001).[6]

Several of the major teachers groups in Texas, together with many Democratic lawmakers, have expressed concerns about the continued expansion of charter schools, fearing that the reform will resegregate the public schools. John Cole, president of the Texas Federation of Teachers, stated: "We seem to be reinventing the old Jim Crow school system" (Mabin 2000, 1). Others, however, point to the demographic make-up of charter schools and assert that they serve a student population that the traditional system has largely ignored. Reflecting on the legislature's expansion of charter schools in 1997 (which created a "flexible cap"), a senior Republican state senator noted: "I think the reason we were able to expand [the cap] is that these [charter schools] were not white flight. . . . The vast majority . . . are being created to address bilingual or at-risk kids from bad socioeconomic circumstances. And the people who were originally afraid of them began to understand that . . . this may be a ticket out for some of those kids. So, I think [raising the cap was based more on] . . . the experience of what type of programs they are offering as opposed to the results or the quality. . ." (Fusarelli 1998, 66). It is too early to tell whether charter schools will resegregate the Texas public school system. However, the system is deeply segregated, to such a degree that charter schools could hardly make the situation worse (and may, in fact, lead to greater integration).

The partisan nature of the battle over charter schools heated up considerably during the 2001 legislative session. In December 2000, Republican comptroller Carole Keeton Rylander issued a series of recommendations on charter schools —recommendations in tune with the Senate Republican leadership and Republican governor Rick Perry. Rylander proposed removal of the charter cap and encouraged lawmakers to increase the number of charter authorizers (Rylander 2000). Universities, for example, would be given a small fee (perhaps 3 percent) to cover administrative overhead. In spring 2001, the Democrat-controlled House approved a bill establishing a two-year moratorium on the formation of new charter schools (Mabin 2001). House Republicans complained that the legislature was moving too quickly to undo the original charter school plan—that members were overreacting to a few well-publicized charter school failures. In the end, lawmakers gave the state education commissioner more power to oversee charter schools and to close those he found to be failing. The 2001 amendments also mandated preferential treatment for charter applications—and no caps—for charter schools to be operated by colleges and universities but set a new cap of 215 on all other charter schools (Keller 2001).

Impact on Traditional Public Schools

The third-year evaluation of Texas charter schools surveyed 271 public school superintendents with charter schools operating nearby.[7] According to 80 percent of the superintendents, local charter schools had no discernible effect on programs, policies, or practices in the public schools; 15 percent reported mild effects; and 5 percent reported moderate to strong effects (Texas Education Agency 2000b). Of those reporting effects, two-thirds described the effects as detrimental and 8 percent as beneficial. Six percent reported that the presence of the charter school had influenced the district to consider future implementation of new programs or practices. Contrary to expectations, 90 percent of superintendents surveyed reported no detrimental financial effects from charter schools. In Texas, this is likely due to several factors, including small charter school enrollment, relative to the state's total public school enrollment; the fact that many charter schools are located in urban areas, near large districts where the effects are diluted; and the continued growth of public school enrollment throughout the state, with, therefore, no net enrollment loss.

While comprehensive empirical evidence of charter school effects is lacking, anecdotal information suggests that Texas charter schools are inducing a variety of curricular and related reforms in neighboring public schools. For example, a charter school in Irving, Texas, using a rigorous International Baccalaureate (IB) curriculum, prompted the nearby public school district to initiate a similar IB pilot program. In response to a charter school adopting a challenging career and technology curriculum, the local district pushed for a new $50 million middle school explicitly patterned after the charter school's program. Moreover, several districts have initiated school uniform programs after neighboring charter schools implemented similar plans. And after a charter school created a successful exchange program with a "sister city" in Mexico, the local district announced creation of a similar program (Charter School Resource Center of Texas 1999).

Unfortunately, anecdotal evidence aside, it is too early to determine with any certainty whether the charter school challenge will encourage or force traditional public schools to modify their programs to better meet the needs of an increasingly diverse student population. Such "second-order effects" will likely take years to manifest themselves in public schools (Hassel 1999a, 4).[8] Until such effects are clearly documented, their perceived absence weakens one of the central tenets of the charter school (and school voucher) philosophy—that more choice will lead to greater competition and thus improved educational outcomes.

This question, which is critical to the long-term success of both movements, remains largely unanswered in Texas.

Charter School Finance and Support

Charter school funding continues to be controversial in Texas. Although charter schools receive the same per-pupil allotment as public schools, charter schools do not receive funding for start-up costs and facilities and cannot collect local property tax revenue. State money is supplemented only by grants, donations, and limited federal funds for start-ups. Charter schools are unable to save money to build permanent facilities, nor can they pay for facilities through voter-approved bonds.

Related to funding is the lack of technical assistance offered to charter schools. Several charter school directors complain that state auditors show up only to investigate alleged wrongdoing, not to provide advice and support. The Charter School Resource Center of Texas was created to provide technical assistance to charter schools (Markley 1997a). However, the center is a privately funded, nonprofit organization and receives no state funding. The center hosts multiple curriculum and administrative workshops across the state and, in 1998, made over 200 on-site support-service visits.[9] The twenty Educational Service Centers (ESCs) across the state have been directed to offer technical assistance to charter schools (as they do for traditional public schools), but many have resisted the additional workload—particularly given that ESC budgets have not been increased accordingly.[10] The TEA cannot by law offer technical assistance to charter schools, given its role as monitor of the schools.

Conclusion

Charter schools in Texas have progressed from the initiation phase to the implementation phase and are now entering the institutionalization phase. Competition for charters is high in Texas. After the legislature voted to increase the number of open-enrollment charter schools in 1997 by 100, approximately 700 organizations requested applications from the TEA. Many charter schools plan to expand, reflecting high demand from families.

Although charter schools are growing in popularity, the battle over their expansion, even their continued existence, is far from over. The controversies outlined in this chapter are many, and the early results from the Texas charter school "experiment" are far from conclusive. As Vergari (1999, 400) notes: "Although desirable, enthusiasm [and public support for charter schools are] insufficient indicator[s] of the overall performance of a charter school." Ultimately, charter schools must prove they can more effectively educate students, particularly those most at risk, if the movement is to thrive. Early evidence suggests that charter schools are clearly no "magic bullet" for the problems of American education.

Nor is there concrete evidence that the initial enthusiasm for charter schools will be able to sustain itself. As Sarason (1998) points out, founders of charter schools tend to underestimate greatly how difficult it is to create a school from the ground up, particularly the unanticipated conflicts that arise. Many founders, particularly teachers, parents, and community groups, are unfamiliar with the administrative details of actually running a school and are often quite unprepared and ill equipped for the demands and burdens of school administration (Hassel 1999a). Like any cause or revolution, charter schools require an *enormous* commitment of time and resources. Like all causes, such movements are difficult to sustain. It is unclear whether enough good intentions—enough "entrepreneurial spirit and dedication among school leaders"—exist to "expand charter schools into a widespread educational reform movement" (Fusarelli 1999, 222).

Another factor tempering enthusiasm for charter schools is found in the formidable political barriers that exist, making it difficult to sustain the movement. Despite initial bipartisan support, increasing opposition to charter schools is surfacing. Local teachers unions, public school administrators, and school districts in many areas are openly hostile toward charter schools, erecting multiple obstacles in the path of the reform effort and attempting to block efforts at expanding and strengthening charter school laws. One charter school founder has said, "It is as if we were creating a leper colony" (Sarason 1998, 53). This ever-present institutional resistance may, in the end, pose the greatest threat to the success and longevity of the movement.

In the conclusion of his frequently cited book on charter schools, Joe Nathan (1996, 180) asks, "Twenty years from now, will the charter movement be a chapter or a footnote in school reform?" In a similar vein, Hassel (1999a, 147) wonders whether the early momentum will "propel the charter school movement into a future of real impact." Some scholars have suggested that charter schools will usher in a new era of accountability in schools (Hassel and Vergari 1999).[11] This is unlikely to happen with charter schools in Texas, since the statewide accountability system for public schools is so well established. Perhaps charter schools will help other states to develop their accountability systems. In Texas, however, the effect, if any, may be centered on helping state policy makers to rethink and revise the alternative accountability system for nontraditional schools (such as dropout-recovery programs).

Charter schools in Texas appear to be addressing a need within the public school system—the inadequacy of traditional public schools to provide an effective and efficient education to students most at risk of dropping out. Advancing this equity argument, advocates assert that charter schools' responsiveness to the needs of at-risk students has been largely absent in the traditional public education system. Finally, someone is paying attention to the needs of at-risk, predominately minority children, telling them, "You count!" and "We care about you." Imagine: schools that actually focus on children, instead of on special interest groups and bureaucracies. However, if the charter school movement in Texas is to flourish, offering more choice within the public school system and challenging it to improve, charter school performance on the state tests must improve dramatically (and quickly). Anecdotal evidence of individual school and student success (such as winning a spelling bee) is not enough to ensure the continued existence of the movement.

A word of caution, however. If the history of school reform in the United States teaches us anything, it is that we should not underestimate the power of existing institutional and organizational arrangements and the effects of these deep, structural patterns on individual behavior (Peters 1999b; Scott 1995). As charter schools expand, adding grade levels and increasing in size, they risk losing the very features that make them unique—their small size, the greater personal attention they offer to students, and a heightened sense of community.[12] As they become institutionalized, they may evolve into something not unlike traditional public schools, perhaps serving as alternatives for "hard to educate" children. The Texas accountability system, with its heavy emphasis on measurable standards, constrains the flexibility of charter schools to innovate and will gradually force charter schools into one mold—not unlike that of traditional public schools.

Twenty years from now, it is likely that Texas charter schools will be fully incorporated into the traditional public school system, offering, in a best-case scenario, smaller, more attentive schools focused on the needs of children most at risk. The worst-case scenario is that the charter schools will be so greatly influenced by existing institutional structures and organizational processes that the status quo will win out. It is still too early to tell which of these educational futures will prevail.

11 • Charter Schools in Florida

A Work in Progress

*Tracey Bailey, Carolyn Lavely,
and Cathy Wooley-Brown*

FLORIDA'S CHARTER SCHOOL LAW was adopted in 1996, authorizing the creation of charter schools as part of the state's public education system. The original intent of the charter school legislation was to create innovative educational programming by removing the burden of excessive regulation. Since the first legislation passed, the law has been significantly amended to expand the opportunities for charter schools and to provide them with greater flexibility.

In Florida, a charter proposal can "bubble up" from many sources, such as parents, teachers, and interested individuals or groups of individuals wanting the educational choices provided by a charter school. Cities, municipalities, and other legal entities have put forth charter school proposals. Traditional public schools can also convert to charter status with 50 percent of teachers and 50 percent of voting parents supporting the conversion to charter status. Florida has been very slow to convert its traditional public schools. As of 1999–2000, fewer than 2 percent of Florida charter schools were conversions of traditional public schools. Private or parochial schools cannot convert to charter status, although some private or parochial school programs have been the impetus for a new charter school to start up and provide for all children the education that had been previously a privilege of children whose parents could afford private school tuition.

Evolution of the Florida Charter School Law

Initially, charters could be granted only by the local school district in which the charter school was expected to operate. A 1998 amendment to the law stipulated that state universities could sponsor charter schools as developmental research schools. In considering such charters, the university must consult with the district school board in the county of the proposed charter school. In all other cases, charter school organizers must submit an application to the school district in which the charter school is to be located, and the district is required to act on the application no later than sixty days after submission. Significantly, the law also established a process for the appeal of charter applications that have been denied by the local school district. In cases of denial, applicants may appeal to the state board of education. The district may fail to act in accordance with the recommendation of the state board only for good cause as specified in the charter school law.

The law limits the number of charter schools per district according to a formula based on the student population size of the district. In 1998, the caps on the number of schools in each size of district were doubled. For example, school districts with 100,000 or more students, which could previously allow up to fourteen charter schools, can now allow up to twenty-eight. There is a provision, however, that allows a school district to request an increase in the number of charter schools located within the district. In 1996–1997, when the caps were much lower, several districts asked for an extension of the caps to allow more quality charters to open.

Florida charter schools are required to organize as nonprofit corporations under IRS not-for-profit guidelines or to be operated by nonprofit corporations. The schools may be organized as either private or public employers and may participate in the state retirement system. Charter school teachers must be certified in accordance with Florida law, and charter school staff may collectively bargain as a separate unit or elect to be part of the school district's collective bargaining agreement.

In the creation of the charter school statute, the legislature sought to relieve charter schools from many of the regulatory burdens of the traditional public schools. Thus, charter schools are considered exempt from all Florida statutes with the exception of those related to civil rights, health, safety, and student welfare. Charter schools are also responsible for the provisions outlined in the Sunshine Laws related to the maintenance of academic and public records.

The Florida Education Finance Program (FEFP) and the General Appropriation Act determine revenues for charter schools. In general, charter schools are entitled to those funds that would normally be allocated for public school students. Florida charter schools are funded based on state allocations that flow through the school district to the charter school. In Florida the per-student allocation is relatively low (approximately $3,416, plus certain categorical funding). With special education students, the per-student amount increases based on the services noted in the student's individual education plan (IEP).

Given Florida's low base student allocation, many educational management companies (EMCs) have not found Florida to be attractive from a business standpoint. In order to provide the array of services needed in a charter school, the EMCs must charge a fee that is too high to make the operation of the school feasible. EMCs have, however, provided services to charter school founders who could not otherwise realize the creation of a charter school without such assistance. In the fall of 2000, approximately sixteen charter schools in Florida were working with EMCs.

During the 1997 legislative session the charter school law was amended to include several new provisions. The first provision required that in cases of rejected charter applications, local school districts provide a written articulation of the reasons for denial within ten days after the decision. A second provision prohibited school districts from imposing unreasonable rules and regulations that are contrary to the flexibility intended in Florida's charter legislation. A third provision permitted charter schools to receive, at no cost, any property deemed as surplus by the district. In addition, conversion charter schools (i.e., traditional public schools that have converted to charter status) cannot be charged a rental or leasing fee for their facilities.

The charter school law was amended again in 1998. Two of the major changes were the inclusion of municipalities as an eligible group to obtain a charter and the authorization of the creation of charter schools in the workplace. A third addition to the law was the creation of mediation services provided by the Florida Department of Education (FDE). The mediation was intended to afford a resolution to a charter school when the school district (as the sponsor) and the charter school came to an impasse on issues. Requests for mediation have been very limited, with fewer than a handful of schools requesting this service. Many charter schools conclude that since the school district is the one and only sponsor, they may "win the battle, but lose the war." The 1998 amendments also allowed for students not in residence of a district to request an interdistrict transfer. In addition, charter schools were allowed to target their enrollment to students who live within a reasonable distance from the charter school. Targeting students within close proximity to the charter schools was intended to assist charter schools that were transporting students from great distances throughout the school district.

The original law provided that the term of a charter could be only one, two, or three years. Under the amended 1998 charter law, a charter can be renewed for a period of five years. This provision is intended to enhance the ability of charter schools to secure long-term funding for facilities. In a special legislative session in the fall of 1998, capital outlay funding was the focus for all schools, to provide funds for permanent classrooms and remove the growing number of portable buildings that were surrounding many traditional public schools. Funding was provided in this session to build more permanent classrooms. However, a key outcome of this legislative session for charter schools was that they were allowed to participate in the School Infrastructure Thrift (SIT) program. This program was originally designed to reward school districts for building "thrifty" schools or for building a school for less than the state average cost per pupil, approximately $12,000–$18,000 per student depending on grade level.

As the legislation was being drafted it occurred to several legislators that perhaps this "SIT fund" should go to school districts that were serving students in charter schools, rather than to the charter schools directly, in order to build additional "thrifty classrooms or thrifty schools." In exchange, the charter school would house these children in a nondistrict facility and save the taxpayers dollars. It was decided that the school district was permitted to share SIT funds with the charter school as an incentive for the charter school to increase student capacity. This was an important day for Florida's charter schools; they finally had a funding source for capital outlay.

Participation in the SIT funds program showed how desperately charter schools needed a source of capital outlay that was dedicated to their needs and was not dependent on the "sharing" of a percentage of the SIT funds from the school districts that received those funds. Initially, some school districts shared SIT funds equitably, with a fifty-fifty split with the charter school. In other cases the school districts had their own capital needs, and even though the students at the charter school had made the funds available, only a small percentage of the funds actually went to the charter school. In 1998–1999 $44 million in SIT funds flowed to school districts for having children in charter schools (OPPAGA 2000, 3). Of this amount, the school districts reported providing $16 million to the charter schools. Subsequent legislation passed in 1999 allocating capital outlay dollars directly to charter schools through another capital fund. Charter schools would now be eligible on an annual basis for capital outlay dollars. These funds would be dispersed under the requirement that any unencumbered funds from capital outlay provided by the district would revert to the school district in the event that the charter school ceased operation.

Another amendment, effective since July 1999, provided that charters could be renewed for up to fifteen years for those schools that demonstrated exemplary

academic performance and fiscal management. In Florida, the fifteen-year charter
was established to facilitate long-term financing for charter school construction.
The school must annually submit to its sponsor or the school district its audited
financial records, its progress toward meeting the goals in the charter, employee
salary levels, and other data collected on all public schools. Even though the
charter school may have obtained a fifteen-year charter, the reasons for a charter
school being terminated are identical to the reasons for nonrenewal at the end of
the term of the charter. By the fall of 2000, six charter schools had received contract renewals for fifteen years.

Policy Implementation

Only a few months after passage of the charter school law in 1996, five charters
were granted by five different Florida school districts, from the Florida panhandle to Miami-Dade. This first approval process was extremely difficult for districts, due to the short period of time between the passage of the legislation and
the submission of applications. Indeed, several of the school districts involved
had few or no policies in place for processing applications. Subsequently, the
FDE, in conjunction with local school districts, developed a template for charter
school applications. This template is based on the legislation and delineates various essential components of a charter school proposal. This effort has helped to
standardize the charter school application process in Florida, as the vast majority of school districts still use this template as the foundation for their application
requirements.

Since the founding of the first five charter schools in 1996, the number of
schools has grown at a rapid pace. By the end of 1997, a little over a year after the
legislation passed, a total of 33 charter schools were in operation in Florida. By
1998, there were 75 charter schools in operation, and the number increased to 112
charter schools open in the fall of 1999. The number of Florida charter schools
grew to 149 in 2000–2001, with 96 more applications approved for 2001–2002.
During fall 2000, charter schools enrolled over 27,000 students in Florida (Florida
Department of Education 2000).

While legislators debated charter school legislation, some members voiced
concerns that charter schools would become White, upper-class, elitist schools
and leave behind the most difficult to educate students in the traditional public
schools. These concerns have proven to be incorrect. For example, 38 percent of

the students enrolled in Florida charter schools in 1999 were African American. This is similar to the state's overall percentage of African American students. In addition, 48 percent of the charter schools in operation in 1999 targeted special needs populations, including "at-risk" students, "exceptional" students, and those with other nontraditional educational needs (Florida Department of Education 2000).

One of the most challenging aspects of the implementation of charter school policy has been the varying interpretation of the legislation by local school districts. As with any new idea, there is a learning curve. For charter schools and local school districts, the learning curve has been extremely steep. Initially, district staff often were not typically provided with concrete policies to guide them when confronted with various charter school issues. This was partly due to the fact that administrators could not predict what the dilemmas and controversies were likely to be until the schools were actually open and issues had arisen.

Clearly, the school districts have significantly affected the implementation of charter school policy. In some school districts, administrators have conveyed that charter schools (which they did not support) should conform to traditional "in the box" operating procedures. However, this was in direct conflict with two fundamental principles of charter schools: innovation and deregulation. Thus, a great deal of effort on the part of both districts and charter schools has been necessary in order to develop and implement policies that satisfy district requirements while maintaining the unique visions of the charter schools.

Unfortunately, the implementation process in Florida has not yet evolved to the point at which charter schools and districts all have positive, interactive relationships. In some school districts, staff are still resentful of charter schools, and this resentment has made it difficult for charter schools to interact effectively with the districts. Such tensions have occurred with both brand-new charter schools and traditional public schools that have converted to charter status. Moreover, just when districts were getting used to "start-up" charter schools, they were confronted with conversion charter schools, which forced them to reexamine their policies. In some school districts, conversion charter schools in particular are perceived as troublemaking defectors from a cherished public school tradition. The conversion charter schools have opted to remain public employers and lease staff from the school districts. They do not benefit from capital outlay funds or SIT funds, since they have buildings and furniture. They are, as some charter school advocates say, "only half out of the box."

While there are some situations in which policy implementation at the local level is still in transition, it is important to note that state-level policy has continuously reflected and reinforced the original intent of the charter school law. As noted earlier, the twin pillars of Florida's charter law are innovation and deregulation.

"Being Accountable"

The price that the charter schools pay for the flexibility to operate free from excessive regulation is increased accountability. Nathan (1999, 172–73) observes: "All across the country, educators are stepping forward who are willing to be held responsible for improving student achievement. . . . Opponents questioned whether educators would be willing to put their jobs at risk, basing them on whether student achievement improved. Five years later, we know the answer. Yes, teachers all over the country are coming forward." Charter schools are accountable to their local school districts and, most importantly, to their students and families. They are held accountable for fiscal management and for the academic progress, health, safety, and welfare of their students.

Similar to the charter school laws in other states, fiscal accountability is perhaps the most clearly specified accountability item in the Florida law. Charter schools are responsible for providing fiscal management within the guidelines established by governmental accounting standards for nonprofit corporations. Many school district offices receive summaries of charter school revenues and expenditures. This allows the districts to monitor the use of public funds by charter schools and hold them accountable for their fiscal management practices. Each year a charter school is required to obtain an independent financial audit that reviews the procedures and expenditures of the school for the past year. Copies of the independent audit are provided to the chartering school district and the FDE. Charter schools must also provide a written statement specifying a corrective-action plan that addresses any issues raised in the audit. It is then the responsibility of the district to monitor compliance with the corrective-action plan.

The process for determining academic accountability and student progress is mandated in a 1999 amendment to the charter school law. It is the responsibility of each school district and each charter school to agree on the standards of performance for students in the charter school. These standards are part of the original charter application and the actual contract (charter). Failure to achieve the standards set forth in the charter provides grounds for the school district to revoke the charter.

All charter school students are required to participate in the statewide high-stakes test, the Florida Comprehensive Assessment Test (FCAT). Charter school test results are reported to the FDE along with the local school district's figures. The test results are also used in part to "grade" the charter schools in the same manner in which traditional Florida public schools are now graded. Schools with student populations of less than thirty students per grade are exempt from the grading system but not exempt from participation in statewide testing. In addition, public schools that target special populations, such as schools that focus on exceptional student education and alternative education, do not participate in the grading program.

Many charter schools have expressed concerns over the use of standardized testing as a means to gauge charter school efficacy. For example, a student who enrolls in a charter school the day before the statewide testing program would be required to participate in the testing at the charter school. What would be reflected in the student's test score, however, would not be the progress the student has made at the charter school but the achievement of the previous school. As many of the initial charter schools in Florida tended to be small, grassroots schools, most districts required an additional measurement of student progress beyond statewide tests. In many of the smaller charter schools, as few as three students may have been tested under the statewide system. Districts thus did not think such results provided an adequate or accurate picture of the entire academic performance at the charter school. Accordingly, the school district and charter school have typically agreed that student performance will be judged according to data from standardized tests that the charter school administers to students at the beginning of the school year and again at the close of each year.

As is noted earlier, many of the charter schools in Florida are aimed at serving specific student populations. The charters for these schools therefore specify accountability in line with the specific programs of the schools. For example, a school that targets students "at risk of dropping out of school" may use additional indicators of student progress, such as attendance data and discipline records.

One of the key challenges surrounding academic accountability has arisen from the inability of charter schools and school districts to agree on the level of student achievement to be attained. Many charter schools have questioned why they should have to achieve higher rates of student progress than the traditional public schools. In addition, some of the original charters did not contain specific measurable indicators of student achievement. These factors have made it difficult for district staff to monitor compliance and to hold charter schools accountable for student performance. In order to receive approval of their charters, some founders have set their goals so high that they are unable to achieve the goals specified in the charters.

Charter schools are held to a higher academic standard than traditional public schools. If they do not achieve their goals, they can be closed. Traditional public schools have not been subjected to such a threat. Several charter schools have not been renewed or have been closed based partially on academic accountability and the way their goals were specified. Often a charter school applicant will set a reasonable academic goal given a "typical" student population; then, as students enroll, the charter school operators realize they are running a school in which the student population is far from "typical." Many charter schools, as well as traditional public schools, are advocating a "value-added" approach to academic accountability that entails a "pretest" administered when students first enter the charter school and a "posttest" to gauge what they have learned while enrolled at the school.

In the 1999 charter legislation, in an attempt to clarify academic accountability, three components were added that new organizers would address in their charter proposals: (1) determining the baseline of student achievement and prior rate of academic progress; (2) determining how these baselines and academic progress rates will be compared to the rates while the student is at the charter school; and (3) comparing these rates, to the extent possible, to those of comparable student populations in traditional public schools. This was an effort to help charter organizers to address up front an accountability issue that might otherwise come back to "bite" them during the charter-renewal process. Charter schools in Florida need to specify more clearly measurable academic goals that are realistic and obtainable.

When the mass media report standardized test scores, which are not necessarily adequate or accurate indicators of charter school performance, there is potential for gross misinterpretation. Moreover, many small charter schools target populations so specific that there is no traditional public school counterpart to use as a basis of comparison. In addition, where charter schools outperform local district schools, the mass media might compare school districts unfavorably with charter schools. When reviewing test-score data, it is important to always consider that the traditional public school generally deals with a much more diverse population of students than the typical charter school. It is thus worth questioning whether the two entities should be compared using the statewide testing program as the ruler.

Charter schools report annually on fiscal management and academic accountability to the chartering entity—the school district. These annual reports, in combination with the financial audits, become the basis for charter renewal. Many charter schools have developed multifaceted annual reports with graphs and photographs that display their accomplishments and their progress toward achieving the goals specified in their charters. The reports include information on fiscal expenditures, student enrollment, policy changes, facility issues, and the qualifications of charter school staff. Copies of the annual report are forwarded to the FDE, which provides a data template for charter schools to use as a model to make certain that all required data is included.

Controversies

Disputes pertaining to funding, the chartering process, and transportation are among the many controversies that have emanated from the charter school movement in Florida.

Funding

Charter schools, like school districts, cannot operate without revenue. Until 1998, there was no provision in the Florida charter school law for the ongoing provision of capital outlay dollars. Moreover, the provision that was put in place did not provide charter schools with the same level of funding as the school districts received. This has been a serious and politically contentious issue since the inception of the first charter schools. Charter school students should be entitled to attend school in facilities equal to their traditional school counterparts. Lack of capital outlay funding has forced some charter schools to operate in what the districts consider to be substandard facilities. In addition, charter school operators have questioned the fact that local school districts have been able to obtain some capital outlay dollars for students who are served in charter school facilities. School districts continue to earn some types of capital funding based on *all* children in a school district—even those in charter schools. Capital outlay funds do not "follow" the students, as operational funds do in Florida. The charter schools are eligible for a smaller amount of capital funding, as is discussed earlier. The districts have maintained that charter schools do not "draw off" a significant number of students from any one given school to make it possible to reduce the number of needed classrooms and that they have not been located in areas that would prevent the school district from needing to build new schools.

The Chartering Process

In Florida there is only one entity that authorizes nearly all charter schools, the local school district. Universities can sponsor their own "lab" schools (also called "developmental research schools"), but they are not authorizing entities for other charter schools. Concerns have arisen over the fact that charters are granted by the very entities that they allegedly "compete" with, and charter school supporters have advanced proposals for alternative chartering agencies. One charter school founder likened such a state of affairs to McDonald's sponsoring Burger King. One recommendation regarding a change in chartering entities would be to allow school districts to grant charters outside their geographical boundaries. An even more significant change in the chartering process would be to allow state universities and community colleges to grant charters. The University of South Florida had its charter school approved by the local school district because the charter school is not a developmental research school but a school for at-risk students in a neighborhood near the university. And in Michigan, for example, local districts are permitted to grant charters, but universities have authorized the overwhelming number of charter schools. Some advocates of this proposal suggest that expanding the pool of eligible authorizers would give charter schools some flexibility in negotiating administrative fees (as is discussed later in the chapter).

Expanding the pool of authorizers would also allow charter schools to have more autonomy from the local school district. This would enable charter school operators to avoid the tensions that occur when innovation and "out of the box" ideas meet the bureaucracy of school districts. Since the charter school would not be perceived as a "competitor" of universities and community colleges, a more positive working relationship between the authorizer and the school could be established, and high student achievement would be the primary goal for all involved.

The administrative fees charged to the charter schools by school districts have also been a matter of controversy. Initially, the school district was permitted to charge a service fee for administrative services, and the fee's actual cost could not exceed 5 percent. This was later amended to a flat 5 percent fee charged for basic administrative services. School districts argued that their costs exceeded the 5 percent fee, thus draining school district resources. However, districts are still permitted to charge charter schools for services beyond the scope of basic administration, and disputes have arisen over precisely what services are included in the 5 percent district administrative fee. Each school district in part determines what is included in the scope of basic services. For example, in one Florida school district, intradistrict daily mail service to a conversion school was terminated. The district position was that this service did not fall within the realm of services covered by the 5 percent administrative fee. In other districts, however, intradistrict daily mail service *is* covered by the administrative fee. While this may seem like a small technical matter, the service in question is essential and highlights the disparities that can arise due to differing interpretations of rules and regulations by school districts.

The larger the budget for the charter school, the more the district recovers from the 5 percent fee. Many charter schools argue that they do not get the level of service that their 5 percent fee represents. Conversion schools particularly have difficulty with this issue. One question analysts have asked is how much the services would be worth in a free market. One district justified some of the nearly $200,000 administrative fee it charged to a charter school by explaining that it issued the payroll for the charter school's teachers. It was not until the charter school had obtained bids from payroll service providers that the district realized that perhaps this service was not as costly as the district had alleged.

Transportation

The law requires charter schools to provide transportation consistent with the requirements of traditional public schools. For many charter schools, the best option for transportation has been to contract with the local school district for transportation. In certain districts, the cost of transportation exceeds the state funding allocation for transportation. In such cases, the charter school is required to reimburse the district for any difference in cost. The reverse, however, has not always been true. In cases in which the district has been able to provide transportation for less than the allotted funds, the surplus has not been returned to the charter school. In addition, the concern exists that the districts will not necessarily seek out the most efficient transportation routes if they know they can gain additional revenue from the charter schools. In Florida, funding for transportation is based on the percentage of students transported in a school district. This amount is adjusted to account for rural bus occupancy and cost of living.

Charter school students are often placed on buses after other public school bus routes are established. A charter school has paid for a sixty-passenger school bus to go out empty with a driver and bus attendant to pick up one or two students and then bring children thirty miles or more to a charter school. In some districts, a more cost-efficient method has been used, in which students ride to their "home" school, or traditional zoned public school, and the charter school then pays for shuttle service from the home school to the charter school.

The Status of Charter Schools in Florida

Without students, charter schools cannot generate revenue to operate. Many believe that the charter school "experiment" is too new to be assessed adequately and accurately. Indeed, even the four-year national study of charter schools, sponsored by the U.S. Department of Education, did not yield conclusive findings on the implications of the charter school movement for student achievement (RPP International 2000). Some argue that it takes at least five years to determine the effectiveness of a new charter school. Since the oldest charter schools in Florida have been in operation for only five years and there are only five such schools, it will take more time to accurately rate the quality of charter schools overall in Florida. As of the fall of 2000, there had been nine charter school closures or nonrenewals in Florida for a variety of reasons: finances, governance, declining enrollment, and failure to demonstrate academic accountability.

There have, however, been several notable success stories among Florida's charter schools.

- Seaside Academy, one of Florida's first charter schools, received a rating of B+ in the state's new grading system. This is a small middle school in the Florida panhandle. To achieve a B rating the school met the following criteria: current-year reading, writing, *and* math data were at or above high-performing criteria; no subgroup data were *below* minimum criteria; and at least 90 percent of students engaged in a standard curriculum were tested.

- McKeel Academy, Florida's first conversion school, received a rating of A in the grading system. McKeel achieved all the indicators of Seaside. In addition, it met the following criteria: the percentage of students absent more than twenty days, the percentage suspended, and the dropout rate (for high schools) were *below* state averages; students showed substantial improvement in reading; students showed no substantial decline in writing or math; and at least 95 percent of students engaged in a standard curriculum were tested. Significantly, McKeel went from being the poorest-performing school in the district to being one of the highest-achieving schools.

- The Child Development Center was the first charter school in the state to offer educational services to students from birth through age six who were developmentally delayed or at risk for developmental delays. In Florida, like other states, beginning educational services at birth are not mandated and therefore are often left to social service agencies. The Child Development Center provides these services so that developmentally delayed children do not fall between the cracks as agencies transition from programs for two-year-olds to preschools for three-year-olds.

- The University of South Florida (USF) created the first public university–based charter school in the country. The USF Charter School serves at-risk students from a poverty-ridden neighborhood that borders the university. This neighborhood is often called "suitcase city" because of the transient nature of its population. The university, acting as a "good neighbor" to this community, aims to provide a stable school that will give the kindergarteners through third graders an enriched start to their school career. Prior to the opening of the charter school, many of the children from "suitcase city" would be enrolled in school after school as their parents or guardians relocated within the neighborhood. The charter school offers this population of students a stable school that they can attend regardless of where they move, as well as small classes and a diagnostic approach to education.

Overall, it appears that Florida charter schools are providing quality educational services to their students. Charter schools that fail to provide such services lose students and therefore are unable to maintain sufficient revenue to remain in operation. Over 70 percent of the charter schools in Florida have waiting lists. Many charter schools have families that drive students across the district—sometimes over twenty miles—to a particular school so that children may attend a school with a unique program.[1] Finn, Manno, and Vanourek (2000, 71–72) note that "charter accountability is dual: to the customers (families) and to the authority that sponsors the school. The charter approach does not mean blind faith in the invisible hand. While market forces are necessary, they may not be sufficient to assure quality. Neither is the charter strategy an example of 'privatization.' The public retains an interest in the successful delivery of education services paid for by public funds."

One of the fundamental theories of charter schools is that they will create a free market economy that will force change in the traditional public school system. The question then becomes whether the charter school movement has indeed provoked such change. Thus far, on the surface, the movement does not appear to have caused overwhelming change in the overall public education system in Florida. The attitude in many of the school districts is one of "wait and see" if the "experiment" succeeds or fails. School district administrators often perceive charter schools as entities outside their realm of operation and do not see them as a catalyst for change. Some school districts see charter schools as helping with their growing student populations. In other districts, charters are viewed as a place to serve small segments of the population that may get lost in the thousands of children whose needs must be addressed. Still other school districts view charter schools as the outsiders, doomed to failure.

In the fall of 2000, 149 charter schools were in operation in Florida, and there were 95 additional charter schools approved to open in fall 2001. The increase in charter schools is concentrated in high-growth areas such as Central Florida and the southeast coast. A Manhattan Institute study has shown that in general, charter schools have not "induced large changes in district wide operations" (Teske et al. 2000, 3). Looking beyond the surface in Florida, however, we can identify some clear indicators that, in some cases, charter schools are serving as catalysts for change in the traditional school system. The success of Seaside Charter Middle School prompted the local school district to build a middle school in an area that they had previously determined to be too sparsely populated for such a school. In several other regions, a popular charter school has prompted the local school district to enhance its educational programs by adding instruction in technology or foreign languages or thematic instruction in order to compete for students.

Overall, it is abundantly clear that charter schools have had an impact on public education in Florida. In 1999, charter school students in Florida made up .01 percent of Florida's public school students. During fall 2000, there were over 27,000 students enrolled in charter schools in the state, with thousands of children on charter school waiting lists. This has focused national attention on the Florida charter school movement.

So what are the specific impacts that charter schools have made on the educational system in Florida? First and foremost, they have brought choice to parents for whom there were previously no feasible choices available other than the public school to which their child was assigned. Parents have become empowered to take control of the types of educational services that their children receive, regardless of socioeconomic status.

Second, charter schools have provided students with a greater variety of educational programming. Parents in Florida can choose from traditional "back-to-basics" schools, schools that emphasize technology, or less structured "progressive" schools. This range of curricular offerings allows students to participate in educational settings that are most suited to their particular learning styles.

Third, in some cases, charter schools have provided a wide variety of services that local school districts could never provide. It is simply unrealistic to expect that a local school district with a student population in the range of 100,000 children would be able to meet the needs of every single student effectively and efficiently. Charter schools have provided school districts with varied programs and services that previously could not be delivered to targeted groups such as children who are at risk of academic failure and some children with special needs. This combination of factors suggests that the charter school movement in Florida will continue to grow stronger. A committed constituency of parents and educators, bipartisan support in the legislature, and the leadership of a reform-minded governor are likely to ensure that charter schools will be an enduring aspect of the educational landscape in Florida.

12 • Charter Schools in North Carolina

Confronting the Challenges of Rapid Growth

Michelle Godard McNiff and Bryan C. Hassel

WHILE INITIALLY RELUCTANT to enter the growing charter school movement, North Carolina legislators adopted a charter school law in 1996 allowing for three types of charter authorizers, noncertified staff, and guaranteed full operational funding. The North Carolina charter school law is typically rated toward the "permissive" or "strong" end of the continuum (Center for Education Reform 2001a). The state's law has allowed for rapid charter school growth. By May 2001 there were ninety-two charter schools in operation, the sixth-largest number of charter schools in the United States. Among these schools were some of the state's top performers, some very innovative school designs, and a host of options for at-risk children.

However, the sudden emergence of such a large number of charter schools has presented unique challenges to the schools, the school districts, and the state agencies charged with oversight. From academic achievement to fiscal soundness, questions have arisen about the capacity of many of North Carolina's charter schools to provide effective public school options for the state's children. After surveying the state's charter school law, its charter schools, and their student populations, we turn our attention to some of those questions.

Bipartisan Compromise Yields a Strong Law

Charter school legislation in North Carolina came about due to the surprising bipartisan leadership of a liberal Senate Democrat and a conservative House Republican. Believing that charter schools could be a vehicle to increase parental, student, and educator choice, Senator Wilbur Gulley (D) and Representative Steve Wood (R) became effective allies, working together toward the passage of charter legislation. Such legislation was first introduced in 1995 by Wood, as a "carrot offered along with the stick of a tuition tax credit bill" (S. Wood 1999).

The charter school bills first introduced in the House and Senate were strikingly different. House Bill 955 allowed for several charter authorizers (the state board of education [SBE], a local board of education, a board of county commissioners, a community college board of trustees, a University of North Carolina board of trustees, or a town or city council). Senate Bill 940 required applicants first to submit their applications to local boards of education and held the SBE responsible for final approval. HB 955 permitted an unlimited number of charter schools, while SB 940 allowed only three charter schools per school district and required that at least fifteen of the forty schools statewide during the first two years focus solely on at-risk students. SB 940 alone required local districts to relinquish current expense appropriations for each student who transferred to a charter school. SB 940 restricted state funds from being used to purchase buildings or land and required all charter school faculty to hold a state license; HB 955 contained no such restrictions.

HB 955 received strong publicity and support from school choice advocates such as Vernon Robinson, an education reform advocate and lobbyist and unsuccessful candidate for state superintendent of public schools. SB 940 was supported by the business and education communities. A coalition of the state's business leaders; chamber of commerce executives; the state school boards association; the state administrators association; and the Public School Forum, an education policy and research organization, publicly supported SB 940. As opponents of tax credits and vouchers, they viewed the bill as a stopgap measure to other school choice options (Norris 1999).

The tuition tax credit bill was killed. The education committees ironed out differences in the two charter school bills, and on 21 June 1996 the state legislature ratified HB 955 (the Charter Schools Act of 1996), which permitted up to 100 charter schools (with a limit of 5 schools chartered per school district each year).[1]

The official purposes of the charter school law were to improve student learning, encourage creative teaching methods, provide increased choice and learning opportunities, and create new professional opportunities for educators (NCGS 115-238.29A). Informally, some advocates hoped that the charter school experiment could lead to deregulation of North Carolina's other public schools, serve as a laboratory for innovative educational programs, and create competitive pressure on existing public schools to improve.

An application to operate a North Carolina charter school must be made by a private nonprofit corporation. In addition, applications to convert an existing public school to a charter school must include evidence that a significant number of parents with children in the school favor conversion and a statement of support signed by the majority of the faculty.

Charter schools may be granted preliminary approval by one of three charter authorizers: the board of trustees of a campus of the North Carolina university system, a local board of education, or the North Carolina SBE. However, the SBE approves all charters. If a local district or university rejects a charter application, the applicant may appeal directly to the SBE, which can overturn the local or university decision.

North Carolina charter schools are free from many public school state statutes and regulations. However, charter schools must meet the same health and safety standards as other public schools, must be nonsectarian in all practices, and cannot be affiliated with a sectarian school or religious institution. Charter schools must also provide instruction for at least 180 days per year, meet or exceed SBE student performance standards, conduct state assessments, and comply with state policies for students with special needs. Employees are under contract with the charter school's board of directors and are not considered employees of the local school district. If teachers with career status receive leaves of absence, they may return to the local school district with their tenure intact.

Except as provided by law or the mission of the school as spelled out in the charter, admission cannot be limited on the basis of "intellectual ability, measures of achievement or aptitude, athletic ability, disability, race, creed, gender, national origin, religion, or ancestry" (NCGS 115-238.29F(g)(5)). Preference may be given only to siblings of students who are currently enrolled in the school and to the children of charter school staff members. If the number of applicants exceeds available seats, students are accepted by lottery.

The North Carolina charter school law requires that a charter school receive the same state operating allocations per pupil as received by other public schools in the district. Additional state dollars must be given for special needs children and those whose first language is not English. School districts are required to remit to charter schools a per-pupil share of their current expense appropriations for each child who transfers from a regular public school to a charter school. Significantly, districts are not required to share capital expense appropriations. Charter schools must either lease buildings with state funds or purchase land and buildings through nonstate sources. By law, state funds cannot be used for purchase of property or buildings, nor can counties—the traditional source of financing for school facilities in North Carolina—provide charter schools with funding for capital projects.

The charter term is five years. Statutory reasons for charter nonrenewal or revocation include failure to meet student performance requirements noted in the charter; failure to meet fiscal management standards; violation of state or federal law; and abrogation of conditions, standards, or procedures set forth in the charter. The SBE may also close the school if two-thirds of the faculty at the school request it or for "any other good cause" (NCGS 115-238.29G).

There have been few changes in the North Carolina charter school law. A 1998 amendment allowed charter school boards of directors to make a one-time decision to enroll their staff in the state retirement and health plans. While the decision applies to all teachers within the school, individual teachers at schools that opt out of the system may "purchase" credit in the retirement system. For the 1997-1998, 1998-1999, and 1999-2000 school years, the legislature empowered the SBE to reimburse school districts with fewer than 3,000 students that lost more than 4 percent of enrollment to charter schools. Through early 2001, the SBE had invoked this amendment in only one case—when a public elementary school in a small county converted to a charter school, drawing away more than 10 percent of the district's student population.[2] Other amendments include allowing charter schools to set aside seats for founders' children. In May 2001, a bill to create charter school districts was under consideration by the state legislature. Earlier in the 2001 session, bills to remove or raise the cap on charter schools had failed.

Diverse Approaches for a Diverse Student Population

North Carolina's charter school law limits the number of charter schools to 100. A total of 97 charter schools were expected to be in operation in 2001-2002; 2 additional charters had been approved but planned to delay their openings until fall 2003 (see table 12.1, note a). While charter schools are located throughout the state, over 25 percent of those operating in 2001 were in the central Research Triangle area (which includes Raleigh—the state capital—and the university communities of Durham and Chapel Hill).

The majority of North Carolina's charters are new "start-ups." Of the charter schools operating or approved in 2001, seventeen were private school conversions and only two were public school conversions. Charter schools may contract with for-profit educational management companies (EMCs). In 2000–2001, eight charter schools were associated with two EMCs—National Heritage Academies and Advantage Schools.[3] While both of these EMCs have headquarters out of state, the charter movement has also spawned some homegrown entrepreneurship. Several North Carolina–based firms offer financial management services to charter schools, including data entry into the state's financial and student information management system.

North Carolina's charter schools offer extremely diverse approaches to education, ranging from "back-to-basics" to "progressive" and from Montessori to Direct Instruction. There are some strikingly innovative institutions, including a charter school in a juvenile detention facility that allows incarcerated youth to obtain high school credit and a school based within a pioneering science museum. The most common shared characteristic is their small size. Of the charter schools operating in 2000–2001, the median enrollment was 129 students. The smallest charter school served 15 at-risk K–12 students with developmental challenges.[4] The largest charter school served over 700 children in 2000–2001. Table 12.1 provides a snapshot of the characteristics of North Carolina charter schools.

The charter school population in North Carolina does not mirror the general public school population. Rather, charter school students are more likely to be Black, male, and participating in free or reduced-price lunch programs. In 1996–1997, the inaugural year of charter schools, the White proportion of the general public school population was approximately 62 percent; in charter schools, it was 47.4 percent. Nearly one-half (49.9 percent) of the charter school students were Black, and 3.5 percent were members of other minority groups. By 2000–2001, the White proportion in charter schools had increased to 52.6 percent. (The White population in all public schools was approximately 61 percent.) However, the range varied from school to school, from 0 to 100 percent White. As indicated in table 12.2, the 2000–2001 proportion of White students in North Carolina's charter schools was slightly higher than the 1998–1999 national charter school average (RPP International 2000, 30). Of the nineteen charter schools reporting free and reduced-price lunch data in December 1997, fourteen had a greater percentage of needy students than the state average.

Nearly 10 percent of charter school students in North Carolina are labeled as "exceptional," the state's term for students with special needs. Children in the

Table 12.1

North Carolina Charter Schools at a Glance

Number of Charter Schools, Spring 2001	
Number of Charter Schools in Operation	92[a]
Number of Approved Schools	100[a]
Types of Charter Schools in Operation, 2000–2001	
Start-Ups	81
Private School Conversions	17
Public School Conversions	2
Size of Charter Schools	
Average Size, 2000–2001	172
Median Size, 2000–2001	129
Maximum Size, 2000–2001	746
Minimum Size, 2000–2001	15
Student Demographics	
Male Students, 2000–2001	52.2%
Female Students, 2000–2001	47.8%
White Students, 2000–2001	52.6%
Black Students, 2000–2001	43.2%
Hispanic Students, 2000–2001	1.8%
American Indian Students, 2000–2001	1.4%
Asian Students, 2000–2001	1.1%
Students Identified as "Exceptional Children," 1997–1998	9.3%
Students Identified as "Academically Gifted," 1997–1998	2.5%
Students Participating in Free/Reduced Lunch Program, 1997–1998	49.1%

[a] One of the 92 charters operating in spring 2001, LIFT Academy, had its charter revoked by the North Carolina SBE in December 1999 due to financial mismanagement. School officials sued the board on the grounds that it did not receive due process; therefore, the school continued to operate with state funds under a temporary restraining order until summer 2001, when the revocation was made final.

exceptional category range from academically gifted to severely handicapped. Charter schools appear to be serving the same percentage of emotionally handicapped and specific learning disabled students as the state's public schools. However, they may also be serving fewer "educable mentally handicapped" students and a smaller percentage of students who are formally identified as "academically gifted" (North Carolina State Board of Education 1998, 25).[5]

Table 12.2

North Carolina Charter School Students Compared to State Public School, National Charter School, and Public School Averages

	North Carolina Charter Schools	All North Carolina Public Schools	All U.S. Charter Schools	All U.S. Public Schools
Percentage of White Students	52.6[a]	60.9[a]	48.2[c]	59[d]
Percentage of Students Participating in Free/Reduced Lunch Program	49.1[d]	39.6[d]	38.7[c]	37.6[e]
Percentage of Students Who Are "Exceptional"	9.3[d]	11.5[d]	8.4[c]	11.3[d]
Median Size of School	129[a]	568[b]	132[c]	486[d]

Sources: Child Nutrition Section, North Carolina Office of Charter Schools; Statistical Research Section, North Carolina Department of Public Instruction; RPP International 2000

[a] Data from 2000–2001

[b] Data from 1999–2000

[c] Data from 1998–1999

[d] Data from 1997–1998

[e] Data from 1994–1995

The State Grapples with a New Kind of Public School

This section describes six aspects of oversight and accountability in North Carolina: the state role, authorization trends, fiscal oversight, academic accountability, exceptional children compliance, and program evaluation.

The State Role

The SBE provides the primary oversight of the charter school program in North Carolina. In addition to final approval of charters, the SBE is statutorily responsible for ensuring that charter schools are accountable and meet the terms of their charters. The SBE also makes decisions about charter renewal and revocation. The SBE does not have to go it alone, however—the charter school law allows for the establishment of an independent committee to provide the SBE with recommendations about charter approval, renewal, and revocation, as well as to provide technical assistance to chartering entities or charter applicants. The Charter School Advisory Committee—an appointed group of charter school directors, private and public school officials, businesspeople, and parents—meets monthly in open session.

The state's charter school program is administered by the Office of Charter Schools in the Department of Public Instruction (DPI). The Office of Charter Schools and other DPI staff provide technical assistance to applicants and to operating schools. The demands of charter schools on DPI staff have been surprising to agency leadership. Initially, only three staff members were allocated to the Office of Charter Schools to work full time with the first group of charter schools. Because charter schools essentially are treated as independent school districts with separate financial accounts, DPI staff beyond the Office of Charter Schools were increasingly pressed to provide the services required by the new schools. In 1998, the DPI spent over $500,000 in personnel costs to provide services to charter schools.[6]

The DPI began tracking the amount of time spent by other agency staff on charter school issues (e.g., financial services, curriculum sections, testing and accountability sections, exceptional children services, and student information management systems) and determined that more than ten full-time staff members were needed to address the increasing demand of the growing program. The largest impact of charter schools on staff outside the Office of Charter Schools was in the financial and technology service areas to which DPI staff devoted at least 12,193 hours in one year (North Carolina State Board of Education 1998, 4). Additional funds were granted by the legislature in 1999, and by early 2000, the equivalent of ten full-time DPI staff members were working on charter school issues.

Trends in Authorization

The pattern of charter authorization in North Carolina changed dramatically between 1996 and 1999. First, applicants grew less likely to approach local boards for preliminary approval. In the inaugural year, forty-seven out of sixty-five charter school proposals (72 percent) were submitted initially to local boards of education. The trend shifted in 1997, as more applicants bypassed the local board and submitted proposals directly to the SBE—only 33 percent sought local approval. The percentage dropped again in 1998, to 28 percent, and plummeted to 6 percent in 1999. This change appears to represent rational calculation on the part of charter school applicants. All proposals must be approved by the SBE in any case, so approaching the SBE directly in effect saves a step—especially since the SBE has proven unwilling to rubber-stamp local decisions. As of 2001, the

SBE had heard twenty-one appeals from applicants whose charter proposals were denied locally. In ten cases, the SBE overruled the local boards and granted the charters.[7] In addition, local boards became less willing to approve charters than in 1996. In that first year, local boards approved 62 percent of applications received, versus 23 percent and 33 percent in 1997 and 1998 (local boards approved two of the three applications they received in 1999 and 2000). The state approval rate held steadier between 1996 and 1998, ranging from 50 percent to 61 percent before dropping to just 13 percent in 1999. The total number of applications submitted statewide also dropped from an all-time high of sixty-six in 1997 to just half of that in 2000.

In 1999, seven applicants approached university boards for preliminary approval. Prior to 1999, no applicants had approached universities, and universities had not appeared eager to receive applications. All of the 1999 applications were presented to the universities at or near the application deadline with no involvement by the universities in the planning or evaluation of the schools, and none were approved. Three of the applicants made unsuccessful appeals to the SBE. It remains to be seen whether universities will consider more seriously the possibility of crafting policies on charter school approval if the charter cap is raised. In March 2001, the SBE renewed the charters of twenty-one schools for additional five-year terms. In May 2001, six other schools that had mixed student performance results were granted three-year charters.

Fiscal and Compliance Oversight

The North Carolina charter school law subjects charter schools to financial audits and audit requirements adopted by the SBE. Schools are also required to participate in the Uniform Education Reporting System (UERS), the state's electronic reporting mechanism for tracking student and financial information, and they must report at least annually to the chartering entity and the SBE (NCGS 115C-238.29E(g)).

Charter school participation in UERS was a source of great controversy in the program's initial years. Designed for the state's school districts, UERS required schools to account for student and fiscal information according to strict protocols for electronic submission to the state. Though the state commissioned the development of a streamlined software package specifically for charter schools, many charter operators found the system cumbersome and unreliable. Further, some operators argued that the system did not provide the information they needed to handle management tasks, requiring them to keep duplicative accounting systems. The resulting problems, exacerbated by turnover in charter school staff and leadership, contributed to the DPI's need for two staff members in its financial services division dedicated to working full time with charter schools. Though there has been considerable improvement in the software and enhanced charter school training offered by the DPI since 1997, ongoing concerns in this arena provide prime examples of the difficulty of fitting charter schools into preexisting systems of oversight.

The SBE has empowered the Charter School Advisory Committee to hold interviews with and make recommendations about charter schools that are not in compliance with state fiscal requirements. Following the close of the 1999 fiscal year, the DPI found seventeen schools to have financial irregularities. While the advisory committee was satisfied with the remedial efforts of many of the schools, several schools were to be monitored closely by the DPI and the committee. One school had such a severe financial shortfall that the SBE revoked its charter in fall 1999, just after the school had opened for the year.

While twenty charter schools in North Carolina had closed by May 2001, the SBE had revoked the charters of only seven schools. One of the revocations was for a private school conversion, and the other six were for start-ups. While all revocations were due to factors of financial or administrative mismanagement, one revocation was based partially on noncompliance with laws regarding exceptional children. Most of the thirteen schools that voluntarily closed their doors were unable to maintain the minimum number of sixty-five students or were burdened by unresolved legal issues or business difficulties. Three of the schools never got past the preliminary planning stages and turned in their approved charters.

Academic Accountability

While the charter school law does not mandate specific performance standards for charter schools, the SBE requires charter schools to participate in the state assessments known as the "ABCs." The tests are part of the ABCs of Public Education, a reform effort that began in 1995, prior to the adoption of the charter school law. This program is designed to emphasize accountability at the building level, to focus instruction on the "basics," and to give more control to local district officials. In elementary and middle schools, the state tests assess student performance in reading, writing, mathematics, and computer literacy. At the high school level, tests are administered in several core courses.

The assessment model includes both performance and growth standards. Performance standards refer to the percentage of a school's tests scored at or above grade level, and growth standards are the benchmarks set annually to judge the increases an individual school's students have achieved from the previous year. Based on test scores from previous years, schools are given a score or benchmark to be used in measuring improvement over time. The tests are administered each spring, and the results are released in the summer. Each school receives one of four main labels: (1) exemplary: the school exceeded its growth standard by 10 percent or more; (2) expected: the school met its growth standard; (3) no recognition: the school failed to reach its growth standard, but at least half of its tests came out at or above grade level; and (4) low performing: the school failed to reach its growth standard, and more than 50 percent of its tests were scored below grade level.

Schools can receive rewards or sanctions based on their performance. Schools that exceed their growth targets by 10 percent or more receive financial rewards; low-performing schools may receive on-site state assistance teams, and school personnel may be fired. Charter schools may request state assistance if they are found to be low performing and are eligible to receive performance rewards. However, charter school personnel are not subject to dismissal by the state. If a charter school has been low performing for two years, school officials must come before the Charter School Advisory Committee with an account of student performance and a plan of action for improvement. Following the hearing, the committee may recommend revocation of the charter.

Table 12.3 compares charter school performance with the performance of the entire public school system. Charter schools have consistently ranked among both the highest and the lowest performers. The percentage of students performing at or above grade level in charter schools ranged from 2.9 to 96.4 in 1999–2000.[8] In 1997, two out of the three top-performing schools were charter schools, while seven of the lowest-performing schools in the state were charter schools. Two years later, that pattern continued: two out of seventy-one charter schools included in the 1999–2000 ABCs program ranked among the top ten schools in the state, and eighteen charter schools were among the forty-three public schools in the state that were labeled "low performing." Charter school proponents cautioned readers of the charter schools' ABCs results, noting that only nineteen charter schools had participated in the ABCs system for three years and that the

Table 12.3

Charter School Performance on State Assessments

	Charter Schools	All North Carolina Public Schools
1998–1999		
Met Expected or Exemplary Growth/Gain Targets	59.5%	81.2%
No Recognition	24.3%	18.1%
Low Performing	16.2%	0.7%
Average Performance Composite	57.29	69.1
1999–2000		
Met Expected or Exemplary Growth/Gain Targets	36.6%	69.6%
No Recognition	38.0%	28.2%
Low Performing	25.4%	2.1%
Average Performance Composite	59.2	69.8

Source: North Carolina Department of Public Instruction 1999, 2000

Note: Schools that met their exemplary growth/gain targets exceeded their growth standards by 10 percent or more. The term "growth" is used for grades K–8; "gain" is used to describe high school performance on end-of-course assessments.

Schools that met their expected growth/gain targets met their growth standards. The term "growth" is used for grades K–8; "gain" is used to describe high school performance on end-of-course assessments.

Schools that received no recognition failed to meet their growth standards. However, at least half of their tests came out at or above grade level.

Low-performing schools failed to meet their growth standards, and more than 50 percent of their tests were scored below grade level.

average percentage of students at grade level in those schools was equal to the state average. The chair of the SBE concurred, stating, "I don't think that people should put too much emphasis on the low scores at charter schools that have only been open or one or two years" (John Locke Foundation 2000, 2).

In general, though, charter schools have ranked below average in both performance and growth. In 1999–2000, the average public school's grades 3–8 "performance composite"—the percentage of tests scored at or above grade level —was 69.8 percent. For charter schools, the average was 10.6 percentage points lower, at 59.2 percent. Only about four in ten charter schools met or exceeded their growth targets in that year, compared with nearly seven in ten of all public schools. Given the relatively high percentage of at-risk children served by charter schools in North Carolina, it is not surprising that charter schools' test performance lags behind that of public schools overall. However, even after accounting for student background characteristics, nearly 90 percent of charter schools turned in performance composites that were lower than typical public schools with similar populations.[9]

Academic performance played a major role in the first round of the SBE's renewal decisions in 2001. The SBE developed a five-part framework to assess schools' success, examining academic performance, enrollment, governance, fiscal compliance, and special education. In its renewal policy, the SBE stated that any school meeting standards in four of the five areas would receive a five-year renewal. However, when the SBE considered six schools that met standards in four areas, but not in academic performance, it changed its policy, ultimately granting only three-year renewals to these schools.

Exceptional Children

Charter school opponents and some educators have expressed concerns that exceptional children may be turned away from charter schools or may not be receiving the services they have a right to receive by state and federal law.

In late 1998 through mid-1999, the state audited exceptional children services at eleven randomly selected charter schools for compliance with federal and state law. Three to six exceptional children attended each charter school and were most likely to be classified in three disability areas: specific learning disabled, speech impaired, and other health impaired. None of the audited schools were providing services to the severely/profoundly disabled or the autistic. Four of the eleven schools were required to return amounts ranging from $580 to $4,692 when it was determined that the funds were not being used properly (Exceptional Children Division 1999). The most common noncompliance areas were inaccurate reporting, misclassification, and lack of individualized education plans. Due to poor record-keeping, two of the audited schools were unable to provide the state with a head count of their exceptional children on a particular date. One school was cited for having no method in place to determine which children were receiving services, and another school was found not to be providing special services to all identified students due to staff shortage. None of the audited schools were found to be 100 percent compliant; however, the schools were, on average, compliant with more than 94 percent of the requirements.

Charter schools are faced with at least two vexing problems related to exceptional children—funding the services required by law and finding teachers to provide those services. A high-needs child can cost over $60,000 a year to educate. If such a student enrolled in a charter school, the school's annual budget could be spent within a few months. North Carolina provides some state funding for exceptional children's programs, but for various reasons the funding often does not match need.[10] In addition, there is a shortage of special education teachers in the state. Districts with higher salaries for special education teachers provide the biggest lure, leaving charter schools and poorer districts scrambling to find staff. Though the DPI's Exceptional Children office holds meetings to ensure that charter school operators know how to keep exceptional children's records, classify students properly, and create acceptable individualized education plans, some charter school leaders and staff do not attend. In addition, the goal of recruiting special education teachers may be more elusive given the shortage of such professionals, especially in rural parts of the state.

Program Evaluation

In addition to monitoring the performance of individual charter schools, the SBE tracks the charter school system as a whole. The charter school law requires the SBE to report annually to the state legislature on the charter school program. The legislation also asked that the SBE review the "educational effectiveness" of the program and, by January 1999, provide a report including recommendations (NCGS 115C-238.29I(c)). If the report indicated "demonstrable, substantial success" the legislature was free to lift the cap of 100. The SBE's charter school evaluation report, presented in December 1998, examined the impact of charter schools on the DPI and local school districts and provided detailed selected characteristics of charter schools, programs, students, and teachers. Report recommendations included maintaining the cap of 100 charter schools statewide or pursuing controlled growth of charter schools until full evaluation was completed (North Carolina State Board of Education 1998).

Controversies and Questions

Five main issues continue to be controversial in North Carolina's charter school arena: assessment, financing, teacher certification, racial balance, and the cap on the number of charter schools.

Student Assessment

While most charter and traditional public school officials agree that charter schools should demonstrate accountability, there is significant controversy about how best to demonstrate student success. Though SBE policy requires charter schools to use state tests, some charter schools have also chosen to use nationally recognized assessment instruments. Controversy arises when charter school students fare poorly on state tests while succeeding on national tests. The most publicized case of such a discrepancy is that of Healthy Start Academy in Durham, a K–3 charter school that serves mostly minority children from low-income families. Its students have demonstrated outstanding performance on the Iowa Test of Basic Skills for two years. In 1999, Healthy Start kindergartners and second graders scored in the ninety-ninth percentile, first graders scored in the ninety-fifth percentile, and third graders scored in the eighty-first percentile. However, on the state tests, only 41.9 percent were performing at or above grade level. State officials explain that it is possible to do well on national tests and poorly on state tests because national exams are designed to test common material taught in many different states, while end-of-grade exams used in the ABCs program are designed to assess student mastery of the North Carolina curriculum (Simmons 1999). Some charter school proponents question the statewide testing mandate and doubt the validity of the ABCs program.

Concerns about competing on an uneven playing field trouble many charter advocates. All of the charter schools participating in the 1997–1998 and 1998–1999 state tests were either in their first or second year of operation—a time when challenging start-up issues potentially consume much of a school's energy and focus. However, traditional public schools have been under a variety of statewide testing programs since the late 1980s and have grown familiar with the state's system and demands. Another issue makes the student assessment situation even more difficult to resolve: a large number of North Carolina's charter schools serve highly at-risk students—children who rank far below their peers in academic performance. While many educators in the state believe that charter schools need to be subject to the same set of academic standards as traditional public schools, the tests have sparked a policy debate.

In early 2001, charter school officials were participating, albeit reluctantly, in the state tests but contending that the mandate placed premature constraints on the charter school movement. In particular, the constraints preclude opportunities to develop alternative assessment models that could make such limiting outcome analyses unnecessary. The issue has further divided advocates and opponents of the state's accountability program, a system that is simultaneously receiving kudos and coming under increasing scrutiny.[11]

Finances and Facilities

The state allocates to each charter school the same average per-pupil allotment that is given to the local district in which the charter is located (in 2000–2001, state allocations were approximately $4,162 per pupil.) Additional monies are granted for children with special needs (in 2000–2001, the additional allocation was $2,413 per each child with special needs) and for children with limited English proficiency (based on a formula for each district). About a quarter of school funding in North Carolina is provided by counties and cities, with wide-ranging capacity for support. The funding invested locally in public schools ranged from a low of $628 per student to a high of more than $4,167 per student (Public School Forum 2000). Charter schools also receive some federal funds, most of which follow disadvantaged students through programs like Title I.

While school districts must relinquish current expense appropriations to each charter school for each child who transfers, they are not required to share capital expenses. In 1999–2000, county governments spent an average of $674 per pupil on capital expenditures for school districts, ranging from $149 to $1,559. The average traditional public school received $17,524 more per classroom for capital improvements than did the average charter school (Public School Forum 2000). Charter schools also miss out on receiving disbursements from local county fines and forfeitures funds. While state law requires that school systems receive much of the funds generated by local court systems, few districts have shared that money with charter schools. Charter schools are building lawsuits with the goal of gaining some share of the fines and forfeitures collected locally. In 2001, stakeholders were awaiting the state court of appeals decision and possible action on a state Senate bill that would require districts to share fines and forfeitures proceeds.

As noted, school districts are not required to share capital expenses. Charter schools are restricted to using state funds only for leasing facilities or making loan payments, and that money must come out of the general operating budget of the school. As a result North Carolina charter schools have faced the same facilities predicaments reported nationwide (RPP International 1999b, 2000; Charter Friends National Network 1999a, 1999b). They have opened in facilities that were inadequately sized and lacked the amenities needed to implement their academic programs fully, and they have had to devote a large share of their operating budgets to facilities costs. According to one analysis, the average charter school spent 15 percent of its revenue on plant operation and maintenance (Center for Community Self-Help 1999).

In 1998, the legislature made one change with the potential to improve the facilities climate for charter schools: it authorized the North Carolina Educational Facilities Finance Authority to issue bonds on behalf of K–12 educational institutions run by nonprofit organizations. Since interest earned on the authority's bonds is generally exempt from taxation, institutions borrowing through the authority can expect to pay less than they would for regular taxable debt. But through the end of 2000, no charter schools had taken advantage of the authority's offerings. The costs of issuance through the authority have made this avenue unfeasible for all but the largest charter school projects. Moreover, the strict underwriting criteria applied by the authority are difficult for charter schools to meet, as they lack the endowments and decades-long track record of the authority's conventional borrowers.

Self-Help, a statewide nonprofit community development financial institution, has established a loan program to help charter schools meet capital needs. The organization, which specializes in making capital available to borrowers underserved by traditional lending institutions, also engages in charter school advocacy and technical assistance. But without an infusion of risk capital to undergird its efforts, Self-Help has been able to meet only a fraction of the capital needs of charter schools.

Teacher Licensure

North Carolina's charter school law allows 25 percent of elementary school teachers and 50 percent of teachers who teach grades 6–12 to be unlicensed. As many as 34 percent of charter school teachers in the first year were not licensed to teach in North Carolina, and another 15 percent had expired licenses (North Carolina State Board of Education 1998, 30). However, many charter school officials disagreed with the findings, claiming that the lengthy time taken by the state agency to process licensure applications was the root of the problem. DPI officials have stood behind the report figures and argue that there have been three main reasons for the number of noncertified teachers in North Carolina charter schools: the inability to hire licensed teachers, the misconception that out-of-state licenses would suffice, and the assumption that retired teachers had current licenses. In the winter of 2000, the DPI was unable to furnish information about the proportion of charter schools that were complying with teacher certification requirements. The DPI intends to track teacher licensure status and resolve any inconsistencies with each charter school.

Many educators believe that only a licensed teacher is a qualified teacher, and much informal lobbying takes place to encourage legislators to make charter school teacher qualifications much more restrictive. Charter school proponents counter that the success of charter schools requires freedom from regulation and that true innovation will not take place with narrow restrictions on staff qualifications.

Racial Balance

When North Carolina opened the door to charter schools in 1996, many predicted a rush of all-White academies. However, it appears that the opposite has happened. In 2000–2001, in twenty-seven out of ninety charter schools reporting racial data, more than 90 percent of the students were children of color. While one school's seventy-five-member student population was all White, there were twelve schools serving 100 percent students of color. While the law establishing charter schools called upon them to "reasonably reflect" the racial and ethnic composition of their communities, many charters were approved to serve specific populations, such as young people at risk or students in inner-city settings. The student populations of those types of charter schools tend to be disproportionately minority. Ten of the state's charter schools are predominantly White (90 percent or more), but most of these reflect the racial balance of their surrounding communities in the rural western areas of the state.[12]

Some have feared that the state's predominantly Black charter schools may be forced to close. However, in July 1999, the SBE voted to allow the Charter School Advisory Committee to determine, on a school-by-school basis, whether a charter school's racial imbalance is justified and what action, if any, the state should take. Through early 2001, the SBE had taken no action against any charter school on the basis of its racial makeup.

Charter School Cap

Fifty-three of the state's 100 counties were without a charter school in 2001. Charter school advocates have urged legislators to raise the cap of 100 charter schools. With 100 charters approved and several applications waiting, such pressure is increasing. However, those who have been consistently wary of or opposed to charter schools have been increasingly vocal about maintaining the limit. John Wilson, executive director of the North Carolina Association of Educators, the state's National Education Association affiliate, argues that the state first needs to "spend a great deal of time scrutinizing the charter schools that already are open" (Simmons 2000). Some options discussed include allowing new schools to develop only in school districts without charter schools or allowing an increase in the number of charter schools serving at-risk student populations. By 2001, however, with initial test scores mixed, it appeared that most legislators had adopted a "wait and see" stance toward charter schools.

The Uncertain Future of Charter Schools in North Carolina

Those calling for the state to stand firm on the cap are often found in local district school offices. They warn legislators and state board members to wait for proof that the charter school experiment is working before "opening the floodgates." Indeed, many public school officials are quite standoffish about charter schools. While not likely to speak openly against the charter idea, they tend to downplay charter schools in their districts. Two statewide surveys regarding district and charter school collaboration have found little interaction. The SBE's 1997–1998 survey of the first-year impact of charter schools on local education agencies and their traditional schools showed that, while only a quarter of the districts reported poor relationships with charter schools, 83 percent reported limited or no contact with charter school officials or faculty (North Carolina State Board of Education 1998). The majority of districts (85 percent) reported little change in educational programs as a result of charter schools. The largest impact reported by local school officials was budgetary: two-thirds of the districts reported impacts on school district resources, including some with losses of millions of dollars.

Another study, conducted almost two years later by the North Carolina League of Women Voters, echoes the findings of the 1997–1998 survey. The league sought to gauge the perceptions of superintendents about the impact of charter schools on district resources and educational strategies. Of the superintendents with charter schools in their districts, 19 percent reported that charter schools had a strong impact on the district. These superintendents claimed an average loss of 3 percent of their total funds as a result of charter schools, and one district reported losing 12 percent of its total funds for education (North Carolina League of Women Voters 1999).[13] Over 14 percent of the superintendents reported that charter schools offer an incentive to improve schools, yet none of the respondents viewed charter schools as laboratories for educational innovation. The majority of superintendents hoped relationships with charter schools would improve; however several superintendents preferred that charter schools "just go away."

With little support from local districts and an under-resourced state agency, many charter schools seek support elsewhere. For example, the Association of North Carolina Charter Schools is a four-year-old group of charter school directors and staff. In addition, the Charter League is a charter school membership group that provides consulting services and workshops and conducts outreach to the state education agency, the media, and others.[14] In 2001, the league hired a professional lobbyist to assist with the objective of lifting the charter cap. Early in the history of the charter school program, two resource centers—the North Carolina Charter School Resource Center and the North Carolina Education Reform Foundation—emerged.[15] Both centers offered a variety of services to charter school applicants and operators, and the Education Reform Foundation engaged in lobbying for charter schools. The relationship between the two organizations proved adversarial at times, due to philosophical differences. The Charter School Resource Center viewed charter schools as an important and potentially substantial piece of the whole public education pie and sought a cooperative relationship with the DPI in helping charter schools navigate challenges. The Education Reform Foundation viewed charters as the gateway to a much wider system of school choice and was more highly suspicious of the motives of the DPI, as well as other mainstream education organizations. In 1999, the Education Reform Foundation turned its attention largely to promoting privately funded voucher programs, and two years later, the Charter School Resource Center ran out of funding. As of spring 2001, there was no active nonprofit organization with paid professional staff providing technical assistance to the state's charter schools.

As a result, substantial responsibilities remain on the shoulders of the state. The charter school law gave the SBE two weighty responsibilities—holding charter schools accountable for fiscal and academic performance and providing technical assistance to the fledgling institutions. Not only are these two responsibilities individually challenging, carrying them out simultaneously creates a complex and politically tenuous role for state officials.

Since the number of charter schools has grown so rapidly in North Carolina, the SBE and its delegates have had little time to craft systematic policies and practices. As difficulties have arisen (e.g., fiscal problems and chronically low academic performance at individual schools), state officials have had to react in an ad hoc fashion. While the uniqueness of each charter school demands some degree of case-by-case response, state officials and charter schools alike have struggled to arrive at and understand the standards and processes by which important decisions will be made. As additional years of academic and compliance data become available—and as the first charter schools near the ends of their initial charter terms—clarification of these standards and processes will become all the more important. In the meantime, it remains to be seen whether the charter school movement will fulfill the broad purposes of the charter school law.

By spring 2001, the focus of education policy makers in North Carolina had shifted from school choice to other issues—how to recruit and retain teachers; how to tweak the state's school accountability system; and how to cope with the state's burgeoning student population and inadequate, aging facilities. Some believe that there is no leader left in the state legislature to "carry the torch" for the charter school cause; that until new legislators and a new governor who encourage the growth of charter schools arrive in the state capital, the reform will take a back seat to other education priorities. However, there is one education issue in 2001 that has gained unprecedented attention—determining ways to improve minority achievement, which may lead the school-improvement focus back to charter schools.

With less than 50 percent of the state's Black students passing state tests in mathematics and reading in 1999 and with scores only slightly improved for Native American and Hispanic students, state education leaders, parents, and other stakeholders are earnestly searching for ways to better meet the educational needs of these children. In early 2001, nearly one-half of the state's charter schools were already serving student populations that were more than 50 percent minority, suggesting that the charter school approach may be attractive to minority families. If more minority parents and others seek out charter schools as an alternative, the pressure to lift the cap of 100 schools could increase significantly. However, substantial financial woes among many charter schools and the absence of a well-funded technical assistance effort raise questions about whether they will get the help they need to succeed.

Whether charter schools expand in North Carolina will depend largely on the legislative lifeline—whether legislators will provide the political and financial support necessary to allow the public education program to flourish. That, in turn, depends on the results charter schools can show for students. But as in other states, North Carolina legislators are unsure as to how to interpret the complex test results of charter schools. If some charter schools do extremely well and others do poorly, how should the legislature respond? And what should it make of the fact that more mature charter schools are performing comparably to district schools, even though they have higher proportions of at-risk students? What seems clear is that when the SBE releases its next evaluation of the charter school program, it will not provide any definitive thumbs up or thumbs down on the charter experiment. Legislators will be left, as they were when they enacted charter school legislation five years before, to make complicated judgments about the value of school choice and a diversity of providers of public education.

13 • New York

Over 100 Charter Applications in Year One

Sandra Vergari

SEVEN YEARS AFTER the nation's first charter school law was adopted, New York became the thirty-fourth state to permit charter schools.[1] While the state is a relative latecomer to the charter school scene, charter school advocates have been actively making up for lost time. In this chapter, I discuss the charter school law and the dynamics of the implementation process. I also review the challenges stakeholders encountered during the launching and initial two years of operation of the New Covenant Charter School in Albany. New Covenant was the largest of the state's first three new start-up charter schools that opened in fall 1999. The case illustrates various problems that new charter schools may experience and financial concerns faced by school districts. Finally, I assess the status of the charter school movement in New York State (NYS).

New York State Gets a Charter School Law

The NYS Charter Schools Act was adopted in the wee hours of the morning during a special session of a lame-duck legislature in December 1998. Republican governor George Pataki had been promoting such legislation for three years, but his efforts were thwarted by opposition from the politically powerful teachers unions and the Democratic majority in the state assembly.[2] As in other states, the teachers unions enjoy lobbying power rooted in their ability to make campaign contributions and mobilize members at the ballot box.[3]

On 2 December 1998, lawmakers approved legislation to give themselves a significant pay raise. However, at the close of November, Pataki had indicated that he was not ready to approve such legislation, avowing: "I don't think a pay raise for legislators, standing alone, is justified" (Perez-Pena 1998). Pataki planned to use the pay raise as a bargaining chip through which to finally secure a charter school law. Thus, the law was the product of a masterful political bargain. State lawmakers would get a 38 percent pay raise, their first salary increase in ten years, and the governor would get charter schools.[4] Lawmakers faced a deadline of 21 December 1998 to come to an agreement on charter school legislation. On that date, the governor would have to act on the pay raise bill.

Opponents of charter schools, such as the New York State School Boards Association (NYSSBA), characterized the initiative as a "distraction" that would divert attention from other school reform efforts (see NYSSBA 1999; Hammond 1998). State board of regents chancellor Carl Hayden expressed concerns that charter schools could divert focus from New York's new system of student standards and assessments. State education commissioner Richard Mills characterized charter schools as a "small strategy" unlikely to provide a solution for more than a few children (Stashenko 1998, A1). In December 1998, the NYS League of Women Voters sent a letter to state officials expressing opposition to charter schools, warning that they would drain money from public schools "while continuing to require them to function as educators of last resort" (Gallagher 1998).

Supporters of the charter school legislation included minority interests such as the Urban League, religious leaders, members of the business community, and Change–New York (a conservative antitax group). The Reverend Floyd Flake, now an official at Edison Schools, Inc., is a prominent African American minister and former New York City (NYC) congressman. Acting as a policy entrepreneur, he contributed to the formation and maintenance of an advocacy coalition in support of charter schools.[5] Through his political contacts and linkages with financial supporters of school choice, Flake helped to mobilize support for the charter school law in NYS (Morken and Formicola 1999).

During December 1998, closed-door negotiations between the governor and legislative leaders produced an agreement on charter school legislation. On 17 December, the Senate passed the charter school bill (SB 7881) by a vote of thirty-nine to twenty.[6] At 3:20 A.M. on 18 December 1998, the Assembly passed the bill by a vote of ninety-three to forty-five.[7]

Shortly after the bill's passage, Governor Pataki declared that the "creation of charter schools represents the single greatest improvement in education in state history" (Dicker and Birnbaum 1998, 1). Pataki had traveled outside of NYS frequently in 1998–1999, and some analysts speculated that he had championed the charter school reform as a means to advance his ambition for national political office (Levy and Hartocollis 1998). The president of the National Education Association–New York, Gregory Nash, offered less enthusiastic rhetoric: "The work that was done would never have been supported had it been held in the light of day with open hearings and public discussion. Votes were sold last night at the expense of children in our classrooms, and those responsible should be ashamed" (Jakes 1998, 2). When asked about the political process by which the charter school law was secured, Governor Pataki remarked, "You know how the system works" (Levy and Hartocollis 1998, D2).

Elements of Political Compromise

Four "charter entities" can approve new charter schools in NYS. First, the state board of regents (SBR) is a charter entity and also formally issues all charters. Second, the board of trustees of the State University of New York (SUNY) can approve charter schools. Third, a local board of education can approve charter schools to be operated within district boundaries. Finally, the NYC schools chancellor can approve applications for charter schools within the NYC school district. Conversion charter schools must be approved by the relevant school district board or, in NYC, by the chancellor.[8] In permitting both the gubernatorially appointed SUNY board and the legislatively appointed SBR to authorize charter schools, the charter school law reflects pure political compromise. The SBR is commonly viewed as an ally of Democrats, while the SUNY board has a decidedly Republican flavor.[9]

The law permits 100 newly created charter schools. SUNY is eligible to authorize 50 charter schools, and the SBR, school boards, and the NYC schools chancellor may approve 50 new charter schools. There is no limit on the number of conversion charter schools formed from previously existing public schools. Upon the recommendation of one of the four charter entities, the SBR issues the charter. The SBR can refuse to approve a charter; however, it cannot overrule SUNY decisions to award charters. If a charter entity rejects a charter school application, its decision is final and not subject to an administrative or judicial appeals process.

Analysts classify the NYS Charter Schools Act as "strong" or "permissive" (Vergari 1999). More than one public authority is authorized to approve charter schools, public school conversions and start-up charter schools are permitted, charter schools are generally autonomous from the local school district and enjoy freedom from most state and local school regulations, and the law permits a relatively substantial number of charter schools. Charter schools receive state and local per-pupil funding from the school district in which the charter school student resides. Moreover, in contrast to some other states that leave transportation matters to be determined in individual charters, the NYS law requires that school districts provide transportation for charter school students in the same manner as is required for private school students.[10]

Noncertified teachers may number five or constitute 30 percent—whichever is less—of a charter school's teaching staff. Teachers and staff in conversion charter schools are automatically represented by the local union and covered under pre-existing collective bargaining agreements.[11] For start-up charter schools with pupil enrollments of 250 or below during the initial year, employees are not deemed to be members of the local district bargaining unit, and the school and its employees are not subject to any existing bargaining agreement between the district and its employees. In start-up charter schools in which the initial pupil enrollment exceeds 250 in the first year, instructional employees are represented in a separate negotiating unit at the charter school by the same employee organization that represents like employees in the district in which the school is located. Thus, it is not surprising that a number of charter applications have proposed enrollments just below 250 students. The provision regarding mandatory representation by the local union can be waived in ten schools that are chartered by SUNY; it had issued four such waivers by July 2001. This waiver authority is yet another political compromise included in the charter school law.

The SUNY Board of Trustees and the Charter Schools Institute

A short time after the adoption of the Charter Schools Act, the SUNY board formed the Charter Schools Institute (CSI) to run its charter school program and make recommendations to the board regarding charter school approval. The initial CSI staff included a president, a vice president, a business manager, and an attorney.[12] In September 1999, CSI announced that Robert Bellafiore, an aide to Governor Pataki, had been appointed CSI executive director and would assume responsibility for its day-to-day operations.[13] Bellafiore was appointed CSI president a year later.[14] By 2001, the CSI office included Bellafiore and fifteen additional staff members: senior vice president and general counsel, vice president for applications and grants, vice president for accountability, vice president of evaluation and research, senior fellow, senior analyst, director of fiscal account-ability, director of public affairs, director of administration, director of operations, assistant counsel, and four other staffers.[15]

Soon after its formation, CSI posted its Website and enthusiastically promoted the charter school law across the state. The institute was clearly eager to facilitate the emergence of charter schools for operation in fall 1999, less than a year after the Charter Schools Act had been adopted. Accordingly, CSI encouraged appli-cations for its initial "fast-track" charter school approval process: charter school applications submitted to CSI by 15 June 1999 would be considered for fall 1999 opening dates. CSI received fifteen applications during this fast-track process, and SUNY approved three charter schools—one in Albany and two in NYC—for fall 1999 openings; all opened that fall. SUNY also granted preliminary approval to five additional applications for fall 2000 openings.

The second round of applications—for charter schools planning fall 2000 openings—were due to CSI by 30 September 1999. CSI received over ninety ap-plications during this round, including nine from Buffalo, eleven from Rochester, three from Syracuse, and twenty-seven from NYC. Thirty-six of the applications included management partners. A handful of these partners were nonprofit orga-nizations, while the majority were for-profit educational management companies (EMCs).[16] Several provisions of the NYS Charter Schools Act (e.g., funding, mul-tiple authorizers, union provisions) make the state relatively appealing to EMCs.

CSI uses its own staff as well as external review teams to evaluate applications. The teams have included certified public accountants; directors of charter au-thorizer offices and charter school associations; charter school consultants and directors; and professors. For example, during 1999, charter school experts from thirteen different states and Washington, D.C., traveled to NYC to participate on CSI review panels. The diverse teams have enabled CSI to gain firsthand knowl-edge of what works and what does not in the charter school arena.[17] Each 1999 review team discussed five applications during the course of a day. In January 2000, SUNY approved fourteen new charter schools, thirteen for fall 2000 open-ings and one for fall 2001.[18]

In the third round, for schools planning to open in fall 2001, there was a marked drop-off in the number of applications submitted to SUNY. By 21 September 2000, SUNY had received thirty-seven applications. Significantly, twenty of these ap-plications were resubmissions from previous applicants.[19] About half (eighteen) of the applicants planned to partner with an EMC (Charter Schools Institute 2000b, 1).[20] In January 2001, SUNY approved seven new charter schools. Two of these prospective schools had EMC partners.[21] In both the 2000 and 2001 charter application cycles, the SUNY approval rate was below 20 percent.

The New York State Board of Regents

As a charter entity, the SBR acts upon charter applications submitted directly to it. As the formal issuer of all charters, the SBR must also act upon proposed charters that have been approved by other charter entities. The SBR is obligated to act within sixty days of receipt of a recommendation from another charter entity, either by approving the charter or returning it to the entity with comments and recommendations. The charter entity may then choose to resubmit the charter (with or without modifications) to the SBR, which again has sixty days to act. In the case of a charter resubmitted by SUNY, the law provides that even if the SBR does not approve the charter, the charter is to be issued thirty days after the resubmission date. As noted earlier, the SBR does not have veto power over charters approved by SUNY. This feature of the Charter Schools Act ensures that SUNY has genuine authority to open fifty charter schools.

The SBR has approached implementation of the charter school law with less zeal than SUNY. Paul Hayford, a New York State Education Department (NYSED) researcher who worked on Goals 2000 initiatives, was assigned initial responsibility for the charter school program. In 1999, NYSED provided charter school "application guidelines" on its Website and conducted several regional forums in concert with CSI. The SBR did not publicize a fast-track application process and by mid-1999 had received one charter application.

Turnover in the leadership of charter authorizer offices is common, and such change occurred early in both of the state-level authorizer offices. Similar to the leadership turnover at CSI, primary responsibility for the charter schools program at NYSED changed hands during fall 1999. Darlene Mengel, who had worked on school reform initiatives at NYSED, including charter schools, was appointed supervisor of NYSED's Charter Schools Unit (CSU). By July 2001, CSU included Mengel, Hayford, an assistant, an aide, and a secretary. CSU draws upon the expertise of other NYSED units for assistance with issues such as curriculum, special education, and bilingual education, and NYSED funds an attorney who works solely on charter school issues.[22]

On 9 August 1999, the SBR approved the two new, SUNY-authorized charter schools for NYC and two conversion charter schools for NYC. However, the SBR voted seven to four to send the New Covenant Charter School application back to SUNY with a request for further details on the new school and how it would impact the Albany City School District in which it would be located.[23] Eight days later, SUNY approved the revised New Covenant application and submitted the proposed charter to the SBR. By July 2001, two charters approved by SUNY had been issued by operation of law, rather than by an affirmative SBR vote. Despite SBR reservations, SUNY upheld its approvals of the New Covenant Charter School and the Roosevelt Children's Academy Charter School. (In 2000, the SBR approved the current, revised New Covenant charter.)

By 30 September 1999, in contrast to the ninety charter school applications received by SUNY, the SBR had received only five applications. CSU uses an internal application review process and forwards its recommendations to the SBR. Of the five applications, one was withdrawn and three had legal problems.[24] In January 2000, the SBR granted final approval to the fifth charter application for a fall 2000 opening, in the Bronx, NYC (the school later decided to open in fall 2001). In the round of applications for 2001 charter schools, the SBR received twenty-six applications; by June 2001, it had approved a total of eight charter schools as a charter entity.

New York City

In 1998, then–NYC schools chancellor Rudy Crew lobbied against the passage of the charter school law. He suggested that only the SBE and the SBR should be able to grant charters in NYC. Crew noted that the law could divert funds from other public schools and that by permitting SUNY to grant charters, it would usurp his ability to maintain high standards in all public schools, including charters (Crew 1998; Levy and Hartocollis 1998).

Nonetheless, in February 1999, Crew announced his plan for charter schools in NYC. By law, conversion charter schools in NYC must be approved by the schools chancellor, and Crew proposed that six city schools convert to charter status for fall 1999. That fall, two of the six schools, both located on the campus of LaGuardia Community College in Queens, began operating as charter schools. In singling out six schools for conversion to charter status, Crew displayed an unusual interpretation of the charter school concept. One of the hallmarks of the concept is that power devolves to the school and "consumer" levels. Moreover, schools seeking to convert to charter status are typically expected to do so as a result of their own, grassroots initiative, not because of a strong suggestion from district administration. Thus, some charter school advocates looked askance at Crew's proposals for conversion charter schools.[25]

In January 2001, Crew's successor, Harold Levy, completed an agreement with Edison Schools, Inc., to manage five failing NYC public schools he had selected for conversion to charter schools.[26] By law, conversion charter schools must be approved by the parents or guardians of a majority of the students then enrolled in the existing public school. Levy's effort to privatize the schools was met with well-organized, active opposition from the teachers union, community groups, and local Democratic politicians. While only half of the eligible parents cast votes, the initiative went down to defeat, as it was opposed by 80 percent of the voters.

By June 2001, NYC had a total of fourteen charter schools. Eight were start-up schools—seven approved by SUNY and one by the NYC schools chancellor— and six were conversion schools. One additional conversion school and six start-up schools had been approved for fall 2001 (four by SUNY and two by the SBR).

Charter Schools Approved for Operation

As indicated in table 13.1, there were twenty-three charter schools in operation in NYS during 2000–2001. Sixteen of these were new schools approved by SUNY. There were also six conversion charters and one start-up charter school approved by the NYC schools chancellor. Several additional charter schools had been approved for fall 2001 openings, including seven new schools approved by the SBR as a charter entity. By July 2001, a total of forty-two charter schools had been approved, including seven conversion schools in NYC. The remaining thirty-five were start-up charter schools, and SUNY was the charter entity for a majority (twenty-four) of these schools.

Nurturing the Policy Innovation

Charter school founders need access to substantial managerial and financial resources. Support activities in NYS mirror what has occurred elsewhere. The New York Charter School Resource Center (NYCSRC) was founded by Gerry Vazquez

Table 13.1

Charter Schools Approved for Operation in New York State

Charter Entity (Authorizer)	Total Number of Charter Schools Operating in 1999–2000	Total Number of Charter Schools Operating in 2000–2001	Additional Charter Schools Approved for Operation in 2001–2002[a]	Additional Charter Schools Approved for Operation in 2002–2003	Total Number of Charter Schools Approved as of July 2001
Board of Regents			7	2	9
SUNY Board of Trustees	3	16	6	2	24
NYC Schools Chancellor Start-Up Schools		1		1	2
NYC Schools Chancellor Conversion Schools	2	6	1		7
Total	5	23	14	5	42

Sources: Charter Schools Unit, New York State Education Department; Charter Schools Institute, SUNY Board of Trustees; Office of Charter Schools, NYC Board of Education

[a] July 2001 data. Charter schools do not always open on the originally planned opening date.

in 1998, prior to the passage of the charter school law.[27] The center is affiliated with the Empire Foundation and is funded through private-sector sources.[28] The center offers free services to charter school applicants and has been particularly active in helping to forge links between EMCs and charter school founders. In 2000, a resource center aimed at assisting charter schools in NYC emerged. The New York Charter Schools Association was formed in early 2000. The association's executive director, Lisa O'Brien, is a former director of human resources and communications for Advantage Schools.[29] The association provides advice and technical support to charter schools and engages in political advocacy on their behalf. It is supported by donations and membership fees.

Formal coalitions in support of charter schools have emerged in Rochester and Buffalo. The Rochester coalition is noteworthy in that its membership includes many officials associated with the traditional "educational establishment." The coalition includes the school district superintendent; the presidents of the Rochester Teachers Association and the Administrators and Supervisors Association of Rochester; the mayor; the county executive; members of the Rochester school board; former members of the SBR; business leaders; and other community members. The coalition has endorsed several applications to establish Rochester charter schools. The Buffalo-Niagara Partnership has established a "Charter School Initiative" that links charter school founders with members of the business community who have expertise relevant to the development of a charter school.

Charter school founders face formidable financial challenges, particularly during the start-up phase. Obtaining funds to purchase or rent adequate facilities is a key challenge. In 1998, the state legislature approved a new "stimulus fund" to provide grants for charter school start-up costs, including facilities costs. The fund contained $1 million as part of the 1999–2000 state budget, and the bulk of the funds were allocated to SUNY. In 2000–2001, the SBR controlled access to $600,000 and SUNY to $3.1 million from the fund. NYS has also been awarded $4.2 million in both 2000 and 2001 from the federal Public Charter Schools Program to be used for charter school planning and implementation grants. In November 2000, NYC mayor Rudolph Giuliani announced a new Charter School Improvement Fund to assist NYC charter schools with facilities acquisition and renovation. In 2001, fourteen charter schools were set to receive grants of up to $250,000 each (Lueck 2000; Shin 2001).

Finally, several nongovernmental sources offer financial support for charter schools. For example, charter school founders can apply to the NYCSRC and to the Gleason Foundation (a member of the Rochester coalition) for start-up grants. Finally, when charter schools contract with EMCs, the companies typically offer start-up capital.

The New Covenant Charter School

The New Covenant Charter School in Albany is one of three charter schools approved by SUNY in June 1999 for fall 1999 openings. New Covenant was set to begin with 550 students in grades K–5. The applicants received one of the ten SUNY "wild-card" exceptions from the union requirement for charter schools with more than 250 students.

Aaron Dare, then president and chief executive officer of the Urban League of Northeastern New York, is the public entrepreneur who launched and executed the plan for the new charter school in Albany's predominantly Black Arbor Hill neighborhood, where he grew up. Dare explained his motivation for fast action on getting the school up and running: "If growing up in Arbor Hill taught me anything, it's that you can grow old waiting for change" (Karlin 1999b, B1). According to Dare, "Children's lives cannot be suspended to accommodate slow-moving reform, however well-intentioned. A single child allowed to slip through the cracks is an unconscionable sacrifice, and we've witnessed the loss of far greater numbers. . . . New York's new charter schools law allows parents, educators, concerned citizens, and community groups like the Urban League to create an entirely new model for public education—in effect a new system delivering a new product" (Dare 1999, B1). The name "New Covenant" was intended to symbolize a new compact with the community.

The New Covenant Charter School's board contracted with Advantage Schools, Inc., an EMC based in Boston, to operate the school.[30] Advantage charter schools have used the highly structured "Direct Instruction" pedagogical method, which some analysts characterize as "teacher proof." Direct Instruction stands in contrast to the philosophy of some charter school advocates who maintain that teachers should be permitted to exercise a measure of their own creativity and professional judgment in determining what occurs in the classroom.

Successful charter school founders display the qualities of public entrepreneurs (Doig and Hargrove 1997; Schneider, Teske, and Mintrom 1995). Skillful public entrepreneurs have access to financial and human capital and are able to mobilize resources. In 1999, Dare drew upon his political capital and network of contacts to carry out his vision for a charter school. Support from key state and local officials enhanced his ability to achieve this objective just nine months after the Charter Schools Act was passed and just weeks after the school's charter was approved. Governor Pataki stood to gain from the politically attractive symbol of a successful charter school in the capital, and Albany's Democratic mayor, Jerry Jennings, could enhance his standing with the governor by facilitating the swift opening of New Covenant.

The Urban League would purchase land from the city, tear down several dilapidated buildings, and build temporary school facilities. In contrast to zoning tensions in some communities in other states in which charter schools have been proposed, New Covenant did not encounter any roadblocks from the Albany City Board of Zoning Appeals.

Getting Ready in a Hurry

During August and early September 1999, subcontractors worked day and night to construct the temporary units for New Covenant in order to meet the school's official opening date of 16 September. However, on 15 September, the school failed to secure an occupancy certificate—the modular classrooms lacked electrical power, fire and smoke alarms could not be tested, much of the plumbing was not hooked up, and not all exit stairways were installed. The Albany building and codes director said he was prepared to issue the certificate as soon as New Covenant was ready: "If they call me at 6 [A.M.], I'll be there" (Karlin 1999c, B6). New Covenant planned to have its crew working through the night of the 15 September and have another inspection at 6:00 A.M.

At 4:30 A.M. on 16 September, Dare and his colleagues decided to delay the opening of the school until 21 September; New Covenant had yet to meet many code requirements. City inspectors made an initial visit at midnight on 21 September and returned seven hours later to complete the inspection and issue a temporary certificate permitting the school to open. In December 1999, in a symbolic indication of New Covenant's presence in the community, the school's student chorus performed at the official opening ceremony for the much-celebrated holiday lights display at Albany's city park.

Transportation Tensions

By law, a school district must provide transportation for charter school students just as it does for private school students within its boundaries who live up to fifteen miles away from their schools. In early August 1999, the Albany City School District (ACSD) asserted that the Urban League had failed to meet the district's 1 June deadline for transportation requests so that New Covenant students could be included on district bus routes.[31] However, the charter school had not received its formal approvals from SUNY until 15 June and 17 August.

Superintendent Lonnie Palmer explained: "If there are any children who live along existing bus runs, we will try to accommodate them, but we didn't schedule any runs to the school. We are trying to follow the rules that [the state Department of Education] has given us" (Benjamin 1999, B1). Dare remarked: "He knows transportation is the lifeline of this school, and he's playing games. This community will not back down from Lonnie Palmer and his intimidation tactics" (Benjamin 1999, B8). About one week later, the ACSD agreed to provide bus service to New Covenant students while the state education commissioner determined whether the bill was to be paid by the ACSD or New Covenant. In March 2000, the commissioner ruled that New Covenant had a legally reasonable excuse for filing a late transportation request and that the ACSD would have to pay the $124,000 bill for bus service (Mills 2000).

Impact on the Albany City School District

The ACSD enrolls about 10,000 students, and New Covenant enrollment was set to be about 5 percent of total ACSD enrollment. Accordingly, ACSD officials expressed concern that the charter school would cause a significant cash short-fall for the district. Referring to Advantage Schools, Bill Ritchie, the head of the district's teachers union, complained that citizens' "tax money could well end up in the profits of a Boston company" (Karlin 1999a, A6). ACSD officials characterized the development of New Covenant as "devastating." Theresa Swidorski, a member of the Albany board of education, and ACSD Superintendent Palmer accused SUNY of dropping a "$4.1 million bombshell" in its approval of New Covenant (Swidorski and Palmer 1999, B1). The ACSD would be required to turn over $7,570 for each of the 550 students set to be enrolled at New Covenant, a net loss of over $4.1 million. Swidorski and Palmer stated: "The idea of the money following the child sounds great in theory but it's a nightmare in practice" (Swidorski and Palmer 1999, B1). Since New Covenant was expected to draw students from several schools, grade levels, and classrooms, ACSD officials maintained that it would be difficult to close a school or consolidate classes. Swidorski and Palmer (1999, B3) asserted that without additional state aid, the ACSD would be left with two unacceptable choices: "slash and burn or impose a tax hike in excess of 10 percent."

New Covenant was the main discussion item at an August 1999 ACSD board meeting. About 300 people attended the meeting, most of whom were minority families planning to send children to New Covenant. Board members emphasized the cash shortfall that would be created by the diversion of funds to the charter school and raised the possibility of firing or demoting teacher aides and custodians. The meeting lasted late into the evening as parents, and some children, lined up before the board to offer personal testimonials about their experiences with the ACSD and to express their hopes for New Covenant.

On 3 August 1999, state lawmakers adopted a state budget that included a record level of school aid.[32] The ACSD was set to receive about $2.7 million more in state aid than had been anticipated, still short of the $4 million budget gap expected as a result of New Covenant. Combined with other cost-saving measures, the ACSD predicted a budget gap of between $1 million and $1.5 million, and the board voted to borrow funds to cover the gap.[33]

When the ACSD board was deliberating upon the 2000–2001 budget, it reviewed proposals for replacing all teacher aides with lower-cost teacher assistants, modifying school cleaning schedules to save money on custodial services, and closing School 26. At a board meeting in March 2000, Superintendent Palmer blamed the charter school for the proposal to close School 26: "This is a financial decision forced on us by the charter school. We would never have considered this in the absence of the charter school because [School 26 is] a great little school."[34] ACSD officials ultimately made the decision to keep School 26 open.

ACSD board member Katharine Webb has commented: "If we have a good school system, we will have students who want to stay with us [as opposed to attending charter schools]."[35] In 1999–2000, the ACSD concentrated largely on making up for the funds lost to New Covenant, rather than on the adoption of programmatic changes in an effort to "win back" educational "consumers" who had chosen a charter school over a district-run school. Toby Michelena, director of a citizen budget advisory committee that scrutinized district finances and delivered recommendations for the 2000–2001 budget, asserted that while New Covenant was having a financial impact on the district, the charter school was not the sole cause of the district's budget problems.[36] In assessing the impact of New Covenant on the ACSD in 2000, Michelena observed: "It's hard to step outside of the box and say 'we need to look at this as a challenge.' Right now, the district views New Covenant as a threat."[37] There has been at least one significant programmatic change that was implemented after the founding of New Covenant. New Covenant offers a full-day kindergarten, and the ACSD had been offering such only in its magnet schools; in 2000–2001, the ACSD expanded full-day kindergarten to ten of its twelve elementary schools.

In formulating its 2001–2002 budget, the ACSD operated on the assumption that New Covenant would enroll 600 students rather than the 750 that the charter school hoped to draw. The ACSD is likely to face additional budget pressures in 2002–2003, as the SBR has approved two companion single-sex charter schools for fall 2002 openings in Albany.

In 2000, ACSD officials mobilized a lobbying effort with other education interests to gain state assistance in meeting the district costs of charter schools. Assemblywoman Sandra Galef (D-Ossining) sponsored a bill that would require the state to pay charter schools directly for each student enrolled and asserted that legislators were "robbing [school districts] of their money" (Wechsler 2001). Such a position holds that public school tax dollars belong solely to school districts. Charter school proponents challenge this claim.

Problems at New Covenant

In December 1999, the public learned that all was not well at New Covenant. Charter school opponents could be heard muttering phrases such as "I told you so," while advocates were concerned that the capital city's much-heralded charter school was not living up to enthusiastic and high expectations. New Covenant parents and others expressed concerns about a leadership vacuum in the school (following the departure of two interim directors, a permanent director was appointed only in December 1999); overcrowding and lack of organization; poor-quality food; weaknesses in the Direct Instruction pedagogy; and gaps in services to special education students. The Charter Schools Act provides that the committee on special education of a charter school student's school district of residence is responsible for developing his or her individual education plan, and the ACSD had informed NYSED that some New Covenant special education students were not receiving adequate attention. A large percentage of New Covenant special education students have returned to ACSD schools. The New Covenant board formally expressed its dissatisfaction with Advantage Schools and established a two-month timeline by which the EMC was to address board complaints.

Further complicating matters in 2000, New Covenant's nonprofit partner, the Urban League of Northeastern New York, suffered a "meltdown."[38] The league was plagued by an array of serious financial problems, including a federal tax lien, and had to lay off employees. In March 2000, there were continuing indications of problems at New Covenant; parents complained about inadequate discipline at the school, and it was still unclear as to how the capital for the permanent school facility would be obtained.

In September 1999, Dare had asserted that the permanent school facility would be ready in February 2000, yet the target date was later pushed to November 2000. In early 2000, Albany's Mayor Jennings raised some eyebrows when he offered to help fund the permanent facility with the stipulation that he control half of the seats on the New Covenant board. His proposal was rejected. Advantage Schools offered to help fund the building but not an attached community center that Dare wanted. In March 2000, Dare announced that the charter school would attempt to cover the facility costs by marketing bonds.

When New Covenant opened, there were about 500 students enrolled, and over the course of the first year, enrollment declined by about 100 students. In June 2000, results of the state-mandated fourth-grade English language arts exam indicated that 91 percent of New Covenant fourth graders had failed the exam, among the worst results in public schools across the state. Some observers raised questions about the extent to which the New Covenant curriculum was aligned with items on the fourth-grade test. Significantly, the test was administered in January 2000, just a few months after New Covenant had opened. While quite disappointing and the subject of much discussion, the test scores were arguably more reflective of the students' previous educational experiences than of the instruction received at New Covenant during the entire 1999–2000 academic year.

In June 2000, the New Covenant board announced a "mutual, amicable" separation from Advantage. Edison Schools, Inc., would be the school's new EMC in 2000–2001. At the same time, the state education department announced that it would send a special team of education officials to advise and question the school. This was the first salient reminder that, as a charter school, New Covenant is subject to the threat of closure.

The charter school was put on probation by SUNY, which issued a seventeen-point remedial action plan that included requirements pertaining to board training and fiscal expertise, a fiscal audit, and an enrollment cap of 400 students due to the limited capacity of the school's temporary facility. New Covenant began its second year with a new governing board; a new EMC; and a new director— Eleanor Bartlett, an experienced Albany public school administrator and a member of the SBR at the time of her appointment as director.

The second-year fourth-grade test scores at New Covenant were better than those of the previous year. Twenty-two percent of fourth-graders passed the exam in early 2001, compared to just 9 percent one year earlier.[39] The scores were still very low, however. In May 2001, it was announced that New Covenant would fire ten of its twenty-four teachers at the close of the academic year. As a charter school, New Covenant enjoys the autonomy to engage in such firings, but concerns were raised about the lack of public explanation for the action. An Albany newspaper editorial noted that the charter school was not exempt from "reasonable standards of public accountability" and thus owed taxpayers an explanation as to why so many teachers were judged problematic after only a year under the new school administration ("Answers Please" 2001).

Lessons from the New Covenant Case

The New Covenant case raises many questions for both prospective charter school founders and prospective authorizers. Charter opponents in NYS are quick to emphasize apparent shortcomings of charter schools.[40] In the rush to get charter schools up and running, did advocates neglect to consider the possibility of un-intended negative political and educational consequences? Would an additional year of planning have prevented some of the problems at New Covenant? Despite its reputation for charter school advocacy and its receipt of numerous charter ap-plications, SUNY has indicated that it will not approve charter schools blindly. Indeed, some charter advocates lament that SUNY's approval rate was not higher during the first two full rounds of application submission. Some also maintain that the charter school accountability system worked in the New Covenant case: parents voiced complaints; CSI witnessed problems, and SUNY placed the school on probation; and several key changes aimed at improving the school were adopted.

The presence of an EMC introduces an additional line of complexity to the accountability process. There is potential for the charter school governing board and the EMC to shirk responsibility for shortcomings at a charter school by plac-ing blame on each other. Thus, it is critical that members of the governing board be adequately trained and willing to fulfill their obligation to oversee school op-erations effectively. It is noteworthy that the New Covenant board was able to sever ties with an EMC that was not meeting expectations and choose a new company. Of course, such choices must be made very carefully given that chil-dren's educational development is at stake and that the public has invested in the tax-funded school. The case raises questions about efficiency and effectiveness, two key goals of the charter school movement. The transition to the new EMC has the potential to yield positive results over time, but it also required adjustments on the part of teachers, parents, and students who had spent a year implementing the Advantage program.

Charter school opponents have viewed New Covenant as a school in an inade-quate facility, managed by a profit-hungry EMC, selfishly taking precious funding away from the majority of ACSD students. However, despite declining enrollment in the first year and a host of parental concerns, many families remain committed to the school. In 2000–2001, about 385 students attended New Covenant, and the school hoped to attract 750 students for 2001–2002, when its new permanent fa-cility was scheduled to be complete.

In a different political context, the viability of the school might be more doubt-ful. However, a range of stakeholders (e.g., public officials and other charter school advocates, parents, and the new EMC) now face political, personal, professional, and/or profit incentives to try to ensure that New Covenant thrives rather than fails.

In the unfortunate event that the school is eventually forced to close, advocates are likely to note that a closure demonstrates that the accountability component of the charter school reform is genuine—in other words, that in contrast to deficient traditional public schools that continue to operate, failing charter schools are closed. However, in theory, a charter authorizer does not approve an application unless it reflects a strong potential for operational success. Obviously, the closure of a charter school may be disruptive for students, parents, and teachers. A closure, and especially multiple school closures, may also be harmful to the reputation of the authorizer and the broader charter school movement. Further, a charter school closure means that the public has received a negative return on its financial investment in the school. All things considered, then, the necessary closure of a failing charter school is something to be mourned rather than celebrated by reform advocates.

Oversight and Accountability

The charter authorizer and the SBR are the public agents authorized to oversee charter schools (§2853.1(c)). However, as in other states, the NYS charter school law is vague regarding oversight responsibilities, stating simply that "oversight by a charter entity and the board of regents shall be sufficient to ensure that the charter school is in compliance with all applicable laws, regulations, and charter provisions" (§2853.2). The law also provides that the school district in which the charter school is located has "the right to visit, examine into, and inspect the charter school for the purpose of ensuring that the school is in compliance with all applicable laws, regulations, and charter provisions" (§2853.2-a). The school district may forward evidence of noncompliance to the charter entity and the SBR for action pursuant to revocation or termination of the charter.

Charter schools must meet or exceed New York's recently overhauled education standards, and charter school students must take the same state tests as all NYS public school students.[41] Charter schools are also required to submit annual reports to the charter authorizer and the SBR (§2857.2(a)). In turn, the SBR must provide an annual report on the NYS charter school system to the governor and state legislature.

In April 2001, the commissioner of education issued the first such report. The brief document focuses on the five charter schools in operation in 1999–2000. It indicates that the overall fiscal impact of the four charter schools in NYC was "negligible," while New Covenant expenses were 2.76 percent of the ACSD budget (New York State Education Department 2001, 7). About two pages of the report are devoted to observations and recommendations for possible amendments to the Charter Schools Act. Perhaps the most controversial recommendation is that a definition or formula be provided that would assist a charter entity in determining whether it should reject a charter application because of excessive programmatic and fiscal impact on a school district (New York State Education Department 2001, 12).[42] In a memo to the commissioner of education, the New York Charter Schools Association expressed its adamant opposition to such an amendment. The memo noted that such an amendment implies that public school funds belong to school district administrators, rather than students, and that it would reward inadequate districts by inhibiting charter schools from being established, thereby penalizing students most in need of school choice (New York Charter Schools Association 2001, 2).

According to CSI policy, each SUNY-approved charter school must develop a detailed accountability plan after the first year of operation. The first such plans were being finalized in spring 2001. CSI makes several unannounced visits and a formal, year-end visit to each SUNY-chartered school every year. SBR policy requires two visits per year to charter schools for which it is the charter entity and annual visits to all NYS charter schools. SUNY and the NYC chancellor bear initial responsibility for overseeing charter schools they have authorized, but the SBR has authority to hold all charter schools accountable for upholding applicable laws and regulations. Moreover, the charter entity and the SBR each have statutory authority to revoke a charter (§2855).

Lawsuits

Contemporary U.S. policy making and implementation occur in the context of pervasive claims to rights, a spirit of adversarial legalism, and a practice of turning to the courts to resolve policy disputes (J. Anderson 2000; Peters 1999a; Kagan 1995; Melnick 1995; J. Wilson 1995). Lawsuits challenging the charter school reform are not uncommon, and the first such lawsuit in NYS was filed in October 1999. New York State United Teachers (NYSUT), the NYSSBA, and the Roosevelt Union Free School District (where SUNY had granted preliminary approval for a charter school for fall 2000) filed suit seeking to annul the new charters approved to date.

The Charter Schools Act requires that "at each significant stage of the chartering process" the charter entity and the regents provide "appropriate notification" to the school district in which the charter school is to be located and to public and nonpublic schools in the same geographic area as the proposed charter school (§2857. 1). Prior to charter issuance or renewal, the school district must be given an opportunity to comment on the proposed charter to the charter entity.

The plaintiffs complained that SUNY had approved the charter schools without providing adequate district notification, leaving insufficient time for the districts to plan for the impact of the schools. The day before the filing deadline for the lawsuit, CSI released the list of the applications it had received for fall 2000 openings, and the lawsuit was dropped about a month later. CSI has since released its charter application lists to superintendents statewide in the fall preceding the proposed opening dates for the schools.[43]

A second lawsuit is potentially more significant. In the case of *Board of Education of the Roosevelt Union Free School District v. Board of Trustees of the State University of New York* (2001), the local board of education challenged the issuance of a charter for Roosevelt Children's Academy Charter School. The board argued that the charter school would aggravate district financial problems by diverting up to $1.7 million to the school and would have a major impact on the district's ability to provide education programs to students who continued to be enrolled in district schools.

In a unanimous decision on 19 April 2001, the NYS Appellate Division, third department of the state supreme court, upheld a lower court's ruling that school districts cannot mount constitutional challenges to the charter school law.[44] As creatures and subdivisions of the state, school districts generally lack standing to levy constitutional challenges to state laws. However, the court also overturned the decision of the lower court that school boards may not challenge administrative decisions of a charter entity.

The state's Charter Schools Act prohibits charter school applicants from appealing to an administrative or judicial body to overturn a charter entity's decision to *deny* a charter school application (§2852.6). However, the appellate court ruled that the act does not expressly prohibit school districts from seeking review of a determination to *grant* a charter. Significantly, the appellate court permitted the lawsuit to proceed on the issue of whether SUNY's decision to grant the charter was "arbitrary and capricious." Thus, barring a successful appeal, the ruling opened the way for school districts to mount legal challenges to the issuance of charters.

Assessing the Charter School Movement in New York State

There are over 4,000 public schools in NYS, over 1,100 of which are in NYC. More than 2.8 million students attend public schools in NYS, and over 1 million of these students attend NYC public schools.[45] Allowing for some approved schools that may not open on schedule, NYS is set to have about 35 charter schools operating in 2001–2002. If and when NYS has the 100 new charter schools permitted by law, they will constitute just 2.5 percent of all public schools in NYS.

Focusing purely on the potential number of charter schools overall, we might expect minimal impact on the public school system. However, enrollments and location matter. In a public school system as vast as that of NYC (the largest school district in the United States), a handful of charter schools poses little threat to the system. Elsewhere, however, the appearance of one or more charter schools within district boundaries may have significant implications in terms of the loss of students and the funding that follows them to the charter school.

Raising or lifting the legal cap of 100 new charter schools would increase the chances that charter schools would have an impact on the traditional public school system. Yet the Charter Schools Act is young, and an increase in the cap does not look politically feasible at this time. However, once SUNY nears its cap of 50 charter schools, charter advocates may call for turning over a portion of any unused SBR charter slots to SUNY.

Charter school advocates such as Kolderie (1990b) emphasize the importance of having multiple authorizers eligible to approve charter schools in order to break the "exclusive franchise" enjoyed by school districts. Thus far, the majority of charter applications have been submitted to SUNY, the only charter entity whose members are not a part of or closely associated with the traditional K–12 educational establishment. To date, school districts are not active authorizers in NYS. With the exception of the NYC schools chancellor, no other school district has approved a charter school. Many education interests fervently oppose any effort to legitimize the charter school concept, and this passion may be preventing some districts from even considering the potential benefits of converting one or more schools to charter status.

Table 13.2 provides a list of the six objectives of the NYS Charter Schools Act as enacted. It is too early to meaningfully assess whether each of these objectives is being met. First, it will take several years—and scientific research designs—before accurate conclusions can be drawn about the academic performance of charter schools. Second, most of the charter schools approved to date are aimed at serv-

Table 13.2

Objectives of the New York State Charter School Law

- Improve student learning and achievement
- Increase learning opportunities for all students, with special emphasis on at-risk students
- Encourage the use of different and innovative teaching methods
- Create new professional opportunities for teachers, school administrators, and other school personnel
- Provide parents and students with expanded educational choices
- Provide schools with a method to change from rule-based to performance-based accountability systems by holding charter schools accountable for meeting measurable student achievement results

Source: New York State Charter Schools Act of 1998 (SB 7881, §2850, 2, a-f)

ing at-risk students, yet it is unclear whether charter schools will "increase learning opportunities for *all* students" (NYS Charter Schools Act of 1998, SB7881, §2850, 2, b [emphasis added]). In order for this to occur, one of two conditions would have to exist: there would need to be a high-quality charter school available to every student in NYS; or charter schools would have to demonstrate strategies that boost student learning opportunities, and other public schools would need incentives to adopt these strategies. Such incentives might exist in the competitive threat of charter schools, citizen demand, or perhaps a grant program.

Third, the meaning of "different and innovative teaching methods" is subject to debate; depending on the local context, a "back-to-basics" curriculum might be viewed as "innovative." Fourth, it appears clear that charter schools do present new professional opportunities for public school personnel. Kane (2000, 83) suggests that the charter school law "holds great promise for liberating teachers and administrators from the constraints of an encumbered system" in NYC. However, particularly in the case of EMC-operated charter schools, it is probable that such opportunities will flow primarily to younger, less experienced teachers, for whom the salary costs are lower than for more seasoned teachers. Moreover, as demonstrated in the New Covenant case, many charter school teachers face yearly employment contracts, as opposed to the job security enjoyed by many other public school teachers.

Fifth, charter schools are providing families with expanded educational choices. However, to date, these new choices are concentrated in urban regions, including Albany, Buffalo, NYC, Rochester, and Syracuse. Finally, the extent to which charter schools will be held accountable for performance—by both authorizer practices and market mechanisms—remains to be seen. The charter term is generally five years (barring early closure), and charter-renewal processes and decisions of the charter entities will offer important insights on the accountability issue.

Much to the delight of some and the dismay of others, the charter school movement is off to a running start in NYS. Over 100 charter school applications were submitted to charter entities in the first year. The number of new applications submitted in the second year declined significantly, and as noted earlier, about half of the applications received by SUNY were resubmissions from previous applicants. These statistics suggest that applicants may be navigating a learning curve regarding the complexities and challenges involved in founding new public schools and that charter entities are cautiously exercising their power to award charters.

Of the seventeen start-up charter schools in operation in 2000–2001, eight (47 percent) were operated by EMCs. Of the seventeen additional start-up charter schools approved by May 2001, six (35 percent) had EMC partners. This state of affairs is certain to be watched closely by opponents and proponents of EMC involvement in the delivery of public education.

While the charter school policy innovation enjoys significant political support from the governor, the SUNY board, and others, traditional education interests such as superintendents, school boards, and teachers unions continue to voice concerns and oppose the reform via legislative lobbying and court-based strategies. The political compromises in the state's unique charter school law and the politically charged charter school arena make NYS a rich site for analysts of charter school issues and the politics of education reform.

14 • Conclusions

Sandra Vergari

EACH OF THE PRECEDING chapters zooms in on particular tracts of the charter school landscape in North America. In this chapter, I provide a panoramic analysis of the findings and insights presented by the authors. My discussion focuses on patterns across the locales and on questions provoked by the charter school policy innovation.

Breaking the Exclusive Franchise

Statutes structure the policy implementation process through delineation of objectives, selection of implementing institutions, provision of resources, and regulation of opportunities for participation by nonagency actors in the implementation process (Mazmanian and Sabatier 1983, 25). Laws that permit a public entity other than a school district board to authorize charter schools promote the breakup of the "exclusive franchise" noted by Kolderie (1990b). In states such as Arizona, Michigan, and New York, the results of such statutory provisions have been significant. Hess and Maranto emphasize that the independent state board for charter schools in Arizona has played a consciously active and effective role in facilitating the rapid growth of charter schools in that state. Mintrom notes that in Michigan the majority of charter schools have been authorized by public universities. Similarly, the State University of New York board of trustees has enthusiastically embraced the charter school concept, and this board is the charter entity for the majority of start-up charter schools approved to date in the state. By mid-2001, with the exception of New York City, no school district had approved a charter school in New York State.

Given the competitive element built into the charter school concept, designating school districts as the primary authorizers is somewhat analogous to expecting that a McDonald's franchise would happily authorize the existence of a Burger King next door, as noted by Bailey, Lavely, and Wooley-Brown. While it is noteworthy that Wisconsin had ninety-two schools chartered by sixty-one different authorizers in 2000–2001, it is equally significant that the overwhelming majority of those authorizers were school districts with a direct interest in the exclusive franchise.

While no two charter school laws are identical, one of the common features of most charter school statutes examined in this book is that they continue to evolve over time. Indeed, many of the charter school laws have been amended in significant ways. While there are several notable exceptions—such as in Michigan and Texas, where some amendments have favored charter school opponents—amendments have generally supported the policy innovation. Hirsch notes that in Colorado, policy makers have taken steps toward ensuring that the charter school concept becomes an institutionalized feature of public education, rather than a marginalized experimental program. Similar patterns are evident elsewhere. For instance, in addition to Colorado, charter school laws in California, Florida, Massachusetts, Minnesota, and Wisconsin have been amended to eliminate or ease caps on the number of charter schools permitted.

Competition versus Cooperation

Charter school advocates (and many charter school laws) posit that the reform is intended in part to foster innovations that can be replicated in traditional public schools. In order for this to occur, several conditions must obtain. First, charter schools must be "innovative"; second, there must be must be incentives for the traditional public school system to adopt the innovations; and third, there must be mechanisms that facilitate the transfer of such innovative practices from charter schools to traditional public schools.

A number of analysts have begun to examine the extent to which charter schools are actually "innovative" (e.g., Wong, Shen, and Novacek 2001; Mintrom 2000a; Rosenblum Brigham Associates 1998). By definition, an innovation is something "new." When considering education, we must ask in what context a practice or approach is "new"—new in a particular school district or state or in a historical context? In a study of school districts and charter schools in Massachusetts, New Jersey, and Washington, D.C., Teske et al. (2000, 15) assert that charter schools and public school officials define innovation differently and that this inhibits the transfer of charter school practices to traditional public schools. Teske et al. (2000, 22) suggest that if traditional public schools and charter schools "can learn to communicate better, even as they remain competitive, the worthwhile lessons from the charter school experiment will spread much more quickly." However, the prospects for more frequent and productive communication between the two systems do not look promising. This is because systems in competition face disincentives to willingly share successful "trade secrets" with each other.

Bridges that promote cooperation between charter schools and their neighbors in the traditional public school system are typically tenuous or nonexistent. As noted by Bosetti and O'Reilly, the Alberta minister of education envisioned charter schools and traditional schools as forming "one seamless public education system." However, attempts by the Alberta government to encourage cooperation between charter schools and the traditional school system have yielded few results. Instead, as reported by all of the authors in this book, there are significant tensions between charter schools and the traditional public school system. This state of affairs is not surprising. The competitive element inherent in the charter school reform inhibits cooperation between charter schools and traditional public schools. For instance, Bosetti and O'Reilly highlight a question confronting charter school operators in Alberta, where charter schools are supposed to offer "unique and innovative programs." If such programs were to be adopted by traditional public schools, would the rationale for charter schools be significantly diminished?

Mintrom (2000a, v) avows that "until efforts are made to seriously engage questions of information dissemination, credence cannot be given to the claim that charter schools hold the potential to transform the whole system of public schooling." He notes that such needs might be met through the development of a central clearinghouse for information collection and dissemination. In his chapter, Mintrom suggests that state departments of education are uniquely positioned to facilitate the identification and dissemination of best practices among charter schools and traditional public schools. The qualities of capacity and will are critical determinants of whether this task is likely to be performed by education departments. The chapters included here indicate that in states such as Arizona, Michigan, North Carolina, and Texas, the charter school units of the education departments lack the personnel and resources for fulfilling such a mission. Commitment to statutory objectives on the part of implementing officials is also essential for achievement of the objectives (Mazmanian and Sabatier 1983). However, personnel in some state departments of education have demonstrated a lack of enthusiasm for the charter school reform.

Equity and Diversity

It is appropriate to next consider matters of equity and diversity in relation to charter schools and the dilemmas that they present for the charter school movement.

Special Education

Given that at least half of the charter schools in Texas were created to meet the needs of students at risk of dropping out, Fusarelli argues that enrollment of special education students in Texas charter schools should be higher than the statewide average, rather than lower, as is the case. Special education students are widely considered to be the most difficult and expensive children to educate. Indeed, McNiff and Hassel note that a high-needs child can cost over $60,000 a year to educate. Accordingly, Fusarelli raises the possibility that special education students who wish to attend charter schools in Texas may suffer implicit or explicit barriers to enrollment and access to special education services. Hess and Maranto note that allegations of discrimination against disabled children have also been levied in Arizona.

In New York, the Albany City School District (ACSD) informed the state education department that the New Covenant charter school was not providing special education students with adequate services in accordance with the students' individual education plans (which are developed in conjunction with the school district as per state law). Significantly, a large number of the special education students who attended New Covenant have returned to ACSD schools. According to Herdman, adequate attention to the needs of special education students has also been a challenge for Massachusetts charter schools. He observes: "Without the economies of scale of a large district, charter schools face the possibility of providing a range of special needs services that exceeds their available revenue." In North Carolina, in addition to shortfalls in funding for special education services, there is a shortage of special education teachers. As noted by McNiff and Hassel, districts with higher salaries for special education teachers leave charter schools and poorer districts scrambling to find staff.

Mintrom summarizes the incentives that appear to motivate many parents and charter school operators on special education in Michigan. First, parents often do not want a stigmatizing label thrust upon their children, and charter schools are viewed as bastions of hope. Second, for charter school operators, financial considerations may motivate neglect of signs of special needs among students. Salient support for this observation is found in Mead's discussion of the attempt by the city of Milwaukee to have charter schools classified as private schools, particularly when it came to matters of special education.

Ethnic and Racial Balance

A number of charter school laws indicate that the student population of a charter school should be reflective of the community surrounding the school. According to Mead, many Wisconsin charter schools have failed to meet the requirement that they specify how they will achieve a racial and ethnic balance that reflects the school district population. Moreover, an official audit found that some Wisconsin charter schools failed to use random selection processes for admissions and instead filled seats on a first-come, first-served basis. Such practices can hamper the achievement of racial and ethnic representation and, as noted by Mead, violate federal requirements that available seats be filled randomly from the applicant pool.

The California charter school law also requires that a charter school application include a description of how the school will achieve an ethnic balance reflective of the general population of the school district in which the charter school is to be located. Wohlstetter, Griffin, and Chau observe that meeting this ethnic diversity requirement has been a challenge for many California charter schools. Nonetheless, as of mid-2001, no charters had been revoked by the state or by authorizers in cases where the charter school student population did not meet the ethnic balance of the district.

As indicated by Fusarelli, it can be argued that the disproportionate concentration of minorities in Texas charter schools is not the product of "White flight," but rather due to the fact that many charter schools are created specifically to try to meet the needs of heretofore underserved at-risk children. Similarly, in North Carolina, where the charter school law requires that charter schools "reasonably reflect" the racial and ethnic composition of their communities, many charter schools were approved to serve at-risk students. Indeed, charter school laws in a number of other states (e.g., Connecticut, Delaware, Illinois, New York, and Virginia) require or encourage that preference be given to applications for charter schools designed to serve at-risk students. The Oklahoma charter school statute permits a charter school to limit admissions to students residing within an "academic enterprise zone." The law defines such a zone as a geographic area within a school district in which 60 percent or more of the children who reside in the area qualify for free or reduced-price lunches. McNiff and Hassel note that the student populations of these types of charter schools tend to be disproportionately minority.

The North Carolina state board of education has decided to determine, on a school-by-school basis, whether a charter school's racial imbalance is justified and what action, if any, the state should take. Similar to the California case, as of mid-2001, no action had been taken against any North Carolina charter school on the basis of its racial composition. According to Wong, Shen, and Novacek (2001), charter schools in California, Michigan, and Texas appear to be serving student populations that are similar to the neighborhoods surrounding the schools. Wohlstetter, Griffin, and Chau observe that while diversity issues are the subject of much attention from researchers, few California policy makers have voiced concerns about diversity. Fusarelli concludes that the Texas school system is already so segregated that charter schools could hardly make the situation worse and may instead lead to greater integration. Hirsch raises diversity concerns of a different type, noting that the supply of charter schools in Colorado is uncommonly concentrated in isolated pockets of the state, primarily in suburban areas.

Conclusions about the public policy implications of evidence depend on the values of the analyst (Brighouse 2000; Peters 1999a). The charter school concept emphasizes the value of choice: "By definition, charter schools cannot be all things to all people: They must focus on and attract students from a selected segment of the educational market" (McCabe and Vinzant 1999, 367). Accordingly, the student population of a charter school with an Afro-, Euro-, or Hispanic-centric curriculum is not likely to encompass the demographic diversity of the individuals featured in the famous 1970s Coca-Cola commercial. Families choose charter schools. If a charter school uses nondiscriminatory admissions processes and its curriculum promotes understanding and tolerance across racial and ethnic groups, there may be little cause for concern. On the other hand, if a charter school "chooses families" by discouraging the enrollment of particular types of students and if its curriculum implicitly or explicitly emphasizes racial and ethnic division rather than the commonalities shared by members of the same society, then social fragmentation is likely to be an unsavory outcome of an emphasis on the choice value. As is discussed later, an emphasis on the choice value necessarily involves trade-offs in terms of other values.

School Finance Equity

Another key equity issue is charter school finance. Do charter schools enjoy public funding at levels similar to traditional public schools? Lack of start-up funds and inadequate operating funds have been cited by most charter schools as serious obstacles to their viability (RPP International 2000).[1] A majority of states do not provide financial assistance for charter school facilities (American Federation of Teachers Educational Foundation 2000). Several of the chapters here report that facilities costs have consumed significant portions of charter school instructional budgets. The formidable challenges of locating and financing adequate charter school facilities were recognized by Congress in 2000 with its approval of a new federal charter school facilities demonstration program.

The most comprehensive examination of charter school finance issues to date is a study commissioned by the U.S. Department of Education and completed by the American Federation of Teachers Educational Foundation (2000). The report indicates that looking only at the raw numbers of charter school and school district funding yields an incomplete assessment of funding comparability between the two systems. Financial comparability is uncertain in states such as Colorado, where charter school funding is determined partly by negotiations over the charter, and in states that fund charter schools based on average school district costs or revenues. The assessment of comparability is a complex undertaking in these states because charter school funding is comparable to the funding of the host district "only when the student body resembles the host district's student body" (American Federation of Teachers Educational Foundation 2000, 84). The report suggests that "charter schools can configure their grade level structure and enrollment in order to generate optimal funding. They can set limits on enrollment and use waiting lists to maximize funding efficiency (e.g., optimal class sizes and staffing ratios) by quickly replacing students leaving the school" (American Federation of Teachers Educational Foundation 2000, 84). However, the report also concludes that charter schools with high-cost students and programs are not funded equitably and may be substantially underfunded (American Federation of Teachers Educational Foundation 2000, 83–84). This is a significant finding in light of the fact that many charter schools are aimed at serving at-risk children. A study of charter schools in California concluded that charter schools usually need access to private resources in order to survive and that the ability to secure private resources varies greatly across schools (Wells and Research Associates 1998).

Legal Issues and the Courts

Charter school policy implementation has been subjected to various legal challenges. As noted in my chapter on New York State, barring a successful appeal, a 2001 court ruling opened the way for school districts across the state to mount legal challenges to the issuance of charters in their districts. In addition, Hirsch highlights the ruling of the Colorado Supreme Court that the power of the state board of education (SBE) to require school districts to authorize charter schools in appeal cases is constitutional. In Colorado, only school districts are permitted to authorize charter schools. However, the court ruling appears to favor those who advocate breaking the exclusive franchise of local districts in Colorado. Hirsch observes that in a state with long-standing cultural and legal adherence to the principle of local control, the decision might lift any constitutional barriers to the introduction of state-level authorizers.

Wisconsin has also been the setting for some intriguing legal questions. For example, Mead notes that the Wisconsin charter school law does not explicitly define charter schools as public schools. In 1998, the city of Milwaukee was unsuccessful in its attempt to make a case that charter schools are not public schools and therefore not subject to the special education rules (and resulting expenses) mandated for public schools.

Accountability

Accountability is the most compelling issue on the charter school landscape today. As noted by Hassel (1999a, 160): "Until charter-granting agencies have policies in place that define charters schools' accountability for results, taxpayers cannot feel confident that the bargain of autonomy for accountability is working. From the perspective of charter schools, the absence of clear accountability systems makes it difficult to act decisively in the development of their schools." Viewing accountability matters through a somewhat different lens, Henig (1999, 101) avows: "To avoid the risks of greater segregation, fragmentation, and stratification that unregulated choice brings into play, we would have to ensure that choice programs are fundamentally fair and are embedded in an institutional context that provides oversight and accountability to democratic values."

When "accountability for results" is mentioned in the policy discourse on charter schools, the "results" inevitably refer to scores on standardized tests. However, B. Levin (2001b) identifies three additional types of student outputs that merit attention. First, school-based student outcome indicators such as attendance rates, rates of disciplinary incidents, and graduation rates might be examined. Second, student satisfaction measures are important, because they provide a gauge of student motivation. Third, postschool outcomes such as university attendance, employment status, and civic participation could be assessed. In addition to student outputs, charter school accountability can also be assessed in terms of institutional outcomes (e.g., effects of the reform on teacher expertise) and social outcomes (e.g., effects of the reform on equity across demographic groups and social cohesion) (B. Levin 2001b).

Charter schools may supplement state-mandated student tests with a range of additional indicators of performance accountability. For instance, Fusarelli writes that charter schools in Texas design their evaluation programs to include more performance measures (e.g., student projects and indices of parental and student satisfaction) than are used for traditional public schools. Similarly, Nathan points out that many Minnesota charter schools have proposed such additional forms of accountability as one year's growth on national standardized tests for each year a student attends the school and reductions in the number of students involved in the juvenile justice system.

According to the authors collected here, many charter school jurisdictions emphasize fiscal accountability over academic and other forms of accountability. An emphasis on oversight of finances is not a bad thing, of course, particularly given that weaknesses in financial administration are a leading cause of charter school closures, and without adequate funds, a charter school cannot afford to operate. However, it is also important to hold charter schools accountable for academic performance and a range of other operational and procedural matters in the public interest (e.g., admissions procedures, conflict of interest rules and service on public boards, open-meetings requirements, teacher certification rules and legislative intent with regard to noncertified teachers, and special education rules).

Standardized procedures of fiscal accounting are mandated and typically utilized with little controversy. Funds are either spent appropriately, or they are not; the school budget either balances, or it does not. In contrast, figuring out how to assess accountability in other areas of school operations is less straightforward (Hassel and Vergari 1999). Bailey, Lavely, and Wooley-Brown indicate that charter schools and their district authorizers have encountered difficulties in agreeing upon acceptable levels of student achievement. Interestingly, they note that charter schools may set high goals in the quest to gain charter approval but have problems meeting those goals once in operation. Thus, the authors advise that "charter schools in Florida need to specify more clearly measurable academic goals that are realistic and obtainable." Bosetti and O'Reilly report that in Alberta, charter schools that are making "reasonable" progress on academic matters are judged to be performing well enough to remain open; this sort of subjective evaluation is not uncommon in other jurisdictions.

The absence of a widely accepted theory of causation in education leads reasonable people to often disagree radically about education policy (Peters 1999a, 352). A number of factors unique to education make it difficult for third parties to determine responsibility for student performance. The educational process is difficult to evaluate because of the social interactions at its heart (e.g., many facets of the teacher-student relationship shape educational outcomes). Learning depends on the capacity and will of both the teacher and the student. Moreover, much of the educational process is hidden and difficult to monitor. In addition to individual-level factors, the quality of the educational process is influenced by institutional, economic, and social factors (Mintrom and Vergari 1997b).

Herdman advises that developers of charter school accountability schemes need to address three fundamental questions: (1) how good is good enough? (2) to what should charter schools be compared? and (3) what is a reasonable time frame in which to make judgments about performance? Nathan points out that the question of how much progress a school should have to make within a particular time frame in order to justify its existence is a new question in public education. In return for regulatory relief, charter schools are supposed to face high standards of accountability for overall performance. Indeed, it can be argued that in their pure form, charter schools are intended to be held to a *higher* standard of accountability than traditional public schools (see Nathan 1996).

Hess and Maranto refer to the "relaxed approach" to charter school regulation in Arizona, and Wohlstetter, Griffin, and Chau report that "strong accountability is lacking" in California. While California charter schools are required to include educational goals in their charters, the authors note that a majority of schools have reported few consequences for not meeting these goals. Hirsch indicates that in Colorado there is wide variation in the level of district communication and interaction with charter schools, as well as in the performance expectations for charter schools. A voluntary, privately initiated pilot accountability program is now underway for fifteen charter schools in Colorado. However, Hirsch states that the results of the data gathering and external site visits that are a part of the program are not compiled and systematically analyzed and distributed.

In Alberta, accountability matters have been the subject of much confusion, and there has been a lack of clarity in the oversight criteria for charter schools. Bosetti and O'Reilly note that systematic evaluation of charter schools in Alberta did not begin until three years after the first charter was issued. In Minnesota, where about 90 percent of the charter schools are not sponsored at the state level, Nathan reports that nine years after the passage of the first charter school law in North America, there is still a need for clarity on who is responsible for what on charter school oversight matters. In Wisconsin, Mead notes that the real oversight of any charter school comes from the chartering authority itself; yet there are no statutory guidelines as to how this task might be accomplished. As a result, the specific terms of the charter are critical in shaping the oversight framework for a given charter school.

According to Mintrom, charter school authorizers in Michigan face considerable public pressure because they "represent the primary conduit through which anything like 'the public will' can be imposed upon charter schools." He observes that authorizers have been caught in the midst of broader battles over the degree to which charter schools should be held directly accountable to charter school parents versus the broader public. This points to a key question for analysts of charter school policy: To what extent is such policy responsive to individual interests as opposed to the collective interest (see, e.g., McCabe and Vinzant 1999; Stone 1988)? Further, can these two types of interests be reconciled and incorporated into the same reform policy?

Technical Complexity

Charter school accountability processes in California and North Carolina have been made more complicated by particular technical problems. Wohlstetter, Griffin, and Chau explain that flux in the standardized testing mandates at the state and local levels has made it difficult to track changes in student achievement over time and to compare charter school students to other public school students as part of a systematic accountability process. In North Carolina, charter schools are required to use the state's electronic reporting mechanism for tracking student and financial information—a system designed for school districts—and many charter operators have found the system to be unwieldy. McNiff and Hassel assert that ongoing concerns over such matters "are prime examples of the difficulty of fitting charter schools into preexisting systems of oversight."

The concerns raised in broader debates about the merits of various uses of standardized testing in public education also apply to charter schools. Fusarelli reports that the Texas accountability system for public education is well developed and places a heavy emphasis on Texas Assessment of Academic Skills scores. This, notes Fusarelli, will encourage uniformity among charter schools, rather than innovation and diversity. Hirsch and McNiff and Hassel raise similar concerns in their respective discussions of Colorado and North Carolina. Many charter schools choose to administer national norm-referenced tests in addition to state-mandated assessments. The accountability debate is further complicated when charter school students perform very well on a national standardized test yet poorly on a state test (as has occurred in North Carolina).

Capacity Issues

Hess and Maranto explain that Arizona policy makers intentionally limited the funding for regulation and administration of the charter school system in order to prevent a new bureaucracy from developing around the reform. However, Mintrom asserts that while opponents of "big government" might applaud the limited role that the Michigan Department of Education plays in the oversight and coordination of the charter school system, such exuberance is misplaced. He suggests that restricting state monitoring means that serious forms of waste and abuse at different levels can go unchecked.

Regardless of intent, the state-level capacity for ensuring charter school accountability is typically limited. Thus, the fundamental question becomes one of how to allocate limited resources most effectively. For instance, the unique charter school renewal inspection process in Massachusetts is outsourced, but Herdman suggests that the $19,000 renewal inspection cost is likely to become prohibitive if charter schools proliferate in Massachusetts. A top official in the state education agency in Texas has asserted that the agency is devoting a disproportionate amount of resources to charter school matters. Accordingly, Fusarelli expects that the problem of limited oversight capacity will continue to be a compelling issue in Texas.

One of the challenges in the task environment of charter school authorizers is how to balance the roles of overseer and helper (Vergari 2000). As noted by Nathan, another challenge is delineating the respective oversight responsibilities of state departments of education and authorizers. In the case of the charter school in Albany, discussed in the chapter on New York, would it have been useful or desirable for the charter school authorizer and/or the state department of education to engage in more intrusive oversight activity during the school's first several months of operation, rather than primarily at the close of the year? Should those charged with oversight also be engaged in the provision of direct assistance or advice to a charter school? These types of philosophical and logistical questions need to be sorted out by the relevant stakeholders. Interestingly, Fusarelli reports that the Texas state education agency cannot by law offer technical assistance to charter schools, because of its role as the monitor of the schools. Given that charter school authorizers have limited resources for fulfilling their public responsibilities, a case can be made that charter schools in their first year —when problems are likely to be the most numerous and serious—should receive more frequent attention than older charter schools.

Analytical navigation of the charter school accountability terrain across North America yields somewhat disappointing findings. It is not uncommon for public officials to think of their respective states as unique in terms of the legal-political context or the technical challenges surrounding charter schools. Certainly, there are some significant differences in enabling legislation and politics across charter school jurisdictions. However, weaknesses in charter school accountability schemes appear remarkably similar across North America. Among other things, this state of affairs suggests that interjurisdictional networking among charter school operators, authorizers, and officials from state departments of education could be quite beneficial. The U.S. Department of Education has facilitated such networking through its sponsorship of national conferences on charter schools in 1997, 1999, and 2000.[2]

If the charter school concept is to be embraced as something significantly better than what is found in the traditional public school system, charter school advocates will need to engage in a concerted effort to develop and implement sound, rigorous, systematic accountability systems. The Massachusetts model discussed by Herdman merits broader consideration, and Finn, Manno, and Vanourek (2000, 126–47) have developed a three-pronged system of accountability that emphasizes transparency. Charter school authorizers have much to gain from discussions with each other on such matters, as recognized by the directors of several authorizer offices when, in 2000, they organized the new National Association of Charter School Authorizers.

Educational Management Companies

One of the most controversial features of the charter school landscape is the presence of educational management companies (EMCs). As I note in the chapter on New York, several provisions of the New York charter schools act make the state relatively appealing to EMCs. About 50 percent of the start-up charter schools operating in New York in 2000–2001 were operated by EMCs. Wohlstetter, Griffin, and Chau report that Edison Schools, Inc., operated about 2 percent of all charter schools in California in 2000–2001; Nathan reports that EMCs help operate about 10–15 percent of Minnesota charter schools; and Mintrom notes that in Michigan 65 percent of charter schools made some use of EMCs in 2000–2001.

Some analysts perceive the introduction of the profit motive to the delivery of public education to be an ugly feature of the charter school environment. Mead indicates that when a couple of charter schools to be operated by Edison Schools, Inc., were authorized by the University of Wisconsin-Milwaukee, concerns were raised within the university community and the city about the propriety of an organization "profiting" from participation in the publicly funded charter program. Similarly, when the charter school in Albany was being founded, the head of the district teachers union expressed dismay that the tax dollars of New Yorkers could end up as profits for an EMC with headquarters in Boston. Other observers note that traditional public schools have long contracted with private providers for a variety of goods and services. Moreover, many school districts have embraced exclusive contracts with particular soda companies, and some traditional public schools willingly display company logos (e.g., on the rooftop of a school near an airport, on athletic scoreboards) in return for particular benefits.

As noted by Herdman, a former state education official in Massachusetts expressed indifference regarding the profit factor, emphasizing instead that an EMC must please the charter school board of trustees and the board of trustees must please the authorizer. Thus, the profit motive need not preclude accountability to the public. However, charter school advocates Finn, Manno, and Vanourek (2000, 243) express concern that if large franchise operations obliterate "mom and pop" charter schools, "the charter movement will lose much of its character, variety, and popular appeal."

The existence of for-profit companies engaged in running all facets of school operations, including instruction, adds another line of accountability to the delivery of education. Through the charter school application and oversight processes, charter school authorizers can help to prevent situations in which the charter school board lacks the capacity and will to fulfill its public duties and defers too much decision-making power to the EMC.

Political and Technical Support for Charter Schools

Individuals matter in the processes of policy adoption and implementation, and turnover in positions of power creates openings for policy change (Mintrom 2000b; Kingdon 1995; McLaughlin 1987). These insights are useful for considering the politics of charter schools in a number of jurisdictions. For example, Hess and Maranto emphasize that charter schools would not have proliferated in the absence of the "promarket regulatory regime" in Arizona. In states such as Michigan, New York, and Wisconsin, governors have played significant roles in promoting charter school initiatives. Bosetti and O'Reilly note that turnover in key government positions has led to diminished political support for charter schools in Alberta. They surmise that in the absence of stronger advocates who hold authority to make decisions, the charter school reform is not likely to thrive in Alberta. Skillful advocates of policy reform craftily "hook" their policy solutions to problems that are on the minds of politicians (Mintrom 2000b; Kingdon 1995). Thus, while political support for charter schools is lacking in North Carolina, McNiff and Hassel suggest that charter school advocates may be able to gain agenda status by linking the solution of charter schools to the much-discussed problem of how to improve the educational plight of many minority students in North Carolina.

Potentially, state departments of education could fulfill an important role in ensuring that the charter school landscape receives nourishing fertilization that fosters the identification and dissemination of best practices across public education, as well as the weeding out of features that are not conducive to a healthy educational environment. In cases where such leadership and service are lacking (for reasons of capacity and/or will), other organizations have attempted to fill some of the gap. As noted by contributors to this volume, privately funded state-level institutes, resource centers, and associations have emerged to provide technical assistance to charter school founders, authorizers, and policy makers. Well-known resources at the national level include the U.S. Department of Education, the Charter Friends National Network, and the Center for Education Reform, each of which has sponsored and disseminated various reports on charter school issues.

Making Sense of the Charter School Landscape

We now return to the questions posed at the beginning of the book. Are charter schools merely "another flawed educational reform" or, worse, a "dismal failure" in education policy? Are they the beginning of the "reinvention of public education"? Or are they something in between these extremes? Nearly a decade after the passage of the first charter school law in North America and over 2,000 charter schools later, there is little evidence to support the casual dismissal of charter schools as an unsuccessful reform. On the other hand, whether charter schools will spur a full-blown "reinvention of public education" remains a matter of uncertainty. What is clear is that the reform is challenging traditional assumptions about the delivery of public education and what the public has a right to expect from public education.

It is still too early to write a definitive report on charter schools' "ripple effects," but the contents of this volume suggest that the traditional public school system cannot afford to ignore charter schools.[3] As observed by U.S. education secretary Rod Paige, "public schools face increasingly tough competition from private schools, parochial schools, charter schools, home schools, and even Internet schools. Public schools are no longer the only show in town. . . . If we don't bring real reform to public schools, more families will leave the system in droves. It will be too late" (Paige 2001).[4] Charter schools can have an impact beyond what their numbers suggest. For any given school district in a state with a strong charter school law, even if there is no immediate indication that a charter school will be formed that attracts district students, the possibility of such may spur positive preemptive action on the part of the district. Thus, the presence of charter schools has the potential to encourage greater attention to "customer service," community building, personal outreach and public relations, and other efforts to maintain and enhance school district legitimacy. On the other hand, school districts may instead emphasize petty rhetoric, legislative lobbying, and court challenges in an effort to thwart the charter school policy reform. The former approach is likely to yield more favorable results for school district interests over the long term.

As in the case of any bold new initiative, there are imperfections across the charter school landscape, some more significant than others. The ability to boast of consistently impressive academic performance among charter schools would be a major political arrow in the quiver of charter advocates. However, existing data indicate that the academic achievement of charter school students overall has been mixed. Making sense of student achievement data for charter schools is a complex undertaking. The methodological dilemmas and controversies surrounding analyses of student achievement under voucher programs (e.g., selection bias, control groups, sample attrition over time, sample size, analytical time frame) also apply to charter schools. These challenging factors, combined with the relatively young age of charter schools in many states, probably account for the void in our knowledge about the academic performance of charter schools overall. Given that the federal government continues to support the reform both symbolically and financially, it would be logical and useful for it to conduct or commission systematic analyses of the academic performance of charter schools.

While the overall academic performance of charter schools remains uncertain, it is safe to say that charter schools are not a magic bullet for boosting student achievement. Nor should they be held to such a lofty standard. The fact that some charter schools are struggling with student achievement confirms what the traditional educational establishment has long known: equipping students with the skills to meet reasonable academic standards, especially students with special challenges and needs, is not an easy undertaking. Finn, Manno, and Vanourek (2000, 98, 153) observe "troubling signs" that charter schools are being held to a different standard than traditional public schools. One rational response to this observation is that, as originally conceived, the charter school concept indicated that charter schools were indeed intended to be held to a *higher* standard of performance than traditional public schools. If the charter school policy innovation is not about demonstrating how to perform *better than* traditional public schools, then on what basis is the regulatory relief that only charter schools enjoy justified? Moreover, if the overriding objective of the charter school movement is not to demonstrate performance superior to that of traditional public schools (in several areas, including student achievement), opponents will have cause to suspect that charter proponents actually seek the achievement of other, possibly "less noble" objectives (e.g., social stratification or opening the doors to a full voucher system).

A Significant Precedent in Education Policy

Some analysts argue that to date, the performance of charter schools is less than impressive and is not commensurate with the amount of public, private, and human capital being pumped into the policy reform (see Fuller 2000; Good and Braden 2000; Wells and Research Associates 1998). However, government endorsement of the charter school concept marks a turning point in education policy that has already had important effects that appear likely to endure. As noted by Tyack and Cuban (1995, 9), "most Americans have been to school and know what a 'real school' looks like. Congruence with that cultural template has helped maintain the legitimacy of the institution in the minds of the public." In the absence of an adequate degree of public confidence in traditional public schools, public schools will suffer from a lack of essential financial, political, and moral support (Sergiovanni et al. 1999, 34–35). As implied in the remarks by Secretary Paige noted earlier, the very legitimacy of the traditional educational establishment is now under challenge by charter schools and other alternative conceptualizations of the "real school." As implemented in some places, and for good or ill depending upon one's perspective, charter school policy has demonstrated that a "real school" can exist in a shopping mall, a warehouse, a museum, or over the Internet; can be operated by a private corporation for profit; can be devoid of a playground, gymnasium, library, or cafeteria; can be governed by a self-selected, appointed board; can use an Afrocentric or Eurocentric curriculum; and can establish its own personnel policies, calendar, grade configuration, and enrollment numbers.[5]

Given that the standard grammar of schooling in the United States has been highly resistant to change (Tyack and Cuban 1995), it is remarkable that charter school laws have been adopted in a majority of the states, that most charter schools have waiting lists, and that the innovation enjoys significant support from the state and federal governments. The charter school statutes and the schools that have developed in response are likely to continue to provoke new ways of thinking about the notion of the "real school."

Policies are often oversold during the formulation and adoption stages. Since expectations about what an initiative can achieve are often unrealistically high, there is likely to be disappointment with the actual results (Ripley and Franklin 1982, 201). In many cases, successful implementation is possible only through a lowering of standards or alteration of the evaluative criteria (Majone and Wildavsky 1979, 179). As in the case of other school choice initiatives, charter school policy has characteristics that can be held at least partially responsible for some shortcomings in producing desired outcomes (Brighouse 2000, 34). Most notably, as public schools, charter schools exist in a context of constraints on their freedom of action. For example, L. Anderson and Finnegan (2001) assert that the individualized goal-setting that was supposed to be a key feature of charter schools is likely to be usurped by externally imposed accountability mandates (e.g., state rules regarding student testing).

During implementation, policies are redesigned by actions that alter resources and objectives (Majone and Wildavsky 1979, 170). Proponents of a program may strategically frame outcomes in a way that favors the program; for example, if proponents of the Head Start program are unable to demonstrate sustained educational improvement in children, they may emphasize that the program increases parental involvement, which may lead to educational improvement (Majone and Wildavsky 1979, 172). Similarly, even if the data clearly suggested that charter schools were not performing well academically, proponents might protect the reform by showing that it promotes the accomplishment of other worthy objectives that are expected ultimately to yield improvements in student achievement and other outcomes.

It is difficult to change institutional structures, but when they do change, there are often dramatic and long-lasting changes in policy outcomes (Baumgartner and Jones 1993, 12). For any given issue, once a precedent has been set and a new principle has been established through the passage of legislation, public policy in that area is significantly altered—because future policies are based on the new principle, because people become used to new practices, and because "it becomes as difficult to reverse the new direction as it was to change the old" (Kingdon 1995, 191) Second, when an old coalition (e.g., the "traditional educational establishment") that was blocking a reform is defeated, "life is never quite the same," because the coalition can no longer be viewed as invincible or as *the* sponsor or opponent of legislation in the policy area (Kingdon 1995, 191). Third, once in place, programs are not often abolished. Programs generate organizations and constituents who are likely to defend the reform in the face of challenges (Peters 1999a). Nonetheless, opponents of an adopted policy need not give up, and proponents cannot necessarily relax after their objectives have been legitimized via statute (Ripley and Franklin 1982, 19). The policy arena contains numerous access points through which different interests may influence outcomes and formal decisions may be appealed or amended (Ripley and Franklin 1982).

If the charter school movement cannot live up to its promise of high standards of accountability for performance—and, again, I emphasize that "performance" here is construed broadly to include a range of issues in the public interest, from finances and academics to admissions policies and governance practices—then policy makers may be hard-pressed to justify continued public financing of the reform. On the other hand, even under such circumstances, the reform might still endure as a limited program that caters to certain "niche markets" or "isolated pockets" of the public school environment.[6] There is a third possible scenario. Consider that "evidence is only [one] of many factors that shape policy, and it may often be among the less important of these" (B. Levin 2001a, 20). Research does not typically occupy a privileged position in the policy-making arena. Research findings may inform policy, but they do not substitute for policy itself. Policy makers are frequently inclined to adopt policy more on the basis of values and preferences than on the basis of research (Sergiovanni et al. 1999, 58). Thus, even if the reform were found to display serious deficiencies, significant political support might still be forthcoming because the reform embodies values cherished by power elites and/or because continued support for the reform is deemed to be politically advantageous. In any case, given the recency of the charter school policy innovation in many jurisdictions, comprehensive, accurate, and adequate assessments of its various long-term outcomes will not be possible for a few more years.

Tyack and Cuban (1995, 140) observe that the discourse about public education has focused on individual school choice yet has neglected collective choice issues that are critical for civic welfare, "choices made through the democratic process about the values and knowledge that citizens want to pass on to the next generation." As noted by H. Levin (2000, 140), school choice initiatives emphasize sending children to schools that cater to the particular values and objectives of individual families, rather than to the objectives of the broader society. Thus, the charter school reform provokes questions about whether public education is a consumer good rather than a common good and about whether parents and children are appropriately viewed as "citizens" or as "customers" (McCabe and Vinzant 1999, 369; Tyack and Cuban 1995, 140–41). Henig (1999, 101) aptly notes that the deficiencies of existing democratic institutions do not mean that the appropriate course of action is to bypass the challenge of making them work. Yet, addressing such challenges takes time, and children grow up. Thus, who can blame those parents who have decided to try the customer-exit option when they seek only what is best for their children and when their earnest citizen voices have proved ineffective?

Some elements of the common school perspective may be preserved in the charter school system via certain state mandates applied to all public schools, including charter schools. For example, civil society concerns may be addressed in part through a state mandate that all public schools deliver a particular character-education curriculum based on important core values on which there is consensus. Charter school advocates are averse to any mention of the term "mandate," yet it is reasonable to subject charter schools, as publicly funded entities, to selected mandates that are widely agreed to serve the public interest. Interests that favor the values of choice, deregulation, and individual goals, which are central to the charter school concept, would need to compromise with interests that are especially concerned about civil society, civic capacity, and the nurturance of common core values among the nation's youth.

Overall, at present, the vista looks promising in terms of the viability of the charter school policy innovation. Symbolically, politically, and substantively, the reform appears to hold more long-term significance than the typical fad in educational policy and administration. Charter schools enjoy bipartisan support at the state and federal levels. The charter schools now in operation, those approved to open, and the frequency of waiting lists for student admissions provide tangible evidence of citizen demand for better options in public education. The charter school movement has also involved an extraordinary demonstration of energy and dedication at the grassroots level on the part of charter school founders, educators, and families.

This volume is intended to make an informed contribution to the research literature and the policy debate on education reform. As readers are left to ponder the broad expanse of charter school issues presented, I hope they come away with a clearer view of this multifaceted policy innovation.

Notes

Chapter 1

1. On vouchers, see Moe 2001 and Witte 2000.

2. The charter school reform and other contemporary school choice proposals incorporate now-influential themes expressed earlier by Milton Friedman (1955, 1962).

3. On information issues and school choice, see M. Schneider, Teske, and Marschall 2000.

4. The Center for Education Reform maintains on-line summaries and analyses of charter school laws at <http://www.edreform.com>.

5. For a comprehensive theoretical and empirical analysis of policy entrepreneurs, with a focus on school choice, including discussion of Joe Nathan as a policy entrepreneur, see Mintrom 2000b.

6. A sample of the most recent work addressing the problem of charter school accountability includes Griffin and Wohlstetter 2001; Hess 2001; Hill et al. 2001; Finn, Manno, and Vanourek 2000; Hassel and Herdman 2000; and Vergari 2000, 2001.

7. This statistic does not reflect the considerable variance across the states.

8. However, as noted earlier, charter schools overall are serving fewer special education students than public schools are in charter school states. Further discussion is provided in chapter 14.

Chapter 3

1. The amending legislation is AB 544.

2. In California, the "base revenue limit" is the maximum amount of general-purpose state and local revenue that a district can receive (Wells 1998).

3. The 1997 evaluation was conducted by SRI International, a private-sector research firm. The Legislative Analyst's Office will contract for a neutral evaluator for the 2003 evaluation.

4. The amending legislation is SB 434.

5. The amending legislation is AB 1242.

6. The Anderson Valley Charter Network, with a reported enrollment of 3 students, is located in Mendocino and is designed to provide independent home study, work experience, and trade programs. The Options for Youth Charter School in Sacramento has a reported enrollment of 4,500 students and serves home study students.

Chapter 4

1. Our discussion of the Arizona case is based on published sources and on interviews of forty-six Arizona educators and policy makers that took place from November 1997 to March 2001.

2. The number of campuses is approximate, since operators may count two nearby sites as a single campus or as multiple ones.

3. Open-enrollment plans permit students from one school district to attend a public school in another district, if there is sufficient room in the receiving district's schools. Under open enrollment, per-pupil funding follows the student from one district to the next.

4. The push for voucher legislation continued even after the passage of charter legislation. In 1997, voucher advocates were able to pass a tax-credit measure that encouraged taxpayers to support educational scholarship funds to help students attend private schools.

Chapter 5

1. Quasi-markets can be established using vouchers, contracting, competitive bidding, et cetera. The major mechanisms are reviewed by Weimer and Vining 1999. For discussion of the increasing use of quasi-markets, see Lowery 1998.

2. Article 8, §2, of the Michigan Constitution was revised by the electorate in 1970 through what is commonly known as the "parochiaid" amendment.

3. TEACH stands for "Towards Educational Accountability and Choice."

4. See Mintrom and Vergari 1996.

5. Telephone interview with the author, 1 March 1994.

6. See Mintrom and Vergari 1997a.

7. In Michigan, state money has never been made available to support charter school start-up costs or other capital costs. Federal funds for these purposes have been dispersed through the Michigan Department of Education since 1995.

8. Some, but not all, of these schools were subsequently reauthorized in accord with the provisions of the 1994 and 1995 charter school laws.

9. Cass and Goenner quoted in Johnson 1997.

10. Harris 1998, 3.

11. See Vergari and Mintrom 1998. The questions were asked in a telephone survey of 971 adult Michigan residents. They were included in the thirteenth quarterly Michigan State University (MSU) State of the State Survey (SOSS) conducted by MSU's Institute for Public Policy and Social Research between December 1997 and March 1998. The overall sampling error was ±3.1 percent.

12. The 1995 charter school law limited Michigan's fifteen public universities to granting no more than 85 charters for 1996 and 100 for 1997, with adjustments to be made for subsequent years. In 1999–2000, the cap stood at 150 schools. Starting in 1997, single universities could authorize no more than 50 percent of all charters, a provision designed to curb the number of charters granted by CMU.

13. The figure of $6,500 is for 2000–2001; the figure typically changes annually.

14. This is not to deny that the demand for charter schools is likely to be minimal in affluent school districts, where residential location decisions might have originally been based, at least partly, on knowledge of school quality. For discussion of information and residential choice, see Teske et al. 1993.

15. See, e.g., Chubb and Moe 1990 and various papers cited in Peterson and Noyes 1997.

16. Hyde 1998 reports similar findings for 1997–1998. See Michigan Prospect for Renewed Citizenship 1998 for analyses of MEAP scores in charter and traditional public schools.

17. Cookson and Weiher (1997) report these statistics for Texas, finding a substantially higher proportion of at-risk students in charter schools than in traditional public schools.

18. There are fifteen state public universities in Michigan. Members of the boards of trustees are elected at three (the University of Michigan, Michigan State University, and Wayne State University) and gubernatorially appointed at the remainder. Only universities with appointed boards have established charter school offices, and word of direct political involvement by the governor is often heard (see Vergari 2000; Michigan Prospect for Renewed Citizenship 1998).

19. These battles underscore Gintis's (1995) point that in seeking to infuse competition into public education through choice, the effective design of regulatory structures is essential for maintaining the potential for debating educational goals in the public arena. With appropriate regulation, "the use of the market [can be] . . . an *instrument of* rather than an *alternative to* democratic policy making" (510).

20. GVSU was the authorizer of twenty-eight charter schools in 2000–2001.

21. CMU was the authorizer of fifty-nine schools in 2000–2001. Authorizers can charge charter schools up to 3 percent of their annual state school aid. Thus, differences in the operating styles of GVSU and CMU cannot be explained by the relative scarcity of resources at CMU. Given expected economies of scale, CMU would appear to be better placed to put resources into cultivating positive relations with the schools it oversees.

22. For further discussion of the regulatory styles of charter authorizers see Vergari 2000.

23. Source: <http://www.edisonschools.com>.

24. Quoted by Stecklow 1997.

25. Brown (1992) suggests that problems of opportunism and regulatory costs can erode potential distinctions in the cost-effectiveness of for-profit, nonprofit, and publicly provided schools.

Chapter 6

1. Data from Colorado Department of Education (CDE).

2. On policy entrepreneurs, see Kingdon 1995 and Mintrom 2000b.

3. See Colorado Revised Statutes, 22-30.5-108.

4. See Colorado Revised Statutes, 22-30.5-109.

5. See Colorado Revised Statutes, 22-30.5-103: "At-risk pupil means a pupil who, because of physical, emotional, socioeconomic, or cultural factors, is less likely to succeed in a conventional educational environment."

6. The committee consists of the commissioner or a designee, a member of the local board of the district in which the school is located, a licensed professional at the school, two parents of enrolled students, a principal of a school at the same grade level appointed by the governor, a teacher at the charter school, and a business representative who resides in the neighborhood of the school appointed by the governor.

7. While these data provide some indication of diversity, it is difficult to truly assess the exact proportion of students eligible for free and reduced-price lunch as not all charter schools report the relevant data to the CDE. Without such data, charter schools are reported as having 0 percent eligible even if they are serving students who qualify for free and reduced-price lunch.

8. The Challenge Foundation provides grants for seeking and supporting model charter schools that reach high standards, include character education, show active involvement by parents, and maintain close community ties.

9. Data available for all populations from the CDE.

10. All waiver information compiled by the CDE and published in the *Colorado Charter School Information Packet and Handbook* (Colorado Department of Education 1999).

11. Information compiled by the author as part of an evaluation report for the Alpine Charter School, 1999.

12. Interestingly, under separate statutory provisions, traditional school districts (by request of the school board with support of the majority of a district accountability committee, certified administrators, and teachers) can also request waivers of certain requirements. As is the case in the numerous other states with similar provisions, they are not well used by traditional public schools. Many argue that while there is a general feeling that regulations are burdensome, actually specifying what provision is problematic and having to demonstrate why are too onerous for school districts. From 1994 to 1997, only eighteen waiver requests were granted to traditional public schools, compared to ninety-six for charter schools (Colorado Department of Education 2001).

13. Created by HB 93-1313, the assessment program began in April 1997. A third-grade literacy test is also currently administered. SB 00-186 will now require CSAP testing in grades 3–10.

14. While more charter schools took the exam, data are not publicly reported for schools or districts with fifteen or fewer students tested, affecting eight charter schools. Five charter schools did not administer the CSAP assessment, as they do not serve any of the grades tested.

15. Data from the CDE; comparisons to district averages made by the author.

16. Differences were not significant at the .05 level. Analysis was done by the assessment office of the CDE.

17. In 2000, five charter schools served a student population that was greater than 20 percent minority and free- or reduced-price-lunch eligible. In all five cases, fewer than fifteen students attended the charter school, so CSAP scores could not be reported.

18. *Denver School Board v. Booth* (Colorado Supreme Court No. 97SC609).

19. The districts and charter schools were selected to represent the diversity in size and location of Colorado charter schools and school districts.

Chapter 7

1. Conversation with Scott Hamilton during my tenure at the Massachusetts Department of Education, spring 1996.

2. Information in this section is derived from Herdman 2000.

3. Edgerly was affiliated with the Pioneer Institute, an influential Boston think tank. Pioneer had softened the way for choice and charter schools. In 1991, Abigail Thernstrom wrote a Pioneer publication entitled "School Choice in Massachusetts" that chronicled the lack of educational choices in the state (Thernstrom 1991). The following year, Steven F. Wilson, former executive director of Pioneer and then education advisor to Governor William F. Weld, published *Reinventing the Schools: A Radical Plan for Boston* (S. Wilson 1992), which challenged the bureaucratic culture of Boston public schools and promoted privatization and choice. In addition, the last three executive directors of Pioneer were appointed by Governors Weld and Paul Cellucci to play prominent roles in their respective administrations.

4. Sections 7 and 8 of the charter school law called for a study on the equity of the ACS calculation. Sections 9, 10, and 11 mandated audits by the inspector general of how charter schools (and the charter school office) were spending their funds and also mandated that charter operators become certified in how to spend public funds. This is in addition to the provision that each school complete an independent fiscal audit annually (C.71, s.89, ss.hh).

5. This financial disclosure provision (C.71, s.89, ss.v) was particularly troubling to charter proponents in that it discouraged potential board members from applying, because the paperwork was cumbersome and their financial assets would become public information.

6. Core Knowledge was developed by E. D. Hirsch and specifies the core knowledge each student should know by the end of each grade. The Regio Emilia model is based on the child-centered, preschool curriculum from the Italian village that bears the model's name. It builds on "a child's queries and interests [to] guide the curriculum" (Massachusetts Department of Education 1998, 44).

7. The Parker and City on a Hill Charter Schools have developed involved collaborations with surrounding districts.

8. As LEAs, Commonwealth charter schools in Massachusetts are required to comply with the Individuals with Disabilities Education Act (IDEA), the Rehabilitation Act of 1973 (Section 504), and Title II of the Americans with Disabilities Act (Title II).

9. To meet these demands many charter schools have expanded their administrations to include business managers, development officers, and presidents. These added responsibilities have resulted in higher than expected administrative costs. In 1995–1996, the average charter school spent about 19 percent on administration, as compared to 6 percent for an average district school and 21 percent for an average district (Herdman and Millot 2000).

10. Boston's Renaissance Charter School was cited for being out of IDEA compliance in 1997 but has since corrected the problem.

11. About 4 percent of charters have closed nationally, but virtually none of them have been closed for performance alone (see DeSchryver 1999).

12. The schools were North Star Academy and Boston University Presidential Charter School.

13. This quote is from an interview conducted for Hill et al. 1999; this portion of the transcript was not included in the final draft of the report.

14. Wilson was Advantage board president but no longer CEO in July 2001, when the company was taken over by Mosaica Education, Inc.

15. The MDE has recently adopted a site-visit process for all failing public schools and credits the charter school site visits as having influenced this new policy.

Chapter 8

1. Portions of this chapter were first published in Julie F. Mead, 2000, "Publicly Funded Choice Options in Milwaukee: An Examination of the Legal Issues," a report commissioned and distributed by the Public Policy Forum, Milwaukee, Wisconsin.

2. WI Stat. §118.40.

3. The lawsuit that led to the injunction and the resolution of the dispute are discussed later in the chapter. MPS is the state's largest school district, with 104,914 students (1999–2000 figures). It has many of the problems associated with large urban districts, including high rates of poverty (80 percent of 1999–2000 elementary school students were eligible for free or reduced-price lunch) (Milwaukee Public Schools 2000).

4. In 2001, Indiana joined Wisconsin in granting chartering authority to a specific location by including in its list of sponsors "the executive of a consolidated city." This provision means that the mayor of Indianapolis may now grant charters to schools within the city's boundaries (P.L. 100-2001, Sec. 21; codified at IC 20-5.5-1-15(1)(C)).

5. The MPCP is a private voucher program that allows low-income Milwaukee students to attend participating private schools in Milwaukee with state tuition dollars.

6. CESAs are intermediate educational agencies independent from DPI.

7. This right to appeal is limited to petitioners denied charters. There is no mechanism for persons who may be dissatisfied with the granting of a charter to appeal that decision to the DPI.

8. Charter schools are relieved from Chapters 115 through 121 of Wisconsin Statutes.

9. WI Stat. §118.01.

10. WI Stat. §118.40(2r)(e).

11. For example, the DPI reports that it awarded $4 million in charter school grants for 2000–2001, part of a $13.2 million award for 1 October 1999 to 20 September 2002 from the federal government. Grants were awarded on a competitive basis in four categories: (1) implementation, twenty-five grants totaling $1,835,260; (2) renewal, twenty-two grants totaling $1,231,863; (3) planning, twenty grants totaling $185,400; and (4) dissemination, four grants totaling $75,716.

12. Since school districts control all funding through the negotiated process, the issue of administrative fees is irrelevant for school district charter schools.

13. Given the most recent figures from the DPI for 1999–2000, 877,852 Wisconsin students were educated in 2,086 public schools. By comparison, 148,366 Wisconsin students were educated in 993 private schools.

14. Data from *Milwaukee Journal Sentinel,* 28 December 1999.

15. Of course, there may be other innovations not reflected in the schools' names.

16. Even though §118.32 does not apply to charter schools, another state statute that also prohibits strip searches by school employees remains applicable to charter schools (WI Stat. §948.50).

17. The report states that financial mismanagement was not an issue. Rather, "district officials indicated the school closed when the school board was unwilling to provide funding to rent classroom space for the 1998–1999 school year after parents with children in other district schools expressed their belief that the district was providing the Institute with too much funding" (Wisconsin Legislative Audit Bureau 1998, 32).

18. Contained in a provision of the Charter Schools Expansion Act of 1998, 20 U.S.C. 8066(1)(H).

19. Based on scores obtained by fourth-, eighth-, and tenth-grade students on the Knowledge and Concepts Examinations required by state statutes.

20. Three of the eight charter schools for at-risk students were unable to provide attendance data to LAB. The five remaining charter schools for at-risk students had attendance rates lower than their district counterparts.

21. The instances are when schools are noninstrumentalities.

22. Case No. 97-2110, 1998 WL 762512 (Wis. App. 1998).

23. As mentioned earlier, the Bruce Guadalupe School began operation as an MPS charter school during the 2000–2001 school year.

24. Civil Case No. 98C-554.

25. UWM agreed with this interpretation from the start. MATC took no stand.

26. Letter from Office of City Attorney to John Kalwitz, President of the Common Council of the City of Milwaukee (25 June 1998) (on file with author).

27. Howard Fuller is a former MPS superintendent, a vocal charter school proponent, and director of the Institute for the Transformation of Learning at Marquette University.

28. Letter from Marshall Smith, Acting Deputy Secretary, U.S. Department of Education, to John Benson, Superintendent, Wisconsin Department of Public Instruction (8 October 1998) (on file with author).

29. The Bruce Guadalupe School withdrew its charter application during 1998 after coming to an agreement with MPS to continue as a partnership school. The Marva Collins Preparatory School of Wisconsin declined its charter in 1999 and remains a participating private school in the MPCP.

30. Also in 1999, the legislature adopted a new statute that reiterates the obligation schools chartered by the three special Milwaukee authorities have for compliance with federal law. It also contains a provision that allows, but does not compel, MPS to agree to serve as the LEA for those schools. MPS has not entered into any such agreements as of the 2000–2001 school year (WI Stat. 118.775).

31. *Tinker v. DesMoines,* 393 U.S. 503, 89 S.Ct. 733 (1969).

32. The federal Charter Schools Expansion Act likewise prohibits charter schools from accepting tuition (20 U.S.C. 8066(1)(F)).

33. There is no other mention of "groups operating for profit" in the statute, and any pro-

hibition against contracting directly with for-profit entities is absent from the list of charter school restrictions.

Chapter 9

1. The Canadian Constitution makes provision *only* for the Catholic religion and French language, and these come to bear on only the public education system. Within a public education system there may be a public board and a separate board. The determining factor of whether the public board is Catholic or nondenominational depends on whether the majority of the population in the jurisdiction is Catholic. If it is, then the public board is Catholic and the separate board is nondenominational. If the majority is non-Catholic, the public board is nondenominational and the separate board is Catholic.

2. All dollar amounts in this chapter are in Canadian dollars.

3. Alberta Learning was formerly called Alberta Education.

4. Only Moberly Hall had its charter approved by Fort McMurray Catholic School Board. Prior to that, CAPES school had been approved by Medicine Hat Public School District, and New Horizon had had its charter approved by Elk Island School Board. Upon renewal, both of these charter schools appealed to and were granted approval by the minister of education.

5. A student agenda is a student's personal calendar of school events and assignments.

6. School performance in 1999 was significantly poorer than in 1998 for most subjects across all grade levels.

7. Each department of the Alberta government is required to develop and revise annually its plan of objectives and goals for the coming three years. These plans are public documents and are seen as important means of keeping government visible, open, and accountable.

8. Personal communication to the members of the research team, 19 September 1999.

9. "Differentiated curriculum" refers to a cluster of strategies used in the education of the gifted and talented. The concept is described and operationalized by Susan Winebrenner (1992, 67–69) and is based on the ideas of Gardner (1993) and Renzulli (1988).

Chapter 10

1. I would like to thank Patsy O'Neill, Executive Director of the Charter School Resource Center of Texas, Brooks Flemister, former Senior Director of the Division of Charter Schools for the Texas Education Agency, and their respective staffs for their assistance in the preparation of this manuscript. Any errors of fact or logic, however, are solely the responsibility of the author. This research was supported by a Faculty Research Grant, Fordham University.

2. There is no cap on the number of districts that may receive home-rule district charters ("Texas Charter School Information" 1999).

3. During their first three years of operation, average enrollment in charter schools in Texas has fluctuated from 147 (1996–1997) to 217 (1997–1998) to 198 (1998–1999) (Texas Education Agency 2000b).

4. Recall that charter schools are not rated by the accountability system until after they

have been in operation for two years. According to the TEA, other reasons for charter schools not being rated by the accountability system include insufficient data and lack of peer review.

5. The first comparisons started with seventeen charter schools, increasing up to seventy-one schools in 1999–2000 data.

6. Similar pressures were reported in Hassel and Vergari's (1999) study of charter-granting agencies in Arizona, Chicago, the District of Columbia, Massachusetts, Michigan, and North Carolina, suggesting that this phenomenon is widespread.

7. The response rate was 72 percent.

8. Noting that most of the nation's charter schools have been in operation for two years or less, Hassel (1999a, 3–4) comments that "improvements in the achievement of students who attend charter schools will probably take longer than that to show up."

9. All data in this section was provided by the Charter School Resource Center of Texas.

10. Hassel and Vergari (1999, 410) observe that it is typical for state legislatures to "pass charter laws without appropriating any funds for the activities of CGAs [charter-granting agencies]." When the Texas state legislature passed its charter law in 1995, it created an independent review board to evaluate the effectiveness of the original pilot study (of twenty schools) but failed to appropriate funds for the project (Fusarelli 1998).

11. Others, such as Fusarelli (2001) and Hess (2001), question the political suppositions upon which charter school accountability is based.

12. Small size is a feature that has been noted by several researchers as a key to creating more effective schools, particularly in urban areas plagued by massive, highly impersonal schools (Fusarelli 1999).

Chapter 11

1. Students can obtain interdistrict transfers to attend a charter school outside of the home district.

Chapter 12

1. The bill passed by thirty-seven to eight in the Senate and by seventy-eight to twenty-five in the House.

2. Between 1997 and 1999, the state gave Pamlico County $714,832 each year for that special provision.

3. Advantage Schools, Inc., was taken over by Mosaica Education, Inc., in 2001.

4. The North Carolina charter law requires that at least sixty-five students be served at a charter school. However, exceptions can be made if there is a compelling reason, such as a small student population or geographical isolation, or if the school's curriculum is targeted at serving a special population (e.g., disabled children or incarcerated youth).

5. Several charter schools did not meet the reporting deadline with the headcount of their students and were not included in the evaluation report.

6. Estimated personnel costs were published in North Carolina Office of State Budget and

Management 1999. To reduce the administrative impact of charter schools on the department, the study offered several recommendations, including shifting some technical assistance from the department to the local districts; using automation to help with administrative workload; and treating a charter school as a special school within an existing school district, rather than as an independent school district.

7. Seven of the ten charter schools approved by the SBE on appeal were in operation in 2000; one charter was revoked after one year due to financial mismanagement; and two charters withdrew following final approval but prior to opening.

8. The percentage of students performing at or above grade level in the state's traditional public schools ranged from 23.7 to 98.4 in the 1999–2000 state tests.

9. To reach this conclusion, the authors conducted an ordinary least squares regression analysis in which performance composite was the independent variable and two known student background characteristics—the proportion of students participating in free and reduced-price lunch and the proportion of non-White students—were the dependent variables. Based on the results of the regression, the authors predicted the scores of all charter schools based on the backgrounds of their students. For sixteen of the eighteen schools included in the analysis, actual scores lagged behind predicted scores by an average of over twenty points on the performance composite's one-hundred-point scale. The analysis was very limited, however. Only 1997–1998 data were available, and full data were available for only eighteen of the thirty-four charter schools open at that time.

10. North Carolina's system for funding services to exceptional children in district and charter schools is controversial. First, there is a 12.5 percent cap placed on the number of exceptional children who will receive state funding for exceptional children's programs. If the district identifies more than 12.5 percent of its population as requiring exceptional children's services, it is obligated by law to pay for the additional programs. In 1997–1998, over 50 percent of the state's districts identified exactly 12.5 percent of these students (Public School Forum 1998, 11). The other districts were over the cap and had to provide services to exceptional children out of local funds. Second, the state does not provide a weighted funding scale based on a child's need. Rather, in 2000–2001, a district or charter school received the same amount (an average of $2,412.64) for a multihandicapped student who required a full menu of services as it did for the more easily educated learning disabled child. The state does have a Special State Reserve Fund for Children with Disabilities, which helps schools in situations where a high-cost child enrolls at a school once the budget has been set. By November 1999, two charter schools had received a total of over $40,000 to help meet the costs of services necessary for high-needs students.

11. In 1999, *Education Week* gave North Carolina a B+ for its accountability program (see <http://www.edweek.org/sreports/qc99/>). The National Education Goals Panel has applauded North Carolina's system as producing rapid improvement in student achievement (see <http://www.negp.gov>). However, some parents, teachers, and other education stakeholders were beginning to voice concerns about educators having to "teach to the test" by 1999. The issue of poor minority performance came to the forefront in early 2000 and has placed the state's accountability system under fire.

12. While North Carolina charter schools do have a greater percentage of minority students when compared to the average traditional state public school (47.4 percent compared to 38.8 percent in 2000–2001), several other states with charter school legislation have similar patterns, including Florida, Michigan, Minnesota, and Texas (RPP International 2000, 33).

13. By 2000–2001, 15,523 students were enrolled in North Carolina charter schools, compared to 1,283,945 enrolled in other public schools. This suggests that superintendents may be overestimating the losses, as found by Rofes (1998).

14. Members are able to receive group rates for employee benefits, property and criminal loss, and liability insurance products. To participate, charter schools are assessed one dollar per student.

15. Chapter author Bryan C. Hassel serves on the board of directors of the North Carolina Charter School Resource Center.

Chapter 13

1. Special thanks to Robert Bellafiore, Paul Hayford, and Darlene Mengel for helpful information and insights on prior drafts of this chapter.

2. Charter school bills pertaining only to New York City were introduced in the NYS Assembly during the 1991–1992 and 1993–1994 legislative sessions. These bills died in committee. In subsequent sessions, a couple of statewide charter school bills also died at the committee stage.

3. The New York State United Teachers and the United Federation of Teachers (NYC), affiliates of the American Federation of Teachers, are particularly powerful in NYS.

4. The salary legislation raised the base pay for lawmakers from $57,500 to $79,500 per year, and extra pay stipends for leadership positions were increased by 38 percent. Statewide elected officials, judges, and commissioners also received pay hikes, and the salary for the governor rose from $130,000 to $179,000.

5. On policy entrepreneurs and advocacy coalitions, see Mintrom 2000b; Mintrom and Vergari 1996; Sabatier and Jenkins-Smith 1994.

6. Thirty-two Republicans and seven Democrats voted in favor of the bill, and eighteen Democrats and two Republicans were opposed.

7. Fifty Democrats and forty-three Republicans voted for the bill, while thirty-nine Democrats and six Republicans were opposed.

8. Private schools may not convert to charter status. For a conversion charter school, the parents or guardians of a majority of the students in the existing public school must vote in favor of converting the school to charter status.

9. The regents are elected by a majority of the state legislature, particularly the Democratic majority in the state Assembly. The SUNY trustees are appointed by the governor.

10. Students who reside within a fifteen-mile radius of the charter school are eligible to receive transportation from their school district of residence if the district provides transportation to private schools, as required either by law or district policy.

11. Upon approval of the charter school board, a majority of teachers or noninstructional staff may modify the union contract.

12. Scott W. Steffey, then SUNY vice chancellor for university relations, was appointed president of CSI. Prior to his work in marketing, government relations, and public relations for SUNY, Steffey had worked in marketing and business development in the private sector.

13. Bellafiore joined Pataki's administration as press secretary in January 1995. Beginning in January 1996, he served as the governor's director of special projects, working on policy development and implementation, strategic communications, and interagency coordination. Bellafiore had been director of communications for the Business Council of NYS and had also worked as a news reporter.

14. Steffey, the former CSI president, exited the institute in 2000.

15. CSI also has an office in Purchase, New York.

16. The EMC partners in the most applications for fall 2000 schools were Advantage Schools, Inc. (three); Beacon Education Management (four); Edison Schools, Inc. (six); National Heritage Academies (five); SABIS (three); and Victory Schools, Inc. (five).

17. Each application is also reviewed independently by an expert who did not sit on the relevant team and by a financial analyst.

18. Three of the schools were in the initial group of five schools that had received preliminary approval in 1999. Of the thirteen approved schools, twelve opened in fall 2000 and one in January 2001.

19. In December 2000, SUNY reported receiving a total of forty-two applications during the third round; however, several applications were withdrawn prior to 15 December 2000 (Charter Schools Institute 2000a).

20. The following EMCs were mentioned in at least one application: Advantage Schools, Inc. (two); Beacon Educational Management (two); Edison Schools, Inc. (four); EdServe, Inc. (one); Mosaica Education, Inc. (two); National Heritage Academies (three); Nobel Learning (one); SABIS (one); School Business Management, Inc. (one); and Victory Schools, Inc. (two).

21. An approved NYC applicant was partnered with Mosaica Education, Inc., and an approved Buffalo applicant with Edison Schools, Inc.

22. NYSED also maintains a charter schools office in New York City.

23. The SBR requested a detailed breakdown of the student population for New Covenant and information on special education issues.

24. One had a religion-based curriculum, the second proposed the conversion of a private school to charter status, and the third was for an on-line program offering a GED-preparation program.

25. It should be noted, however, that new, nonconversion charter schools in NYC do not need the blessing of the chancellor.

26. Harold Levy was appointed schools chancellor after Crew resigned in 1999.

27. Vazquez was previously active in several nonprofit school reform initiatives.

28. The Empire Foundation is a conservative think tank affiliated with the antitax group Change–New York. The NYCSRC does not accept financial donations from EMCs.

29. O'Brien had also worked for New York's Governor Pataki and for the former governor of Massachusetts, William Weld.

30. Advantage was taken over by Mosaica Education, Inc., in mid-2001.

31. State regulations require that applications for student transportation be submitted by 1 April. The ACSD had extended the deadline in order to work with a new bus company. State regulations also provide that a district may not reject a late request for transportation if there is a reasonable explanation for the delay (see Mills 2000).

32. The school aid allocation was $12.6 billion of the state's $73.3 billion state budget.

33. The extra $2.7 million in state aid, property tax receipts above anticipated levels, and cost savings from shifting students to the charter school also helped to address the initial $4 million gap (Karlin 1999d).

34. ACSD board meeting, 23 March 2000, Albany School of Humanities.

35. ACSD board meeting, 23 March 2000, Albany School of Humanities.

36. ACSD board meeting, 23 March 2000, Albany School of Humanities.

37. Personal interview with the author, 31 March 2000.

38. Dare resigned in 2000.

39. Statewide, 60 percent of fourth graders passed the exam in 2001.

40. ACSD Superintendent Palmer has asserted: "Instead of a show piece, the New Covenant Charter School turned out to be a poster child for the problems of charter schools" (Wechsler 2001).

41. The SBR replaced the former Pupil Evaluation Program tests with new, more challenging fourth- and eighth-grade tests that measure student skills in reading and math. Science and social studies tests in the fourth, fifth, and eighth grades are also planned. The SBR required that all nondisabled students pass Regents exams in order to receive a high school diploma. The new standards were established in 1996. In 2001, seniors must pass English and math Regents exams. In 2004, they must pass five Regents exams and a foreign-language competency exam.

42. The Charter Schools Act requires applications to include an assessment of the projected programmatic and fiscal impact of the charter school on other public and nonpublic schools in the area (§2851.2 (q)).

43. CSI also sends a copy of the relevant charter application to the superintendent of a district in which a charter school has been proposed.

44. The state supreme court is not the ultimate NYS appellate court.

45. Data from the Office of Information Reporting and Technology Services, New York State Education Department, 1999.

Chapter 14

1. Interestingly, RPP International (2000) indicates that a significantly lower percentage of the charter schools (39) that first opened in the 1998–1999 academic year reported that start-up funding was a major difficulty, as compared to schools that opened in 1997–1998 (59 per-

cent of which reported that start-up funding was a major difficulty). The report suggests that the decline likely reflects support from the federal public charter schools program.

2. The fourth such conference will take place in June 2002.

3. On "ripple effects," see RPP International 2001; Mintrom 2000a; and Rofes 1998.

4. Paige's remarks set "charter schools" apart from "public schools." Legally, charter schools are public schools. I have heard other public officials similarly distinguish charter schools from public schools. These anecdotes support the view that charter schools are actually "quasi-public schools" (see Witte 1996, 161).

5. Charter schools are usually not exempt from state mandates regarding the minimum number of days in the academic year.

6. The two terms quoted are from the chapters by Bosetti and O'Reilly and by Hirsch, respectively.

References

Alberta Chamber of Resources. 1993. *International Comparisons in Education: Curriculum, Values and Lessons.* Edmonton: The Alberta Chamber of Resources.

Alberta Education. 1996. *Charter School Handbook.* Edmonton: Alberta Education.

———. 1998. "Conditions Attached to Charter Approval." Press release. Edmonton: Alberta Education, Communications Branch.

———. 1999a. *The Government of Alberta's Three Year Plan for Education, 1999–2000–2001–2002.* Edmonton: Alberta Education. Available at <http://ednet.edc.gov.ab.ca>.

———. 1999b. "New Policy Benefits Boards and Charter Schools." Press release. Edmonton: Alberta Education, Communications Branch.

Alberta Education, Planning Branch. 1997. *Education Programs and Services Policy Requirements—Charter Schools.* Edmonton: Alberta Education.

Alexander, Lamar. 1986. "Chairman's Summary." In *Time for Results: The Governors' 1981 Report on Education,* 1–7. Washington, D.C.: National Governors' Association.

American Federation of Teachers Educational Foundation. 2000. "Venturesome Capital: State Charter School Finance Systems." Policy report. Washington, D.C.: U.S. Department of Education.

Anderson, James E. 2000. *Public Policymaking.* 4th ed. Boston: Houghton Mifflin.

Anderson, Lee, and Kara Finnegan. 2001. "Charter School Authorizers and Charter School Accountability." Paper presented at the annual meeting of the American Educational Research Association, 10–14 April, Seattle, Wash.

"Answers, Please: Taxpayers Have a Right to an Explanation of Faculty Purge at New Covenant Charter School." 2001. Editorial. *Albany Times Union,* 17 May, A12.

Archer, Jeff. 2000. "Accountability Measures Vary Widely." *Education Week,* 17 May, 1, 18–20.

Arsen, David, David Plank, and Gary Sykes. 1999. "School Choice Policies in Michigan: The Rules Matter." Policy report. East Lansing: Michigan State University.

Banks, Debra, and Eric Hirsch. 1998. "The Charter School Roadmap." Policy report. Washington, D.C.: U.S. Department of Education.

Bardach, Eugene, and Robert A. Kagan. 1982. *Going by the Book: The Problem of Regulatory Unreasonableness.* Philadelphia: Temple University Press.

Barlow, Maude, and Heather Robertson. 1994. *Class Warfare: The Assault on Canada's Schools.* Toronto: Key Porter Books.

Barone, Michael, and Grant Ujifusa. 1999. *The Almanac of American Politics 2000.* Washington, D.C.: National Journal.

Baumgartner, Frank R., and Bryan D. Jones. 1993. *Agendas and Instability in American Politics.* Chicago: University of Chicago Press.

Benjamin, Elizabeth. 1999. "Busing for New School Rejected." *Albany Times Union,* 3 August, B1, B8.

Berglund, Judy. 1993. "Life inside a Charter School." *Minnesota Education Association Advocate,* 17 December, 10–11.

Berman, David R. 1998. *Arizona Politics and Government.* Lincoln: University of Nebraska Press.

Berman, Paul, Beryl Nelson, J. Ericson, R. Perry, and Denise Silverman. 1998. "A Study of Charter Schools: Second-Year Report, 1998." Washington D.C.: U.S. Department of Education.

Bernick, E. Lee, and Charles W. Wiggins. 1991. "Executive-Legislative Relations: The Governor's Role as Chief Legislator." In *Gubernatorial Leadership and State Policy,* ed. Eric B. Herzik and Brent W. Brown, 73–91. New York: Greenwood Press.

Bierlein, Louann A. 1997. "The Charter School Movement." In *New Schools for a New Century,* ed. D. Ravitch and J. P. Viteritti, 37–60. New Haven, Conn.: Yale University Press.

Billingsley, Lloyd, and Pamela Riley. 1999. *Two Steps Forward, One Step Back: The Battle for California's Charter Schools.* San Francisco: Pacific Research Institute for Public Policy.

Bomotti, Sally, Rick Ginsburg, and Brian Cobb. 1999. "Teachers in Charter Schools and Traditional Schools: A Comparative Study." *Education Policy Analysis Archives* 7:22. Available at <http://epaa.asu.edu/epaa/v7n22.html>.

Bosetti, Lynn. 1998. "Canada's Charter Schools: Initial Report." SAEE Research Series No. 3. Kelowna, B.C.: Society for the Advancement of Excellence in Education.

———. 1999. "Alberta Charter Schools: Paradox and Promises." Paper presented at the annual meeting of the Canadian Society for the Study of Education, 9–12 June, Sherbrooke, Quebec.

Bosetti, Lynn, Elaine Foulkes, Robert O'Reilly, and Dave Sande. 2000. "Canadian Charter Schools at the Crossroads: Final Report." SAEE Research Series No. 5. Kelowna, B.C.: Society for the Advancement of Excellence in Education.

Bosetti, Lynn, Robert O'Reilly, and Dianne Gereluk. 1998. "Public Choice and Public Education: The Impact of Alberta's Charter Schools." Paper presented at the annual meeting of the American Educational Research Association, 13–17 April, San Diego, Calif.

Bosetti, Lynn, Robert O'Reilly, Dave Sande, and Dianne Gereluk. 1998. "Manifestations of Choice: Alberta Charter Schools." Paper presented at the annual meeting of the Canadian Association for the Study of Educational Administration, 11 June, Ottawa.

Brighouse, Harry. 2000. *School Choice and Social Justice.* Oxford: Oxford University Press.

Brown, Byron W. 1992. "Why Governments Run Schools." *Economics of Education Review* 11:287–300.

Bruce, Christopher, and Art Schwartz. 1997. "Education: Meeting the Challenge." In *A Government Reinvented: A Study of Alberta's Deficit Elimination Program,* ed. Christopher Bruce, Ronald Kneebone, and Kenneth McKenzie, 383–416. Toronto: Oxford University Press.

Budde, Raymond. 1988. *Education by Charter: Restructuring School Districts.* Andover, Mass.: Regional Laboratory for Educational Improvement of the Northeast and Islands.

Caldwell, Brian J., and Jim M. Spinks. 1998. *Beyond the Self-Managing School.* London: Falmer Press.

California Department of Education. 1999. "Types of Alternative Classroom Instruction in California Charter Schools." Available at <http://www.cde.ca.gov/charter/>.

———. 2001. "Dataquest." Available at <http://data1.cde.ca.gov/dataquest/>.

Center for Community Self-Help. 1999. "Charter School Budget Report." Mimeograph. Durham, N.C.: Center for Community Self-Help.

Center for Education Reform. 2001a. "Charter School Laws: Ranking Scorecard, May 2001." Policy report. Washington, D.C.: Center for Education Reform.

———. 2001b. "Charter School Legislation: Profile of the Texas Charter School Law." Available at <http://edreform.com/charter_schools/laws/Texas.htm>.

———. 2001c. "New Information about Charter Schools Released Showing Only a 4 Percent Failure Rate." Press release. Washington, D.C.: Center for Education Reform.

———. 2001d. Introduction to "Survey of Charter Schools, 2000–2001." Policy report. Washington, D.C.: Center for Education Reform.

———. 2001e. "Making Schools Work Better for All Children." Available at <http://www.edreform.com/charter_schools/>.

Center for Market Based Education. 2000. *Arizona Charter Schools: Five Years of Experience.* Phoenix: Center for Market Based Education.

Charlebois, Kelly. 1999. "Address." Presented at the Professional Development Conference, Alberta Association of Charter Schools, 7–8 May, Calgary.

Charter Friends National Network. 1999a. "Out of the Box: Facilities Financing Ideas for Charter Schools." St. Paul: Charter Friends National Network.

"Charter School Accountability Ratings 2000." 2000. Available at <http://www.tea.state.tx.us/perfreport/account/2000/charters.html>.

Charter School Resource Center of Texas. 1998. "Accountability." San Antonio: Charter School Resource Center of Texas. Available at <http://www.charterstexas.org>.

———. 1999. "Organizational Plan." San Antonio: Charter School Resource Center of Texas.

Charter Schools Development Center. "Charter Schools Development Center Homepage." 1999. Available at <http://www.csus.edu/ier/charter/charter.html>.

———. 2001. "Charter Currents (March)." Available at <http://www.csus.edu/ier/charter/charter.html>.

Charter Schools Institute. 2000a. "Charter Schools Institute Submits Recommendations for Applications to Advance to Next Round of Review." Press release. Albany: Charter Schools Institute, State University of New York.

———. 2000b. "University Receives 37 Proposals for New Public Charter Schools." Press release. Albany: Charter Schools Institute, State University of New York.

"Charter Schools Worse on TAAS." 1999. *Austin American-Statesman,* 19 December, 1–2.

Chubb, John E., and Terry M. Moe. 1990. *Politics, Markets, and America's Schools.* Washington, D.C.: Brookings.

Cibulka, James G. 1999. "Moving toward an Accountable System of K–12 Education: Alternative Approaches and Challenges." In *Handbook of Educational Policy,* ed. Gregory J. Cizek, 183–211. San Diego: Academic Press.

Cibulka, James G., and Roberta L. Derlin. 1998. "Authentic Education Accountability Policies: Implementation of State Initiatives in Colorado and Maryland." *Educational Policy* 12 (1, 2): 84–97.

Clayton Foundation. 1999. "1998 Colorado Charter Schools Evaluation Study." Denver: Colorado Department of Education.

Cohen, David K. 1996. "Standards-Based School Reform: Policy, Practice, and Performance." In *Holding Schools Accountable: Performance-Based Reform in Education,* ed. Helen F. Ladd, 99–127. Washington, D.C.: Brookings.

Colorado Department of Education. 1999. *Colorado Charter School Information Packet and Handbook.* 7th. ed. Denver: Colorado Department of Education.

———. 2001. "The State of Charter Schools in Colorado 1999–2000: The Characteristics, Status and Performance Record of Colorado Charter Schools." Denver: Colorado Department of Education.

Cookson, Chris E., and Gregory R. Weiher. 1997. "Charter Schools in Texas: The Early Returns." Typescript. Houston: University of Houston.

Crew, Rudolph F. 1998. "Charter-School Bill Is Not Good Enough." *New York Daily News,* 17 December, 17c.

Cummins, Cathy. 1997. "Report Cards Still Out." *Rocky Mountain News,* 30 November.

Dale, Angela, and David DeSchryver, eds. 1998. "The Charter School Workbook: Your Roadmap to the Charter School Movement." Washington, D.C.: Center for Education Reform.

Daley, Beth, Doreen Ludica Vigue, and Kate Zernicke. 1999. "Legislature to Consider Raising the Cap on Charter Schools." *Boston Globe,* 6 April, B2.

Dare, Aaron R. 1999. "Law Creates Opportunity to Succeed." *The Times Union,* 15 July, B1, B3.

Darling-Hammond, Linda. 1997. "Doing What Matters Most: Investing in Quality Teaching." New York: National Commission on Teaching and America's Future.

DelVecchio, Rick. 1999. "Jerry Brown Blasts Teacher Unionization Bill." *San Francisco Chronicle,* 22 May 1999, A17.

Derthick, Martha, and Paul J. Quirk. 1985. *The Politics of Deregulation.* Washington, D.C.: Brookings.

DeSchyrver, David. 1999. "Charter Schools: A Progress Report, Part II: The Closures." Washington, D.C.: Center for Education Reform.

Dicker, Fredric U., and Gregg Birnbaum. 1998. "Victorious; George to Pay Up; Gov. Will OK Pol. Raises after Win on School Bill." *New York Post,* 19 December. Available at <http://archives.nypost.com/news/nypost>.

Doig, Jameson W., and Erwin C. Hargrove, eds. 1987. *Leadership and Innovation: A Biographical Perspective on Entrepreneurs in Government.* Baltimore: Johns Hopkins University Press.

Drew, Duchesne Paul, and Anthony Lonetree. 2001. "Charter Schools Face a Tougher Test." *Star-Tribune* (Minneapolis), 9 January, 1A.

ECS and NCSL. 1997. "The Charter School Roadmap." Available at <http://www.ed.gov./pubs/Roadmap/title.html>.

Elmore, Richard F. 1996. "Getting to Scale with Good Educational Practice." *Harvard Educational Review* 66:1–26.

Elmore, Richard F., Charles H. Abelmann, and Susan H. Fuhrman. 1996. "The New Accountability in State Education Reform: From Process to Performance." In *Holding Schools Accountable: Performance-Based Reform in Education,* ed. Helen F. Ladd, 65–98. Washington, D.C.: Brookings.

Eskenazi, Stuart. 1999. "Flunking Out." *Dallas Observer,* 22–28 July, 37.

Exceptional Children Division. 1999. "Program Compliance Audit Reports." Raleigh: North Carolina Department of Public Instruction.

Feller, Jennifer. 2001. "Twin Ridges Charter School Cooperative." *Charter Currents,* March, 12–14.

Ferguson, Ronald. 1991. "Paying for Public Education: New Evidence on How and Why Money Matters." *Harvard Journal of Legislation* 28 (summer): 465–98.

Fiegel, Sy. 1993. *Miracle in East Harlem.* New York: Times Books.

Fikac, Peggy. 1999. "State's Charter Schools Plagued by Financial Problems." *Houston Chronicle,* 4 July, E4.

Finn, Chester E., Jr., Bruno V. Manno, and Gregg Vanourek. 2000. *Charter Schools in Action: Renewing Public Education.* Princeton: Princeton University Press.

Fiske, Edward B., and Helen F. Ladd. 2000. *When Schools Compete: A Cautionary Tale.* Washington, D.C. Brookings.

Florida Department of Education. 2000. *Profiles of Florida School Districts 1998–1999.* Statistical Report, Series 2000-06. Tallahassee: Florida Department of Education.

Friedman, Milton. 1955. "The Role of Government in Education." In *Economics and the Public Interest,* ed. Robert A. Solo, 123–44. New Brunswick, N.J.: Rutgers University Press.

———. 1962. *Capitalism and Freedom.* Chicago: University of Chicago Press.

Fuhrman, Susan H. 1999. "The New Accountability." Policy Brief RB-27. Philadelphia: Consortium for Policy Research in Education, Graduate School of Education, University of Pennsylvania.

Fuller, Bruce, ed. 2000. *Inside Charter Schools: The Paradox of Radical Decentralization.* Cambridge: Harvard University Press.

Furrer, Cheryl M. 1991. "Letter to Senator Ember Reichgott." 11 April. On file with Joe Nathan.

Fusarelli, Lance D. 1998. "The Interplay of Advocacy Coalitions and Institutions on School Choice in Texas: A Case Study of Charter Schools and Vouchers." Ph.D. diss., University of Texas at Austin.

———. 1999. "Reinventing Urban Education in Texas: Charter Schools, Smaller Schools, and the New Institutionalism." *Education and Urban Society* 31 (2): 214–24.

———. 2001. "The Political Construction of Accountability." *Education and Urban Society* 33 (2): 157–69.

Gallagher, Jay. 1998. "Voters Group Raps Charter Schools." *Albany Times Union,* 15 December, B2.

Gardner, Howard. 1993. *Multiple Intelligences: The Theory in Practice.* New York: Basic Books.

Garn, Gregg A., and Robert T. Stout. 1999. "Closing Charters: How a Good Theory Failed in Practice." In *School Choice in the Real World: Lessons from Arizona Charter Schools,* ed. Robert Maranto, Scott Milliman, Frederick Hess, and April Gresham, 142–58. Boulder, Colo.: Westview Press.

Germond, Jack, and Jules Witcover. 1994. "School Voucher Debate Is Taken Up in Arizona." *Baltimore Sun,* 26 January, 2A.

Gintis, Herbert. 1995. "The Political Economy of School Choice." *Teachers College Record* 96 (3): 492–511.

Goins, Keri. N.d. "Pros, Cons of Charter Schools in Texas Still Being Debated." *North Central Sun,* A6.

Good, Thomas L., and Jennifer S. Braden. 2000. *The Great School Debate: Choice, Vouchers, and Charters.* Mahwah, N.J.: Lawrence Erlbaum.

Gormley, William T., Jr. 1998. "Regulatory Enforcement Styles." *Political Research Quarterly* 51:363–83.

Greenwald Rob, Larry V. Hedges, and Richard D. Laine. 1996. "The Effect of School Resources on Student Achievement." *Review of Educational Research* 66 (fall): 361–96.

Griffin, Noelle C., and Priscilla Wohlstetter. 2001. "Building a Plane While Flying It: Early Lessons from Developing Charter Schools." *Teachers College Record* 103 (2): 336–65.

Gutmann, Amy. 1987. *Democratic Education.* Princeton: Princeton University Press.

Hammond, William F. 1998. "Democrats Deplore Rushed Vote on Bill." *Schenectady Gazette,* 4 December, A1, A11.

Harris, Bob. 1998. *Charter School Update.* East Lansing: Michigan Education Association.

Hart, Gary K., and Sue Burr. 1996. "The Story of California's Charter School Legislation." *Phi Delta Kappan* 78 (1): 37–40.

Hart, Jordanna. 1998. "Scrutiny of Charter Firms Sought." *Boston Globe,* 22 March, B1.

Hartley, Mary. 1999. "A Voice from the State Legislature: Don't Do What Arizona Did!" In *School Choice in the Real World: Lessons from Arizona Charter Schools,* ed. Robert Maranto, Scott Milliman, Frederick Hess, and April Gresham, 198–211. Boulder, Colo.: Westview Press.

Hassel, Bryan C. 1999a. *The Charter School Challenge: Avoiding the Pitfalls, Fulfilling the Promise.* Washington, D.C.: Brookings.

———. 1999b. "Paying for the Charter Schoolhouse: Policy Options for Charter School Facilities Financing." Policy report. St. Paul: Charter Friends National Network.

———. 2000. "Politics, Markets and Two Choice Reform Movements: How Charter School and Voucher Programs Interact." Paper presented at the Charter Schools, Vouchers, and Public Education Conference, 9–10 March, Harvard University.

Hassel, Bryan C., and Paul A. Herdman. 2000. "Charter School Accountability: A Guide to Issues and Options for Charter School Authorizers." Policy report. Charlotte, N.C.: Public Impact.

Hassel, Bryan C., and Sandra Vergari. 1999. "Charter-Granting Agencies: The Challenges of Oversight in a Deregulated System." *Education and Urban Society* 31 (4): 406–28.

Hayes, Karen. 1998. "Charter School Debate Now Centers on For-Profit Operators." *Boston Globe, South Weekly,* 8 March, 1.

Heineman, Robert A., William T. Bluhm, Steven A. Peterson, and Edward N. Kearny. 1997. *The World of the Policy Analyst: Rationality, Values, and Politics.* 2d ed. New York: Chatham House.

Henig, Jeffrey R. 1994. *Rethinking School Choice: Limits of the Market Metaphor.* Princeton: Princeton University Press.

———. 1999. "School Choice Outcomes." In *School Choice and Social Controversy: Politics, Policy, and Law,* ed. Stephen D. Sugarman and Frank R. Kemerer, 68–107. Washington, D.C.: Brookings.

Herdman, Paul. 2000. "Accountability in the Third Sector: The Policy Challenges of Holding Charter Schools Accountable in Massachusetts." Qualifying paper, Graduate School of Education, Harvard University.

Herdman, Paul, and Marc Dean Millot. 2000. "Are Charter Schools Getting More Money into the Classroom? A Micro-Financial Analysis of Massachusetts Charter Schools." Policy report. Cleveland: Gund Foundation.

Hess, Frederick M. 1999. *Spinning Wheels: The Politics of Urban School Reform.* Washington, D.C. Brookings.

———. 2001. "Whaddya Mean You Want to Close My School? The Politics of Regulatory Accountability in Charter Schooling." *Education and Urban Society* 33 (2): 141–56.

Hess, Frederick M., Robert Maranto, and Scott Milliman. 1999. "Can Markets Set Bureaucrats Free? The Effects of School Choice on Teacher Empowerment in the Public Schools."

Paper presented at the annual meeting of the American Political Science Association, 2–5 September, Boston, Mass.

Heubert, Jay. 1997. "Schools without Rules? Charter Schools, Federal Disability Law and the Paradoxes of Deregulation." *Harvard Civil Rights–Civil Liberties Law Review* 32 (2): 301–55.

Hill, Paul, Robin Lake, Mary Beth Celio, Christine Campbell, Paul Herdman, and Katrina Bulkley. 2001. *A Study of Charter School Accountability*. Washington, D.C.: U.S. Department of Education.

Hirsch, Eric, and Amy Berk Anderson. 1999. "Colorado Charter Schools: A Comparison of Charter and School District Spending." Denver: National Conference of State Legislatures.

Hirschman, Albert O. 1970. *Exit, Voice, and Loyalty: Responses to Decline in Firms, Organizations, and States*. Cambridge: Harvard University Press.

Hood, Lucy. 1998. "Report Targets Teacher Shortage, Charter Schools." *San Antonio Express-News*, 16 December, C10.

Horn, Jerry, and Gary Miron. 1999. *Evaluation of the Michigan Public School Academy Initiative*. Kalamazoo: The Evaluation Center, Western Michigan University.

Hyde, Justin. 1998. "Charters Trail Public Schools on MEAP Test." *Lansing State Journal*, 15 June, 1B, 3B.

Izu, Jo Ann, Lisa Carlos, Kyo Yamashiro, Larry Picus, Naida Tushnet, and Priscilla Wohlstetter. 1999. "The Findings and Implications of Increased Flexibility and Accountability: An Evaluation of Charter Schools in Los Angeles Unified School District." Los Angeles: Los Angeles Unified School District.

Jakes, Lara. 1998. "Lawmakers Ink Deals on Schools, Milk, Pay." *Albany Times Union*, 19 December, A1.

John Locke Foundation. 2000. "Good News on Charters: Contrary to the Political Spin Advanced by Some, ABC Scores Show Signs of Progress for Charter Schools." Raleigh: John Locke Foundation.

Johnson, Robert C. 1997. "1993 Mich. Charter School Statute Is Legal, High Court Declares." *Education Week*, 6 August, A24.

Kagan, Robert A. 1995. "Adversarial Legalism and American Government." In *The New Politics of Public Policy*, ed. Marc K. Landy and Martin A. Levin, 88–118. Baltimore: Johns Hopkins University Press.

Kane, Pearl Rock. 2000. "The Difference between Charter Schools and Charterlike Schools." In *City Schools: Lessons from New York*, ed. Diane Ravitch and Joseph P. Viteritti, 65–87 Baltimore: Johns Hopkins University Press.

Karlin, Rick. 1999a. "Charter School Plan Approved for Albany." *Albany Times Union*, 16 June, A1, A6.

———. 1999b. "Dare Tells How Charter School Dream Became Reality." *Albany Times Union*, 1 October, B1, B10.

———. 1999c. "School Hammers Out Final Details." *Albany Times Union,* 16 September, B1, B6.

———. 1999d. "Tax Hike Won't Finance Albany Charter School." *Albany Times Union,* 13 August, B5.

Keegan, Lisa Graham. 1999. "The Empowerment of Market-Based School Reform." In *School Choice in the Real World: Lessons from Arizona Charter Schools,* ed. Robert Maranto, Scott Milliman, Frederick Hess, and April Gresham, 189–97. Boulder, Colo.: Westview.

Keller, Bess. 2001. "Texas Legislature Places Restrictions on Charter Schools." *Education Week,* 6 June, 14.

Kemerer, Frank R. 1999. "School Choice Accountability." In *School Choice and Social Controversy: Politics, Policy, and Law,* ed. Stephen D. Sugarman and Frank R. Kemerer, 174–211. Washington, D.C.: Brookings.

Kerns, Peggy. Personal communication. 13 October 1999.

Kingdon, John W. 1995. *Agendas, Alternatives, and Public Policies.* 2d ed. New York: Harper Collins.

Kofler, Shelley. 2001. "Charter School Report Highlights Problems." 29 January. Available at <http://www.wfaa.org>.

Kolderie, Ted. 1990a. "Beyond Choice to New Public Schools: Withdrawing the Exclusive Franchise in Public Education." Policy report. Washington, D.C.: Progressive Policy Institute.

———. 1990b. "The States Will Have to Withdraw the Exclusive." Typescript. St. Paul: Center for Policy Studies.

———. 1992. "Chartering Diversity." *Equity and Choice* 9:28–31.

———. 1993. "The States Begin to Withdraw the Exclusive." Policy report. St. Paul: Center for Policy Studies.

———. 1994. "The Essentials of the 'Charter School Strategy.'" Typescript. St. Paul: Center for Policy Studies.

———. 1995. "The Charter Idea: Update and Prospects, Fall '95." Policy memo. St. Paul: Center for Policy Studies.

———. 1997. "What Does It Mean to Ask: 'Is "Charter Schools" Working?'?" Typescript. St. Paul: Center for Policy Studies.

KPMG Peat Marwick. 1998. "Tuition Rate Study: Study of Charter School Tuition Rate Calculations." Malden: Massachusetts Department of Education. Available at <http://finance1.doe.mass.edu/charter/tuition_study.html>.

Kull, Randy. 1996. "Creationism Gets Equal Treatment: School Flouts Court, State Law." *Arizona Republic,* 30 September, 1.

Ladd, Helen F. 1996. Introduction to *Holding Schools Accountable: Performance-Based Reform in Education,* ed. Helen F. Ladd, 1–19. Washington, D.C.: Brookings.

Leal, David L. 1999. "Congress and Charter Schools." In *School Choice in the Real World:*

Lessons from Arizona Charter Schools, ed. Robert Maranto, Scott Milliman, Frederick Hess, and April Gresham, 58–67. Boulder, Colo.: Westview.

Legislative Analysts' Office. 1993. "Proposition 174: Analysis by the Legislative Analyst." Sacramento: Office of the Legislative Analyst.

"Legislative Panel Calls for Moratorium on Charter Schools." 2000. Available at <http://www.reporternews.com/2000/texas/charter1231.html>.

Levin, Benjamin. 2001a. "A Cross-National Analysis of the Impact of School Choice." Paper presented at the annual meeting of the American Educational Research Association, 10–14 April, Seattle, Wash.

———. 2001b. *Reforming Education: From Origins to Outcomes.* London: Routledge Falmer.

Levin, Henry M. 2000. "The Public-Private Nexus in Education." In *Public-Private Policy Partnerships,* ed. Pauline Vaillancourt Rosenau, 129–42. Cambridge: MIT Press.

Levy, Clifford J., and Anemona Hartocollis. 1998. "Crew Assails Albany Accord on Opening Charter Schools." *New York Times,* 18 December, D1, D2.

Lewington, Jennifer, and Graham Orpwood. 1993. *Overdue Assignment: Taking Responsibility for Canada's Schools.* Toronto: John Wiley.

Lewis, Dan A., and Shadd Maruna. 1996. "The Politics of Education." In *Politics in the American States: A Comparative Approach,* ed. Virginia Gray and Herbert Jacob, 438–77. Washington, D.C.: CQ Press.

Lindblom, Charles E. 1968. *The Policy-Making Process.* Englewood Cliffs, N.J.: Prentice-Hall.

Locke, Deborah. 2001. "Kids Must Come First." *St. Paul Pioneer Press,* 5 April, 10A.

Loveless, Tom, and Claudia Jasin. 1998. "Starting from Scratch: Political and Organizational Challenges Facing Charter Schools." *Educational Administration Quarterly* 34 (1): 9–30.

Lowery, David. 1998. "Consumer Sovereignty and Quasi-Market Failure." *Journal of Public Administration Research and Theory* 8:137–72.

Lueck, Thomas J. 2000. "$10 Million Fund to Help New York City's Charter Schools." *New York Times,* 1 November. Available at <http://www.nytimes.com/2000/11/01/nyregion/01CHAR.html>.

Mabin, Connie. 2000. "Texas Charter Schools Served More Minorities, Study Finds." *Austin American-Statesman,* 17 March.

———. 2001. "Charter School Program Gets Delayed." Available at <http://www.wfaa.com>.

Majone, Giandomenico. 1989. *Evidence, Argument and Persuasion in the Policy Process.* New Haven, Conn.: Yale University Press.

Majone, Giandomenico, and Aaron Wildavsky. 1979. "Implementation as Evolution." In *Implementation,* ed. Jeffrey L. Pressman and Aaron Wildavsky, 3d ed., 163–80. Berkeley: University of California Press.

Malone, Hermoine. 1999. "Charter Schools See Mixed Results in MCAS Scores Not Likely to Bolster Either Side of Debate." *Boston Globe,* 13 December, B1.

Mandala, Cheryl M. 1998. "Study: Less Funding Goes to Charters." *Minnesota Journal,* 25 August, 1, 6–7.

Manno, Bruno V., Chester E. Finn Jr., Louann A. Bierlein, and Gregg Vanourek. 1997. "Charter School Accountability: Problems and Prospects." Policy report. Indianapolis: Hudson Institute.

———. 1998. "Charter Schools: Accomplishments and Dilemmas. *Teachers College Record* 99 (3): 537–58.

Maranto, Robert, and April Gresham. 1999. "The Wild West of Education Reform: Arizona Charter Schools." In *School Choice in the Real World: Lessons from Arizona Charter Schools,* ed. Robert Maranto, Scott Milliman, Frederick Hess, and April Gresham, 99–114. Boulder, Colo.: Westview Press.

Maranto, Robert, Scott Milliman, Frederick Hess, and April Gresham. 1999. "In Lieu of Conclusions: Tentative Lessons from a Contested Frontier." In *School Choice in the Real World: Lessons from Arizona Charter Schools,* ed. Robert Maranto, Scott Milliman, Frederick Hess, and April Gresham, 237–47. Boulder, Colo.: Westview Press.

Markley, Melanie. 1997a. "Chartering New Paths to Learning." *Houston Chronicle,* 15 September.

———. 1997b. "HISD Board Trustees Approve 13 Charters." *Houston Chronicle,* 16 May, A29.

Marshall, Catherine, Douglas Mitchell, and Frederick Wirt. 1989. *Culture and Education Policy in the American States.* New York: Falmer Press.

Massachusetts Department of Education. 1996. "The Massachusetts Charter School Initiative." Policy report. Malden: Massachusetts Department of Education.

———. 1998. "The Massachusetts Charter School Initiative." Policy report. Malden: Massachusetts Department of Education.

———. 2001. "The Massachusetts Charter School Initiative." Policy report. Malden: Massachusetts Department of Education.

Mazmanian, Daniel A., and Paul A. Sabatier. 1983. *Implementation and Public Policy.* Glenview, Ill.: Scott, Foresman and Company.

McCabe, Barbara Coyle, and Janet Coble Vinzant. 1999. "Governance Lessons: The Case of Charter Schools." *Administration and Society* 31 (3): 361–77.

McDonnell, Lorraine M., and Richard F. Elmore. 1987. "Getting the Job Done: Alternative Policy Instruments." *Educational Evaluation and Policy Analysis* 9 (2): 133–52.

McKinney, Joseph. 1996. "Charter Schools: A New Barrier for Children with Disabilities." *Education Leadership* (October): 22–25.

———. 1998. "Charter Schools' Legal Responsibilities toward Children with Disabilities." *West's Education Law Reporter* 126:565–76.

McLaughlin, Milbrey Wallin. 1987. "Learning from Experience: Lessons from Policy Implementation." *Educational Evaluation and Policy Analysis* 9 (2): 171–78.

McQueen, Anjetta. 2000. "Charter Schools Movement Growing." Associated Press, 11 February.

Mead, Julie F. 2000. "Publicly Funded School Choice Options in Milwaukee: An Examination of the Legal Issues." Milwaukee: Public Policy Forum.

Melnick, R. Shep. 1995. "Separation of Powers and the Strategy of Rights: The Expansion of Special Education." In *The New Politics of Public Policy,* ed. Marc K. Landy and Martin A. Levin, 23–46. Baltimore: Johns Hopkins University Press.

Michigan Association of Public School Academies. 1999. "Schools." Lansing: Michigan Association of Public School Academies. Available at <http://www.charterschools.org/schools.html>.

———. 2000. "Schools." Lansing: Michigan Association of Public School Academies. Available at <http://www.charterschools.org/schools.html>.

Michigan Department of Education. 1997. "Michigan Public School Academies: An Overview." Lansing: Michigan Department of Education.

———. 1998. "Updated Public School Academy Listing." Lansing: Michigan Department of Education.

———. 2001. "Michigan K– Database." Lansing: Michigan Department of Education. Available at <http://www.state.mi.us/mde/cfdata/k12db/welcome.cfm>.

Michigan Office of the Auditor General. 1997. "Performance Audit of Charter Schools Office and Michigan Resource Center for Charter Schools, Central Michigan University." Lansing: Michigan Office of the Auditor General.

Michigan Prospect for Renewed Citizenship. 1998. *Charter Schools in Michigan.* Lansing: The Michigan Prospect for Renewed Citizenship.

Miller, Julie A. 1998. "Doing Whatever It Takes." *Education Week,* 8 January, 48–50.

Milliman, Scott, Robert Maranto, and April Gresham. 1999. "Ethnic Diversity and Comprehensive School Choice." Paper presented at the annual meeting of the American Political Science Association, 3 September, Atlanta, Ga.

Mills, Richard. 2000. "Appeal of the NEW COVENANT CHARTER SCHOOL from Action of the Board of Education of the City School District of the City of Albany regarding Transportation." Decision No. 14,327 (17 March). Albany: Office of the Commissioner of Education.

Milwaukee Public Schools. 2000. "Milwaukee Public Schools Accountability Report, 1999–00." Milwaukee: Milwaukee Public Schools.

Minnesota Department of Children, Families and Learning. 2000. "Statistics for Minnesota Alternative Education Programs." St. Paul: Minnesota Department of Children, Families and Learning.

Mintrom, Michael. 2000a. "Leveraging Local Innovation: The Case of Michigan's Charter Schools." Policy report. East Lansing: Institute for Public Policy and Social Research, Michigan State University.

———. 2000b. *Policy Entrepreneurs and School Choice.* Washington, D.C.: Georgetown University Press.

———. 2001. "Policy Design for Local Innovation: The Effects of Competition in Public Schooling." *State Politics and Policy Quarterly* 1 (winter): 343–63.

Mintrom, Michael, and Sandra Vergari. 1996. "Advocacy Coalitions, Policy Entrepreneurs, and Policy Change." *Policy Studies Journal* 24:420–35.

———. 1997a. "Charter Schools as a State Policy Innovation: Assessing Recent Developments." *State and Local Government Review* 29:43–49.

———. 1997b. "Education Reform and Accountability Issues in an Intergovernmental Context." *Publius: The Journal of Federalism* 27 (2): 143–66.

———. 1997c. "Political Factors Shaping Charter School Laws." Paper presented at the annual meeting of the American Educational Research Association, 24 March, Chicago, Ill.

Moe, Terry M. 2001. *Schools, Vouchers, and the American Public.* Washington, D.C.: Brookings.

Morken, Hubert, and Jo Renee Formicola. 1999. *The Politics of School Choice.* Lanham, Md.: Rowman and Littlefield.

Munger, Michael C. 2000. *Analyzing Policy: Choices, Conflicts, and Practices.* New York: W.W. Norton and Company.

Nathan, Joe. 1989. *Free to Teach: Achieving Equity and Excellence in Schools.* Rev. ed. Cleveland: Pilgrim Press.

———. 1996. *Charter Schools: Creating Hope and Opportunity for American Education.* San Francisco: Jossey-Bass.

———. 1999. *Charter Schools: Creating Hope and Opportunity for American Education,* rev. ed. San Francisco: Jossey-Bass.

New York Charter Schools Association. 2001. Memorandum from Lisa Coldwell O'Brien, President, New York Charter Schools Association, addressed to the Honorable Richard P. Mills, Commissioner of Education, 4 April. Albany: New York Charter Schools Association.

New York State Education Department. 2001. "Annual Report on the Status of Charter Schools in New York State in the 1999–2000 School Year." Albany: New York State Education Department.

New York State School Boards Association. 1999. "Charter Schools in New York: An Analysis of New York State's New Charter School Legislation. Albany: New York State School Boards Association.

Nikiforuk, Andrew. 1993. *School's Out: The Catastrophe in Public Education and What We Can Do About It.* Toronto: Macfarlane, Walter and Ross.

Norris, Jo Ann. 1999. Interview by Michelle McNiff, 12 October and 10 November.

North Carolina Department of Public Instruction. 1999. "A Report Card for the ABCs of Public Education, Volume I: Growth and Performance of North Carolina Schools, 1998–1999." Raleigh: North Carolina Department of Public Instruction.

———. 2000. "A Report Card for the ABCs of Public Education, Volume I: Growth and Performance of North Carolina Schools, 1999–2000." Raleigh: North Carolina Department of Public Instruction.

North Carolina League of Women Voters. 1999. "Survey Results: N.C. Superintendents' Perceptions of the Impact Charter Schools Have Had on Their Districts." Chapel Hill: North Carolina League of Women Voters.

North Carolina Office of State Budget and Management. 1999. "The Study of the Effect of Charter Schools on the Department of Public Instruction's Workload and Staffing Requirements." Raleigh: North Carolina Office of State Budget and Management.

North Carolina State Board of Education. 1998. "Report to the Joint Legislative Education Oversight Committee on the Charter School Evaluation Report." Raleigh: North Carolina State Board of Education.

Odden, Allen, and Caroline Busch. 1998. *Financing Schools for High Performance.* San Francisco: Jossey-Bass.

OPPAGA. 2000. "Charter Schools Need Improved Academic Accountability and Financial Management." Program review. Report No. 99-48. State of Florida: Office of Program Policy Analysis and Government Accountability.

O'Reilly, Robert. 1995. "School Councils." *Challenges in Educational Administration* 30 (1): 1–9.

———. 1999. "Assessing Alberta's Charter School Policy." Paper presented at the annual meeting of the Canadian Society for Studies in Education, 14 June, Sherbrooke, Quebec.

Osborne, David, and Ted Gaebler. 1992. *Reinventing Government.* Reading, Mass.: Addison-Wesley.

Osborne, David, and Peter Plastrik. 1997. *Banishing Bureaucracy.* Reading, Mass.: Addison-Wesley.

Paige, Rod. 2001. "Remarks as Prepared for Delivery by U.S. Secretary of Education Rod Paige." Presented at the National Education Association Bargaining and Instructional Issues Conference, 30 June, Los Angeles, Calif. Available at <http://www.ed.gov/Speeches>.

Palmaffy, Tyce. 1998. "The Gold Star State." *Policy Review* 88:30–38

"Panel: Texas Charter Schools Lacking." 2000. Available at <http://www.jsonline.com/news/nat/ap/dec00/ap-texas-charter-s122800.asp>.

Patterson, Dave. 2000a. "California Network of Educational Charters (CANEC) 2000." Available at <http://www.canec.org>.

———. 2000b. Personal communication. 28 January.

Pearce, Kelly. 1998. "Church-State Controversy." *Arizona Republic,* 6 June, A1.

Perez-Pena, Richard. 1998. "Pataki Leaves Room for Deal on Lawmakers' Quest for Raises." *New York Times,* 1 December, B4.

Peters, B. Guy. 1999a. *American Public Policy: Promise and Performance.* 5th ed. New York: Chatham House.

———. 1999b. *Institutional Theory in Political Science: The "New Institutionalism."* London: Pinter.

Peterson, Paul E., and Chad Noyes. 1997. "School Choice in Milwaukee." In *New Schools for a New Century: The Redesign of Urban Education,* ed. Diane Ravitch and Joseph P. Viteritti, 123–46. New Haven, Conn.: Yale University Press.

Pincus, John. 1974. "Incentives for Innovation in the Public Schools." *Review of Educational Research* 44 (winter): 113–44.

Pipho, Chris. 1993. "Bipartisan Charter Schools." *Phi Delta Kappan* 75 (2): 102–3.

Popkin, Samuel L. 1991. *The Reasoning Voter.* Chicago: University of Chicago Press.

Premack, Eric. 1996. "Charter Schools: A Status Report." *School Business Affairs* 62 (12): 10–15.

———. 1999. "1998 California Charter Schools Legislative Summary." Available at <http://www.csus.edu/ier/charter/charter.html>.

———. 2000. Personal communication. 16 February.

"Private School Choice: Arizona Lawmakers at Standstill." 1994. *Daily Report Card*, 15 April, 1.

Province of Alberta. 1997. *Annual Report of the Auditor General of Alberta, 1996–97.* Edmonton: Province of Alberta.

Public School Forum. 1998. "The Things That Matter." Raleigh: Public School Forum.

———. 2000. "Annual Local School Finance Study." Raleigh: Public School Forum.

Public Sector Consultants and Maximus. 1999. *Michigan's Charter School Initiative: From Theory to Practice.* Lansing: Public Sector Consultants.

Reich, Robert B., ed. 1988. *The Power of Public Ideas.* Cambridge: Harvard University Press.

Reijniers, J. J. A. M. 1994. "Organization of Public-Private Partnership Projects." *International Journal of Project Management* 12:137–42.

Renzulli, Joseph S. 1988. "The Multiple Menu Model for Developing Differentiated Curriculum for the Gifted and Talented. *Gifted Child Quarterly* 32 (3): 298–309.

Ripley, Randall B., and Grace A. Franklin. 1982. *Bureaucracy and Policy Implementation.* Homewood, Ill.: The Dorsey Press.

Robertson, Heather. 1999. "Shall We Dance?" *Phi Delta Kappan* 80 (1): 728–36.

Rofes, Eric. 1998. "How Are School Districts Responding to Charter Laws and Charter Schools?" Policy report. Berkeley: Policy Analysis for California Education, University of California at Berkeley.

Rosenau, Pauline Vaillancourt. 2000. "The Strengths and Weaknesses of Public-Private Partnerships." In *Public-Private Policy Partnerships,* ed. Pauline Vaillancourt Rosenau, 217–41. Cambridge: MIT Press.

Rosenblum Brigham Associates. 1998. "Innovation and Massachusetts Charter Schools." Policy report. Malden: Massachusetts Department of Education.

RPP International. 1999a. "A Comparison of Charter School Legislation." Policy report. Washington, D.C.: U.S. Department of Education.

———. 1999b. "The State of Charter Schools: Third-Year Report." Washington, D.C.: U.S. Department of Education.

———. 2000. "The State of Charter Schools 2000: Fourth-Year Report." Washington, D.C.: U.S. Department of Education.

———. 2001. "Challenge and Opportunity: The Impact of Charter Schools on School Districts." Washington, D.C.: U.S. Department of Education.

Rylander, Carole Keeton. 2000. "Recommendations of the Texas Comptroller." Available at <http://www.e-texas.org/recommend/ch06/ed03.html>.

Sabatier, Paul A., and Hank Jenkins-Smith, eds. 1994. *Policy Change and Learning: An Advocacy Coalition Approach.* Boulder, Colo.: Westview Press.

Sanders, William L., and June C. Rivers. 1996. *Cumulative and Residual Effects of Teachers on Future Student Academic Achievement.* Knoxville: Value-Added Research and Assessment Center, University of Tennessee.

Sarason, Seymour B. 1999. *Charter Schools: Another Flawed Educational Reform?* New York: Teachers College Press.

Schnaiberg, Lynn. 1997. "Firms Hoping to Turn Profit from Charters." *Education Week,* 10 December, 1, 14.

Schneider, Anne Larason, and Helen Ingram. 1997. *Policy Design for Democracy.* Lawrence: University Press of Kansas.

Schneider, Mark, Paul Teske, and Melissa Marschall. 2000. *Choosing Schools: Consumer Choice and the Quality of American Schools.* Princeton: Princeton University Press.

Schneider, Mark, Paul Teske, Melissa Marschall, and Christine Roch. 1998. "Shopping for Schools: In the Land of the Blind, the One-Eyed Parent May Be Enough." *American Journal of Political Science* 42 (3): 769–93.

Schneider, Mark, and Paul Teske, with Michael Mintrom. 1995. *Public Entrepreneurs: Agents for Change in American Government.* Princeton: Princeton University Press.

Schultze, Ray. 1993. "Reformers Tout Charter Schools; Establishment Fears Threat to Funds." *Phoenix Gazette,* 13 February, B1.

Scott, W. Richard. 1995. *Institutions and Organizations.* Thousand Oaks, Calif.: Sage.

Sergiovanni, Thomas J., Martin Burlingame, Fred S. Coombs, and Paul W. Thurston. 1999. *Educational Governance and Administration.* 4th ed. Needham Heights, Mass.: Allyn and Bacon.

Shanker, Al. 1988. "Convention Plots New Course—A Charter for Change." Paid advertisement. *New York Times,* 10 July, E7.

Shin, Paul H. B. 2001. "Rudy Rolls Out 3.4M for Charter Schools." *New York Daily News,* 1 May, 32.

Sibley, Krysti. 1998. "NB Charter School Adds Alternative." *San Antonio Express-News,* 8 July, H1, H9.

———. 1999. "Durham Charter School Stumbles on State Test." *Raleigh News and Observer,* 21 July.

———. 2000. "Popularity of Charters Offers Some Insights for Public Schools." *Raleigh News and Observer,* 19 January.

Smoot, Samantha. 2000. "Testimony Before the House Committee on Public Education on Open-Enrollment Charter Schools." 20 June. Available at <http://www.tfn.org/issues/charterschools/testimony.htm>.

Solmon, Lewis C., Kern Paark, and David Garcia. 2001. "Does Charter School Attendance Improve Test Scores? The Arizona Results." Unpublished manuscript.

SRI International. 1997. "Evaluation of Charter School Effectiveness." Sacramento: Office of the Legislative Analyst.

———. 2000. "Evaluation of the Public Charter Schools Program: Year One Evaluation Report." Washington, D.C.: U.S. Department of Education.

Stashenko, Joel. 1998. "Charter Schools at Issue: Mills Reviews Pataki's Proposal." *Schenectady Gazette,* 11 December, A1, A11.

Stecklow, Steve. 1997. "Businesses Scramble to Run Charter Schools." *Wall Street Journal,* 21 August, B1–B2.

Steel, L., and R. Levine. 1994. *Educational Innovation in Multiracial Contexts: The Growth of Magnet Schools in American Education.* Prepared for the U.S. Department of Education, contract #LC 90043001. Palo Alto, Calif.: American Institutes for Research.

Stein, Charles. 1998. "Money vs. Mission: Indignation Follows For-Profits' Foray into Hallowed Industries of Education, Health Care." *Boston Globe,* 15 March, E1.

Stone, Deborah. 1988. *Policy Paradox and Political Reason.* New York: Harper Collins.

Stout, Robert T., and Gregg A. Garn. 1999. "Nothing New: Curricula in Arizona Charter Schools." In *School Choice in the Real World: Lessons from Arizona Charter Schools,* ed. Robert Maranto, Scott Milliman, Frederick Hess, and April Gresham, 159–72. Boulder, Colo.: Westview Press.

Swidorski, Theresa, and Lonnie Palmer. 1999. "Let's Focus on Improving Our Public Schools." *Times Union,* 4 July, B1, B3.

Tapia, Sarah Tully. 1997. "Public Schools Alternative: Arizona Leads the Nation in Schools Chartered." *Arizona Daily Star,* 15 June. Available at <http://www.azstarnet.com/public/packages/charterschools/2chart2.htm>.

Teske, Paul, Mark Schneider, Jack Buckley, and Sara Clark. 2000. "Does Charter School Competition Improve Traditional Public Schools?" Civic Report No. 10. Manhattan: Center for Civic Innovation, Manhattan Institute.

Teske, Paul, Mark Schneider, Michael Mintrom, and Samuel Best. 1993. "Establishing the Micro Foundations of a Macro Theory: Information, Movers, and the Competitive Local Market for Public Goods." *American Political Science Review* 87:702–13.

"Texas Charter School Information," 1999. Available at <http://www.uscharterschools.org>.

Texas Education Agency. 1998. *Texas Open-Enrollment Charter Schools: Second Year Evaluation, 1997–98.* Austin: Texas Education Agency.

———. 2000a. "Snapshot 2000." Available at <http://www.tea.state.tx.us/perfreport/snapshot/2000>.

———. 2000b. *Texas Open-Enrollment Charter Schools: Third Year Evaluation, 1998–99.* Austin: Texas Education Agency.

Texas State Board of Education. 1997a. *Open-Enrollment Charter Guidelines and Application.* Austin: Texas State Board of Education.

———. 1997b. *Texas Open-Enrollment Charter Schools: Year One Evaluation.* Austin: Texas State Board of Education.

Thernstrom, Abigail. 1991. "School Choice in Massachusetts." Pioneer Paper No. 5, Education in Massachusetts Series. Boston: Pioneer Institute for Public Policy Research.

Timmons-Brown, Stephanie, and Frederick Hess. 1999. "Why Arizona Embarked on School Reform (and Nevada Did Not)." In *School Choice in the Real World: Lessons from Arizona Charter Schools,* ed. Robert Maranto, Scott Milliman, Frederick Hess, and April Gresham, 115–28. Boulder, Colo.: Westview Press.

Tucker, Marc S., and Charles S. Clark. 1999. "The New Accountability." *The American School Board Journal* 186 (1): 26–29.

Tyack, David, and Larry Cuban. 1995. *Tinkering toward Utopia: A Century of Public School Reform.* Cambridge: Harvard University Press.

University of California, Los Angeles. 1998. "Beyond the Rhetoric of Charter School Reform: A Study of Ten California School Districts." Los Angeles: University of California, Los Angeles.

U.S. Bureau of the Census. 1997. *Statistical Abstract of the United States: 1997.* 117th ed. Washington, D.C.: Government Printing Office.

U.S. Department of Education. 1998. *Review of Charter School Legislation Provisions Related to Students with Disabilities.* Washington, D.C.: U.S. Government Printing Office.

Vanourek, Gregg, Bruno V. Manno, and Chester E. Finn. 1997. "The False Friends of Charter Schools." *Education Week,* 30 April, 60, 46.

Vergari, Sandra. 1995. "School Finance Reform in the State of Michigan." *Journal of Education Finance* 21:254–70.

———. 1999. "Charter Schools: A Primer on the Issues." *Education and Urban Society* 31 (4): 389–405.

———. 2000. "The Regulatory Styles of Statewide Charter School Authorizers: Arizona, Massachusetts, and Michigan." *Educational Administration Quarterly* 36 (5): 730–57.

———. 2001. "Charter School Authorizers: Public Agents for Holding Charter Schools Accountable." *Education and Urban Society* 33 (2): 129–40.

Vergari, Sandra, and Michael Mintrom. 1998. "Public Opinion on K–12 Education in Michigan." State of the State Survey Briefing Paper No. 98-36. East Lansing: Institute for Public Policy and Social Research, Michigan State University.

Viteritti, Joseph P. 1999. *Choosing Equality: School Choice, the Constitution, and Civil Society.* Washington, D.C.: Brookings.

Walt, Kathy. 1998. "Charter Schools Called 'Mixed Bag' of Success." *Houston Chronicle,* 5 September, A37, A38.

Waters, Betty. 1999. "Charter Schools Crop Up across East Texas," *Tyler Morning Telegraph,* 1 August, 19.

Weimer, David L., and Aidan R. Vining. 1999. *Policy Analysis: Concepts and Practice.* 3d ed. Englewood Cliffs, N.J.: Prentice-Hall.

Wells, Amy Stuart. 1998. "Charter School Reform in California: Does It Meet Expectations?" *Phi Delta Kappan* 80 (4): 305–12.

Wells, Amy Stuart, Cynthia Grutzik, Sibyll Carnochan, Julie Slayton, and Ash Vasudeva. 1999. "Underlying Policy Assumptions of Charter School Reform: The Multiple Meanings of a Movement." *Teachers College Record* 100 (3): 513–35.

Wells, Amy Stuart, and Research Associates. 1998. "Beyond the Rhetoric of Charter School Reform: A Study of Ten California School Districts." Policy report. Los Angeles: University of California, Los Angeles.

Wechsler, Alan. 2001. "Educators' Group Urges State to Fund Charter Schools." *Times Union,* 14 March, B4.

Wilson, James Q. 1995. "New Politics, New Elites, Old Publics." In *The New Politics of Public Policy,* ed. Marc K. Landy and Martin A. Levin, 249–67. Baltimore: Johns Hopkins University Press.

Wilson, Steven F. 1992. *Reinventing the Schools: A Radical Plan for Boston.* Boston: Pioneer Institute.

Windler, William. 1999. Personal communication. 12 November.

Winebrenner, Susan. 1992. *Teaching Gifted Kids in the Regular Classroom.* Minneapolis: Free Spirit Publishing.

Wirt, Frederick M., and Michael W. Kirst. 1997. *The Political Dynamics of American Education.* Berkeley, Calif.: McCutchan Publishing Corporation.

Wisconsin Legislative Audit Bureau. 1998. "An Evaluation: Charter School Program." Report 98-15. Madison: State of Wisconsin.

Wisconsin Legislative Fiscal Bureau. 2001. "General School Aids Amounts for All School Districts." Policy report. 8 February.

Witte, John F. 1996. "School Choice and Student Performance." In *Holding Schools Accountable: Performance-Based Reform in Education,* ed. Helen F. Ladd, 149–76. Washington, D.C.: Brookings.

———. 2000. *The Market Approach to Education: An Analysis of America's First Voucher Program.* Princeton: Princeton University Press.

Wohlstetter, Priscilla, and Lesley Anderson. 1994. "What Can U.S. Charter Schools Learn from England's Grant-Maintained Schools?" *Phi Delta Kappan* 75 (6): 486–91.

Wohlstetter, Priscilla, and Noelle Griffin. 1998. "Creating and Sustaining Learning Communities: Early Lessons from Charter Schools." Philadelphia: Consortium for Policy Research in Education, Graduate School of Education, University of Pennsylvania.

Wohlstetter, Priscilla, Richard Wenning, and Kerri L. Briggs. 1995. Charter Schools in the United States: The Question of Autonomy. *Educational Policy* 9 (4): 331–58.

Wong, Kenneth, and Francis Shen, with Gabrielle Novacek. 2001. "Institutional Effects of Charter Schools: Innovation and Segregation." Paper presented at the annual meeting of the American Educational Research Association, 10–14 April, Seattle, Washington.

Wood, Jennifer. 1999. "An Early Examination of the Massachusetts Charter School Initiative." Boston: Massachusetts Education Reform Review Commission, University of Massachusetts, Donahue Institute.

Wood, Steve. 1999. Interview by Michelle McNiff, 5 October.

Zernike, Kate. 1996. "Weld Bids on Alternative Learning." *Boston Globe,* 15 March, A25.

Contributors

Tracey Bailey (M.S., Florida Institute of Technology) is the National Projects Director for the Association of American Educators. He is the former director of the Office of Public School Choice and Charter Schools in the Florida Department of Education. In 1993, he was selected as the National Teacher of the Year from a field of over 2.7 million public school teachers across the United States. He has been honored by the president in a White House ceremony and has worked with educational leaders nationwide to promote substantive education reform and to foster increased professionalism among teachers. He helped develop and introduce into Florida's classrooms cutting-edge programs in molecular biology and DNA fingerprinting. Bailey also helped to design and establish the National Educational Technology Institute at the Kennedy Space Center.

Lynn Bosetti (Ph.D., University of Alberta) is a professor of policy and administration who has served as vice dean of the Faculty of Education at the University of Calgary, Canada. Her research has focused on educational policy, teacher evaluation, and school choice. She completed a two-year study of the first charter schools in Canada. Her research has been published in journals such as *Social Organization, Educational Policy, Peabody Journal of Education,* and *Alberta Journal of Education,* as well as in various commissioned policy reports.

Derrick Chau (M.A., Loyola Marymount University) is a doctoral candidate in educational policy at the University of Southern California. Before attending USC, Chau was a member of the Americorps-sponsored Teach for America program. He has worked on research projects pertaining to the governance and educational practices of charter schools.

Lance D. Fusarelli (Ph.D., University of Texas at Austin) is an assistant professor of administration, policy, and urban education at Fordham University. His research interests include school choice and the politics of state-level educational policy making. His recent articles on charter schools have appeared in *Education and Urban Society*.

Noelle C. Griffin (M.S.Ed., Ph.D., University of Southern California) is a senior researcher at the Center for Research on Evaluation, Standards, and Student Testing at the University of California, Los Angeles. She has coauthored several papers and policy briefs on charter schools and is coauthor of "Building a Plane While Flying It: Early Lessons from Charter Schools" (*Teacher's College Record* 103 [2]).

Bryan C. Hassel (Ph.D., Harvard University) directs Public Impact, an education and policy consulting firm. He received his M.Phil. in politics from Oxford University, which he attended as a Rhodes Scholar. Hassel has written and consulted widely on such topics as school accountability, facilities financing, and comprehensive school reform. He is the author of *The Charter School Challenge: Avoiding the Pitfalls, Fulfilling the Promise* (Brookings) and coeditor with Paul E. Peterson of *Learning from School Choice* (Brookings).

Paul Herdman (Ed.D., Harvard University) is the director of accountability services with New American Schools, a national nonprofit organization that provides educational consulting services to districts, states, and schools. He has contributed to U.S. Department of Education studies of charter school accountability and a microfinance study of Massachusetts charter schools. Herdman was a lecturer on charter schools at Harvard University, a state-level policy maker in the Massachusetts charter school office and cofounder and director of a school-within-a-school in New York City.

Frederick M. Hess (Ph.D., Harvard University) is an assistant professor of government and education at the University of Virginia and director of the Virginia Center for Educational Policy Studies. His books include *Spinning Wheels: The Politics of Urban School Reform* (Brookings), *Revolution at the Margins: The Impact of Competition on Urban School Systems* (Brookings), and *School Choice in the Real World: Lessons from Arizona Charter Schools* (Westview). He has contributed to scholarly journals including *American Politics Quarterly, Teachers College Record, Educational Policy, Social Science Quarterly,* and *Urban Affairs Review.* He has served on the National Working Commission on Choice in K–12 Education and the Progressive Policy Institute's Twenty-First Century Schools Project.

Eric Hirsch (M.A., University of Colorado) is the executive director of the Alliance for Quality Teaching in Colorado. Formerly, he managed the education program at the National Conference of State Legislatures where he served as the principal analyst for charter school, school choice, governance, and K–12 teacher issues. Hirsch completed the "Charter School Road Map" for the U.S. Department of Education and has provided technical assistance on charter school legislation to numerous states.

Carolyn Lavely (Ph.D., Syracuse University) is professor of special education and director of the Institute for At-Risk Infants, Children and Youth and Their Families and of the Institute for Instructional Research and Practice at the University of South Florida. She is the project director for the development of the University of South Florida Charter School, which serves 130 K–3 "at-risk" children. Lavely was an executive assistant to four Speakers of the Florida House of Representatives (1978–1984 and 1988–1990) and a Head Start director in Syracuse, New York. She has authored and coauthored numerous reports and journal articles.

Robert Maranto (Ph.D., University of Minnesota) is an assistant professor of political science at Villanova University in Pennsylvania. He has authored *Politics and Bureaucracy in the Modern Presidency: Careerists and Appointees in the Reagan Administration* (Greenwood); coauthored *The Politics of Civil Service Reform* (Peter Lang); and coedited *School Choice in the Real World: Lessons from Arizona Charter Schools* (Westview) and *Radical Reform of the Civil Service* (Lexington). Maranto has also authored or coauthored numerous scholarly publications for such journals as *American Journal of Political Science, Administration and Society,* and *Political Research Quarterly.*

Michelle Godard McNiff (M.A., North Carolina State University) is an independent education research consultant in Raleigh, North Carolina. She has conducted extensive research in the areas of state and local school finance, charter schools, and teacher education. She has served as director of public policy research for the Public School Forum and as a program evaluator for North Carolina's state education agency.

Julie F. Mead (Ph.D., University of Wisconsin-Madison) is an assistant professor in the Department of Educational Administration at the University of Wisconsin-Madison. Her research focuses on special education law and legal issues associated with school choice. Mead is coauthor of *Legal Aspects of Special Education and Pupil Services* (Allyn and Bacon) and of *Legal Issues Pertaining to Charter Schools* (Christopher-Gordon). Her work has appeared in such scholarly journals as *West's Education Law Reporter,* the *Journal of Law and Education,* and *Educational Administration Quarterly,* and she is also a regular contributor to the *Yearbook of Education Law.*

Michael Mintrom (Ph.D., State University of New York at Stony Brook) is an associate professor of political science at Michigan State University. His research focuses on the politics of policy change, with emphasis on the politics of school choice. In 1997, he was a National Academy of Education postdoctoral fellow. His work has appeared in books and in such academic journals as the *American Political Science Review* and the *Journal of Politics.* Mintrom is the author of *Policy Entrepreneurs and School Choice* (Georgetown University Press).

Joe Nathan (Ph.D., University of Minnesota) helped write the nation's first charter law and has testified in more than twenty states and before several congressional committees on charter school issues. He directs the Center for School Change at the University of Minnesota. He has written more than 200 articles and guest columns for publications such as *Phi Delta Kappan, Educational Leadership, Education Week, USA Today,* and the *Wall Street Journal.* He has also written a weekly column for ten years that is published by three of the four largest daily newspapers in Minnesota. Nathan has written several books, including *Charter Schools: Creating Hope and Opportunity in American Education* (Jossey-Bass).

Robert O'Reilly (Ph.D., University of Alberta) is Professor Emeritus of Educational Policy and Management at the University of Calgary, Canada. O'Reilly has also served as an educational policy consultant to federal, provincial, and local government agencies. His work has appeared in such journals as *Educational Administration Quarterly, Journal of Educational Administration, High School Journal, Canadian Journal of Education,* and *Journal of Educational Policy.*

Sandra Vergari (Ph.D., Michigan State University) is an assistant professor in the Department of Educational Administration and Policy Studies and a faculty affiliate with the Department of Public Administration and Policy at the University at Albany, State University of New York. Her research focuses on education reform politics and policy, and she has been analyzing the charter school movement for nearly a decade. Her research has appeared in policy reports and academic journals including *Educational Administration Quarterly, Educational Policy, Journal of Education Finance, Publius: The Journal of Federalism, Policy Studies Journal,* and the *Journal of Politics.*

Priscilla Wohlstetter (Ph.D., Northwestern University; Ed.M., Harvard University) is the Diane and MacDonald Becket Professor in Educational Governance at the University of Southern California. She also directs the Center on Educational Governance, focusing on the relationship between school organization and improved school performance. Her research on charter schools has appeared in publications including *Kappan, Educational Policy, Teachers College Record,* and—as the first-ever entry on charter schools—the 1999 *World Book Encyclopedia.* She is principal investigator for a U.S. Department of Education study of strategic alliances in charter schools and recently completed a study of education practices in Los Angeles area charter schools.

Cathy Wooley-Brown (Ph.D., University of South Florida) is the Florida state coordinator for charter schools and directs the Florida Charter School Resource Center. Previously, she was the administrator of instructional services and the director of exceptional student education with the Polk County schools, in central Florida. Her duties included serving as the charter school liaison for the school district that had the first charter school proposal in Florida. Wooley-Brown completed postdoctoral work on school reform at Harvard University. She has been a teacher, program supervisor, and administrator and has developed innovative teacher education programs in cooperation with local universities.

Index